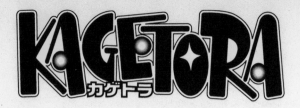

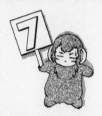

Akira Segami

TRANSLATED BY
Satsuki Yamashita

ADAPTED BY
Nunzio DeFilippis & Christina Weir

LETTERED BY
North Market Street Graphics

BALLANTINE BOOKS • NEW YORK

Kagetora, volume 7 copyright © 2003 by Akira Segami
English translation copyright © 2007 by Akira Segami

Published in the United States by Del Rey Books, an imprint of The Random House Publishing Group, a division of Random House, Inc., New York.

DEL REY is a registered trademark and the Del Rey colophon is a trademark of Random House, Inc.

Publication rights arranged through Kodansha Ltd.

First published in Japan in 2003 by Kodansha Ltd., Tokyo.

ISBN 978-0-345-49616-4

Printed in the United States of America

www.delreymanga.com

9 8 7 6 5 4 3 2 1

Translator—Satsuki Yamashita
Adaptor—Nunzio DeFilippis & Christina Weir
Lettering—North Market Street Graphics

Contents

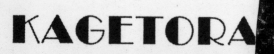

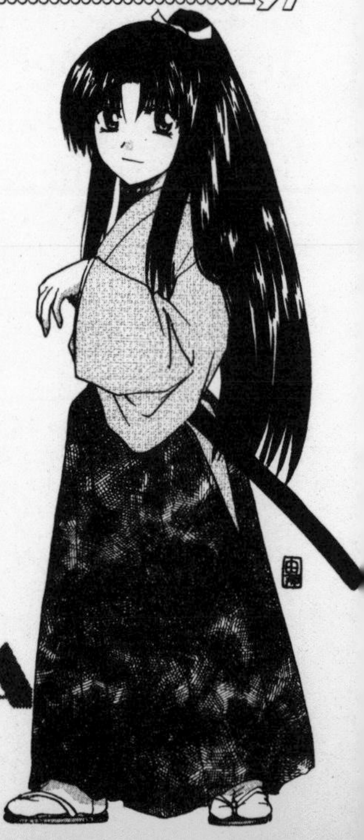

KAGETORA

A Note from the Author

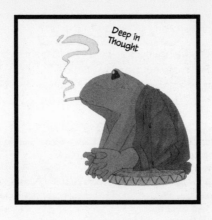

Deep in Thought

After a busy work day, I sometimes want to just sit and space out...Like, at a traditional hot spring inn, drinking sake and gazing out the window...
I know it's impossible but I'm just saying...

Segami

Honorifics Explained

Throughout the Del Rey Manga books, you will find Japanese honorifics left intact in the translations. For those not familiar with how the Japanese use honorifics and, more important, how they differ from American honorifics, we present this brief overview.

Politeness has always been a critical facet of Japanese culture. Ever since the feudal era, when Japan was a highly stratified society, use of honorifics—which can be defined as polite speech that indicates relationship or status—has played an essential role in the Japanese language. When addressing someone in Japanese, an honorific usually takes the form of a suffix attached to one's name (example: "Asuna-san"), is used as a title at the end of one's name, or appears in place of the name itself (example: "Negi-sensei," or simply "Sensei!").

Honorifics can be expressions of respect or endearment. In the context of manga and anime, honorifics give insight into the nature of the relationship between characters. Many English translations leave out these important honorifics, and therefore distort the feel of the original Japanese. Because Japanese honorifics contain nuances that English honorifics lack, it is our policy at Del Rey not to translate them. Here, instead, is a guide to some of the honorifics you may encounter in Del Rey Manga.

-san: This is the most common honorific and is equivalent to Mr., Miss, Ms., or Mrs. It is the all-purpose honorific and can be used in any situation where politeness is required.

-sama: This is one level higher than "-san," and it is used to confer great respect.

-dono: This comes from the word "tono," which means "lord." It is an even higher level than "-sama" and confers utmost respect.

-kun: This suffix is used at the end of boys' names to express familiarity or endearment. It is also sometimes used by men among friends, or when addressing someone younger or of a lower station.

-chan: This is used to express endearment, mostly toward girls. It is also used for little boys, pets, and even among lovers. It gives a sense of childish cuteness.

Bozu: This is an informal way to refer to a boy, similar to the English terms "kid" and "squirt."

Sempai/
Senpai: This title suggests that the addressee is one's senior in a group or organization. It is most often used in a school setting, where underclassmen refer to their upperclassmen as "sempai." It can also be used in the workplace, such as when a newer employee addresses an employee who has seniority in the company.

Kohai: This is the opposite of "sempai" and is used toward underclassmen in school or newcomers in the workplace. It connotes that the addressee is of a lower station.

Sensei: Literally meaning "one who has come before," this title is used for teachers, doctors, or masters of any profession or art.

[blank]: This is usually forgotten in these lists, but it is perhaps the most significant difference between Japanese and English. The lack of honorific means that the speaker has permission to address the person in a very intimate way. Usually, only family, spouses, or very close friends have this kind of permission. Known as yobisute, it can be gratifying when someone who has earned the intimacy starts to call one by one's name without an honorific. But when that intimacy hasn't been earned, it can be very insulting.

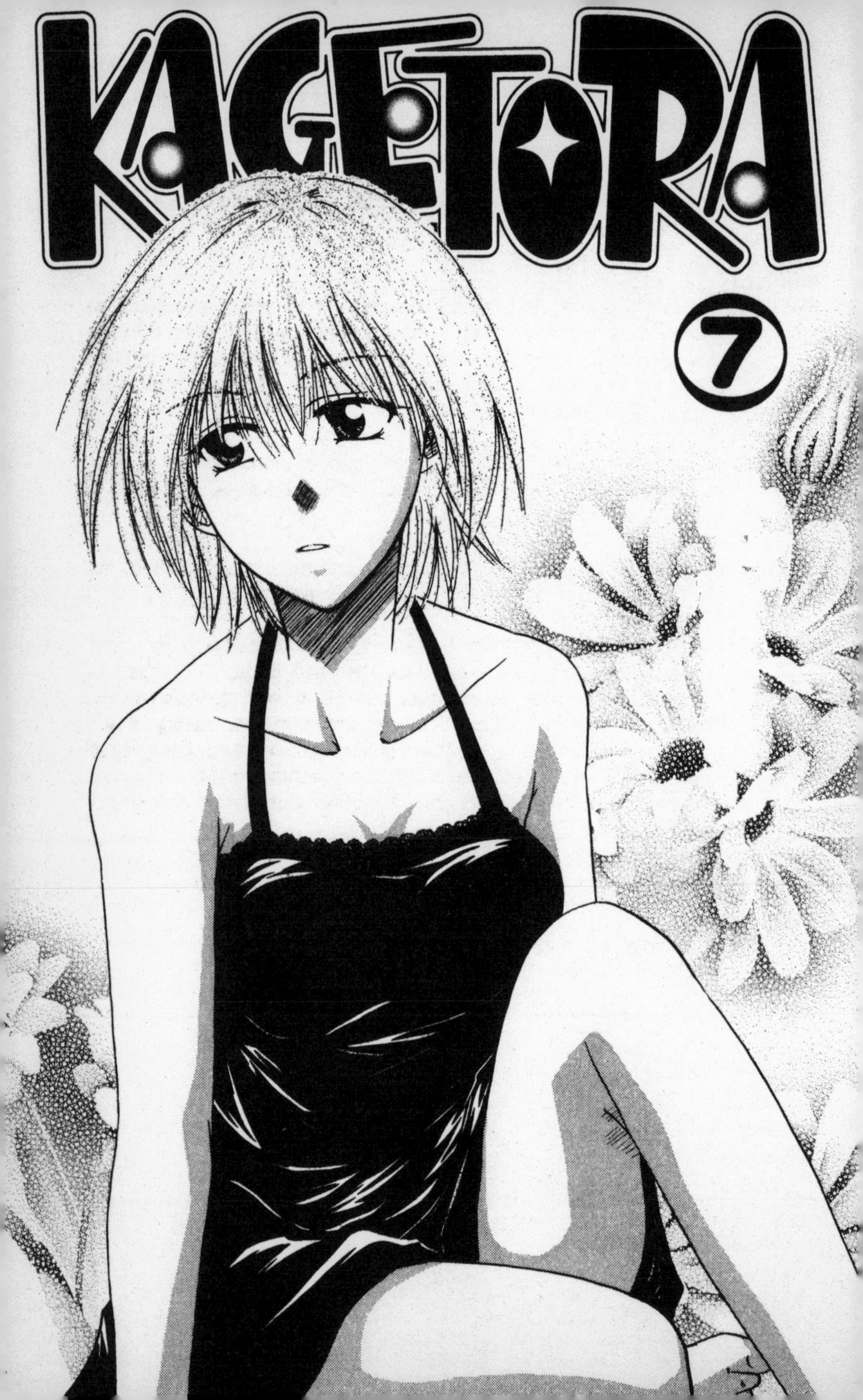
KAGETORA
7

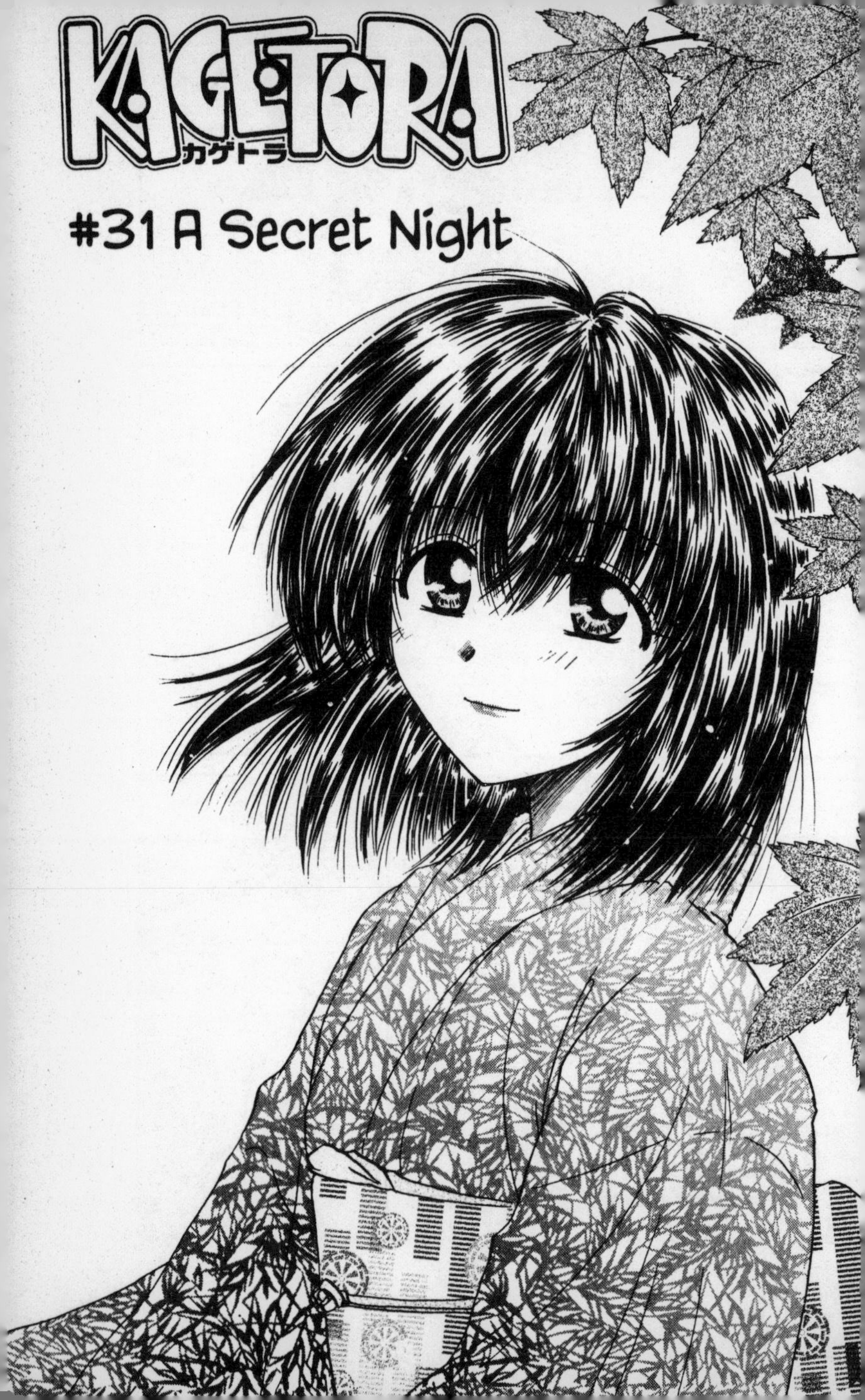
KAGETORA
カゲトラ
#31 A Secret Night

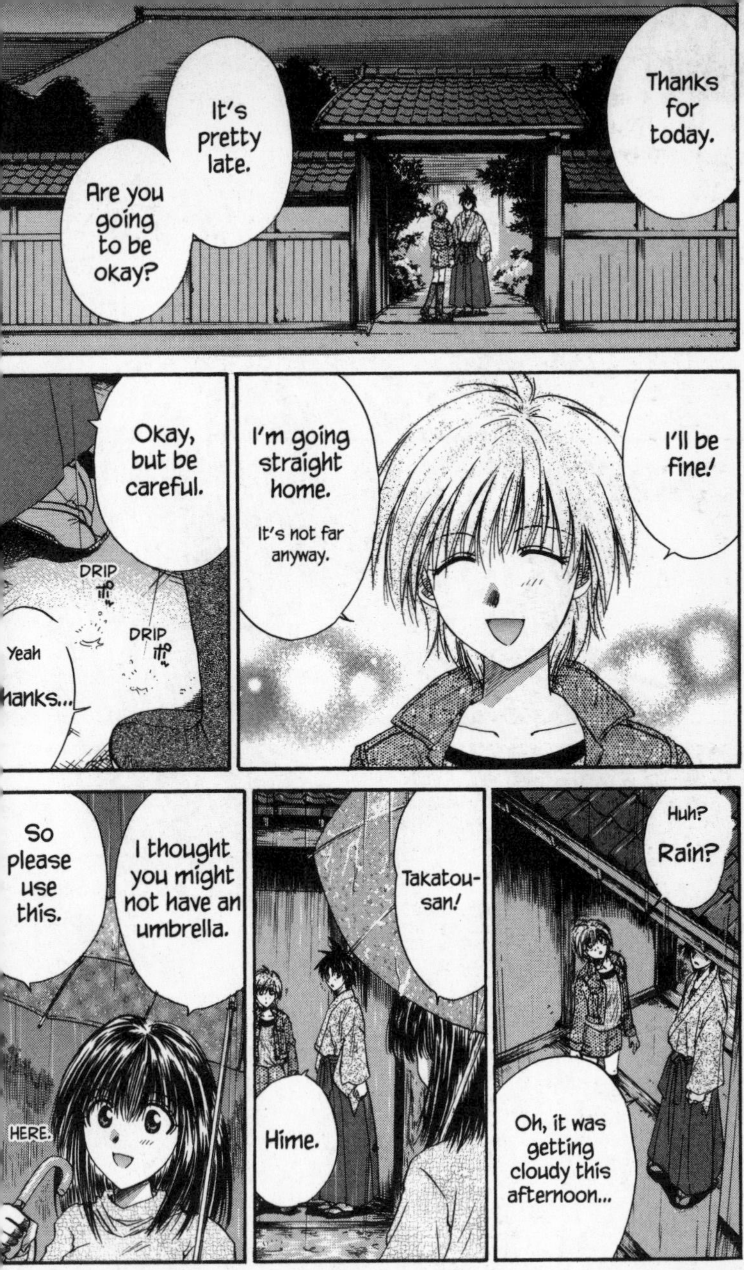
Thanks for today.
It's pretty late.
Are you going to be okay?
I'll be fine!
I'm going straight home.
It's not far anyway.
Okay, but be careful.
DRIP
DRIP
Yeah
hanks...
Huh?
Rain?
Oh, it was getting cloudy this afternoon...
Takatou-san!
Hime.
I thought you might not have an umbrella.
So please use this.
HERE.

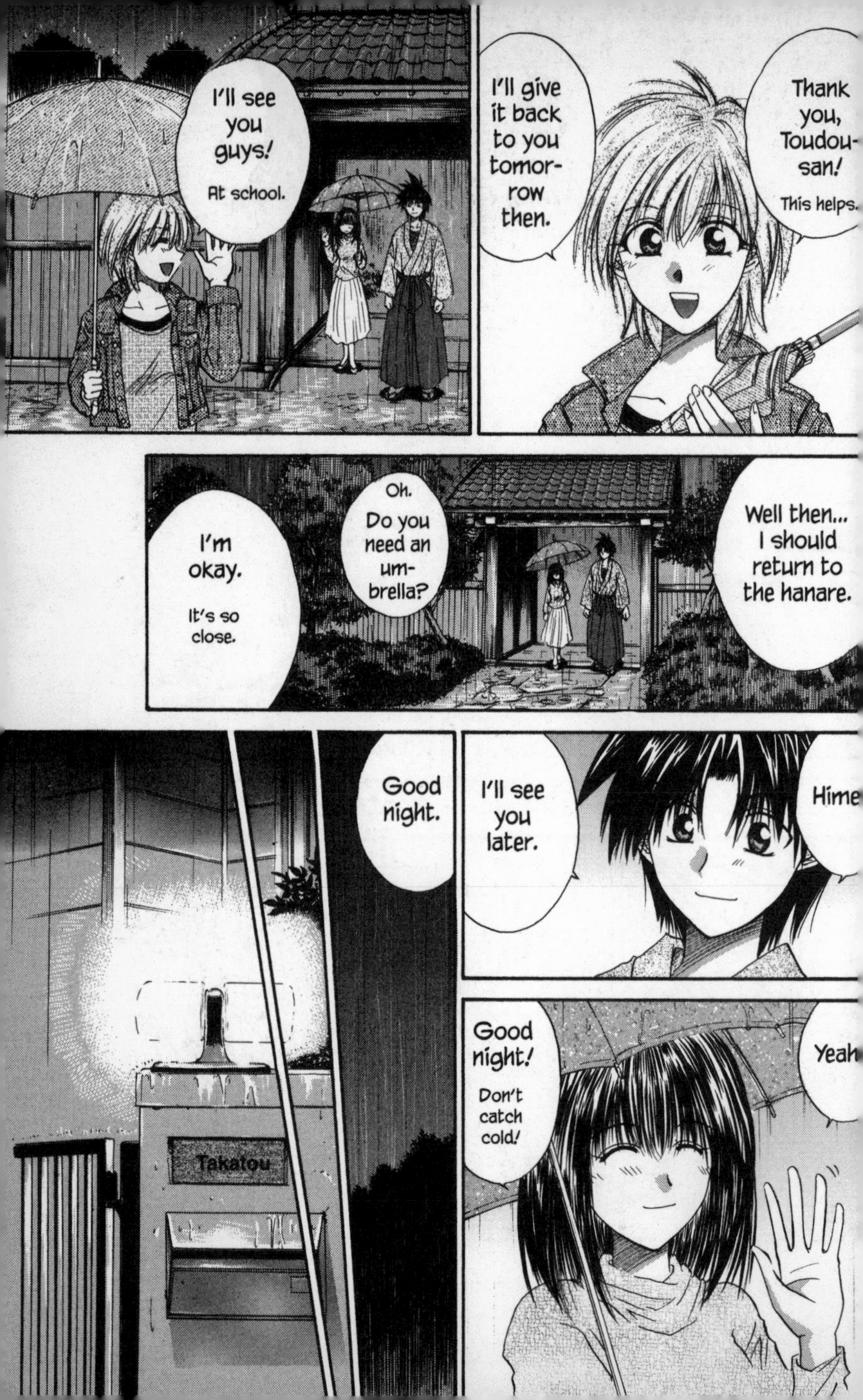
Thank you, Toudou-san!
This helps.
I'll give it back to you tomorrow then.
I'll see you guys!
At school.
Well then... I should return to the hanare.
Oh.
Do you need an umbrella?
I'm okay.
It's so close.
Hime
I'll see you later.
Good night.
Yeah
Good night!
Don't catch cold!
Takatou

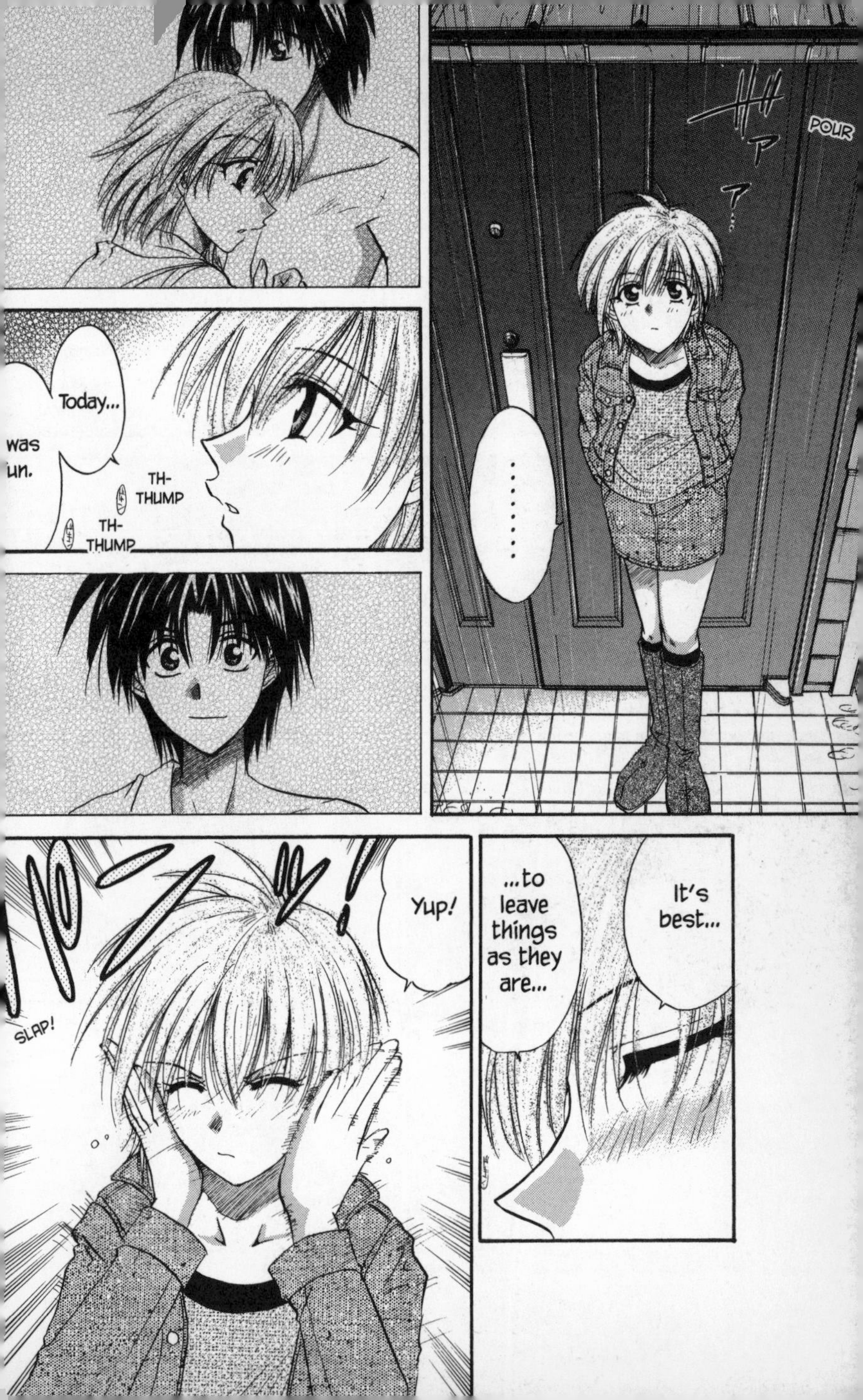
POUR
......
Today...
was
un.
TH-THUMP
TH-THUMP
It's best...
...to leave things as they are...
Yup!
SLAP!

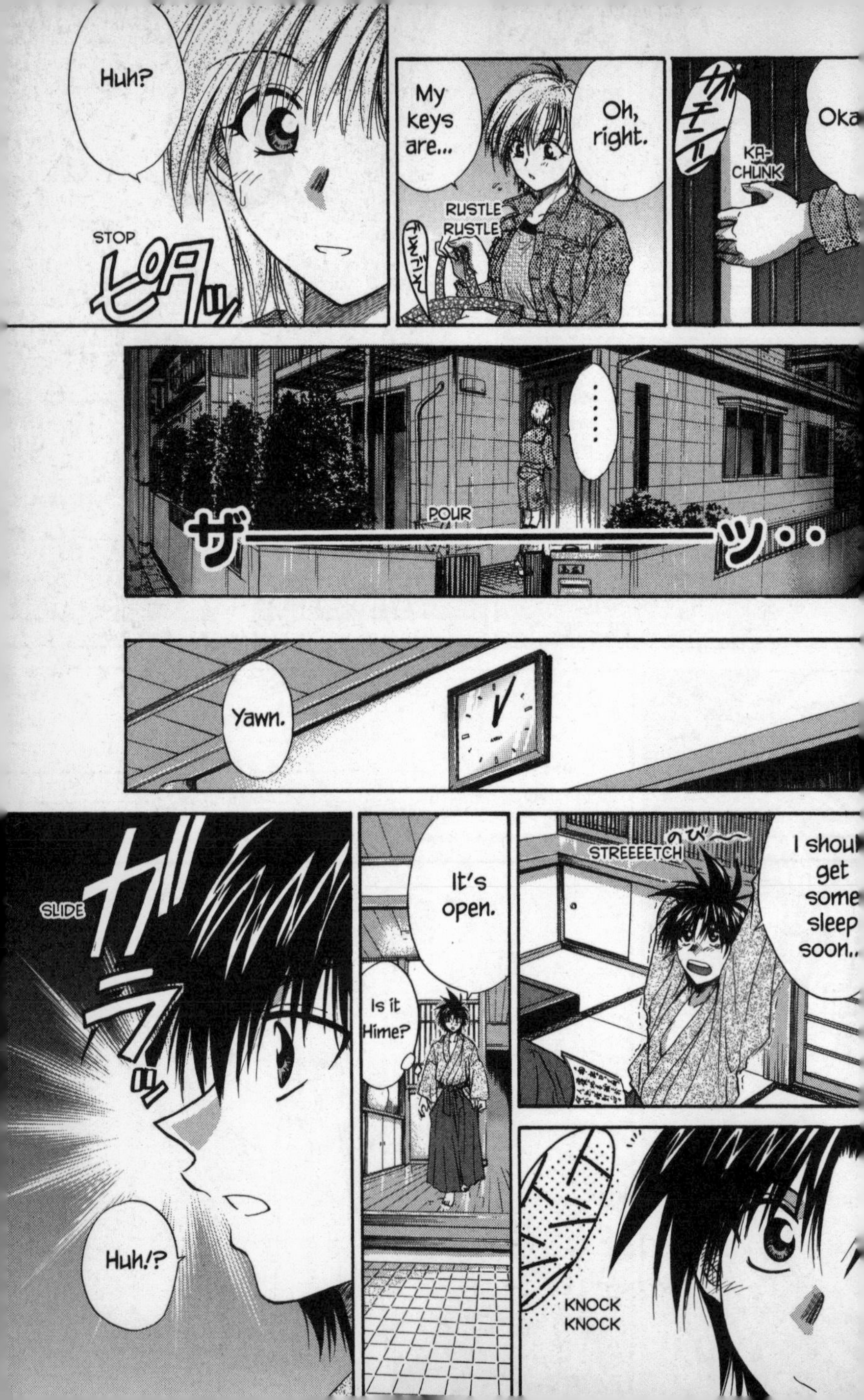
Oka
KA-CHUNK
Oh, right.
My keys are...
RUSTLE RUSTLE
Huh?
STOP
ピタッ
.....
POUR
ザーーーッ・・
Yawn.
STREEEETCH
のび〜〜
I shoul get some sleep soon..
KNOCK KNOCK
It's open.
Is it Hime?
SLIDE
Huh!?

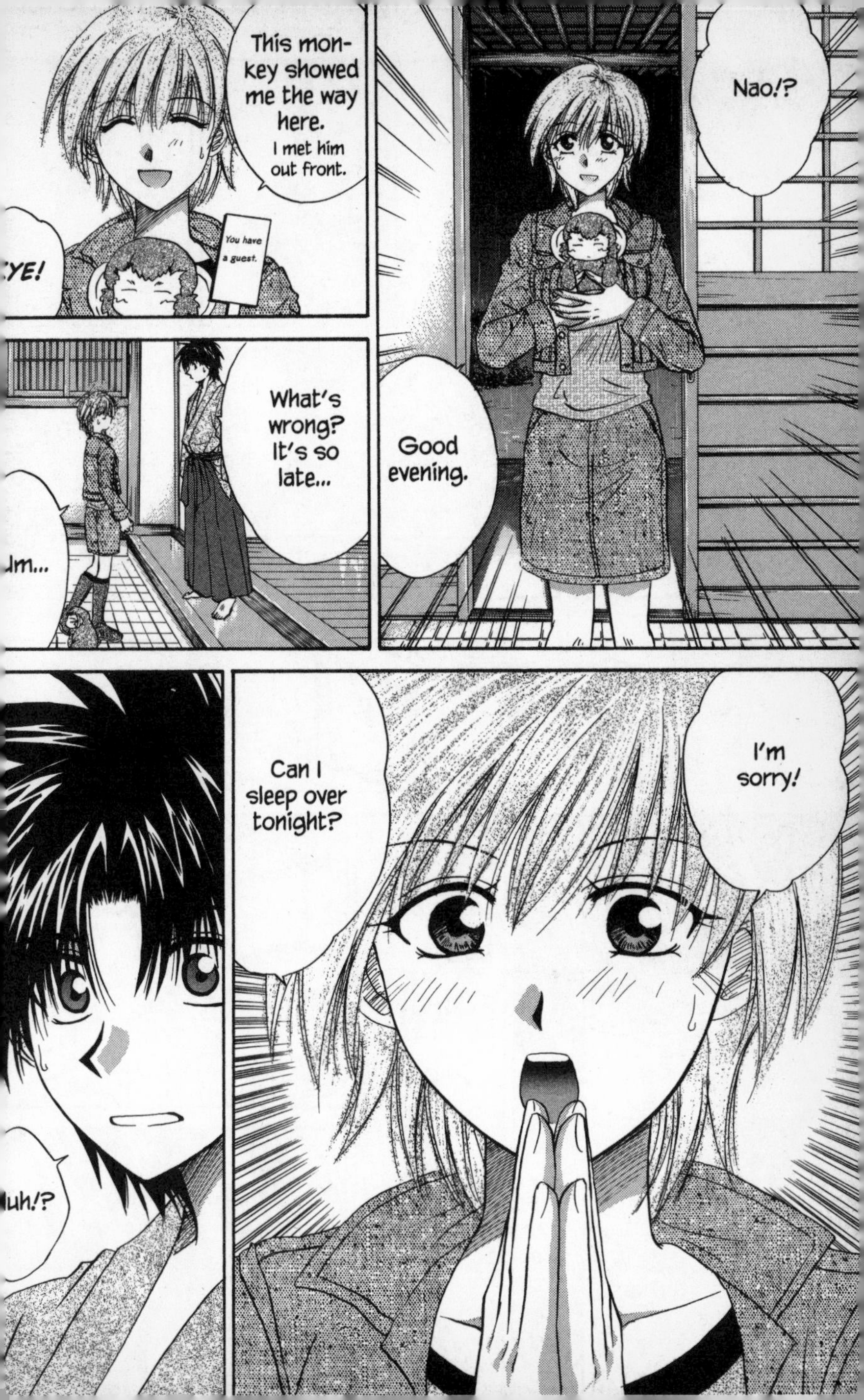
Nao!?
Good evening.
This mon-key showed me the way here.
I met him out front.
You have a guest.
YE!
What's wrong? It's so late...
m...
I'm sorry!
Can I sleep over tonight?
uh!?

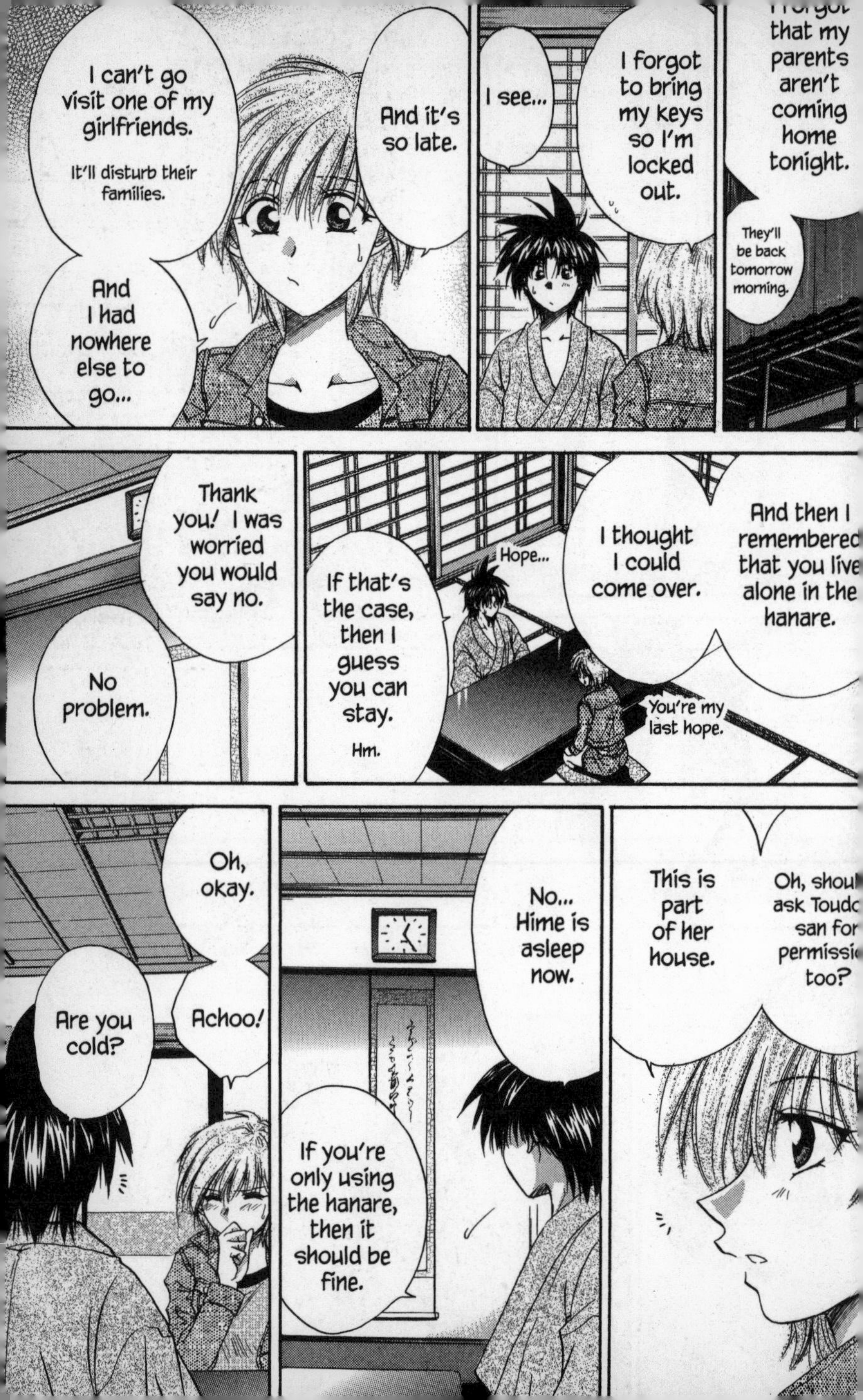
that my parents aren't coming home tonight.
They'll be back tomorrow morning.
I forgot to bring my keys so I'm locked out.
I see...
And it's so late.
I can't go visit one of my girlfriends.
It'll disturb their families.
And I had nowhere else to go...
And then I remembered that you live alone in the hanare.
I thought I could come over.
Hope...
You're my last hope.
If that's the case, then I guess you can stay.
Hm.
Thank you! I was worried you would say no.
No problem.
Oh, shoul ask Toudo san for permissi too?
This is part of her house.
No... Hime is asleep now.
If you're only using the hanare, then it should be fine.
Oh, okay.
Achoo!
Are you cold?

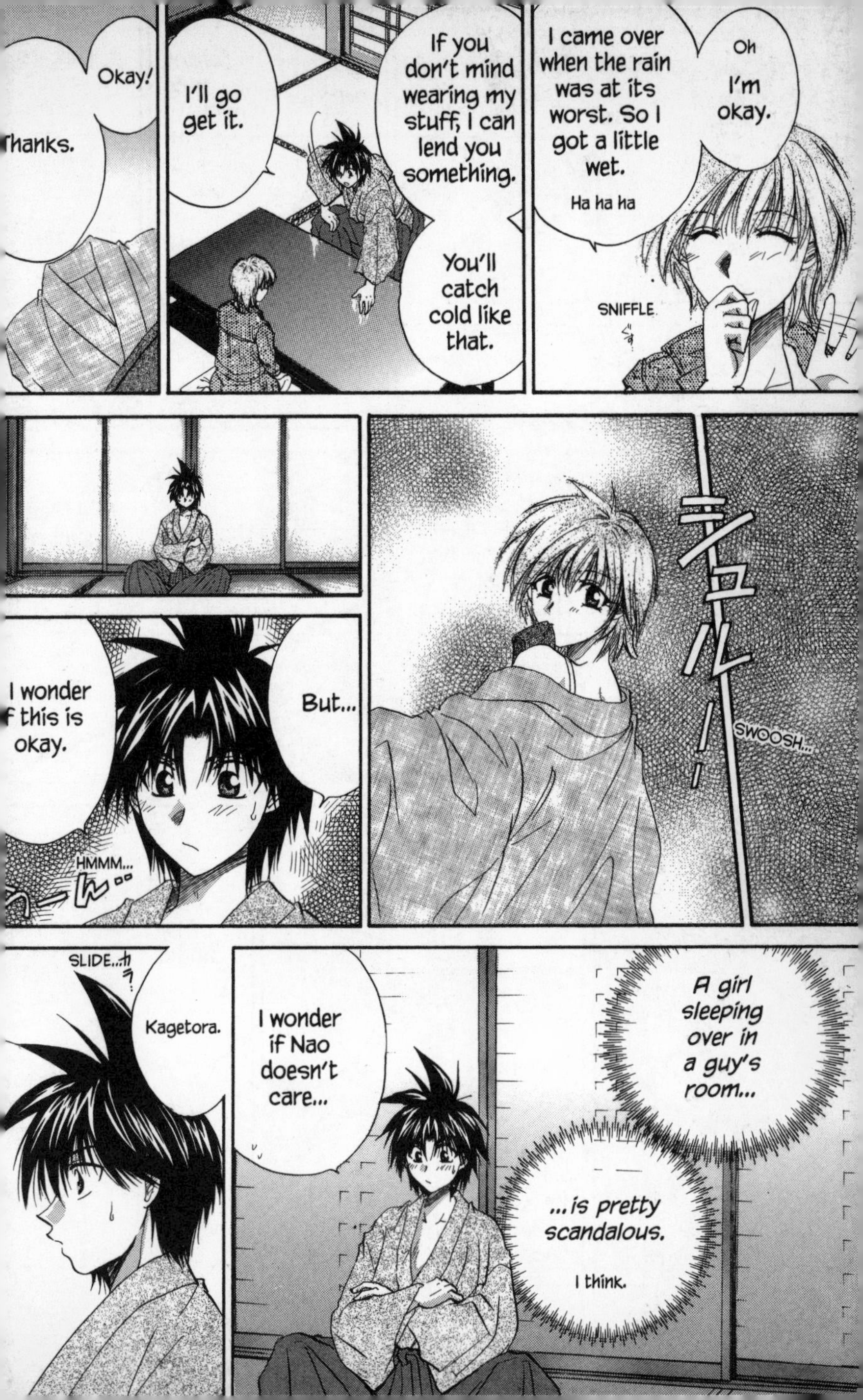

Oh
I'm okay.
I came over when the rain was at its worst. So I got a little wet.
Ha ha ha
SNIFFLE
If you don't mind wearing my stuff, I can lend you something.
You'll catch cold like that.
I'll go get it.
Okay!
hanks.
シュルーー
SWOOSH...
But...
I wonder
f this is
okay.
HMMM...
A girl sleeping over in a guy's room...
...is pretty scandalous.
I think.
I wonder if Nao doesn't care...
SLIDE...
Kagetora.

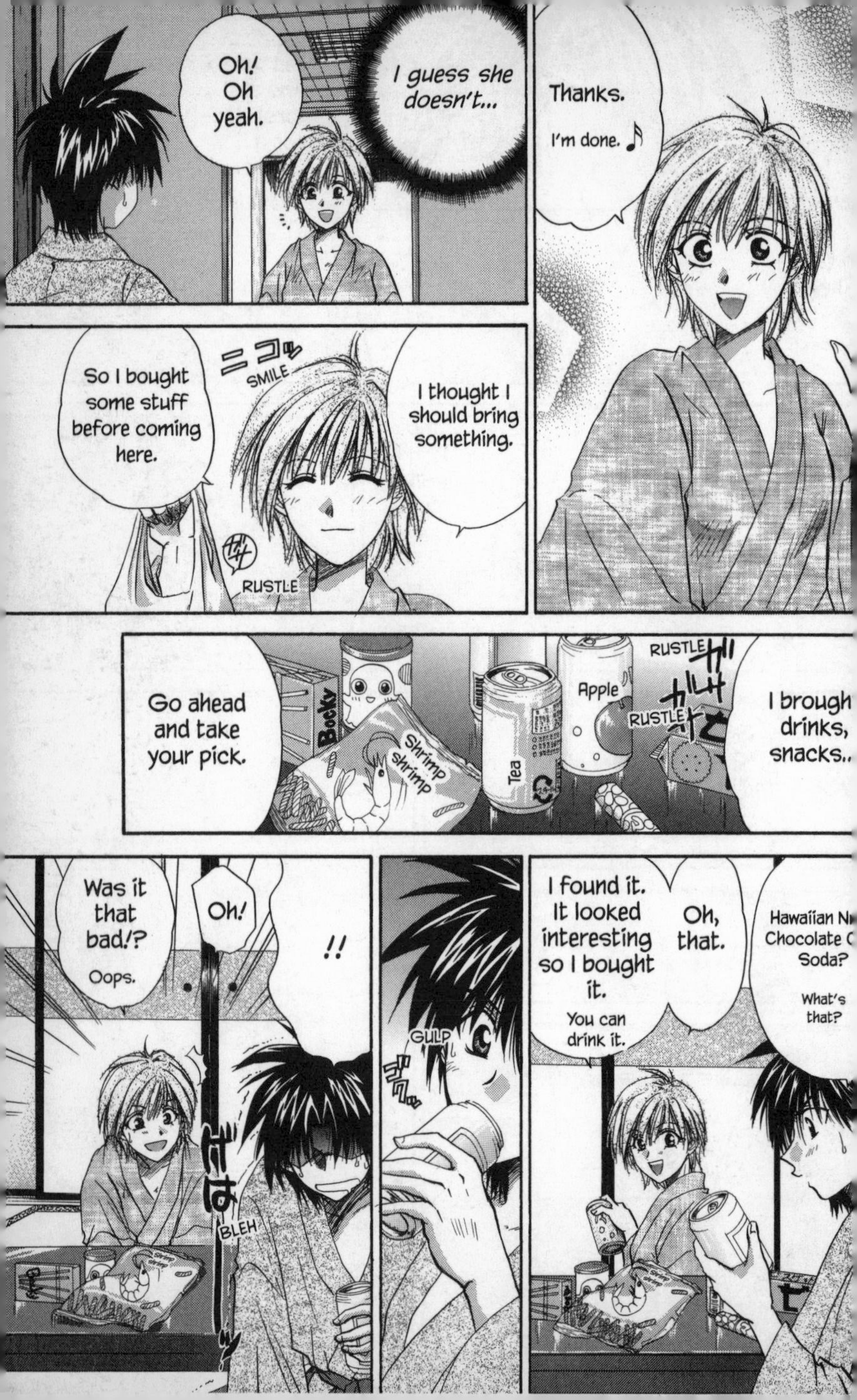

Thanks.
I'm done. ♪
I guess she doesn't...
Oh! Oh yeah.
I thought I should bring something.
ニコッ SMILE
So I bought some stuff before coming here.
RUSTLE
I brough drinks, snacks..
RUSTLE
RUSTLE
Apple
Tea
Shrimp shrimp
Bocky
Go ahead and take your pick.
Hawaiian N Chocolate C Soda?
What's that?
Oh, that.
I found it. It looked interesting so I bought it.
You can drink it.
GULP
!!
Oh!
BLEH
Was it that bad!?
Oops.

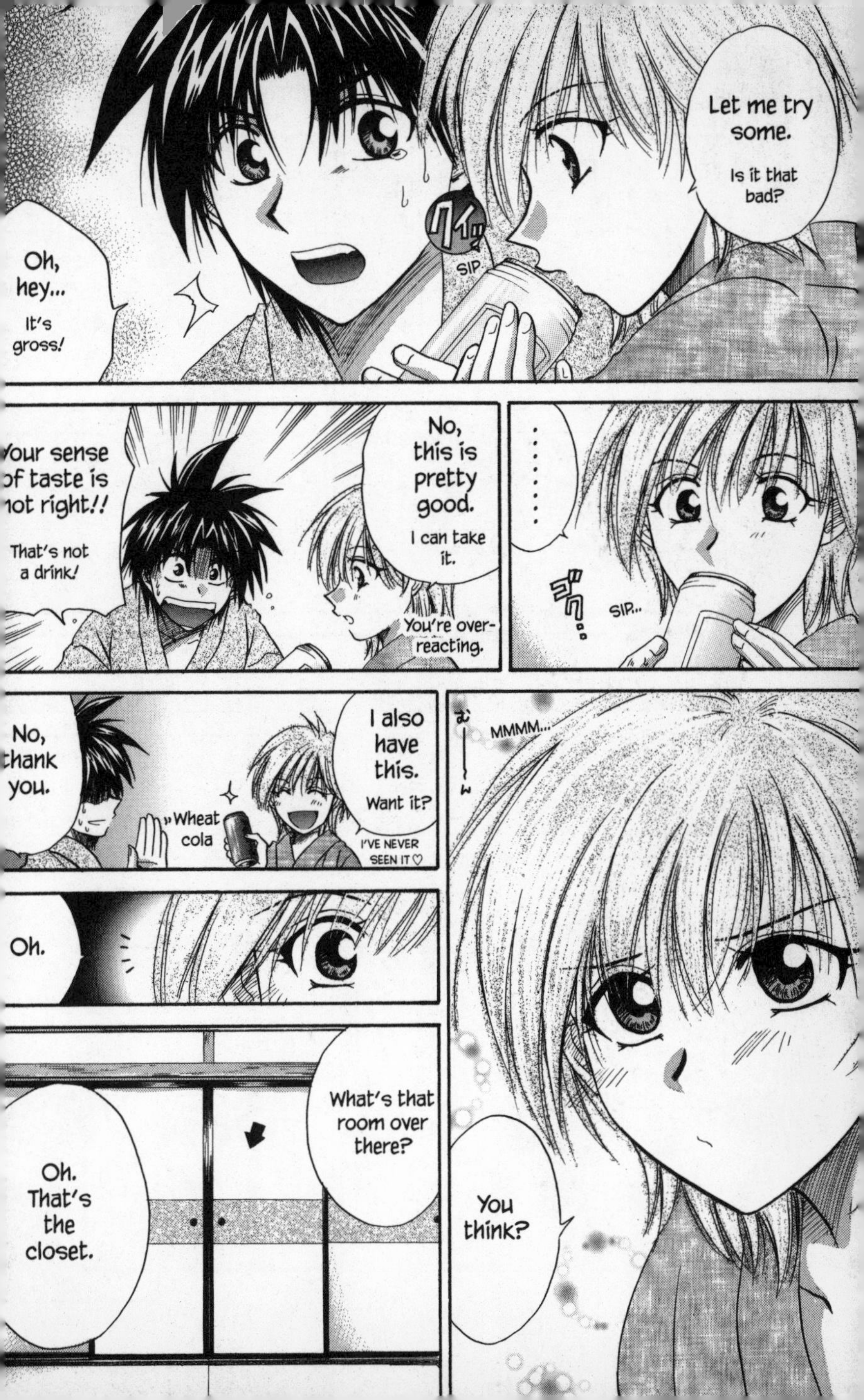
Let me try some.
Is it that bad?
SIP
Oh, hey...
It's gross!
....
SIP...
No, this is pretty good.
I can take it.
You're over-reacting.
our sense f taste is ot right!!
That's not a drink!
MMMM...
You think?
I also have this.
Want it?
I'VE NEVER SEEN IT ♡
Wheat cola
No, hank you.
Oh.
What's that room over there?
Oh. That's the closet.

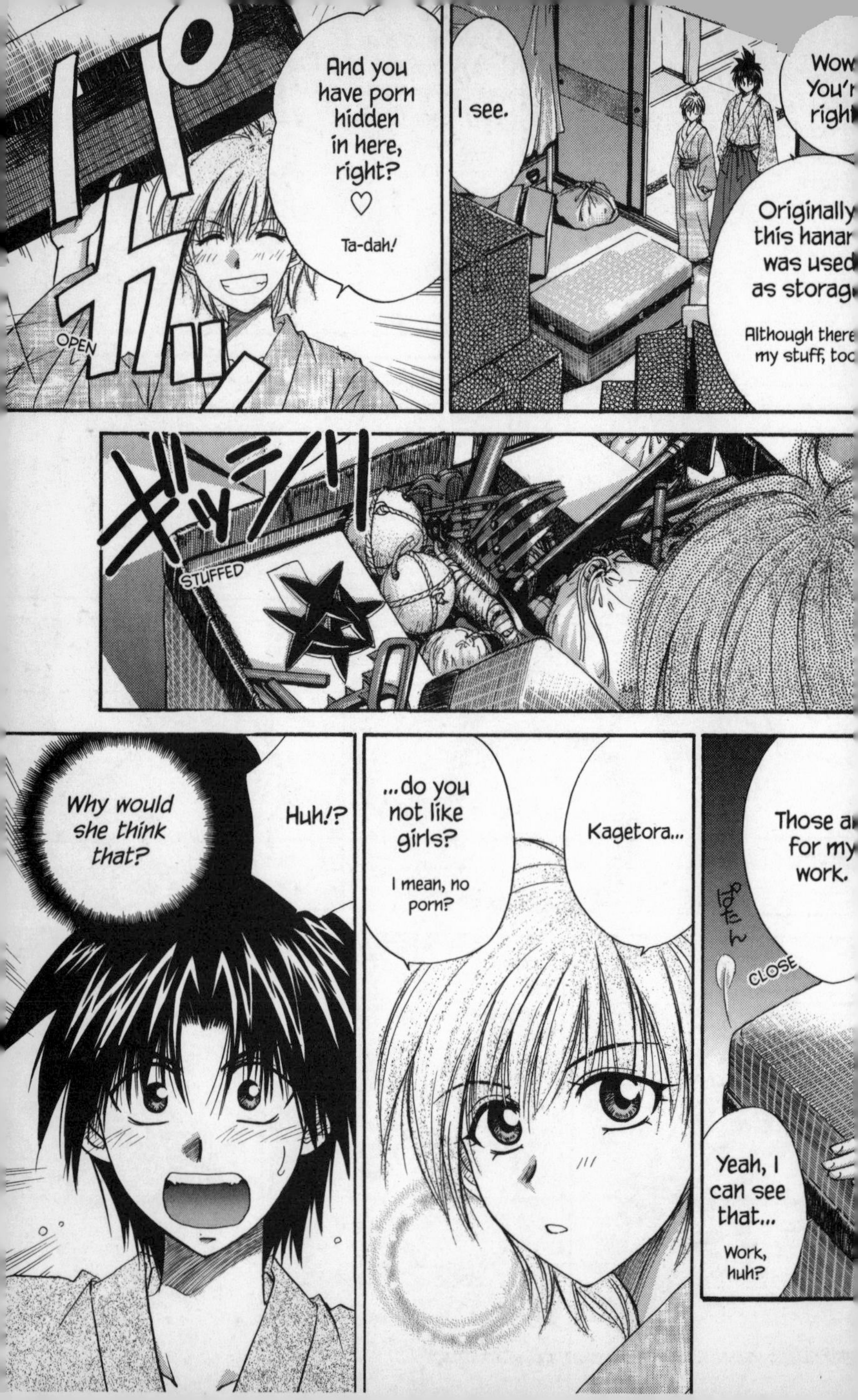
Wow You'r righ
Originally this hanar was used as storag
Although there my stuff, toc
I see.
And you have porn hidden in here, right? ♡
Ta-dah!
OPEN
STUFFED
Those a for my work.
CLOSE
Yeah, I can see that...
Work, huh?
Kagetora...
...do you not like girls?
I mean, no porn?
Huh!?
Why would she think that?

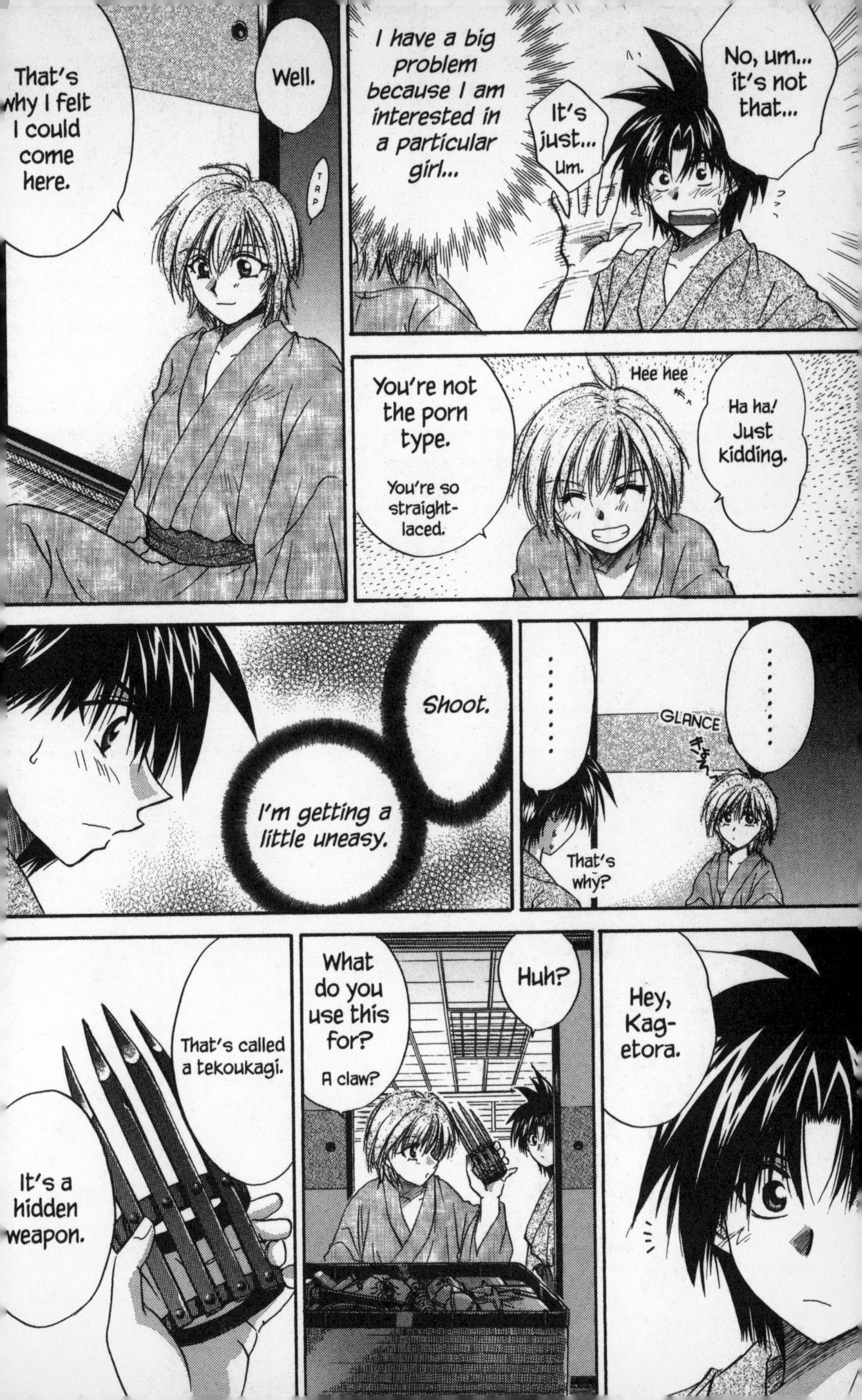

No, um... it's not that...
It's just... Um.
I have a big problem because I am interested in a particular girl...
Ha ha! Just kidding.
Hee hee
You're not the porn type.
You're so straight-laced.
Well.
TAP
That's why I felt I could come here.
......
GLANCE
......
That's why?
Shoot.
I'm getting a little uneasy.
Hey, Kagetora.
Huh?
What do you use this for?
A claw?
That's called a tekoukagi.
It's a hidden weapon.

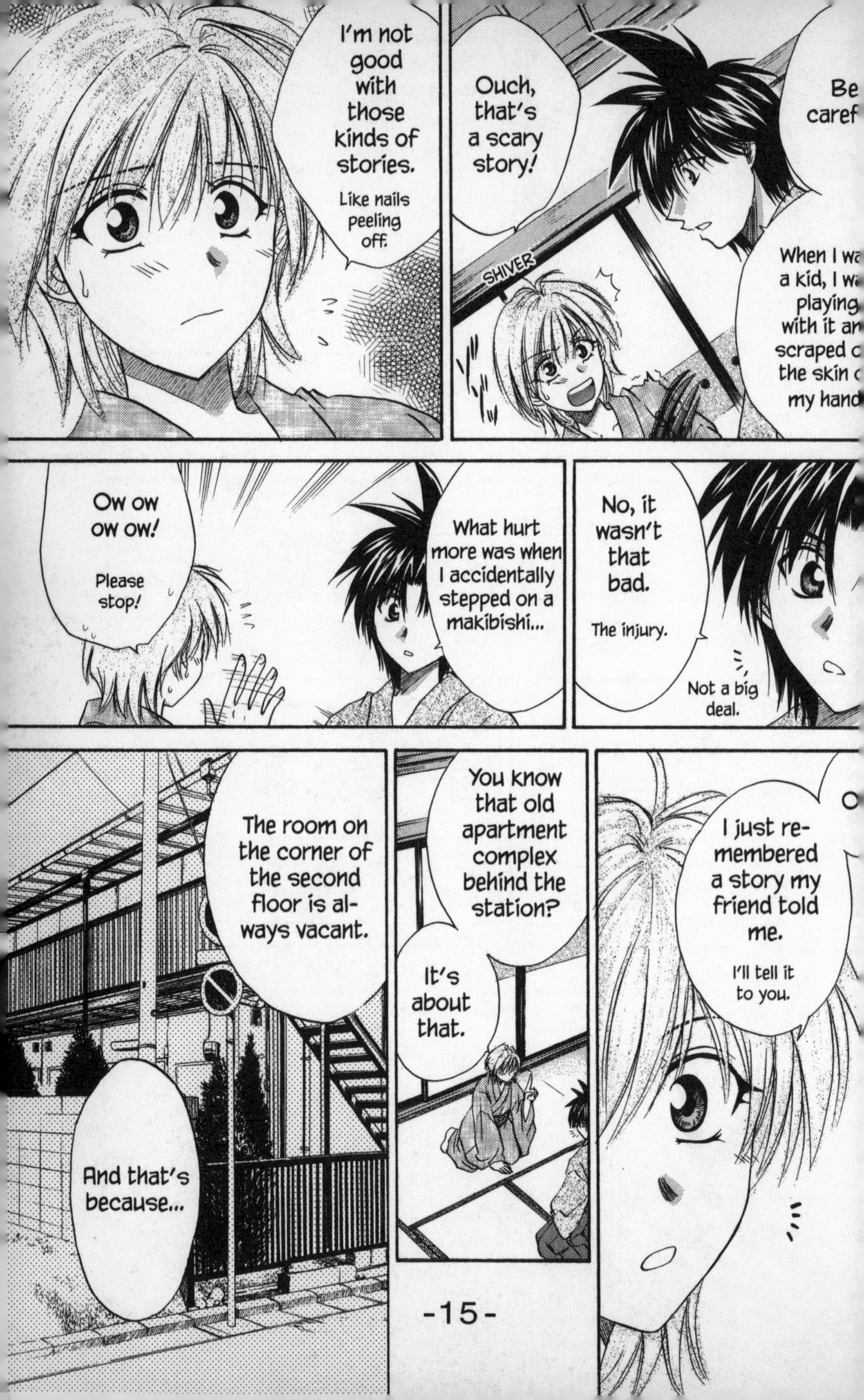

Be caref
When I wa a kid, I wa playing with it an scraped c the skin c my hand
Ouch, that's a scary story!
SHIVER
I'm not good with those kinds of stories.
Like nails peeling off.
No, it wasn't that bad.
The injury.
Not a big deal.
What hurt more was when I accidentally stepped on a makibishi...
Ow ow ow ow!
Please stop!
I just re-membered a story my friend told me.
I'll tell it to you.
You know that old apartment complex behind the station?
It's about that.
The room on the corner of the second floor is al-ways vacant.
And that's because...

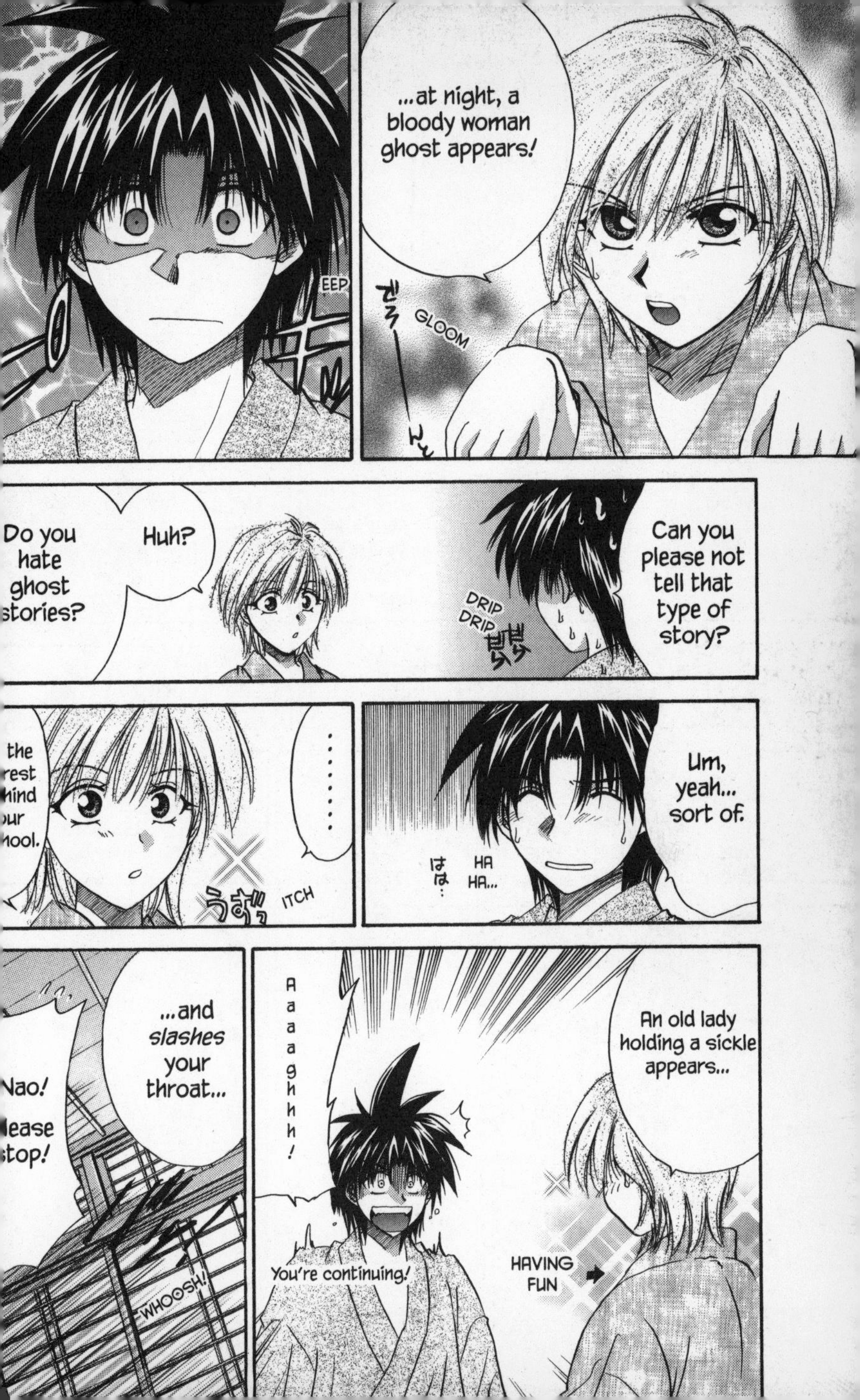

...at night, a bloody woman ghost appears!
GLOOM
EEP
Can you please not tell that type of story?
DRIP DRIP
Huh?
Do you hate ghost stories?
Um, yeah... sort of.
HA HA...
はは...
......
the rest hind ur hool.
ITCH
An old lady holding a sickle appears...
HAVING FUN
Aaaaaghhhh!
You're continuing!
...and slashes your throat...
Nao! lease top!
WHOOSH!

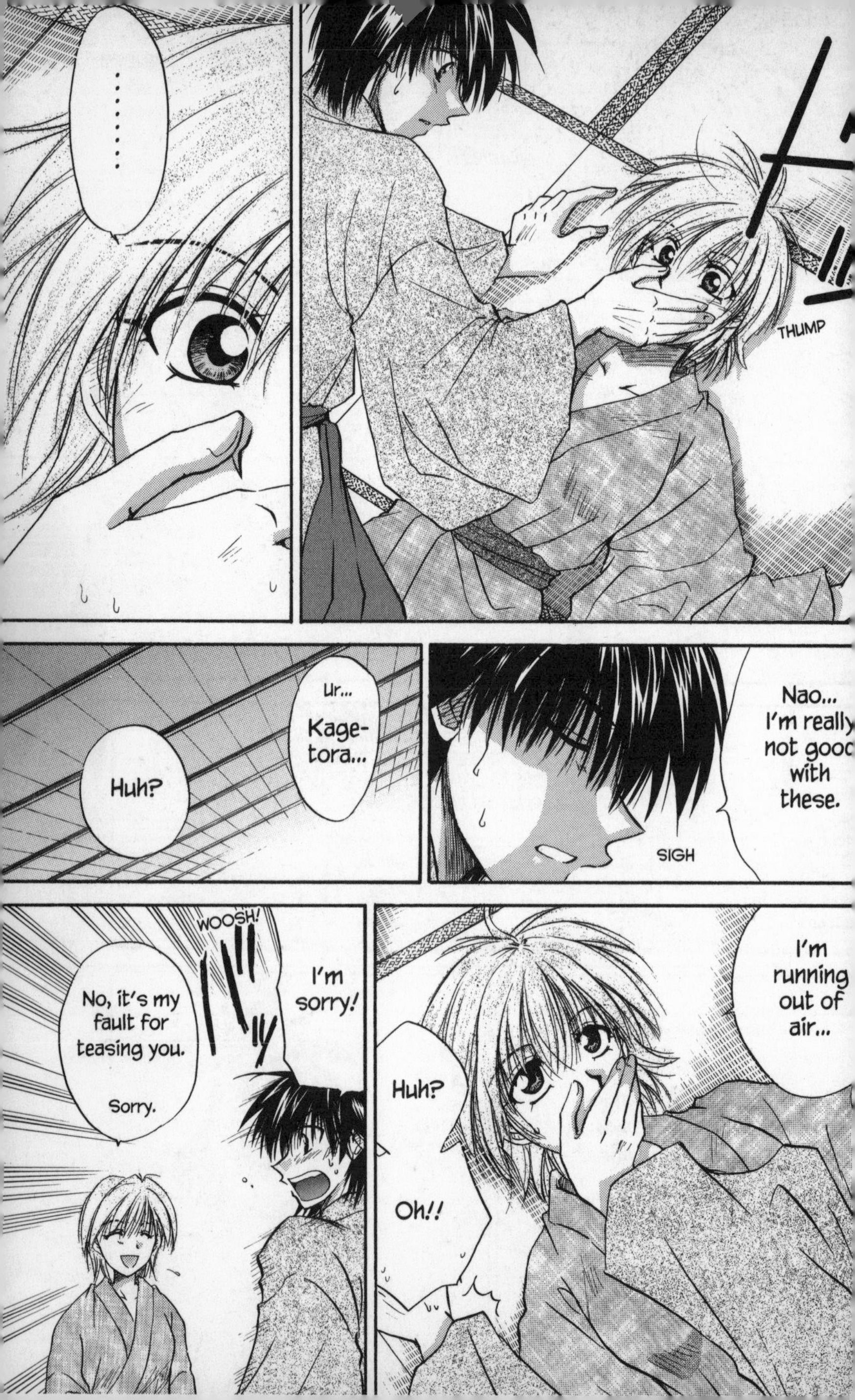
THUMP
......
Nao... I'm really not good with these.
SIGH
Ur... Kage-tora...
Huh?
I'm running out of air...
Huh?
Oh!!
I'm sorry!
WOOSH!
No, it's my fault for teasing you.
Sorry.

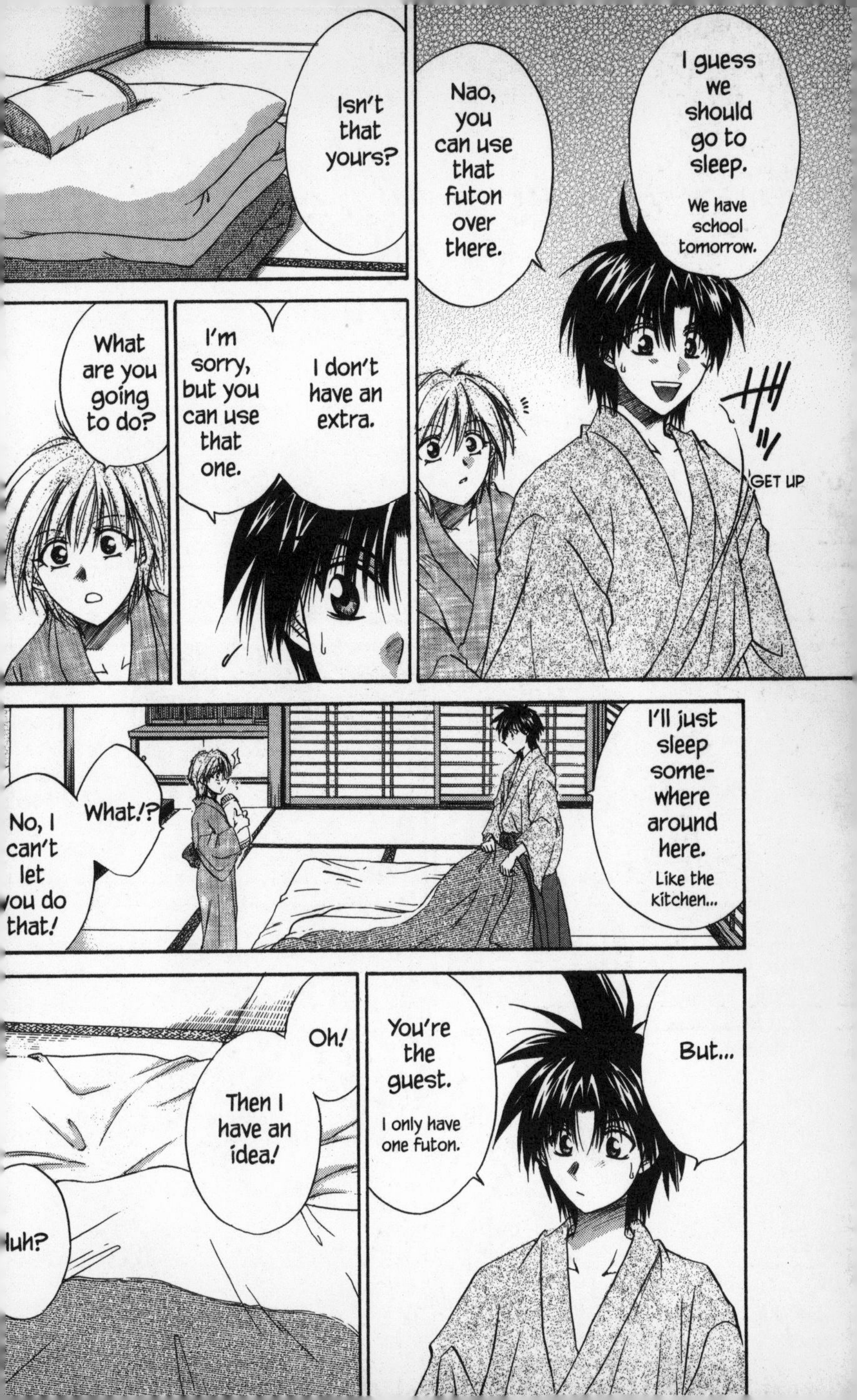
I guess we should go to sleep.
We have school tomorrow.
GET UP
Nao, you can use that futon over there.
Isn't that yours?
I don't have an extra.
I'm sorry, but you can use that one.
What are you going to do?
I'll just sleep somewhere around here.
Like the kitchen...
What!?
No, I can't let you do that!
But...
You're the guest.
I only have one futon.
Oh!
Then I have an idea!
uh?

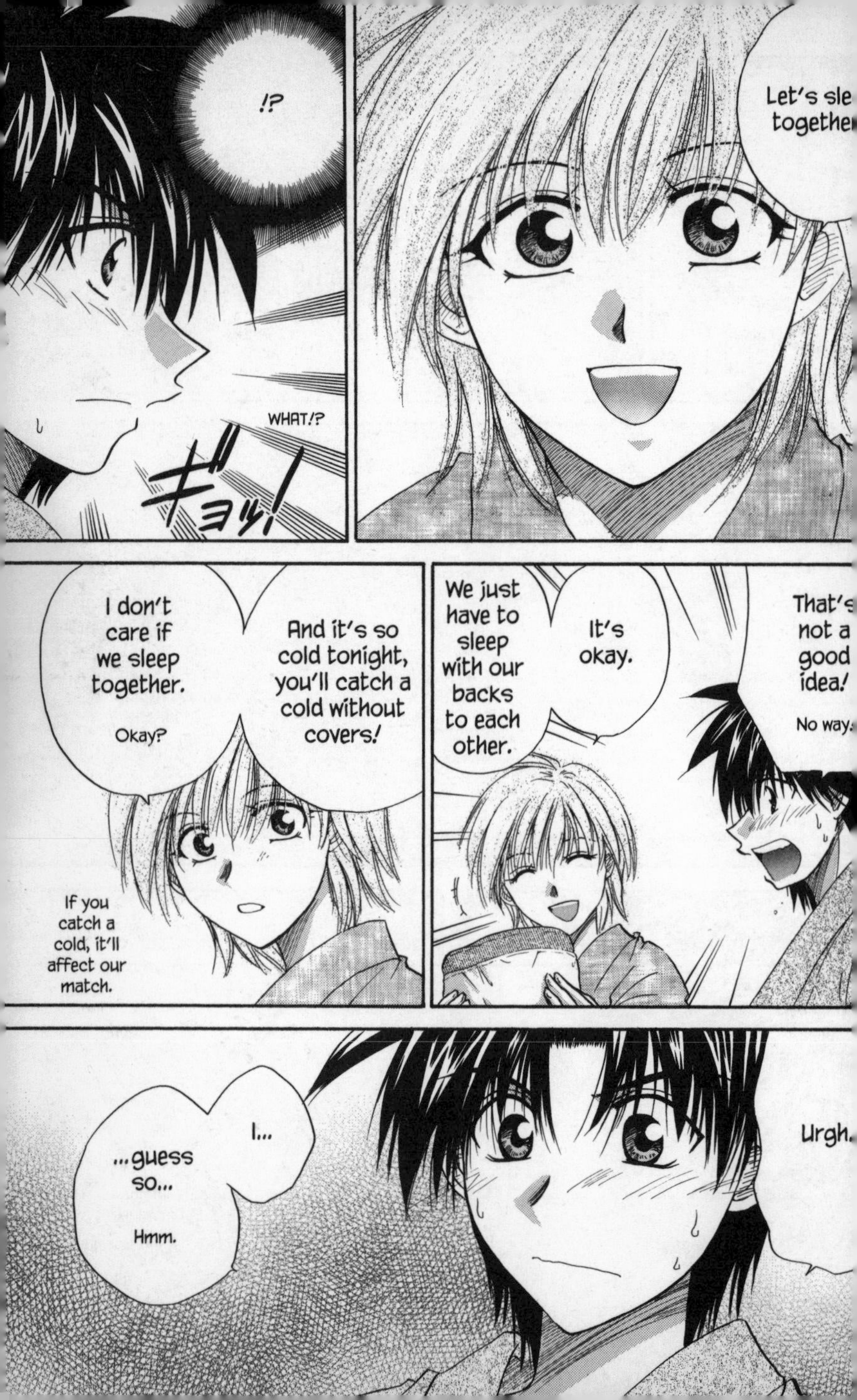
Let's sle togethe
!?
WHAT!?
ギョッ!
That's not a good idea!
No way.
It's okay.
We just have to sleep with our backs to each other.
And it's so cold tonight, you'll catch a cold without covers!
I don't care if we sleep together.
Okay?
If you catch a cold, it'll affect our match.
Urgh.
I...
...guess so...
Hmm.

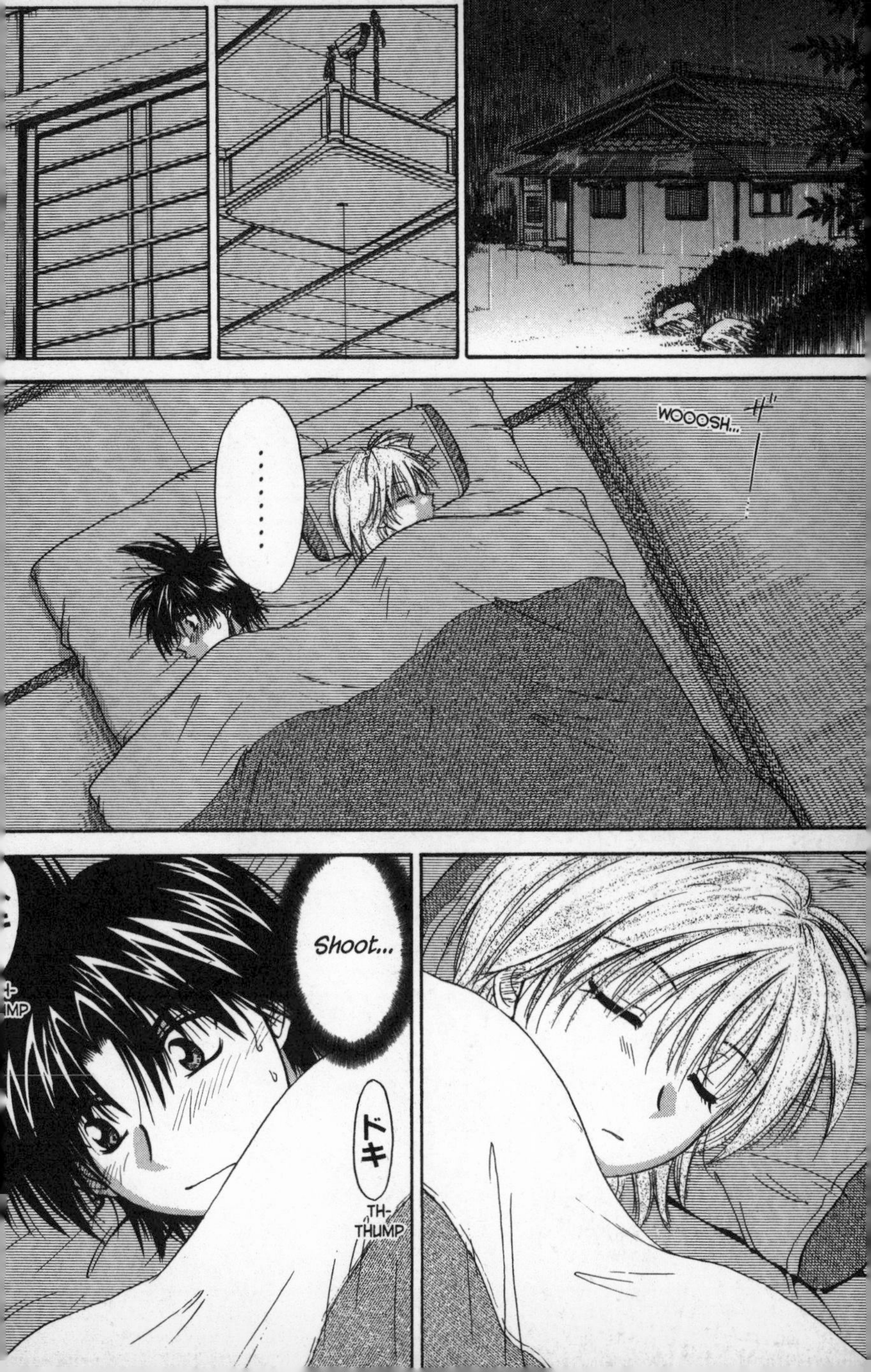
WOOOSH...
......
Shoot...
TH-THUMP

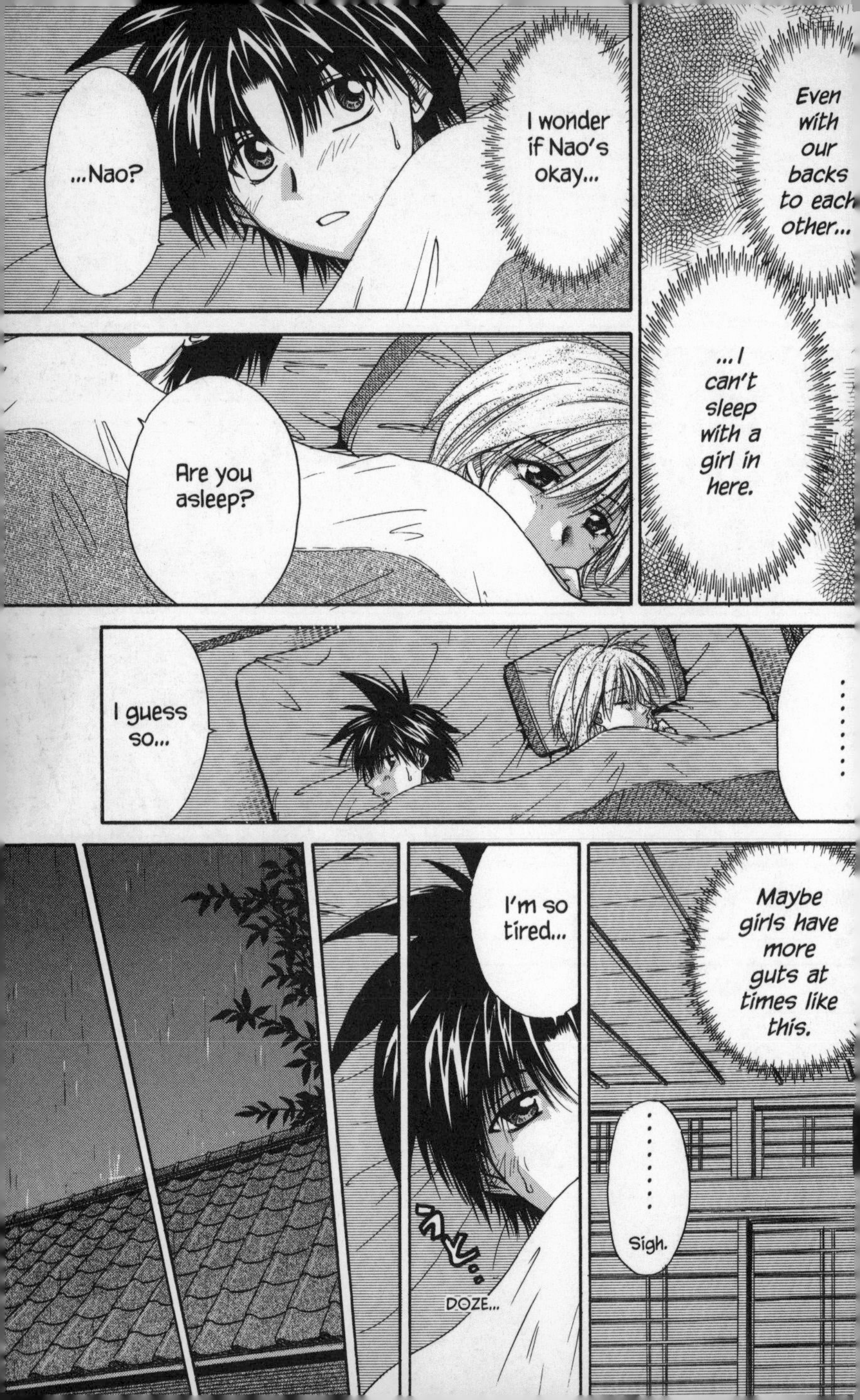
Even with our backs to each other...
...I can't sleep with a girl in here.
I wonder if Nao's okay...
...Nao?
Are you asleep?
......
I guess so...
Maybe girls have more guts at times like this.
......
Sigh.
I'm so tired...
DOZE...

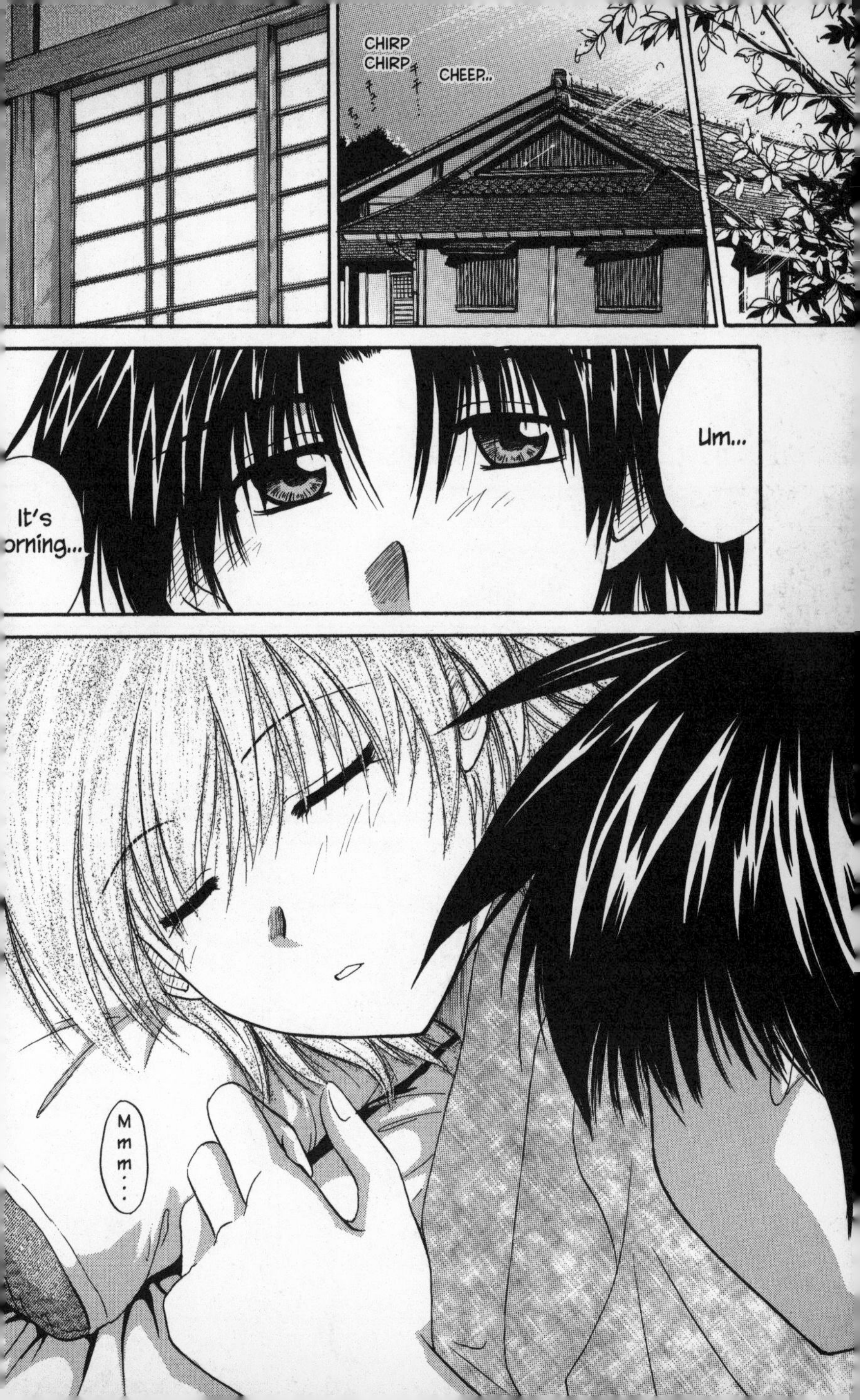
CHIRP CHIRP
CHEEP...
Um...
It's orning...
Mmm...

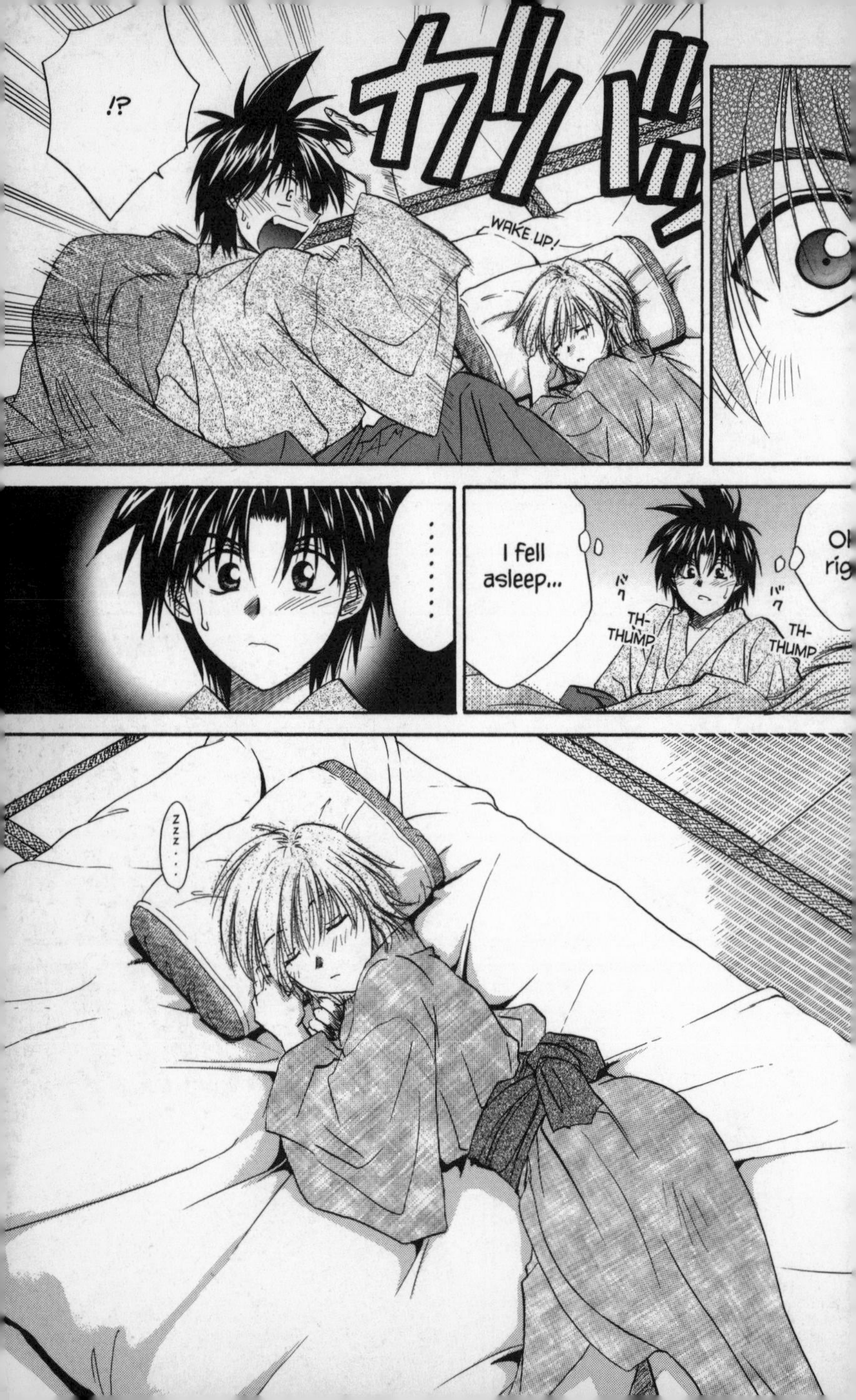
WAKE UP!
!?
Oh rig
TH-THUMP
I fell asleep...
TH-THUMP
....
ZZZ...

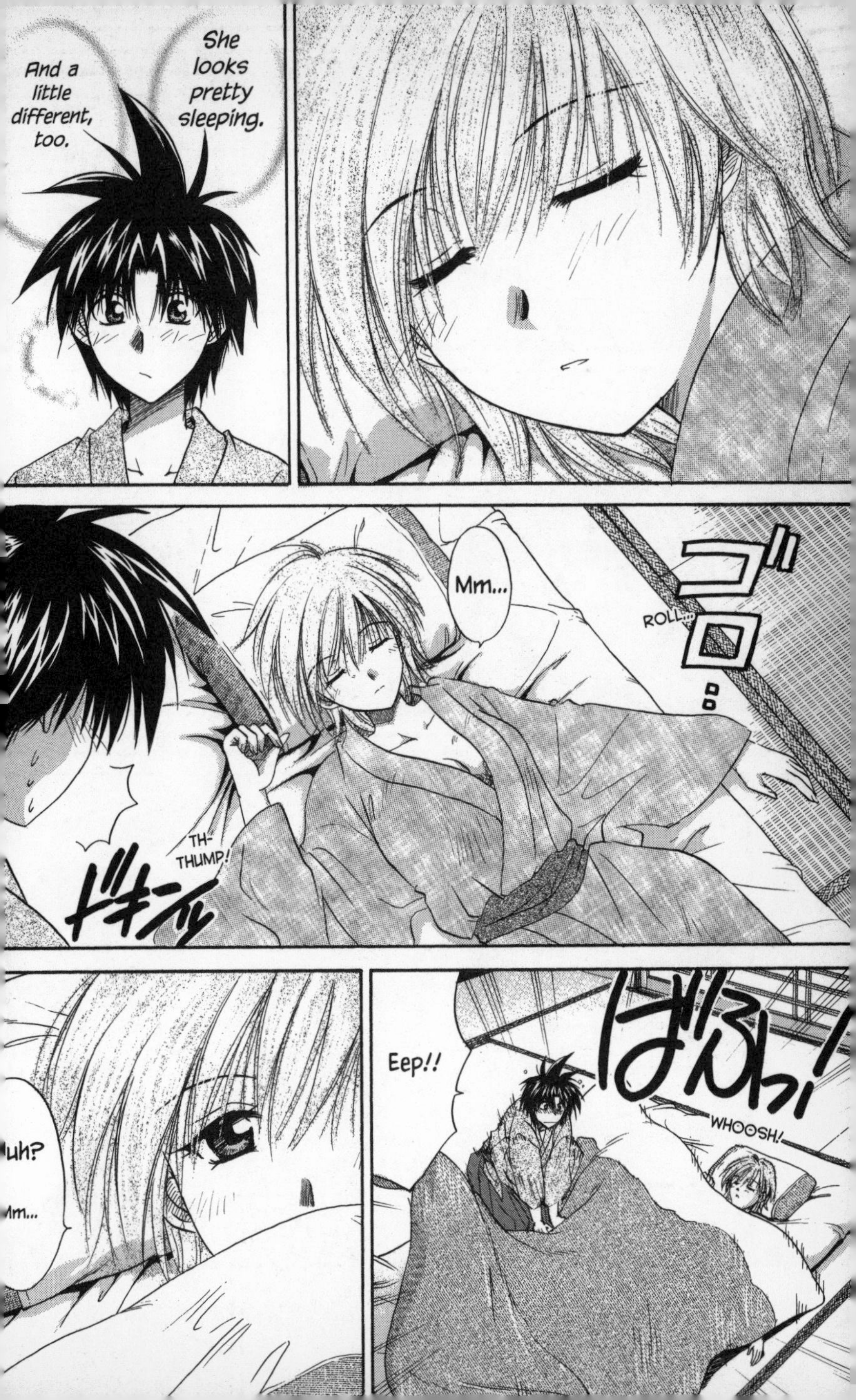
She looks pretty sleeping.
And a little different, too.
Mm...
ROLL...
TH-THUMP!
Eep!!
WHOOSH!
uh?
m...

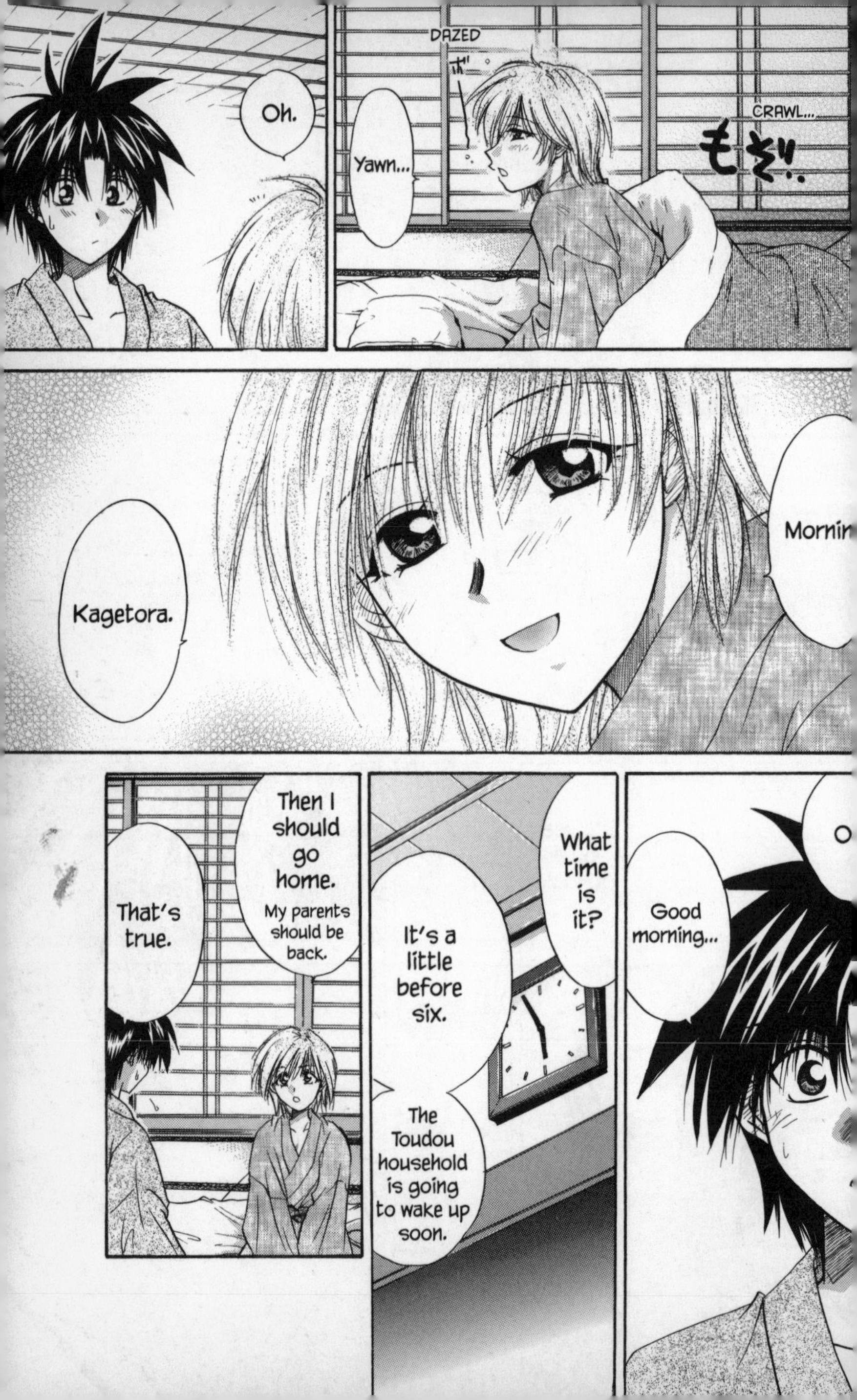
CRAWL...
もそ!!..
DAZED
Yawn...
Oh.
Mornin
Kagetora.
O
Good morning...
What time is it?
It's a little before six.
The Toudou household is going to wake up soon.
Then I should go home.
My parents should be back.
That's true.

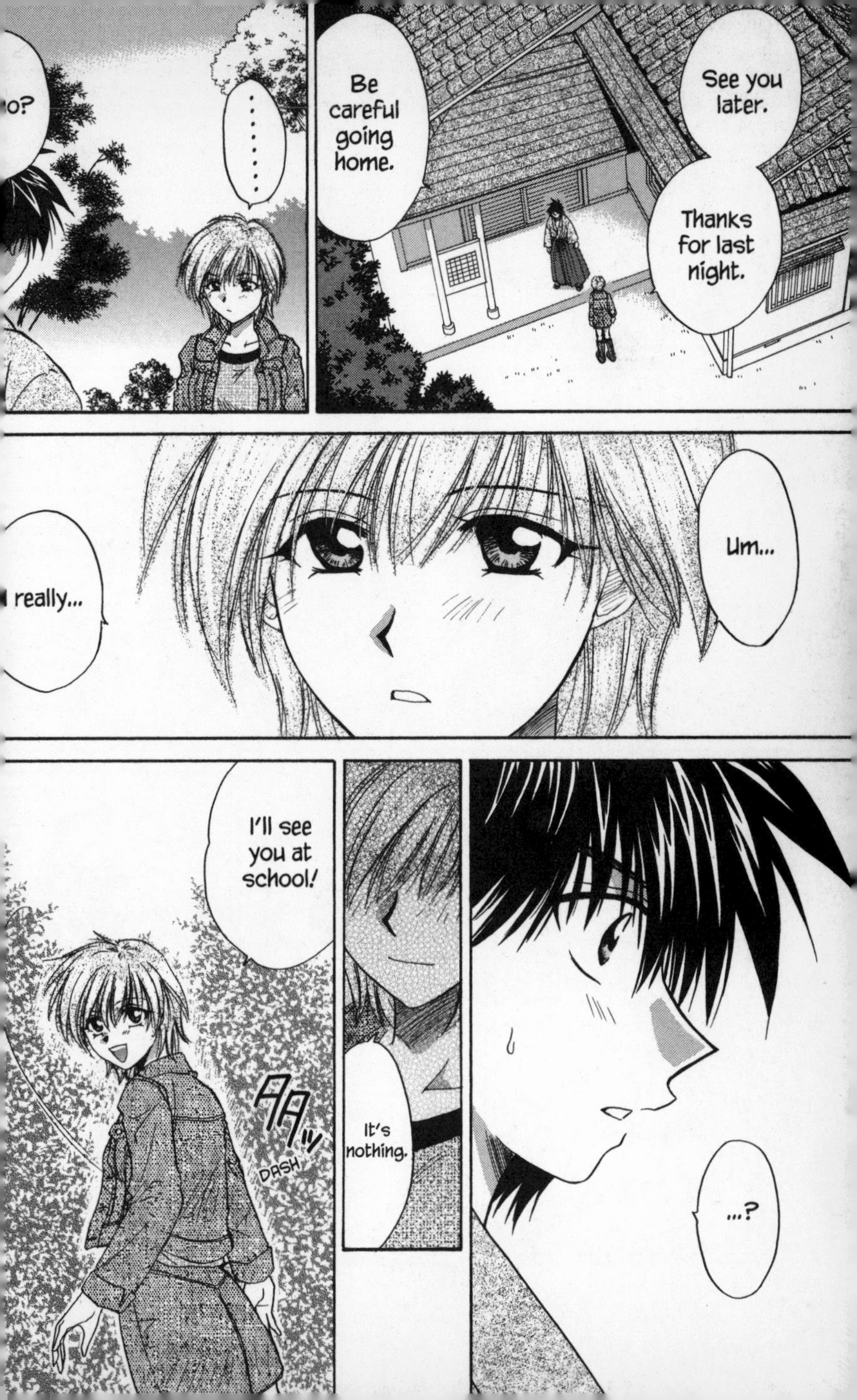

See you later.
Thanks for last night.
Be careful going home.
......
o?
Um...
really...
...?
It's nothing.
I'll see you at school!
DASH

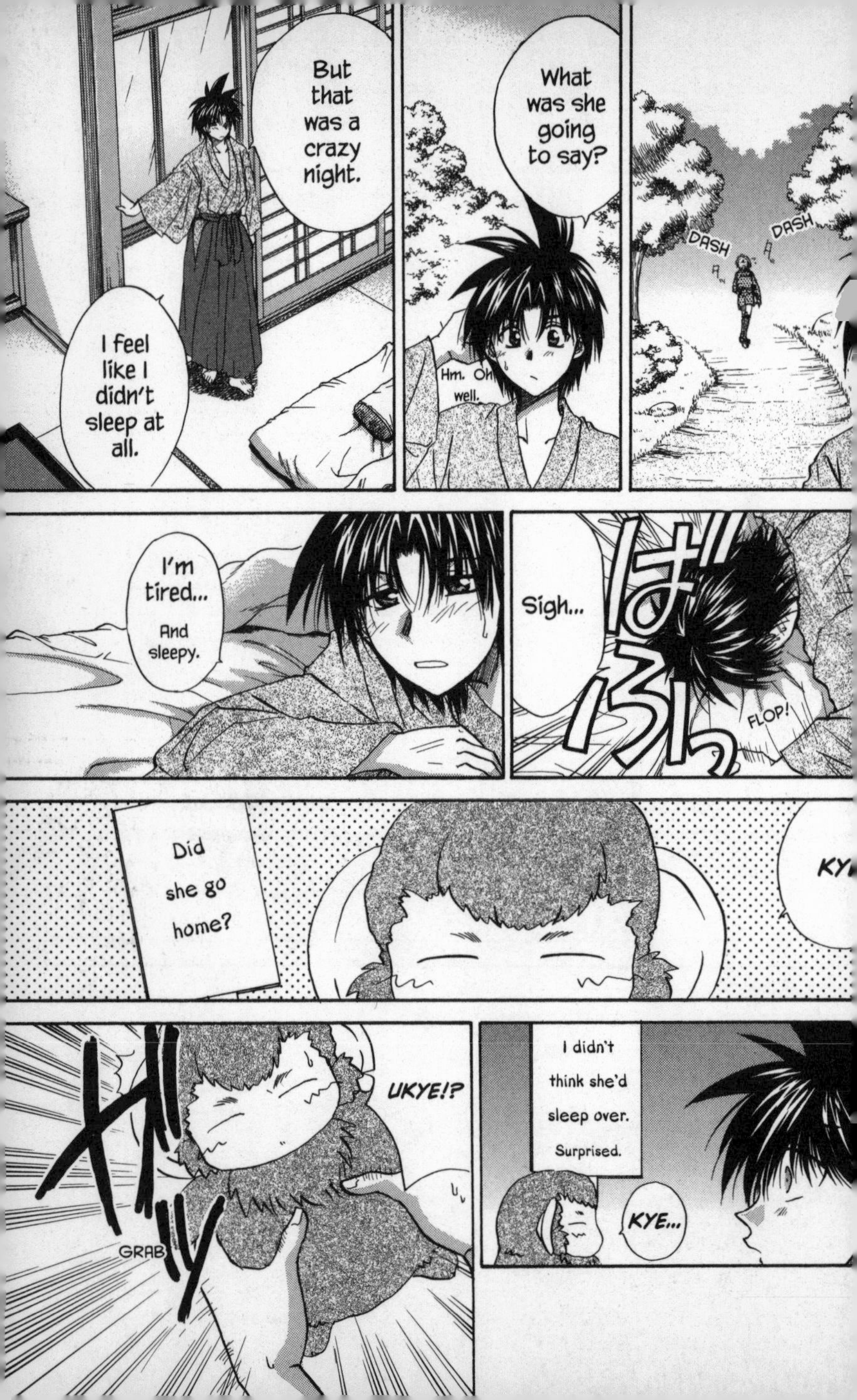
DASH
DASH
What was she going to say?
Hm. Oh well.
But that was a crazy night.
I feel like I didn't sleep at all.
Sigh...
ばふっ
FLOP!
I'm tired...
And sleepy.
KY
Did she go home?
I didn't think she'd sleep over.
Surprised.
KYE...
UKYE!?
GRAB

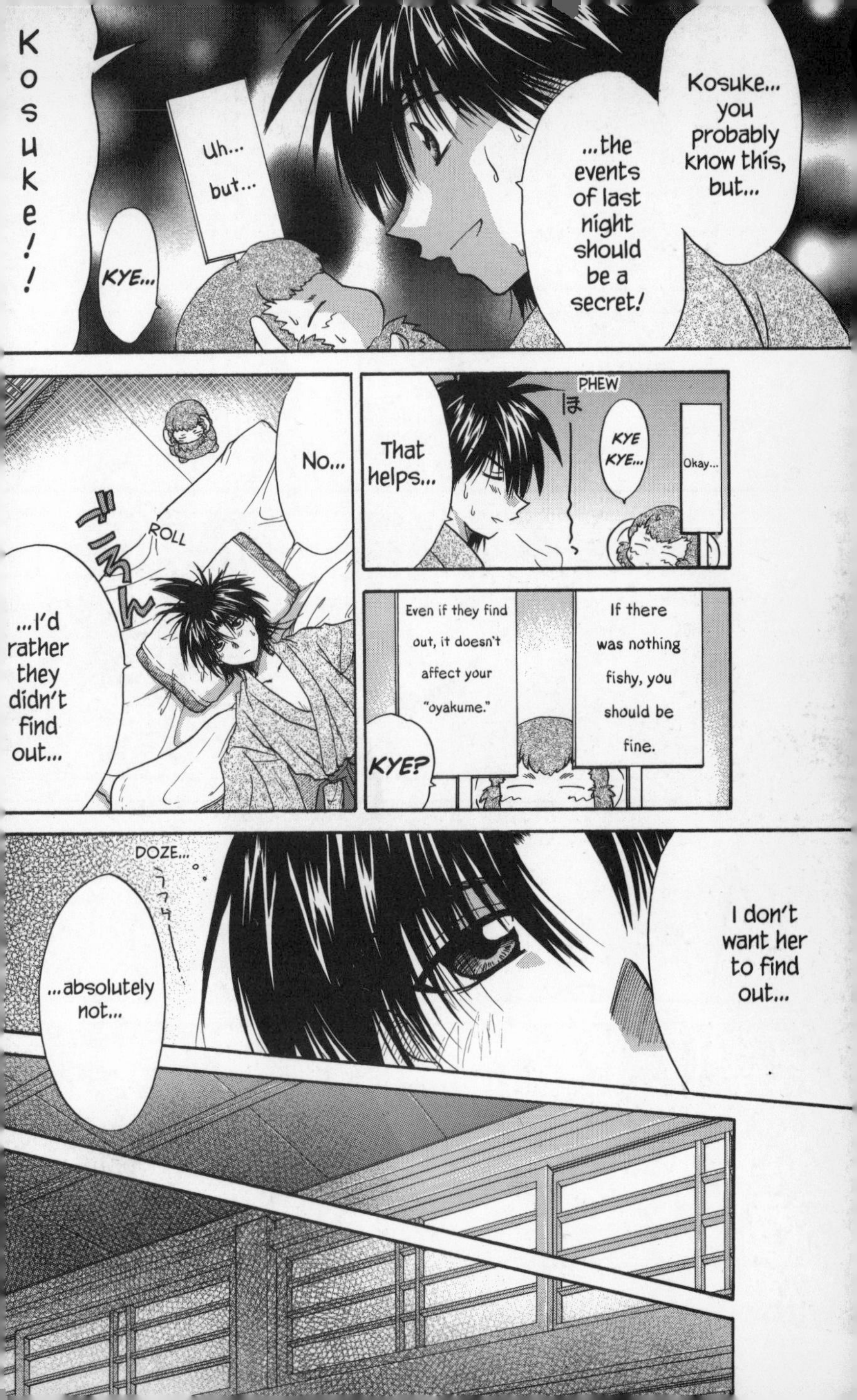
Kosuke... you probably know this, but...
...the events of last night should be a secret!
Uh... but...
Kosuke!!
KYE...
PHEW
Okay...
KYE KYE...
That helps...
If there was nothing fishy, you should be fine.
Even if they find out, it doesn't affect your "oyakume."
KYE?
No...
ROLL
...I'd rather they didn't find out...
I don't want her to find out...
DOZE...
...absolutely not...

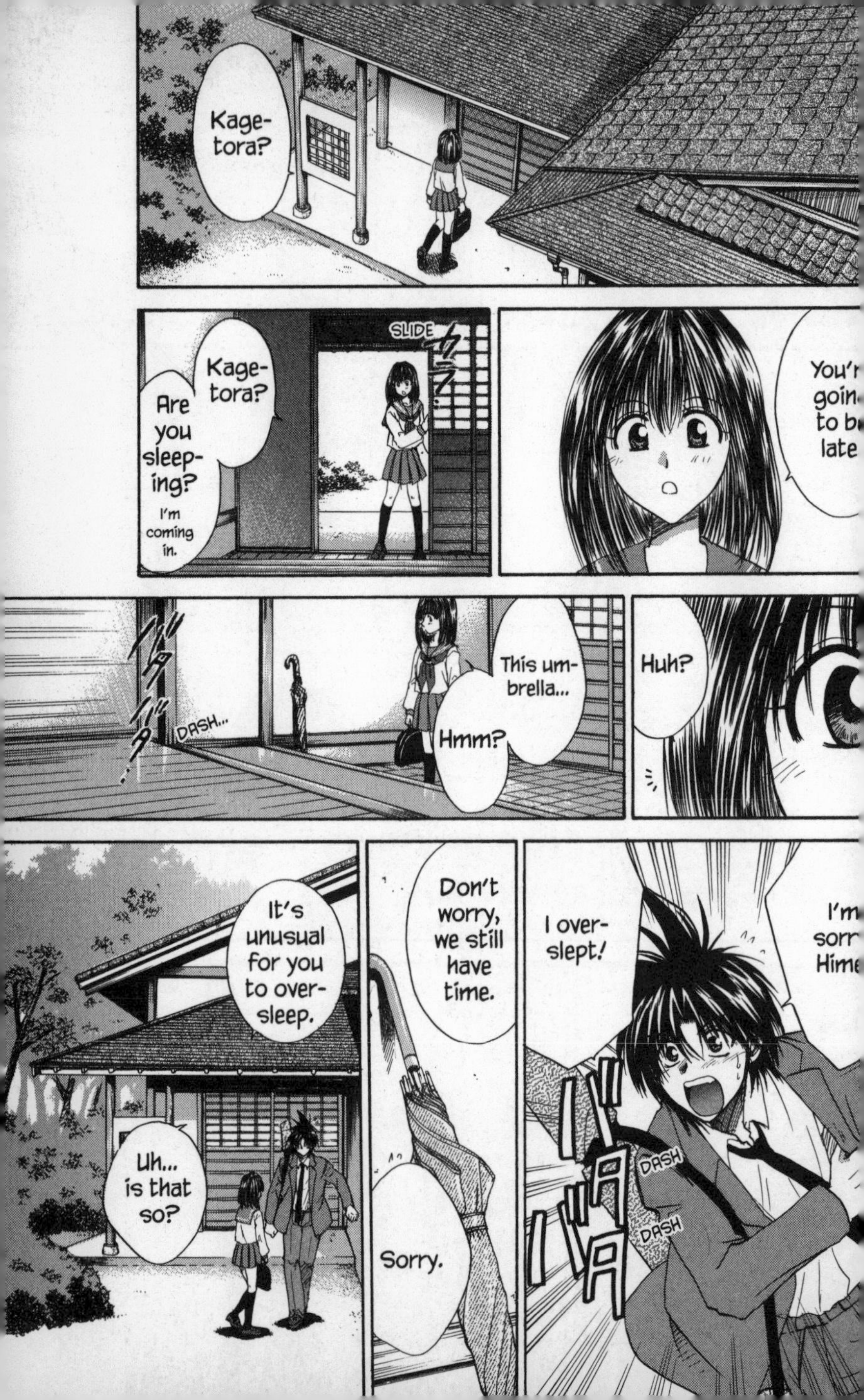
Kage-tora?
You'r goin to b late
SLIDE
Kage-tora?
Are you sleep-ing?
I'm coming in.
Huh?
This um-brella...
Hmm?
DASH...
I'm sorr Hime
I over-slept!
DASH
DASH
Don't worry, we still have time.
Sorry.
It's unusual for you to over-sleep.
Uh... is that so?

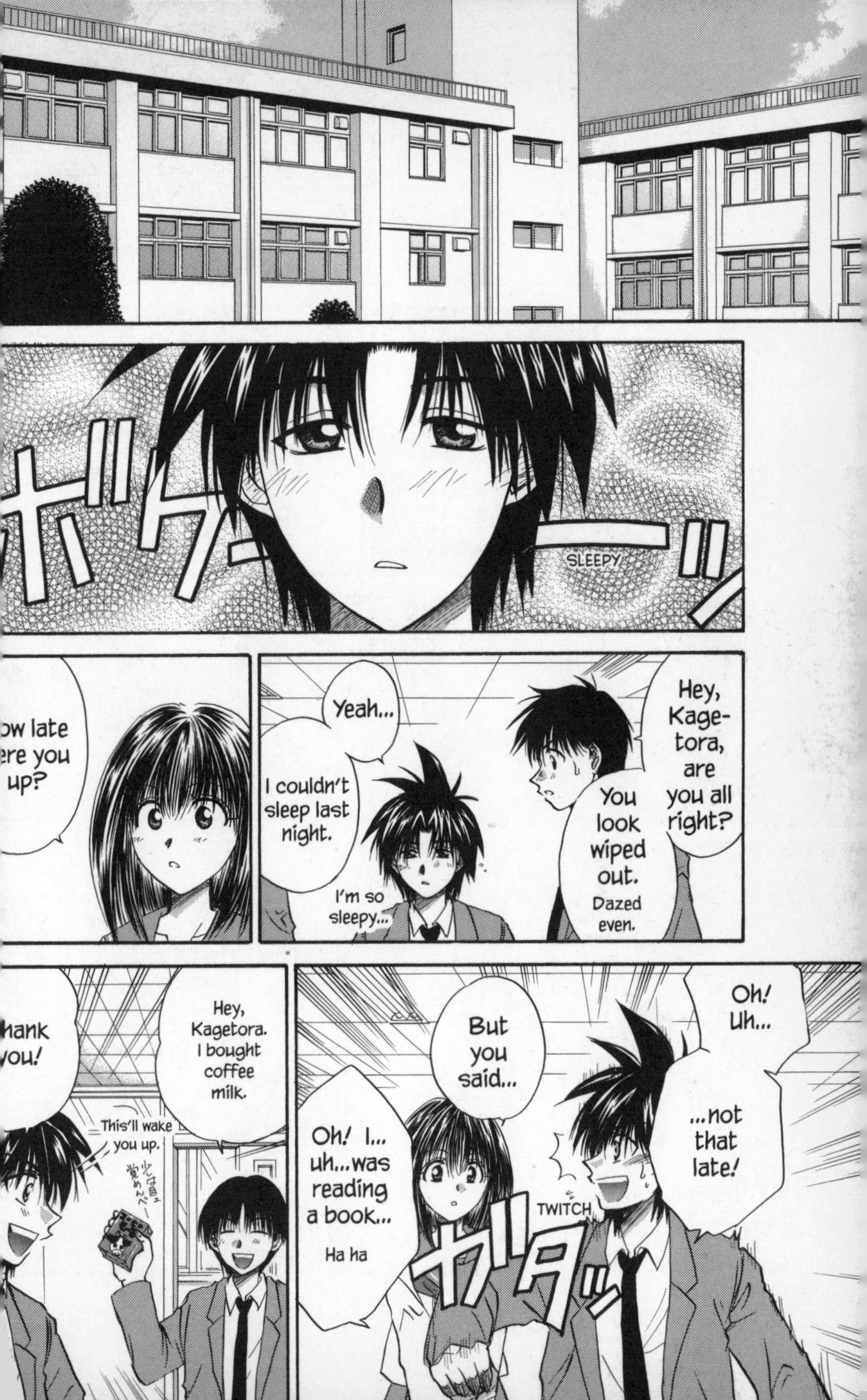
SLEEPY
Hey, Kagetora, are you all right?
You look wiped out.
Dazed even.
Yeah...
I couldn't sleep last night.
I'm so sleepy...
ow late
ere you up?
Oh! uh...
...not that late!
TWITCH
But you said...
Oh! I... uh...was reading a book...
Ha ha
Hey, Kagetora. I bought coffee milk.
This'll wake you up.
hank you!

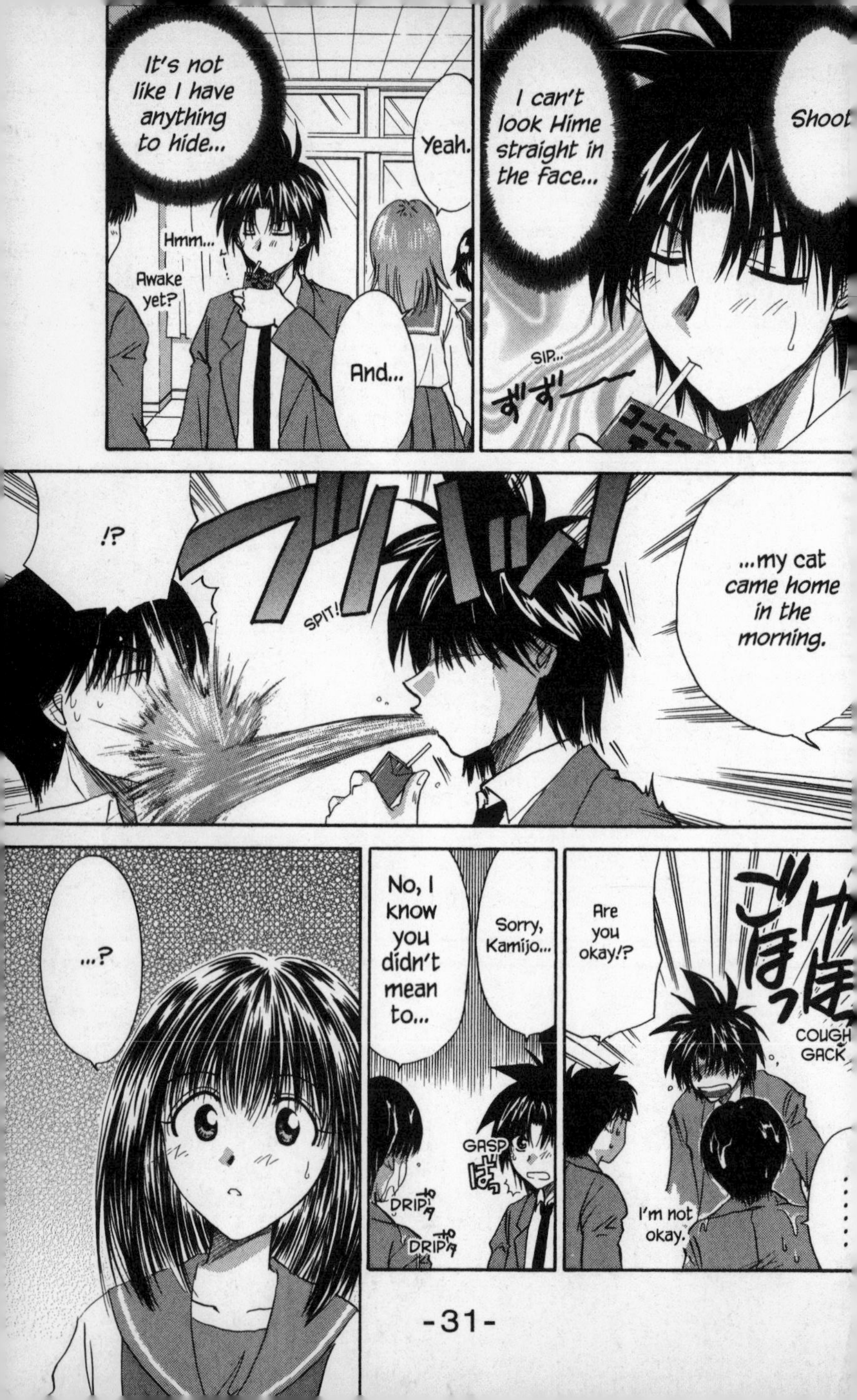
Shoot
I can't look Hime straight in the face...
SIP...
It's not like I have anything to hide...
Yeah.
Hmm...
Awake yet?
And...
...my cat came home in the morning.
SPIT!
!?
COUGH GACK
Are you okay!?
I'm not okay.
...
Sorry, Kamijo...
No, I know you didn't mean to...
GASP
DRIP
DRIP
...?

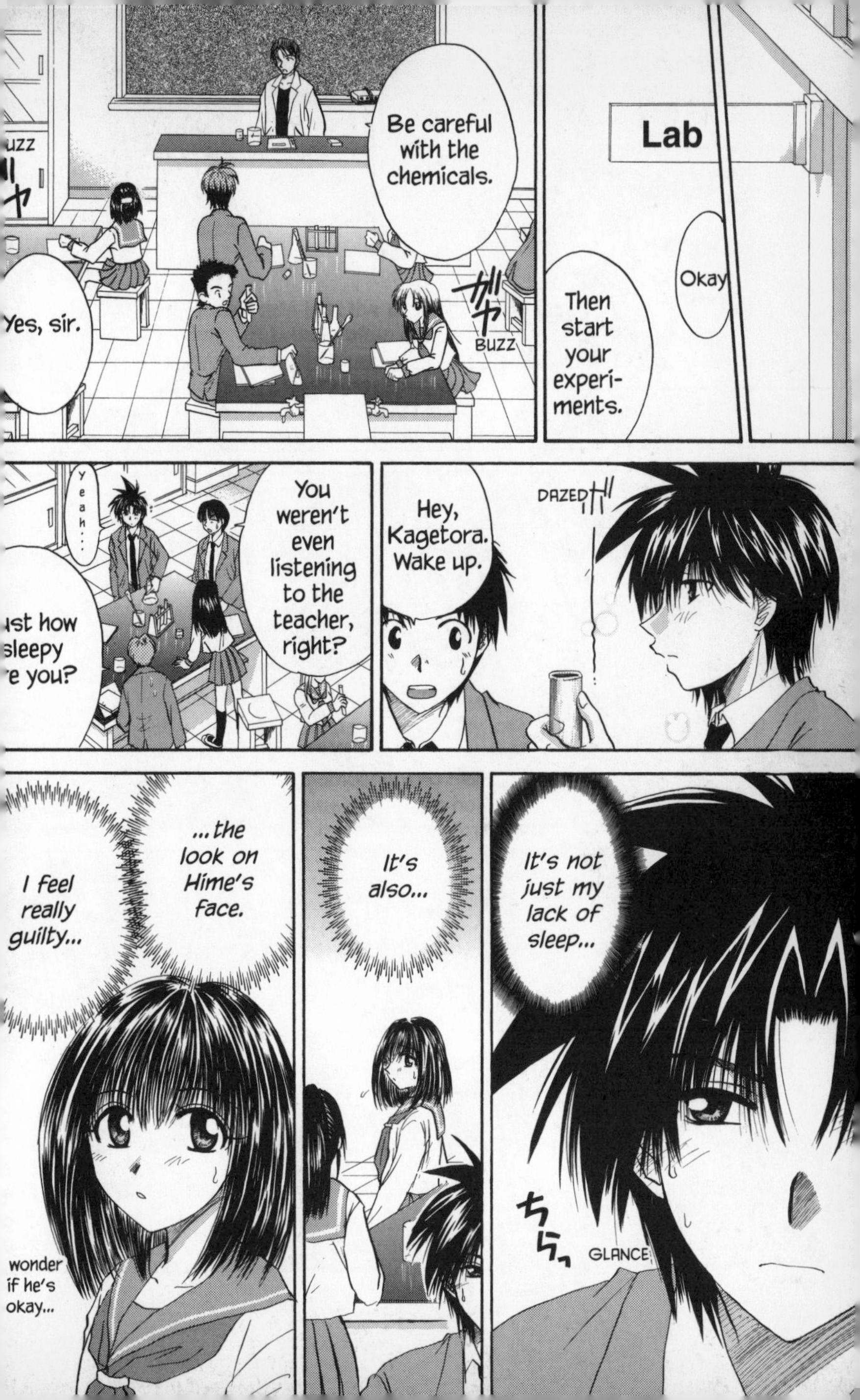
Lab
Okay
Then start your experiments.
Be careful with the chemicals.
BUZZ
Yes, sir.
UZZ
DAZED
Hey, Kagetora. Wake up.
You weren't even listening to the teacher, right?
Yeah...
ust how sleepy e you?
It's not just my lack of sleep...
GLANCE
It's also...
...the look on Hime's face.
I feel really guilty...
wonder if he's okay...

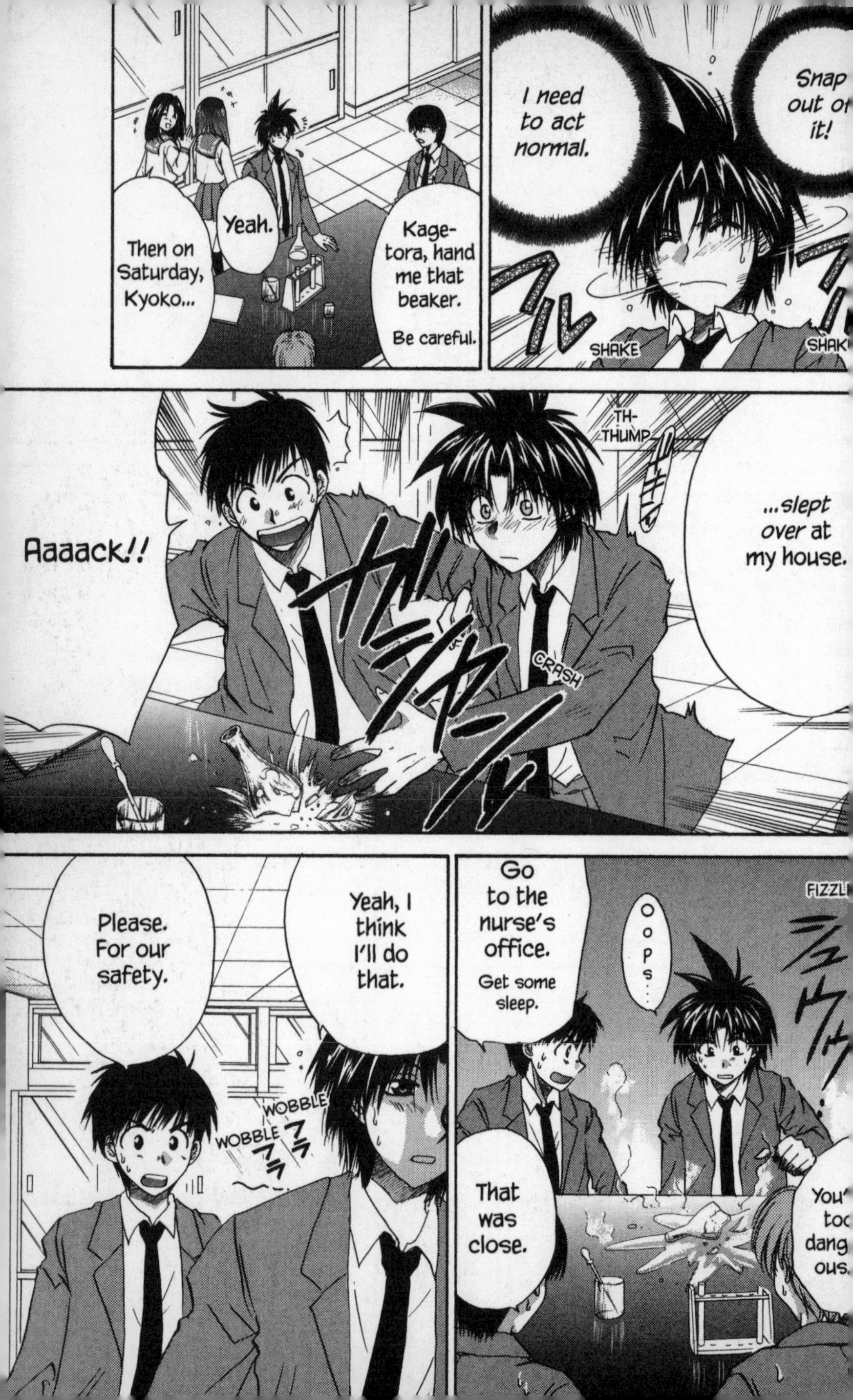
Snap out of it!
I need to act normal.
SHAK
SHAKE
Kage-tora, hand me that beaker.
Be careful.
Yeah.
Then on Saturday, Kyoko...
...slept over at my house.
TH-THUMP
CRASH
Aaaack!!
FIZZL
Oops...
Go to the nurse's office.
Get some sleep.
That was close.
Yeah, I think I'll do that.
WOBBLE
WOBBLE
Please. For our safety.

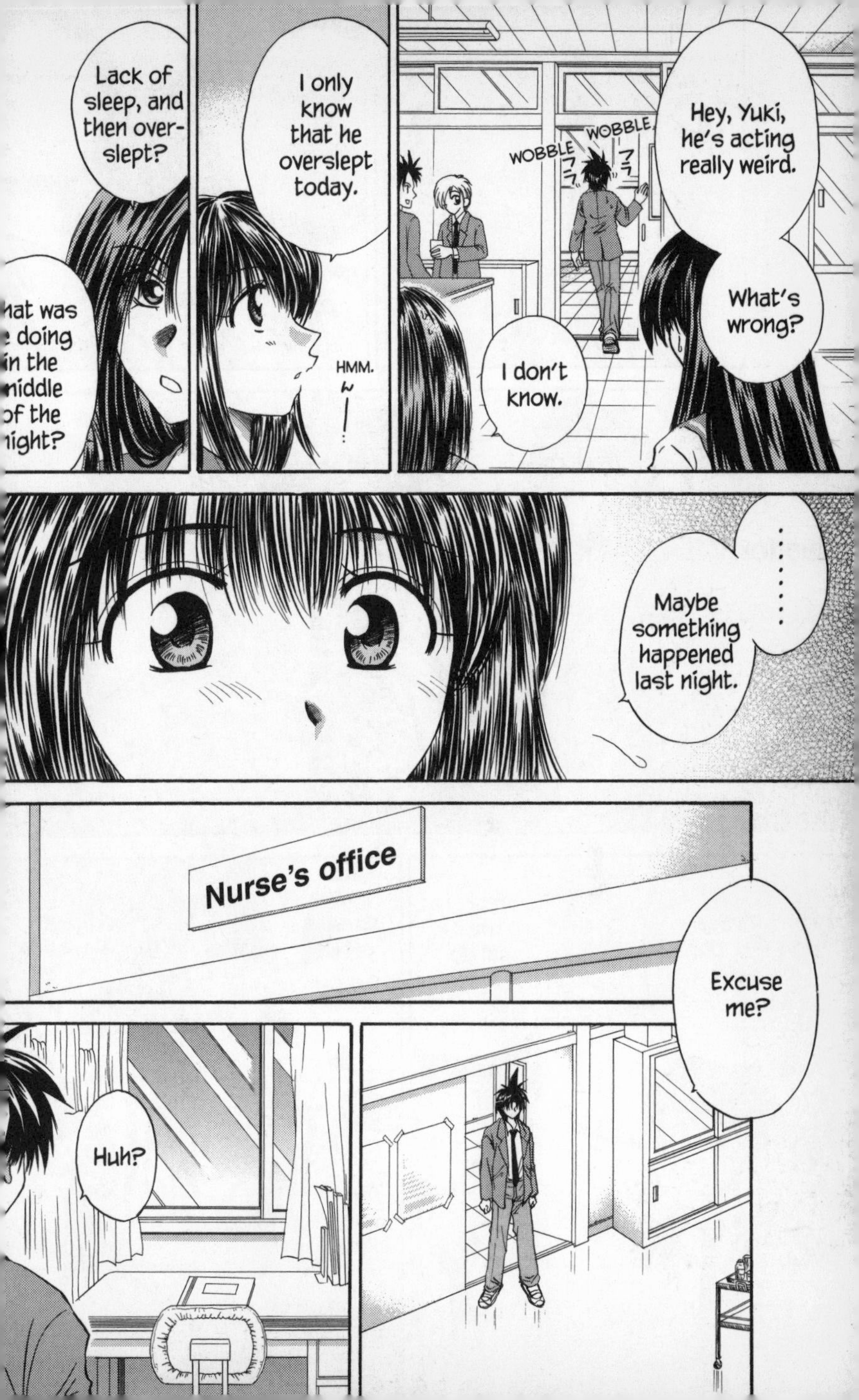
Hey, Yuki, he's acting really weird.
WOBBLE WOBBLE
フラ フラ
What's wrong?
I don't know.
I only know that he overslept today.
HMM.
Lack of sleep, and then over-slept?
hat was e doing in the niddle of the night?
......
Maybe something happened last night.
Nurse's office
Excuse me?
Huh?

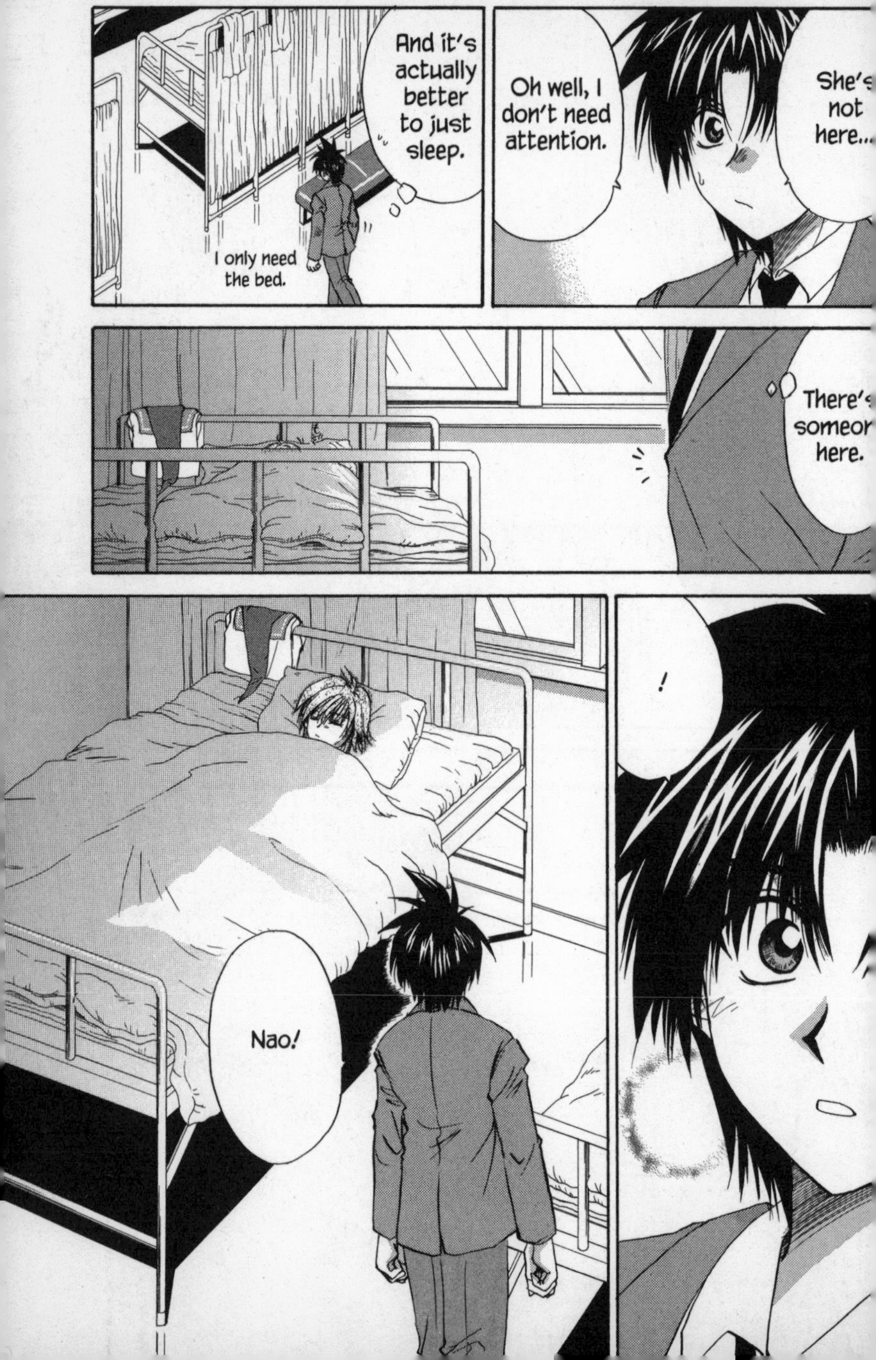
She's not here...
Oh well, I don't need attention.
And it's actually better to just sleep.
I only need the bed.
There's someon here.
!
Nao!

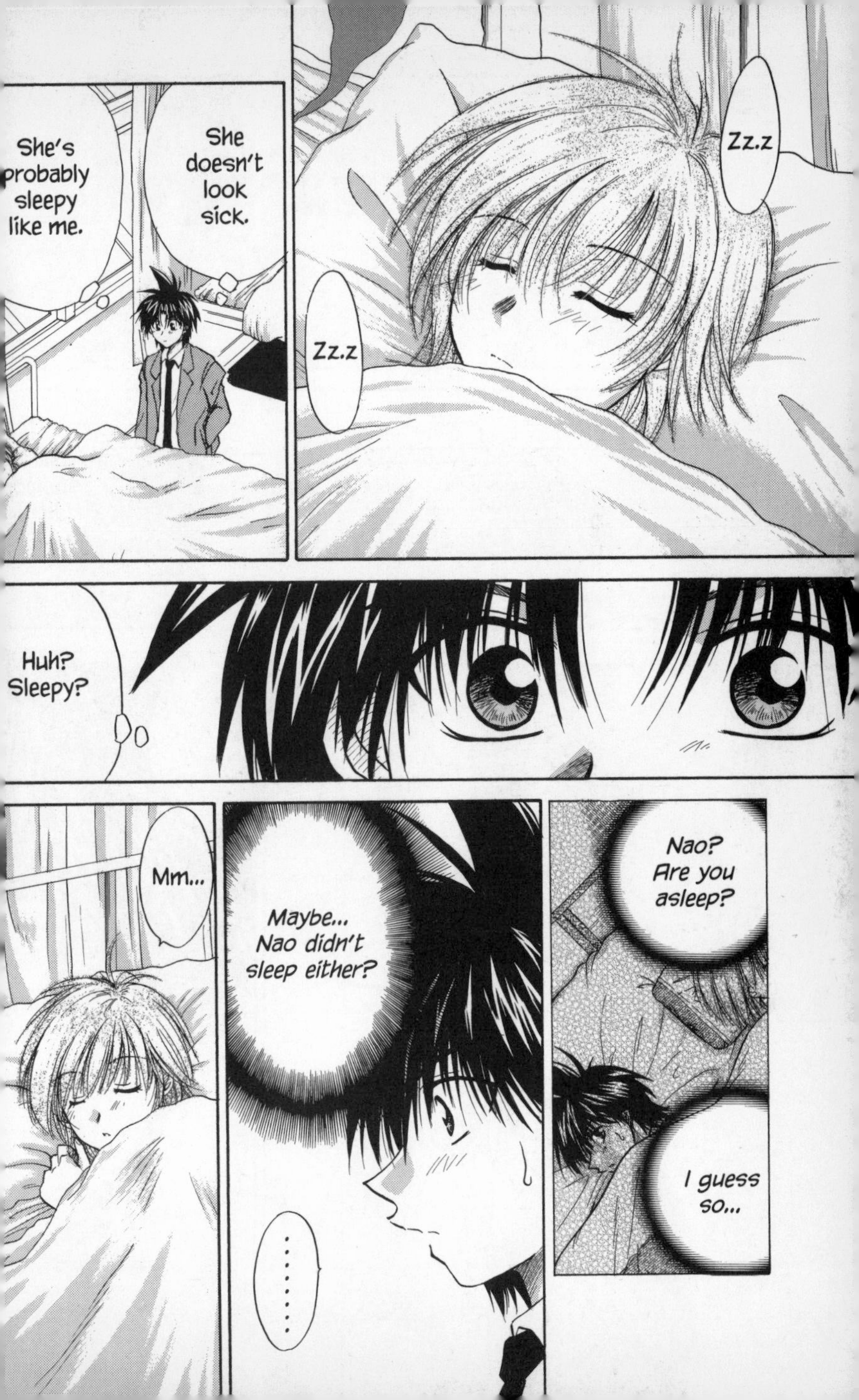
Zz.z
Zz.z
She doesn't look sick.
She's probably sleepy like me.
Huh? Sleepy?
Nao? Are you asleep?
I guess so...
Maybe... Nao didn't sleep either?
....
Mm...

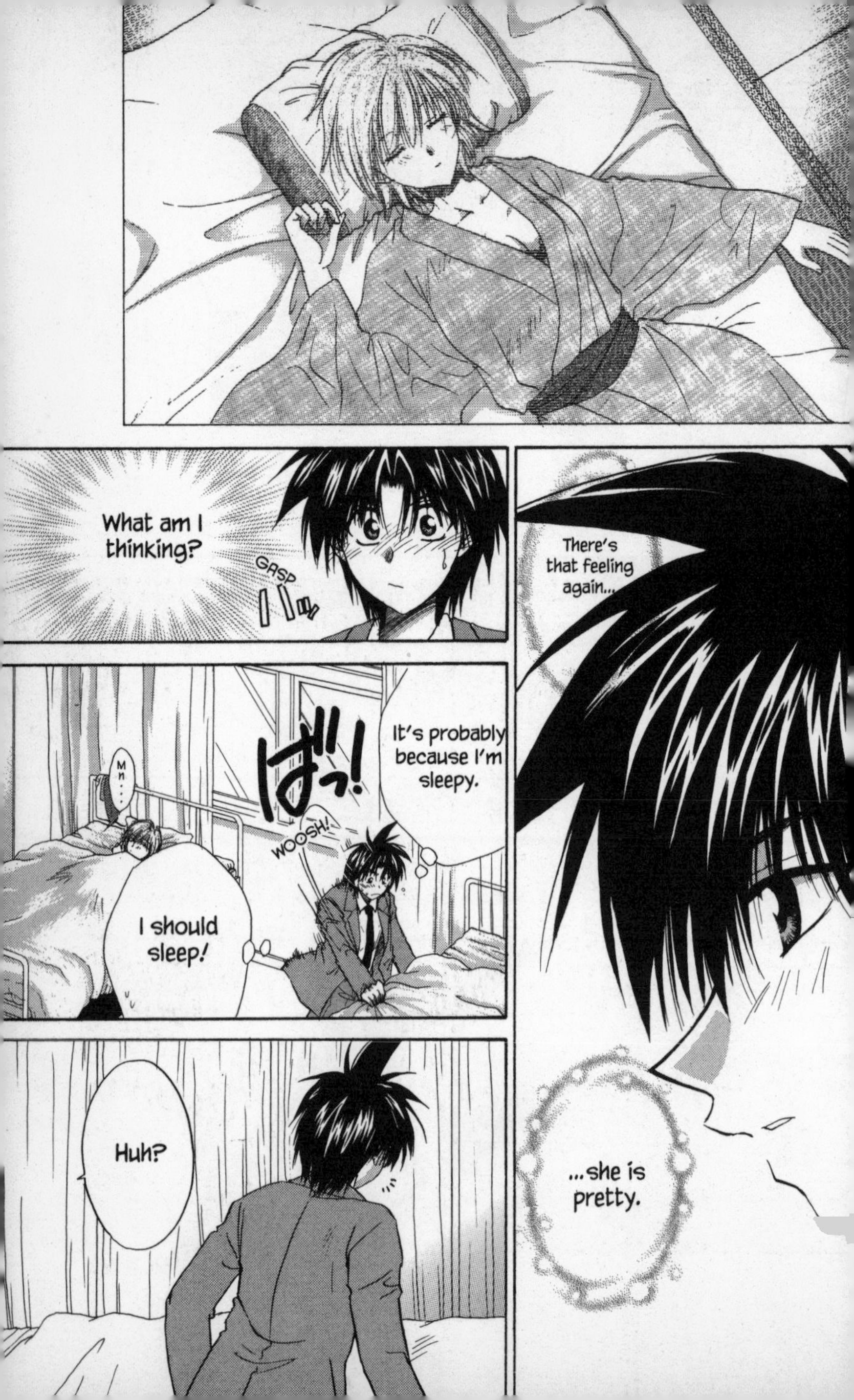
There's that feeling again...
...she is pretty.
What am I thinking?
GASP
It's probably because I'm sleepy.
ばっ!
WOOSH!
Mn...
I should sleep!
Huh?

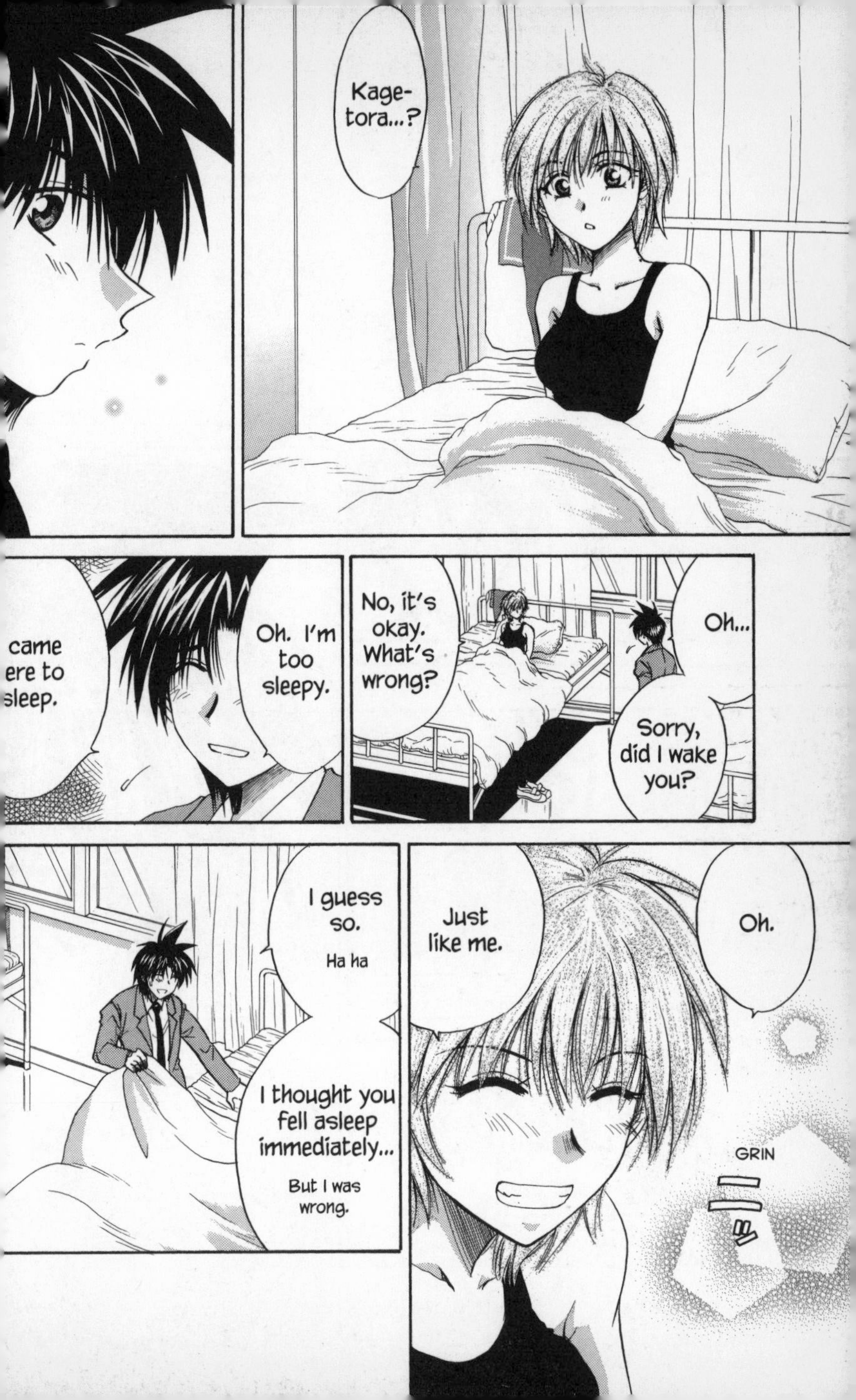
Kage-tora...?
Oh...
Sorry, did I wake you?
No, it's okay. What's wrong?
Oh. I'm too sleepy.
came ere to sleep.
Oh.
Just like me.
GRIN
I guess so.
Ha ha
I thought you fell asleep immediately...
But I was wrong.

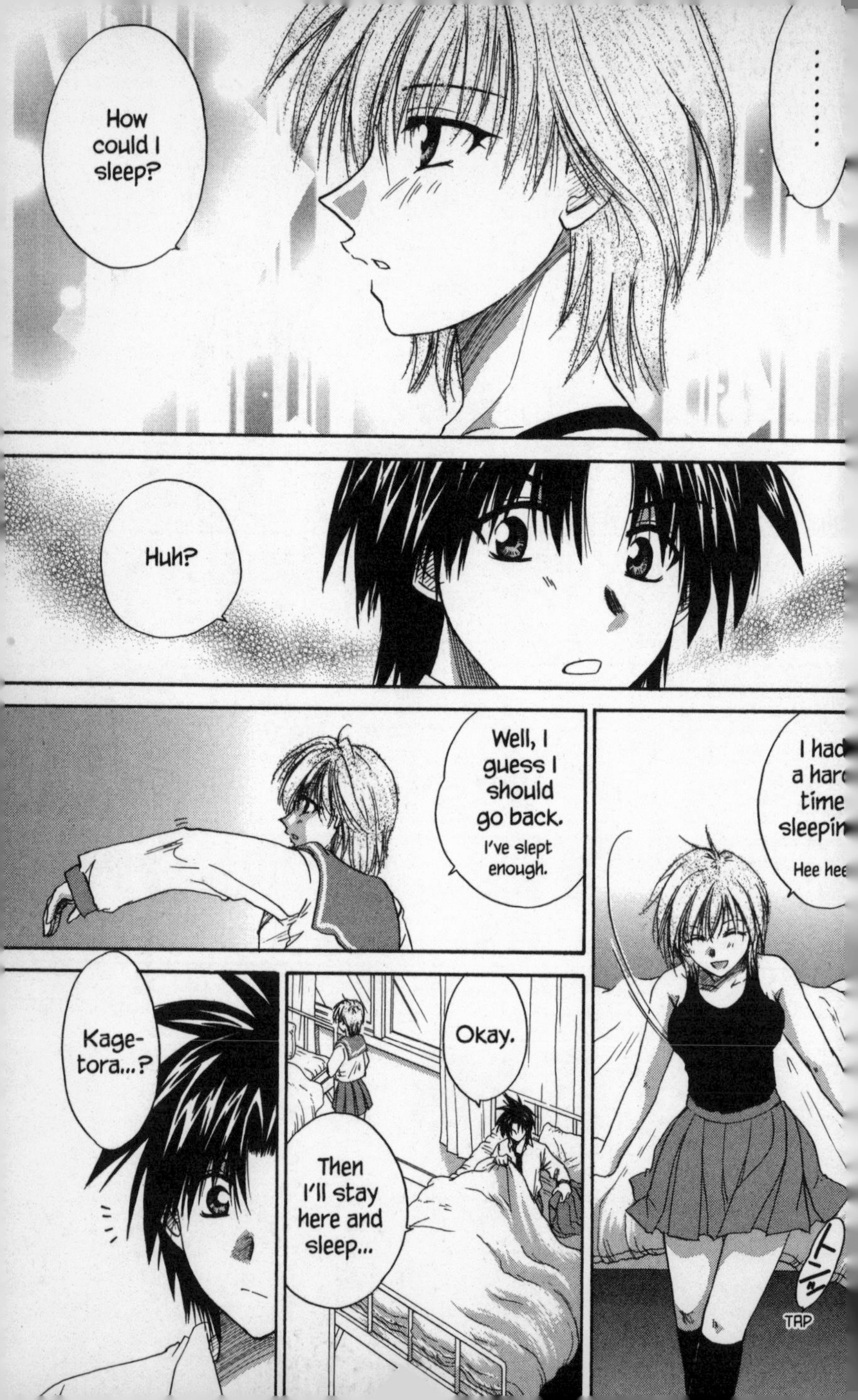
......
How could I sleep?
Huh?
I had a hard time sleepin
Hee hee
TAP
Well, I guess I should go back.
I've slept enough.
Okay.
Then I'll stay here and sleep...
Kage-tora...?

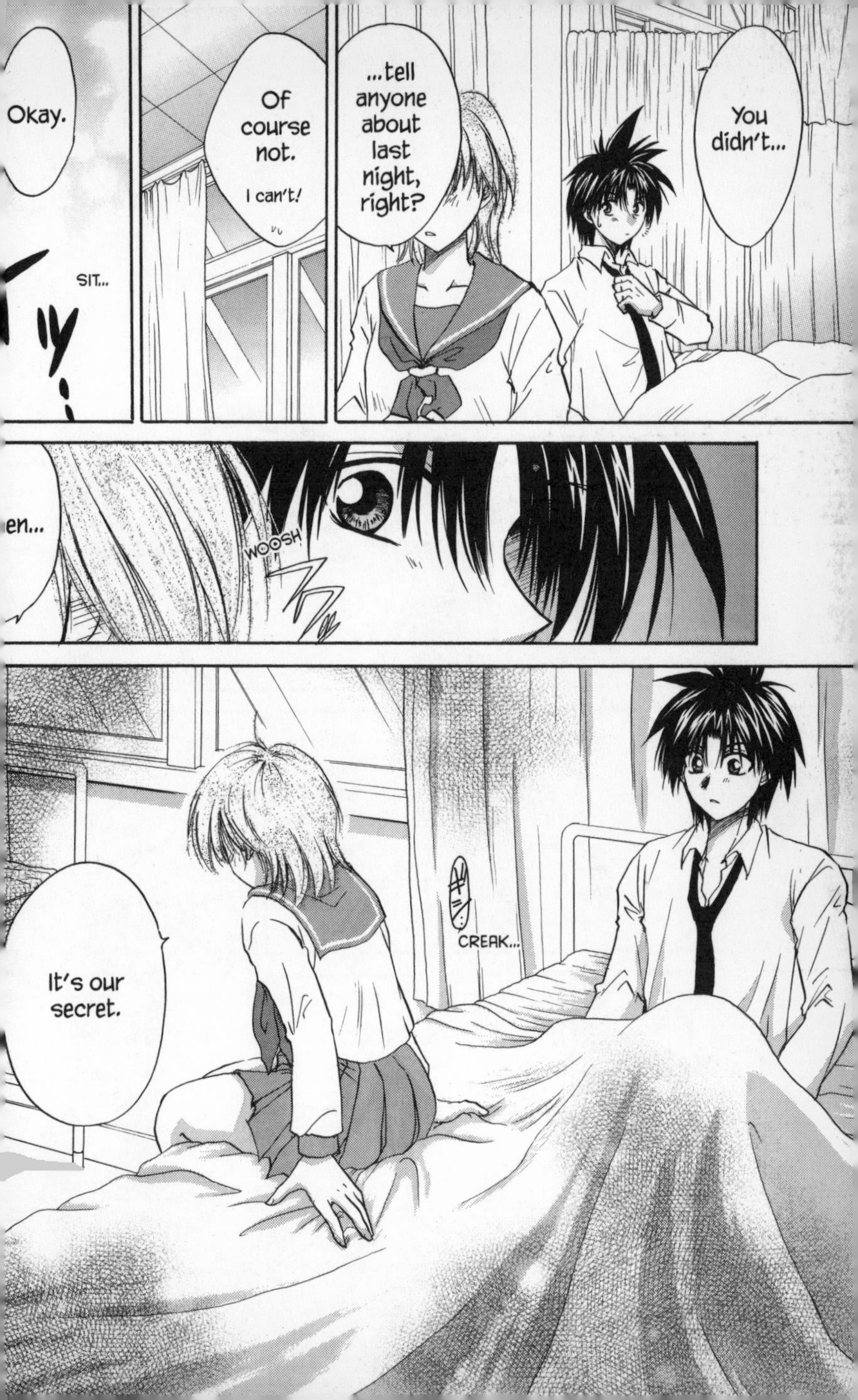
You didn't...
...tell anyone about last night, right?
Of course not.
I can't!
Okay.
SIT...
en...
WOOSH
CREAK...
It's our secret.

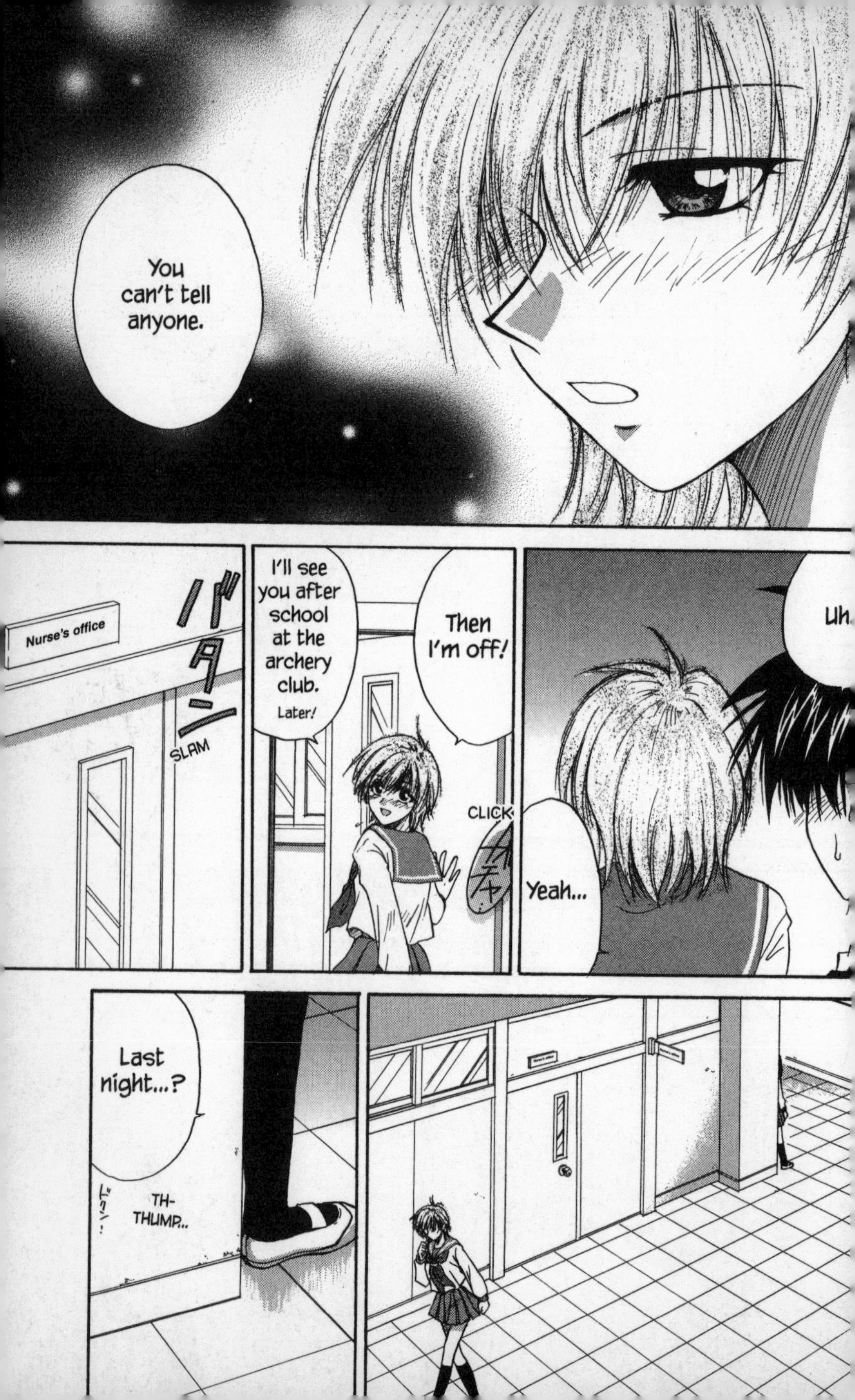
You can't tell anyone.
Uh...
Yeah...
Then I'm off!
I'll see you after school at the archery club.
Later!
CLICK
Nurse's office
SLAM
Last night...?
TH-THUMP...

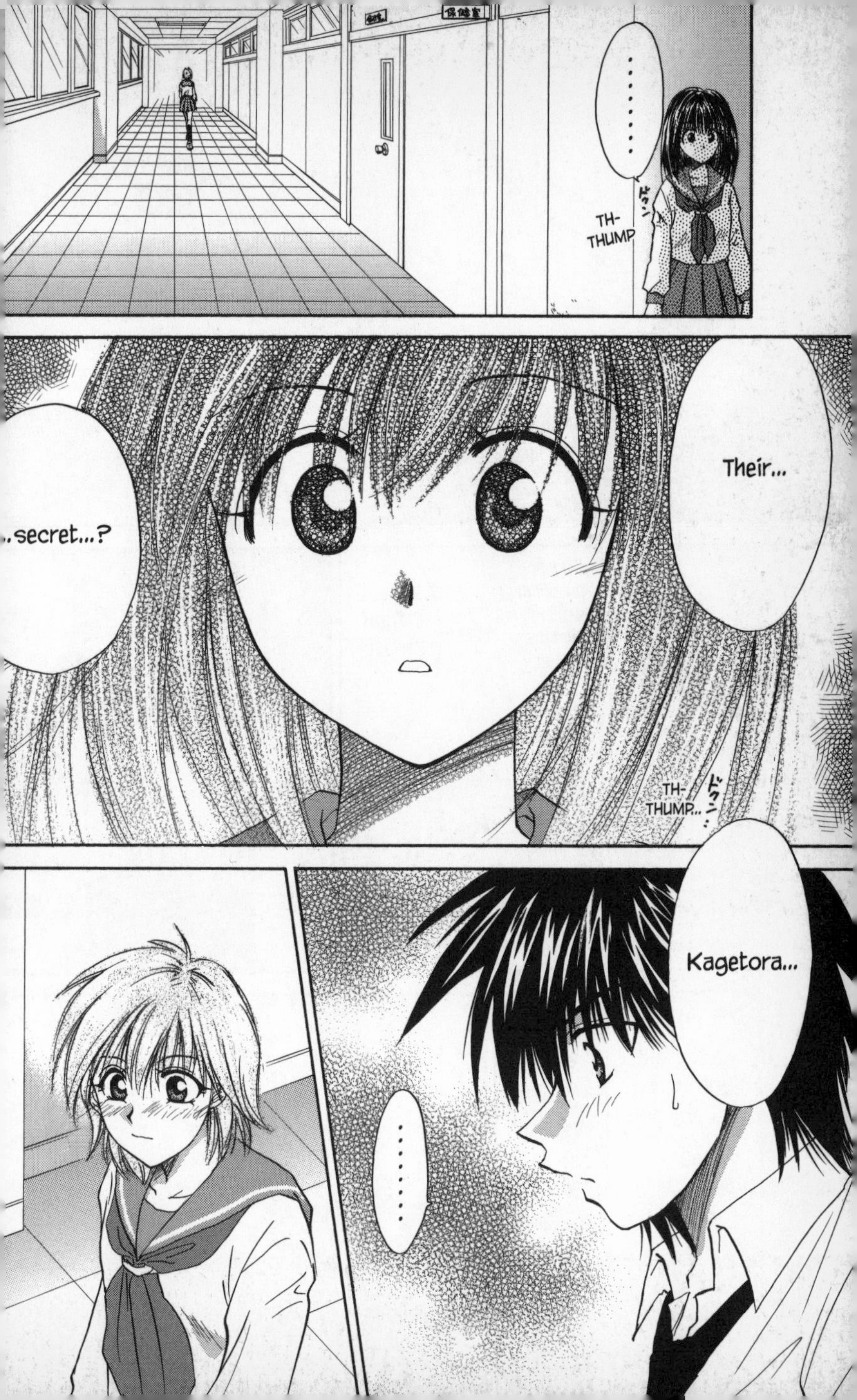
......
TH-THUMP
Their...
...secret...?
TH-THUMP...
Kagetora...
......

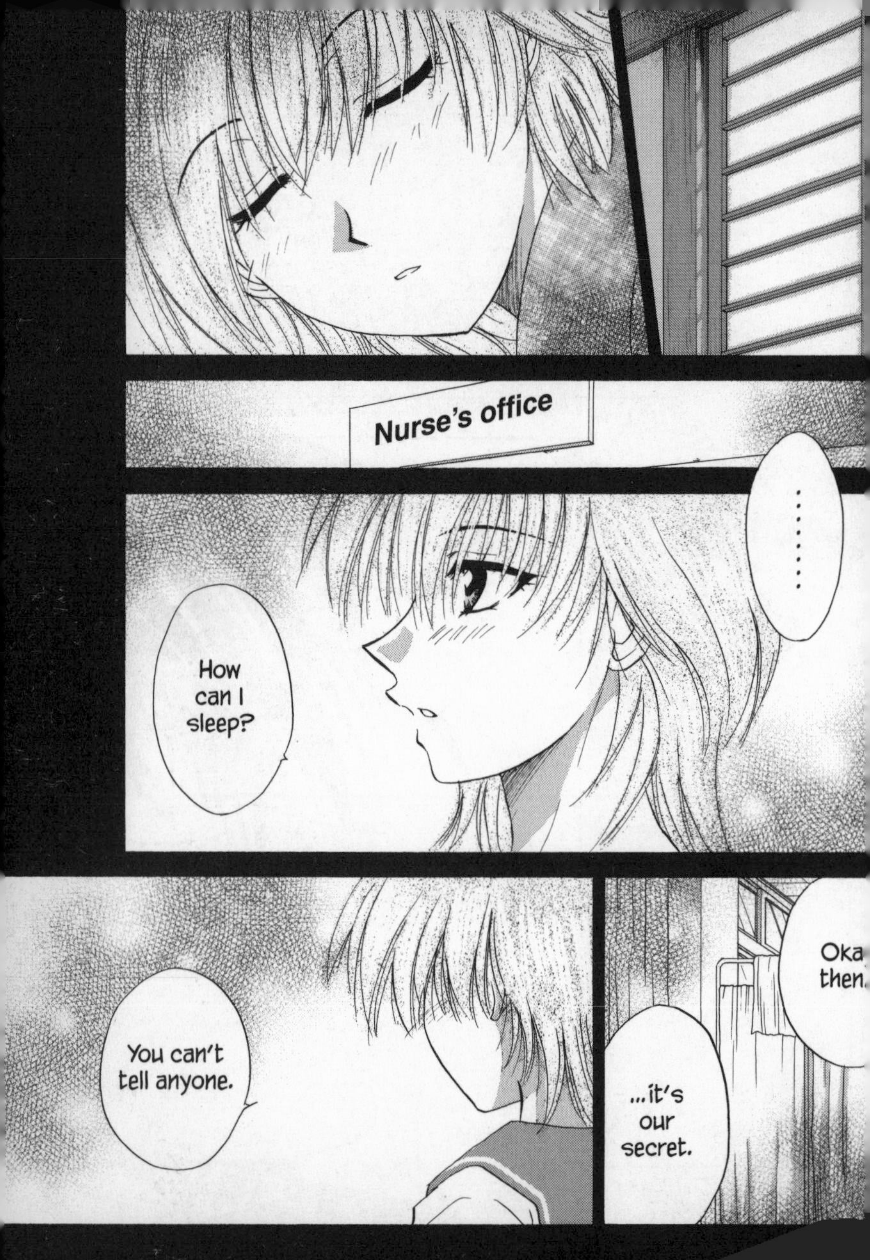
Nurse's office
......
How can I sleep?
Oka then.
...it's our secret.
You can't tell anyone.

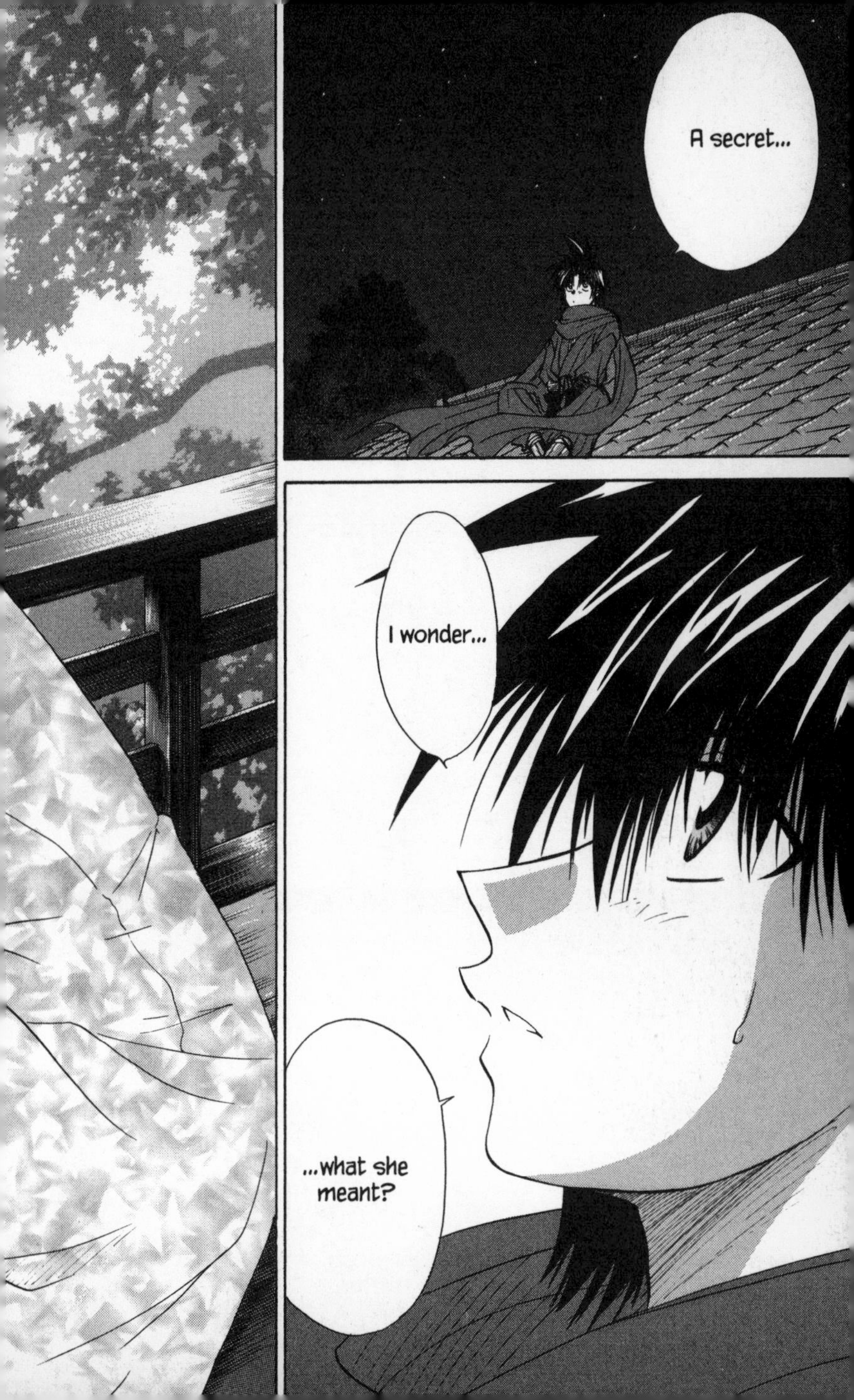
A secret...
I wonder...
...what she meant?

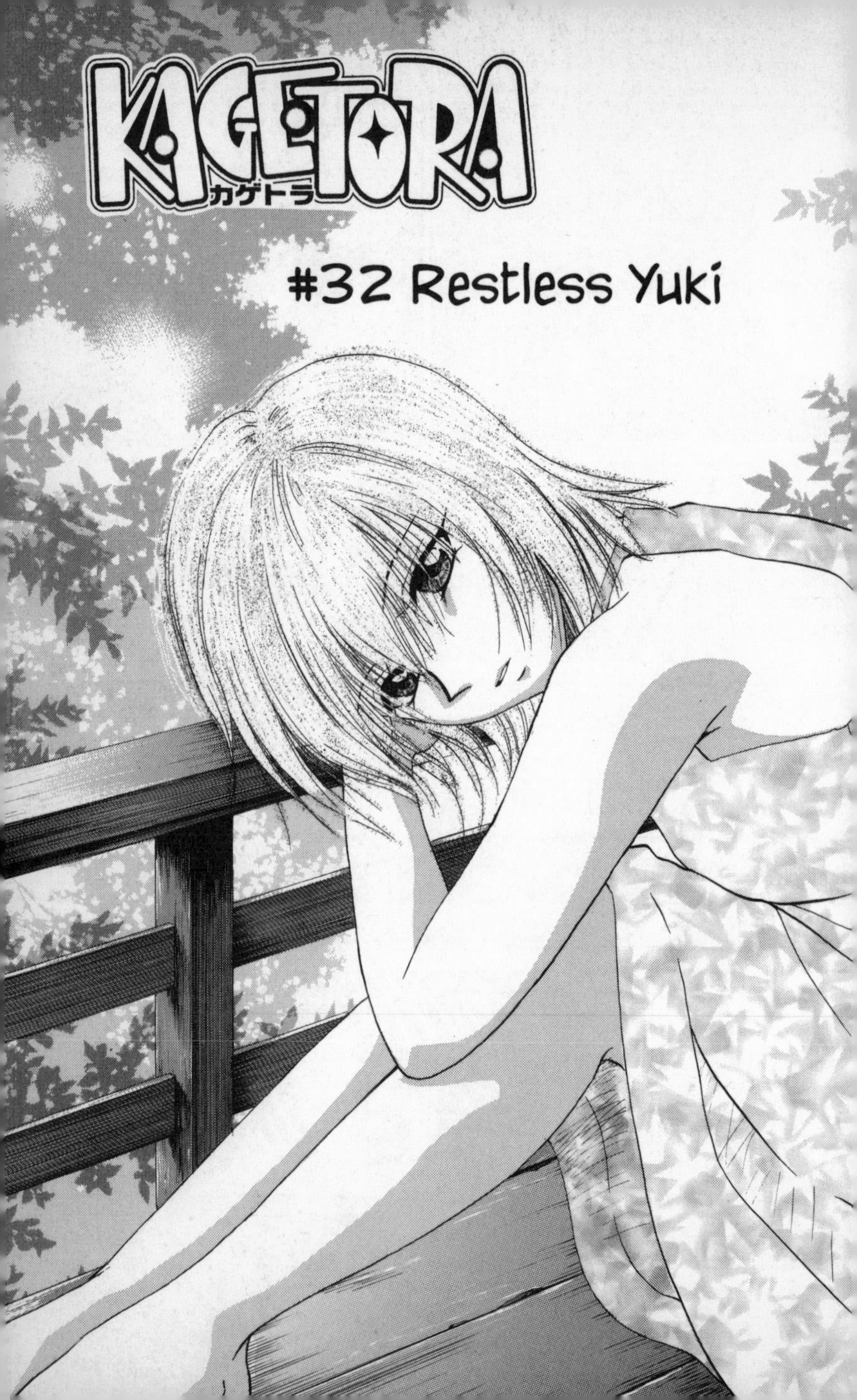
KAGETORA
カゲトラ
#32 Restless Yuki

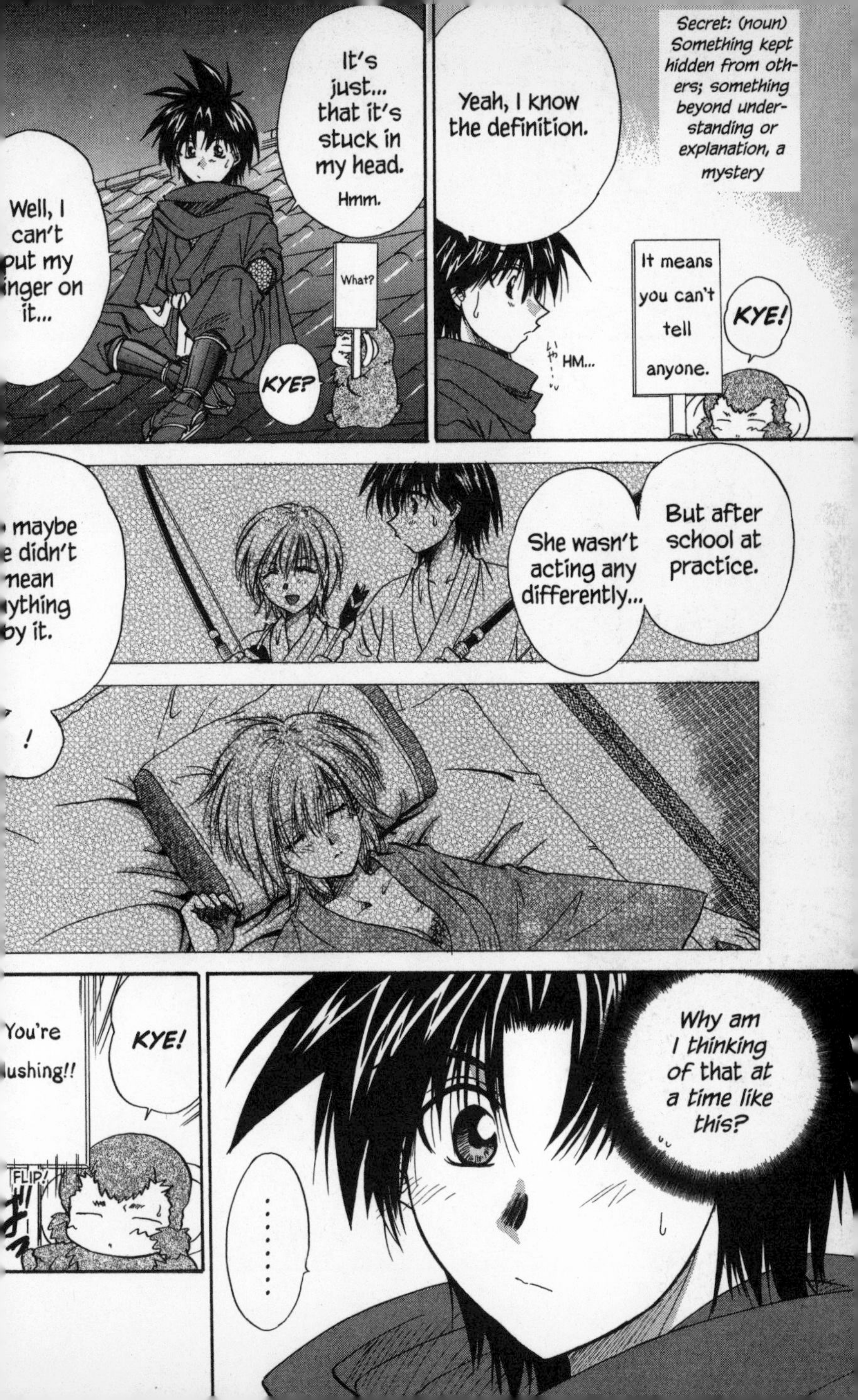
Secret: (noun) Something kept hidden from others; something beyond understanding or explanation, a mystery
Yeah, I know the definition.
It means you can't tell anyone.
KYE!
HM...
It's just... that it's stuck in my head.
Hmm.
Well, I can't put my inger on it...
What?
KYE?
But after school at practice.
She wasn't acting any differently...
maybe e didn't nean ything by it.
!
Why am I thinking of that at a time like this?
......
KYE!
You're ushing!!
FLIP!

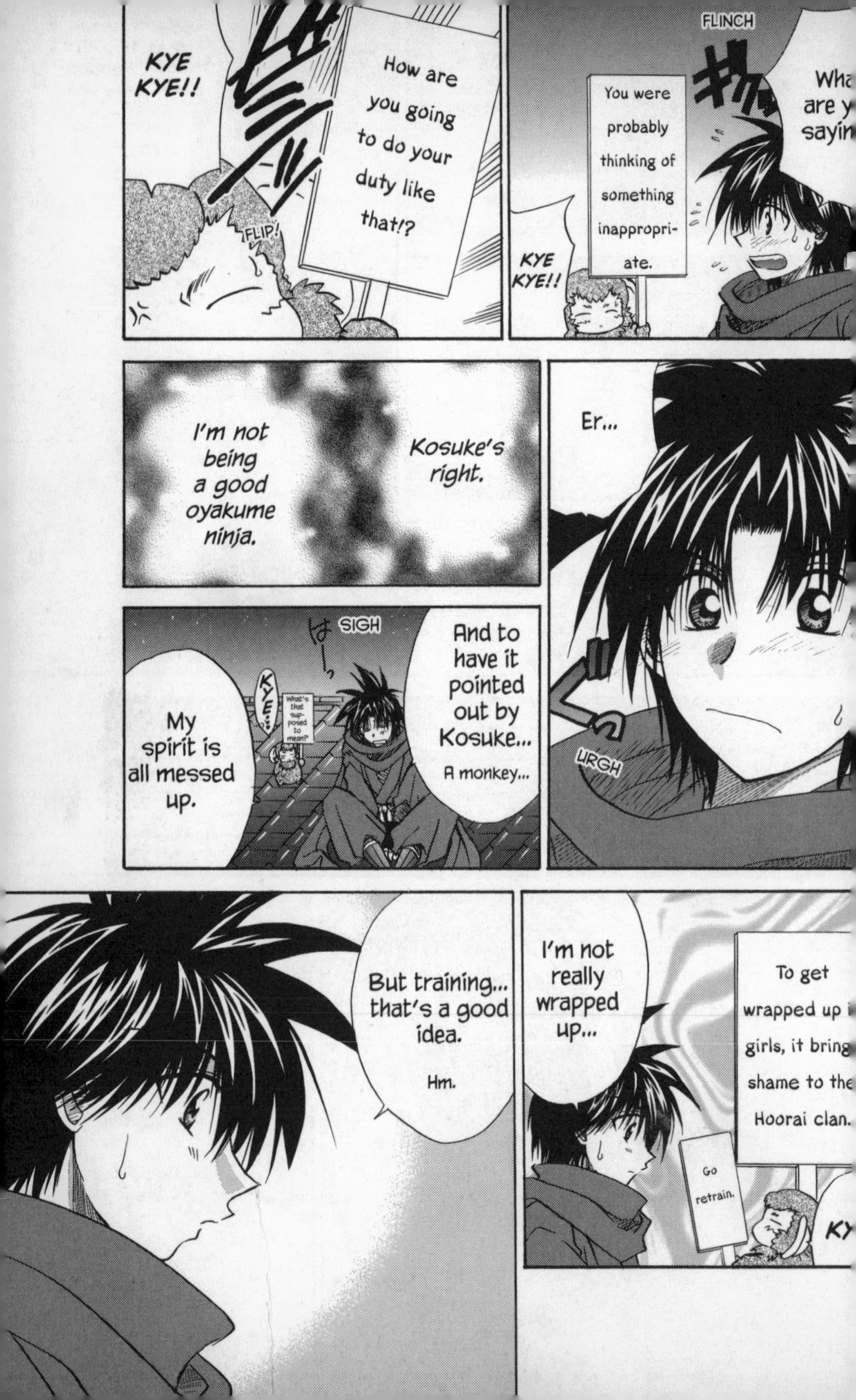
Wha are y sayin
FLINCH
You were probably thinking of something inappropri-ate.
KYE KYE!!
How are you going to do your duty like that!?
KYE KYE!!
FLIP!
Er...
URGH
Kosuke's right.
I'm not being a good oyakume ninja.
And to have it pointed out by Kosuke... A monkey...
SIGH
KYE...
What's that sup-posed to mean?
My spirit is all messed up.
To get wrapped up i girls, it bring shame to the Hoorai clan.
Go retrain.
KY
I'm not really wrapped up...
But training... that's a good idea.
Hm.

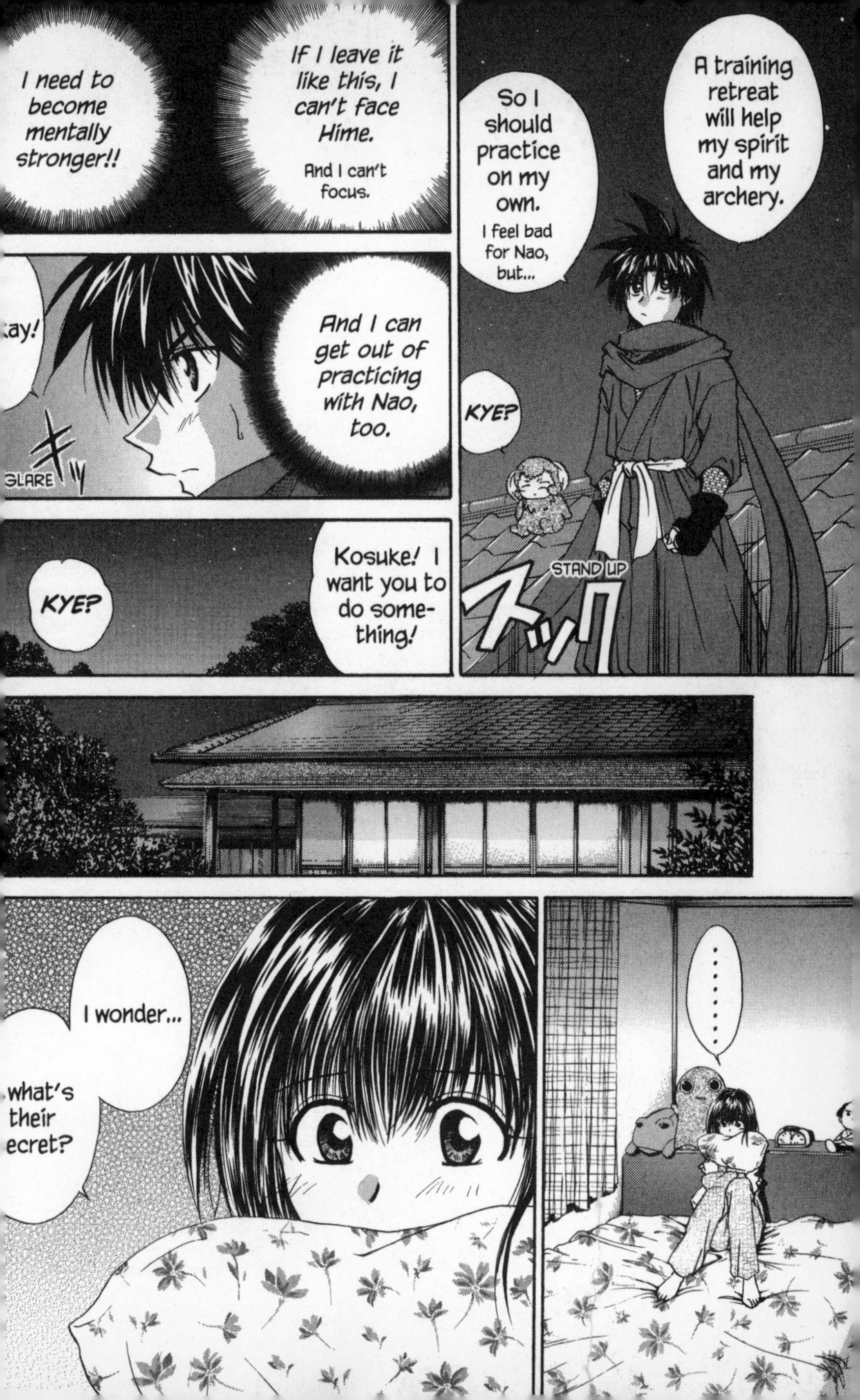
A training retreat will help my spirit and my archery.
So I should practice on my own.
I feel bad for Nao, but...
KYE?
STAND UP
If I leave it like this, I can't face Hime.
And I can't focus.
I need to become mentally stronger!!
And I can get out of practicing with Nao, too.
ay!
GLARE
Kosuke! I want you to do some-thing!
KYE?
....
I wonder...
what's their ecret?

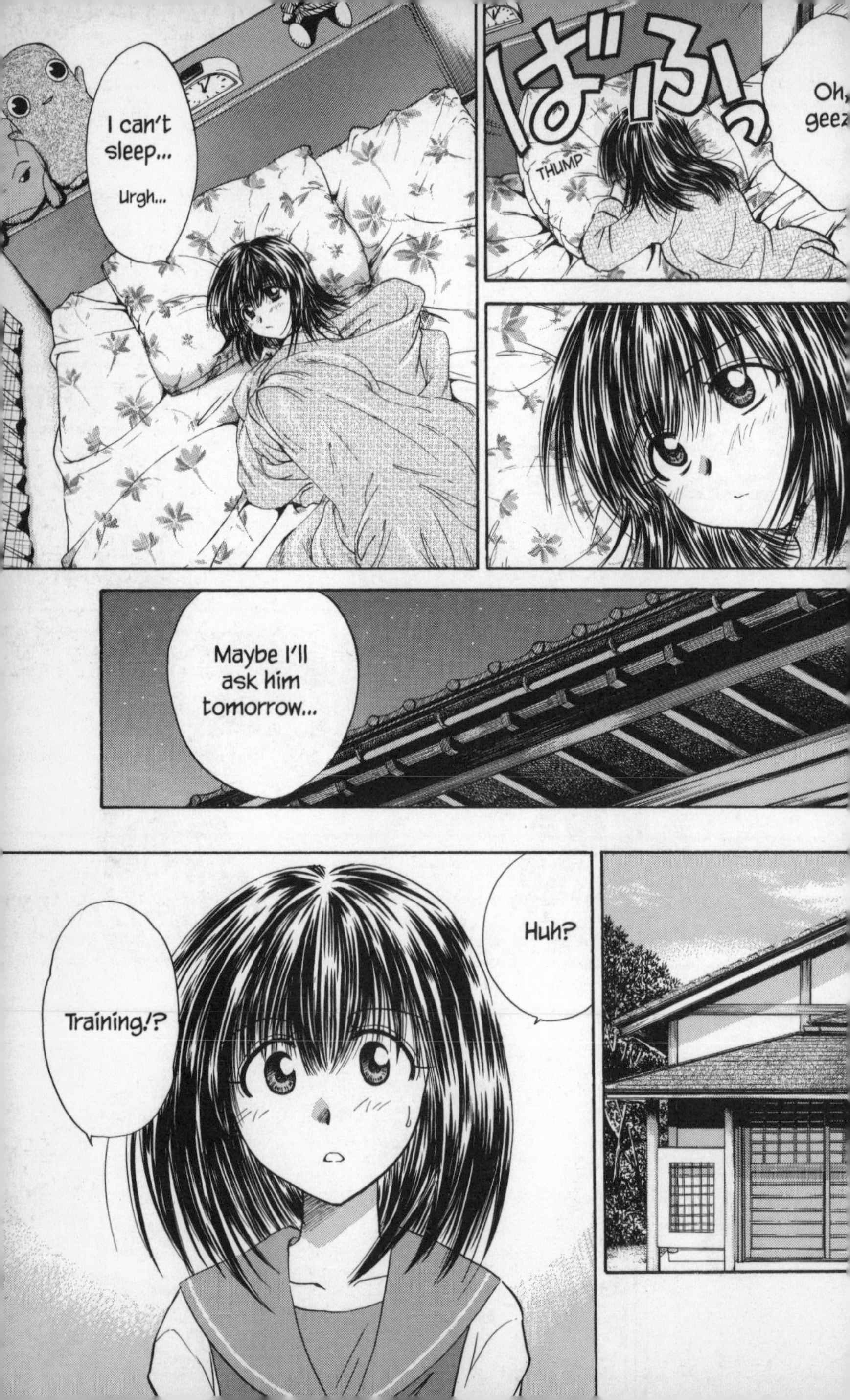
ばふっ
THUMP
Oh, geez
I can't sleep...
Urgh...
Maybe I'll ask him tomorrow...
Huh?
Training!?

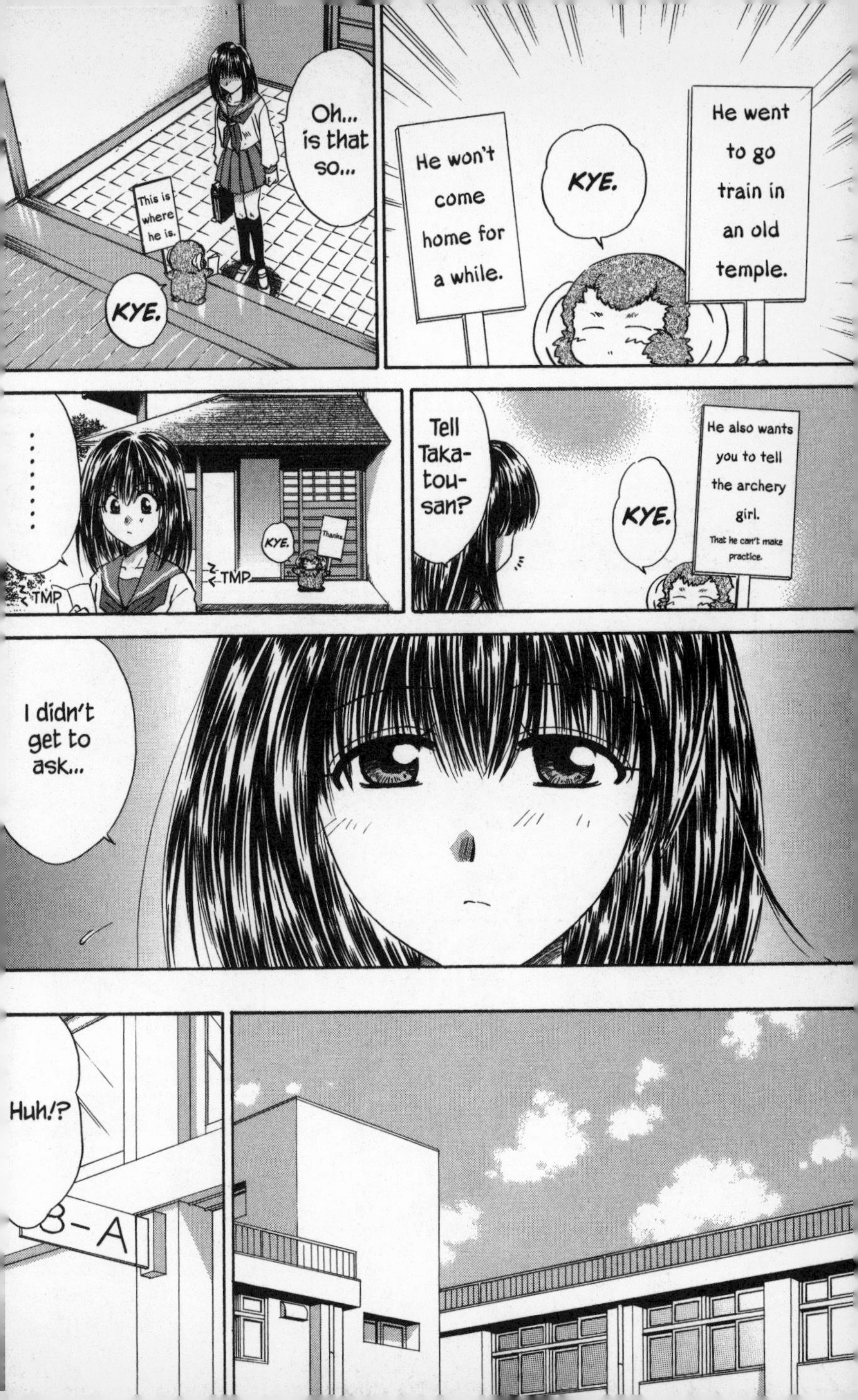
He went to go train in an old temple.
KYE.
He won't come home for a while.
Oh... is that so...
This is where he is.
KYE.
He also wants you to tell the archery girl. That he can't make practice.
KYE.
Tell Taka-tou-san?
Thanks.
KYE.
....
TMP
TMP
I didn't get to ask...
Huh!?
3-A

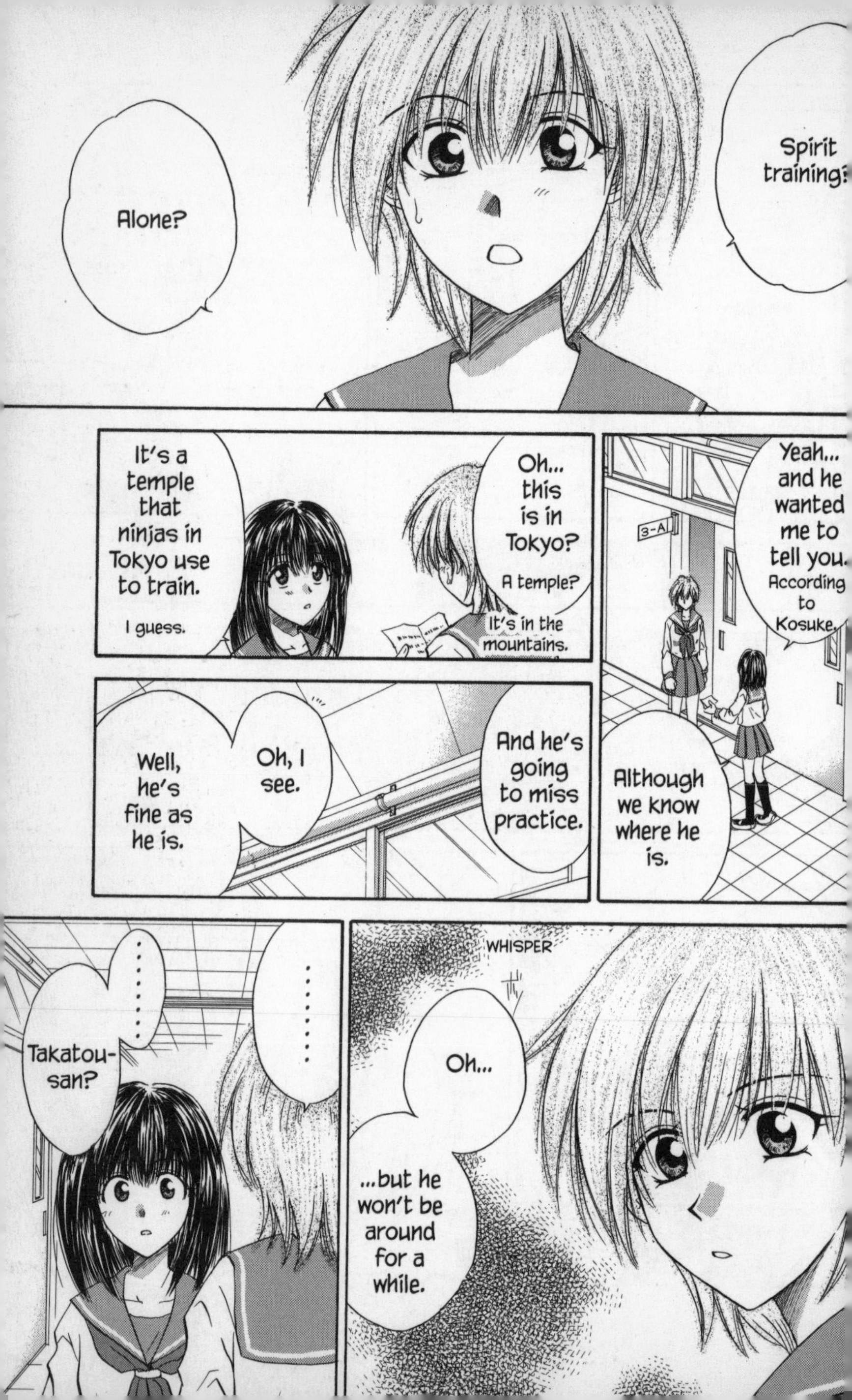
Spirit training?
Alone?
Yeah... and he wanted me to tell you.
According to Kosuke.
Although we know where he is.
Oh... this is in Tokyo?
A temple?
It's in the mountains.
It's a temple that ninjas in Tokyo use to train.
I guess.
And he's going to miss practice.
Oh, I see.
Well, he's fine as he is.
WHISPER
Oh...
...but he won't be around for a while.
......
......
Takatou-san?

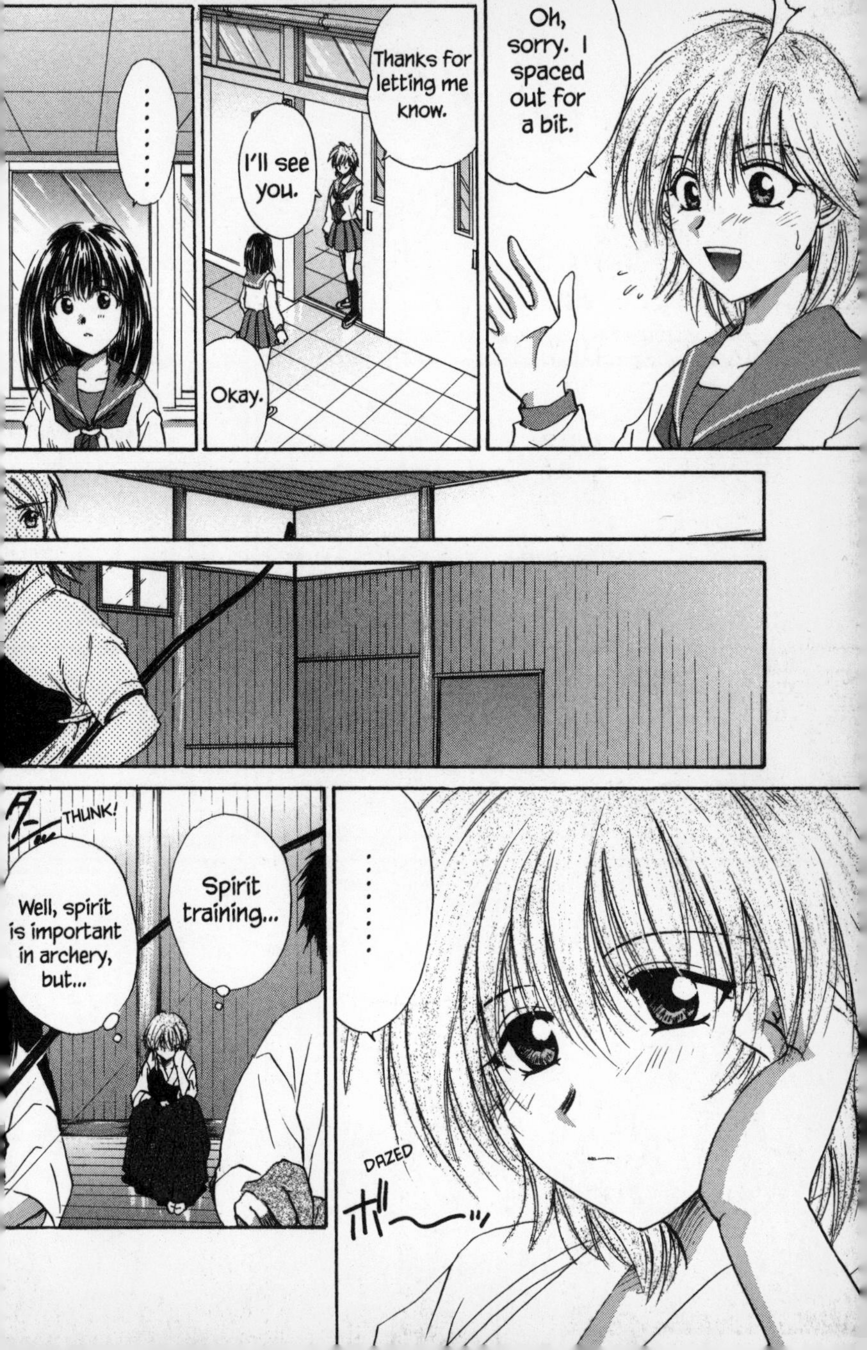
Oh, sorry. I spaced out for a bit.
Thanks for letting me know.
I'll see you.
Okay.
......
......
DAZED
THUNK!
Spirit training...
Well, spirit is important in archery, but...

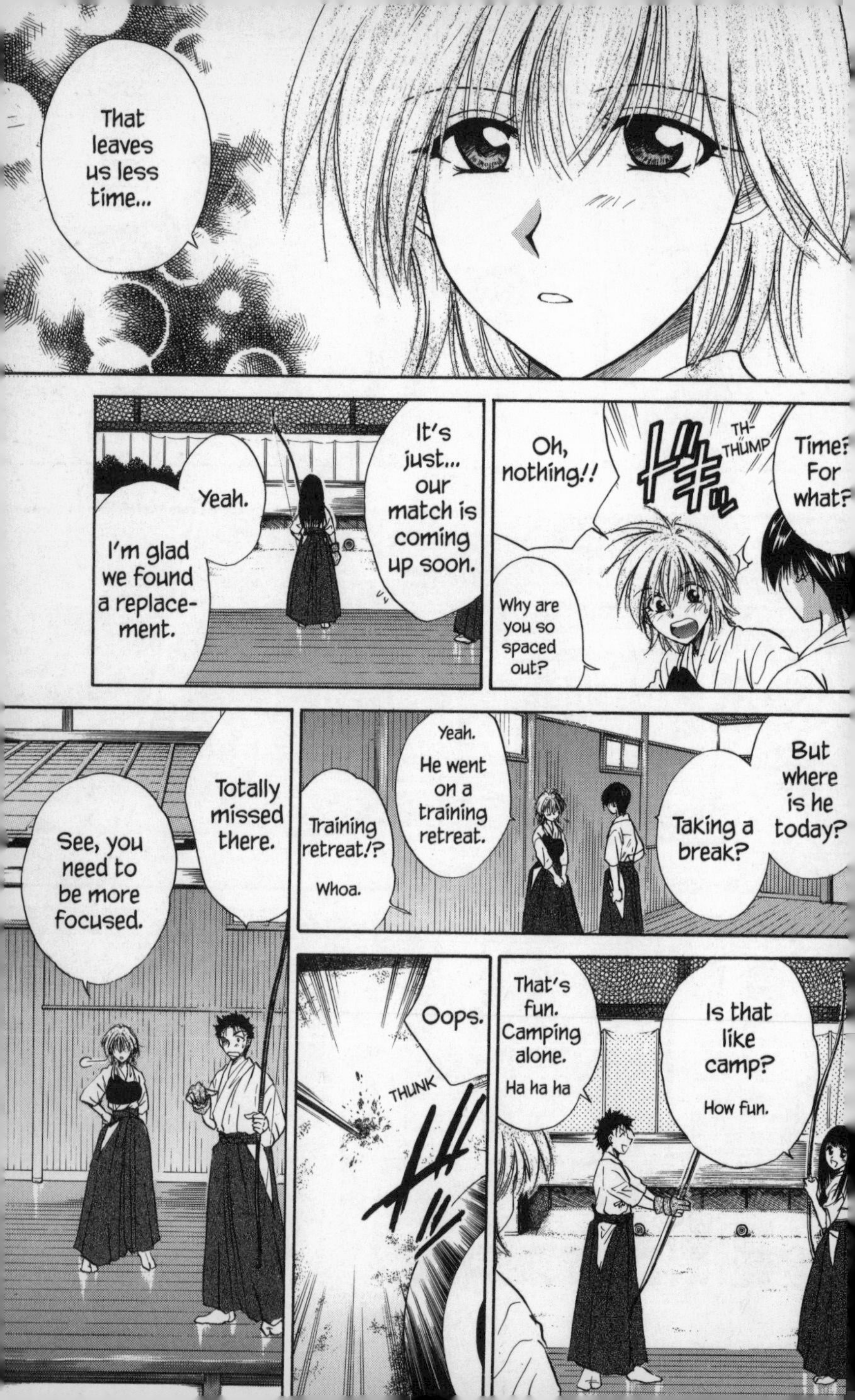
That leaves us less time...
Time? For what?
TH-THUMP
Oh, nothing!!
Why are you so spaced out?
It's just... our match is coming up soon.
Yeah.
I'm glad we found a replacement.
But where is he today?
Taking a break?
Yeah.
He went on a training retreat.
Training retreat!?
Whoa.
Is that like camp?
How fun.
That's fun. Camping alone.
Ha ha ha
Oops.
THUNK
Totally missed there.
See, you need to be more focused.

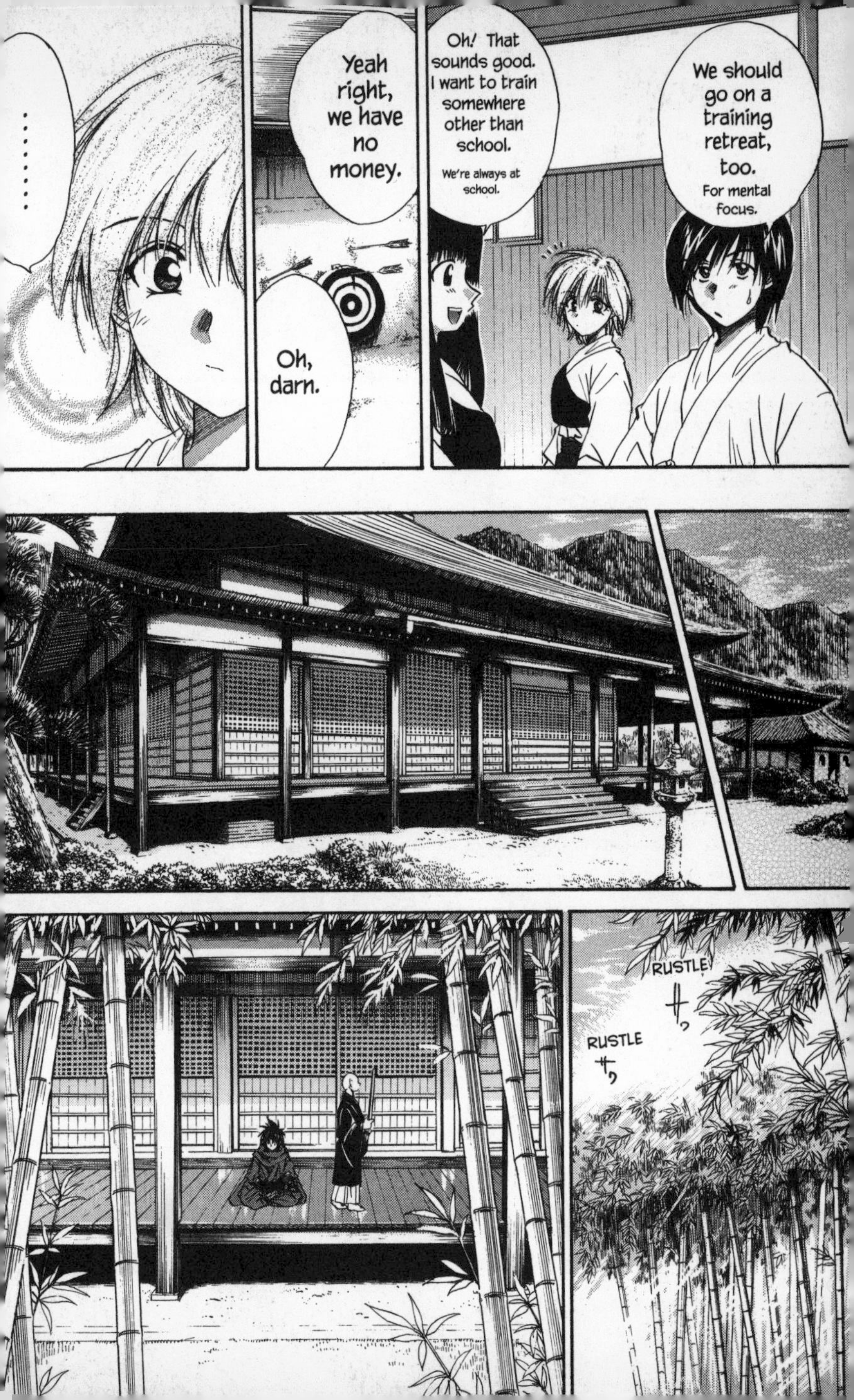
We should go on a training retreat, too.
For mental focus.
Oh! That sounds good. I want to train somewhere other than school.
We're always at school.
Yeah right, we have no money.
Oh, darn.
......
RUSTLE
サッ
RUSTLE
サッ

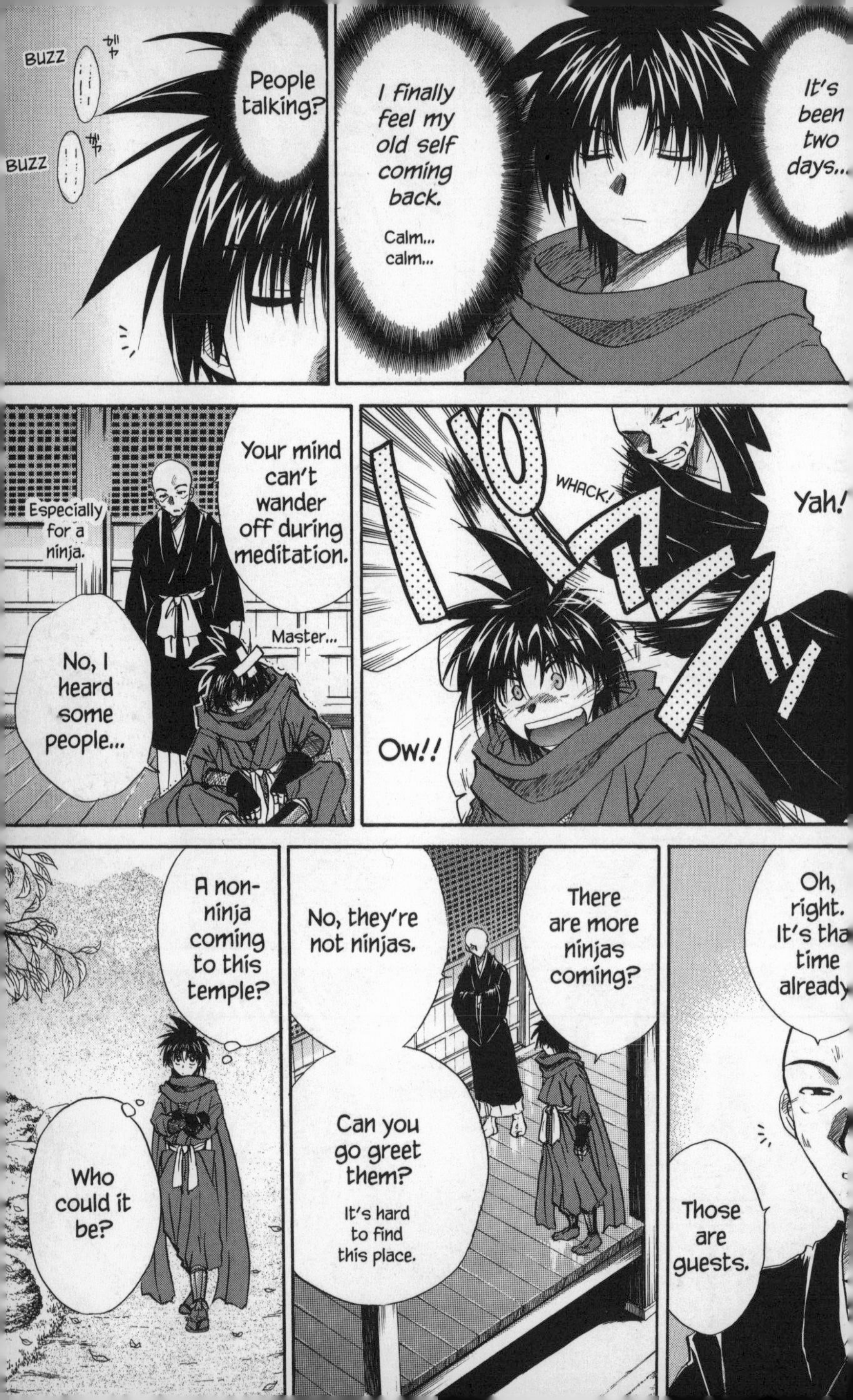
It's been two days...
I finally feel my old self coming back.
Calm... calm...
People talking?
BUZZ
BUZZ
Yah!
WHACK!
Ow!!
Your mind can't wander off during meditation.
Especially for a ninja.
Master...
No, I heard some people...
Oh, right. It's tha time already
Those are guests.
There are more ninjas coming?
No, they're not ninjas.
Can you go greet them?
It's hard to find this place.
A non-ninja coming to this temple?
Who could it be?

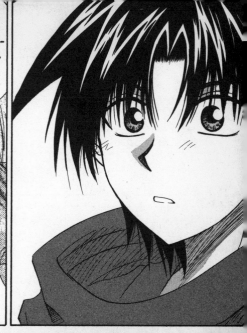

Kage-tora.

PANT...

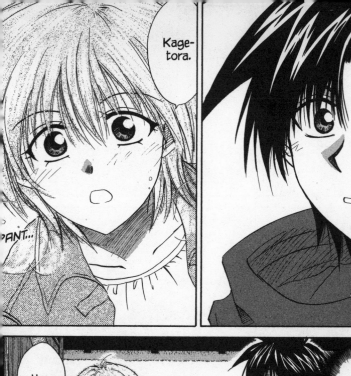

Um...

g time,
see.

guess it
been that
ong.

Why is Nao here!?

· · · · · · · ·

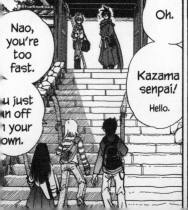

Nao, you're too fast.

u just
n off
your
own.

Oh.

Kazama senpai!

Hello.

Why are you here?

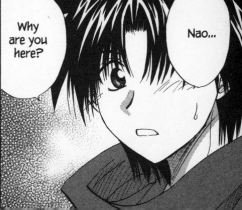

Nao...

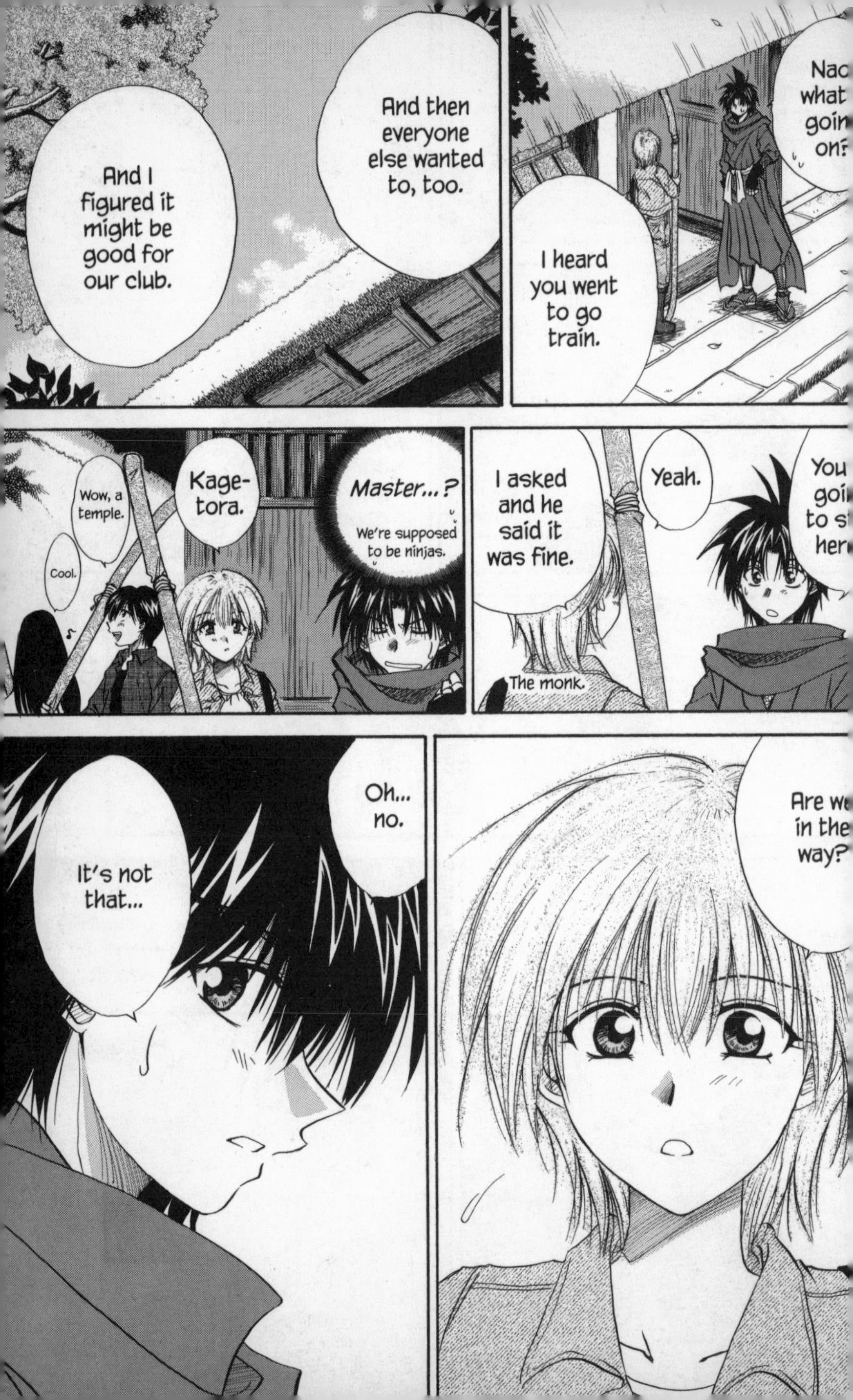
Nac what goin on?
I heard you went to go train.
And then everyone else wanted to, too.
And I figured it might be good for our club.
You goi to s her
Yeah.
I asked and he said it was fine.
The monk.
Master...?
We're supposed to be ninjas.
Kage-tora.
Wow, a temple.
Cool.
Are w in the way?
Oh... no.
It's not that...

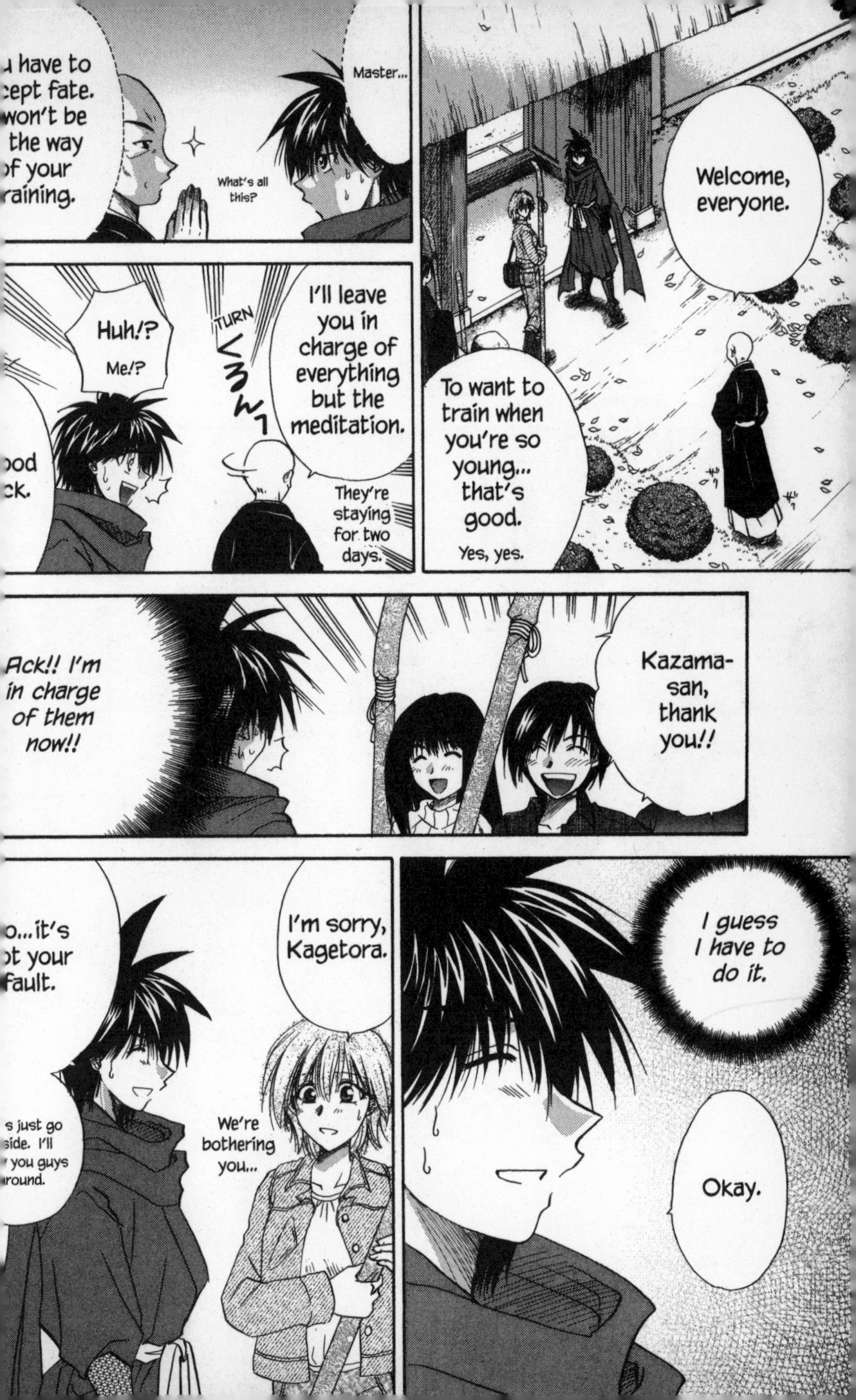

Welcome, everyone.
To want to train when you're so young... that's good.
Yes, yes.
Master...
What's all this?
u have to cept fate. won't be the way of your raining.
I'll leave you in charge of everything but the meditation.
TURN
They're staying for two days.
Huh!? Me!?
ood ck.
Kazama-san, thank you!!
Ack!! I'm in charge of them now!!
I guess I have to do it.
Okay.
I'm sorry, Kagetora.
We're bothering you...
o...it's ot your fault.
s just go side. I'll you guys round.

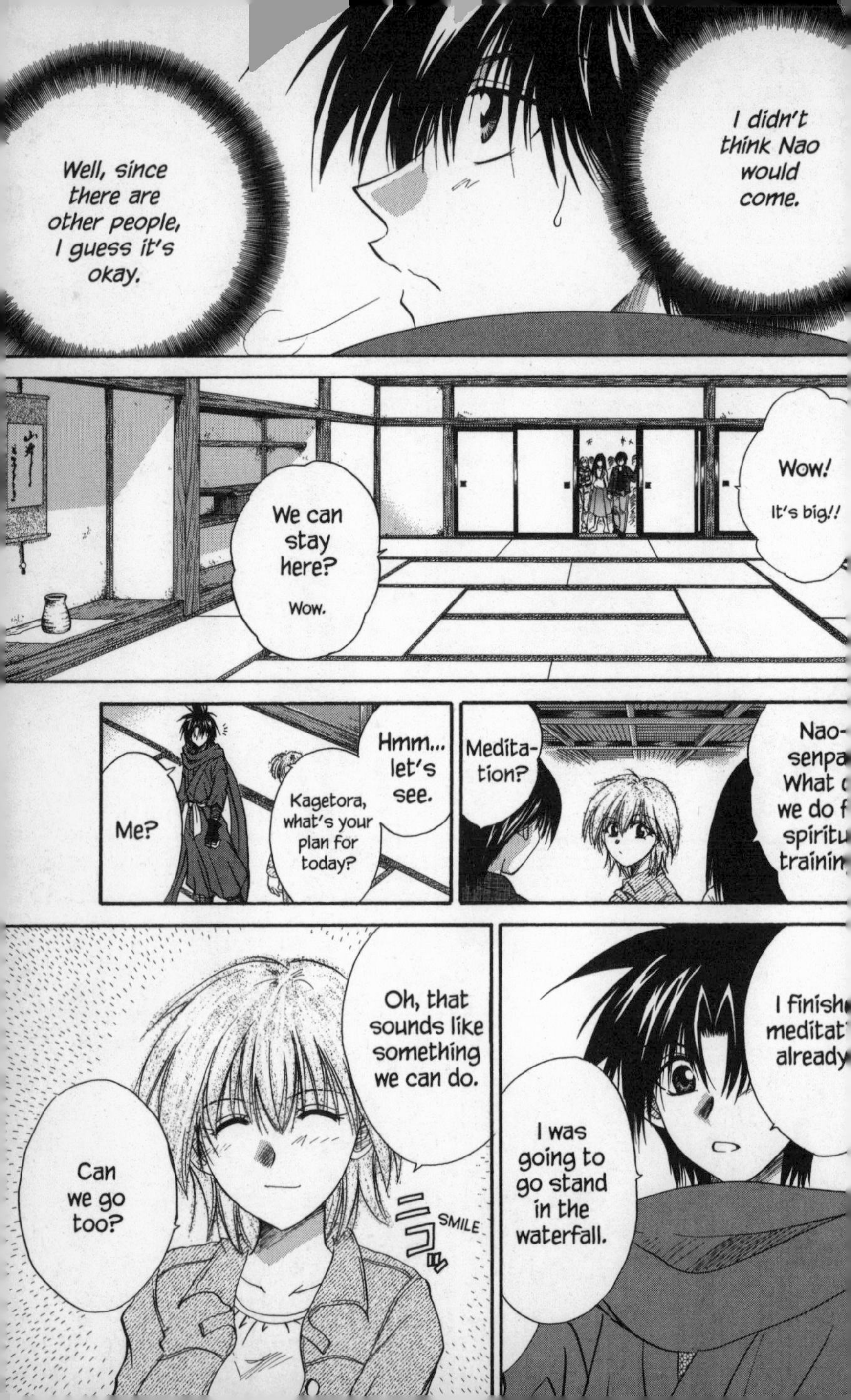
I didn't think Nao would come.
Well, since there are other people, I guess it's okay.
Wow! It's big!!
We can stay here? Wow.
Nao-senpa What we do f spiritu trainin
Medita-tion?
Hmm... let's see.
Kagetora, what's your plan for today?
Me?
I finish meditat already
I was going to go stand in the waterfall.
Oh, that sounds like something we can do.
SMILE
Can we go too?

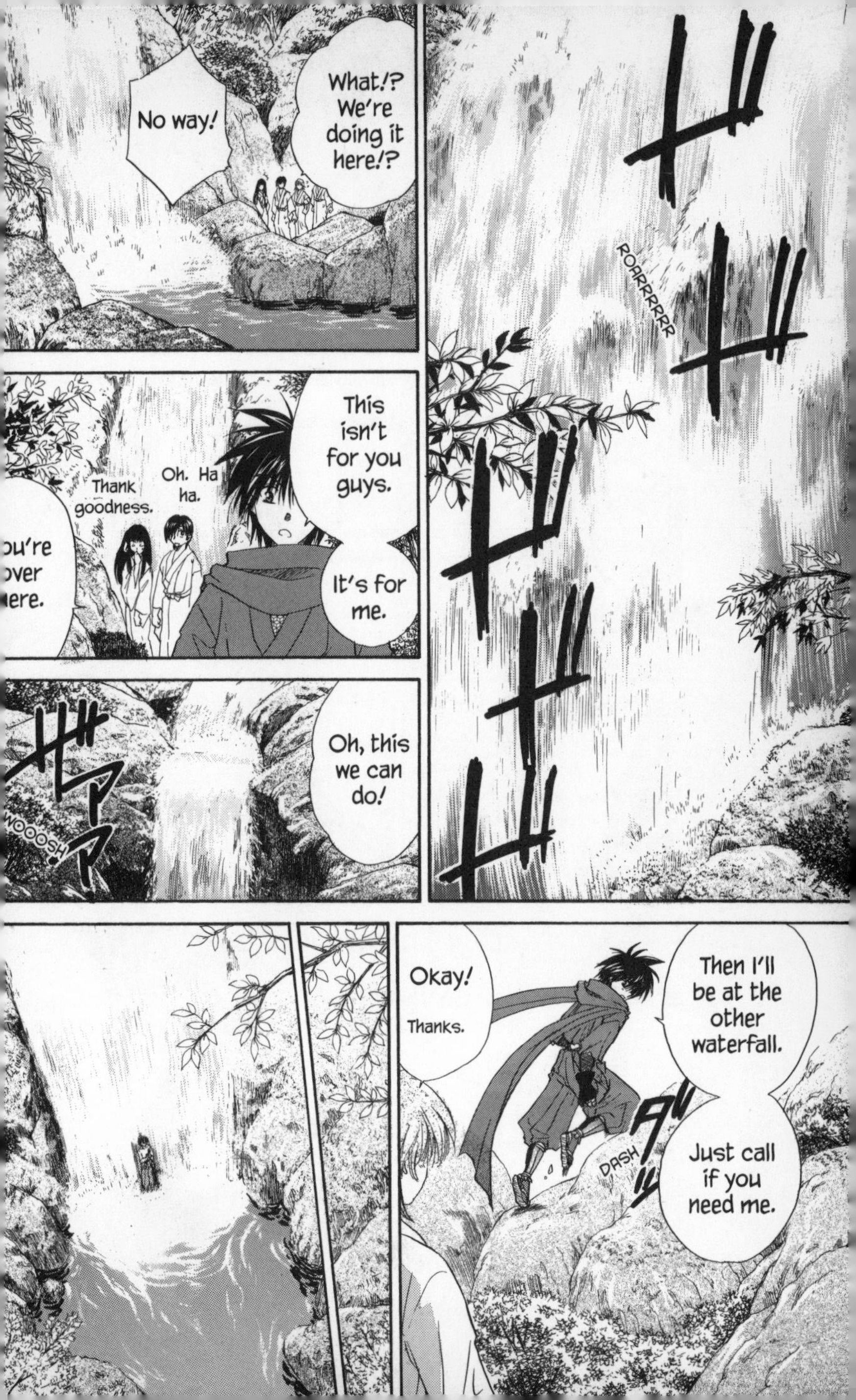
ROARRRRRR
What!? We're doing it here!?
No way!
This isn't for you guys.
It's for me.
Oh. Ha ha.
Thank goodness.
Oh, this we can do!
WOOOSH
Then I'll be at the other waterfall.
Just call if you need me.
DASH
Okay!
Thanks.

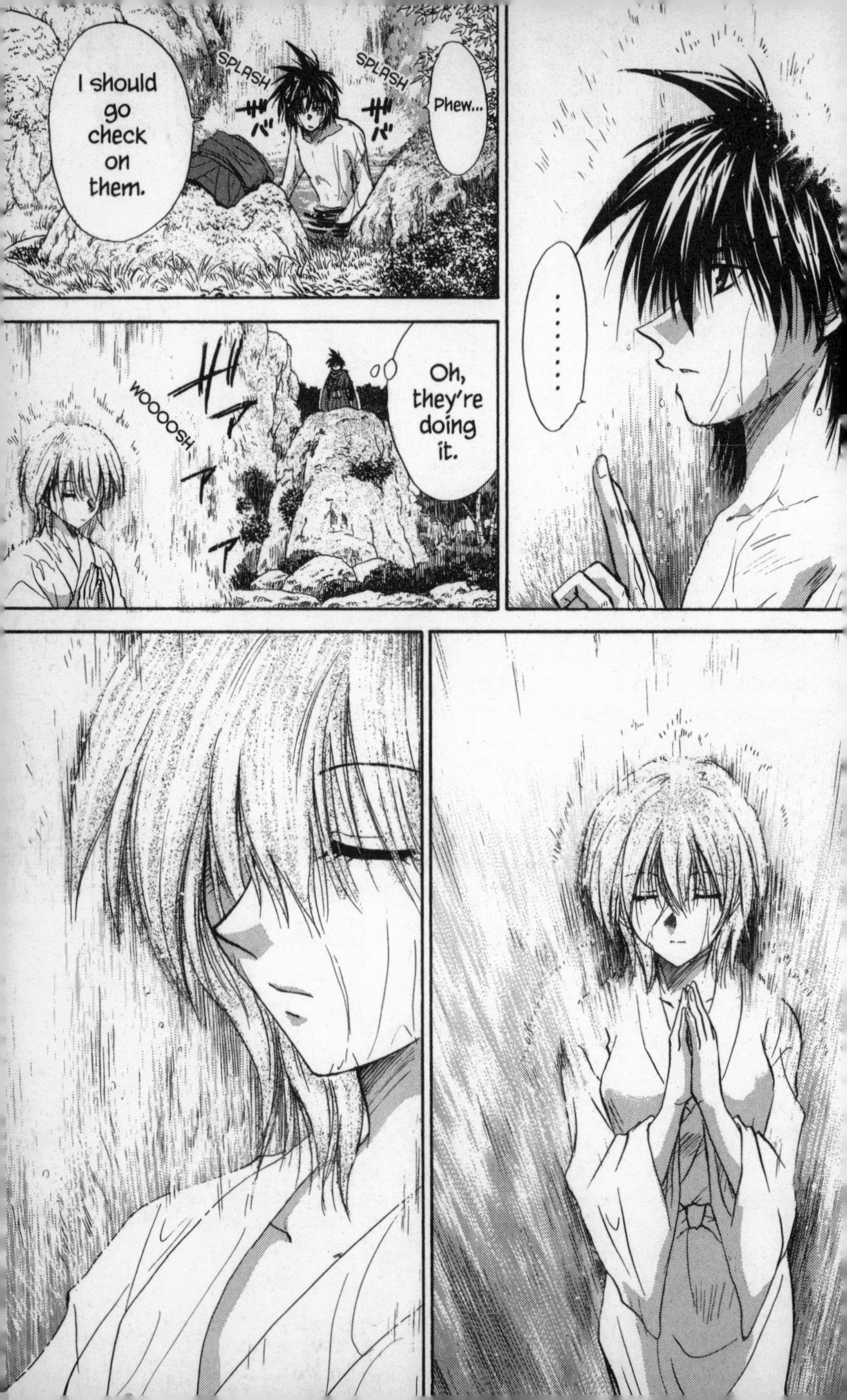
......
SPLASH
ザバ
Phew...
SPLASH
ザバ
I should go check on them.
Oh, they're doing it.
ザァァァ
WOOOOSH

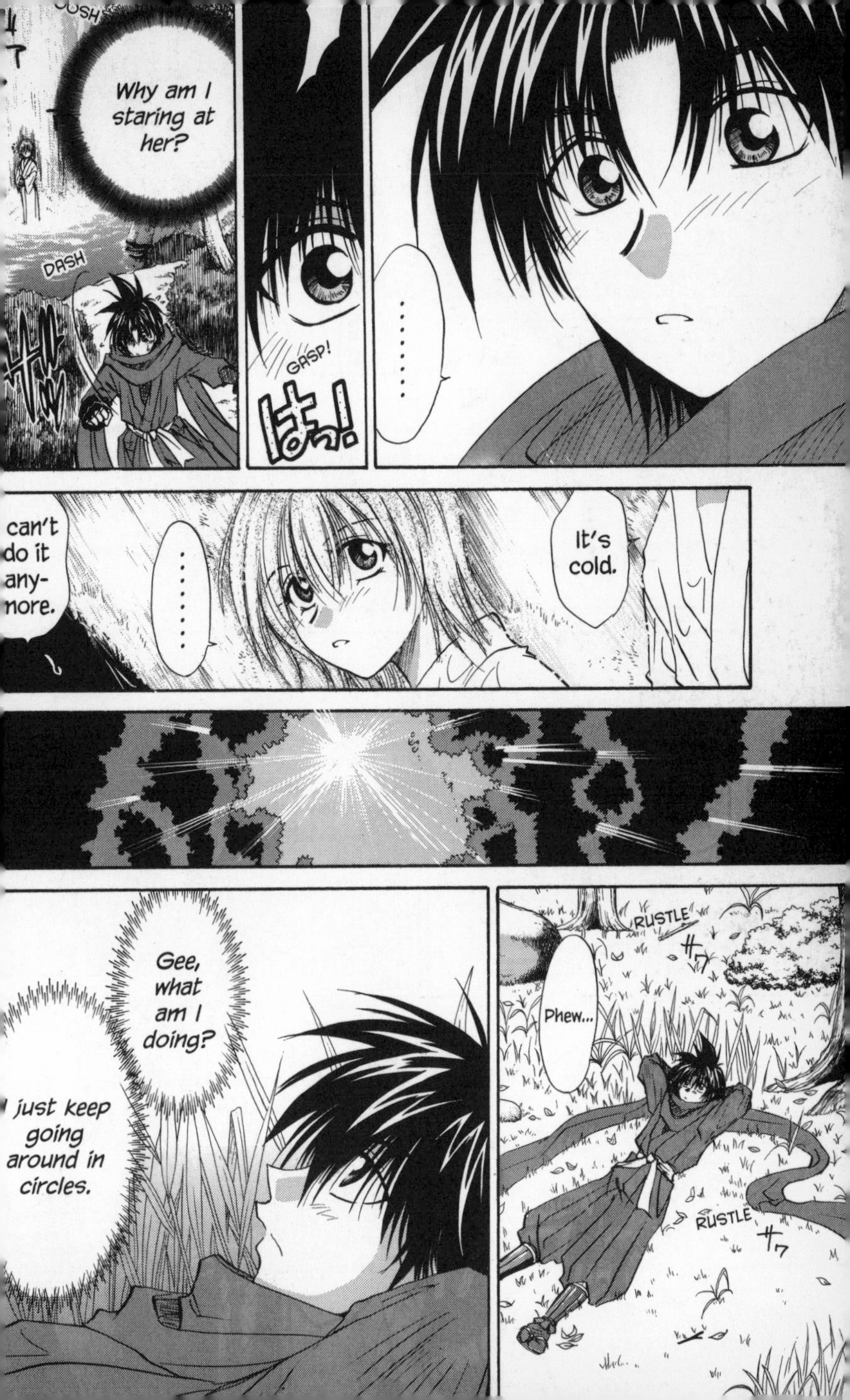

......
GASP!
はっ!
Why am I staring at her?
DASH
It's cold.
......
can't do it any-more.
RUSTLE
Phew...
RUSTLE
Gee, what am I doing?
I just keep going around in circles.

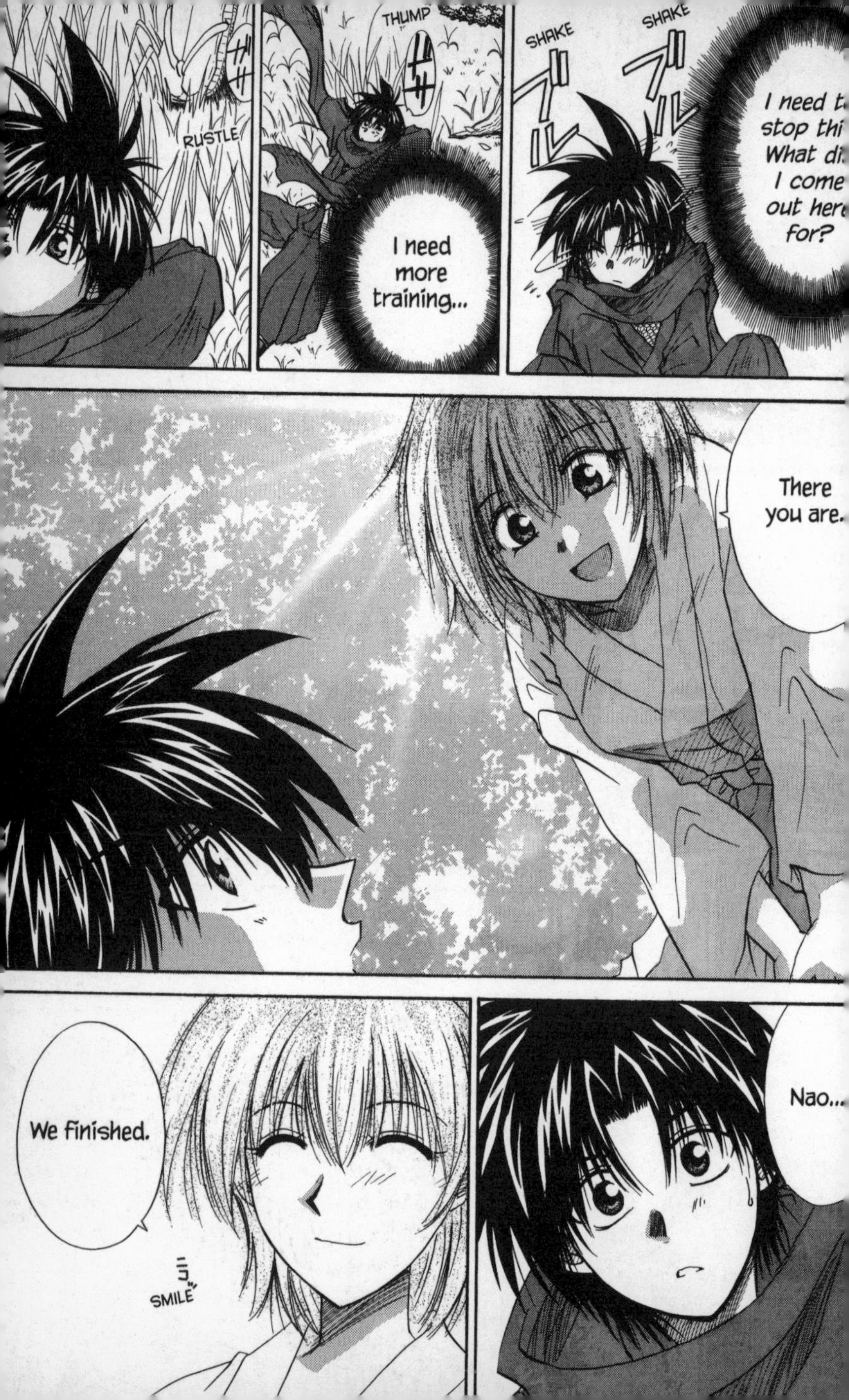
SHAKE
SHAKE
I need t stop thi What di I come out here for?
THUMP
I need more training...
RUSTLE
There you are.
Nao...
We finished.
SMILE

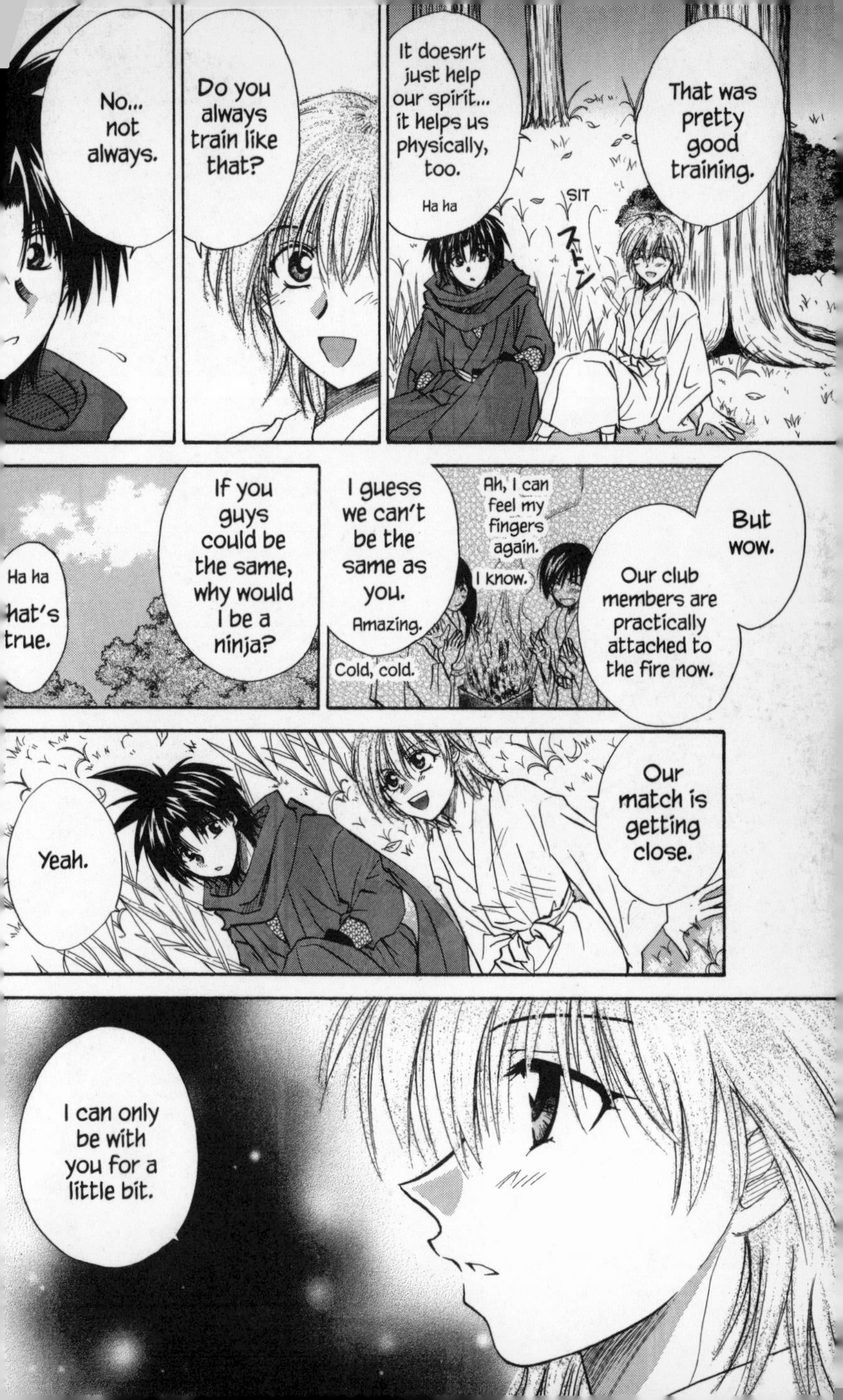
That was pretty good training.
SIT
ストン
It doesn't just help our spirit... it helps us physically, too.
Ha ha
Do you always train like that?
No... not always.
But wow.
Our club members are practically attached to the fire now.
Ah, I can feel my fingers again.
I know.
I guess we can't be the same as you.
Amazing.
Cold, cold.
If you guys could be the same, why would I be a ninja?
Ha ha
hat's true.
Our match is getting close.
Yeah.
I can only be with you for a little bit.

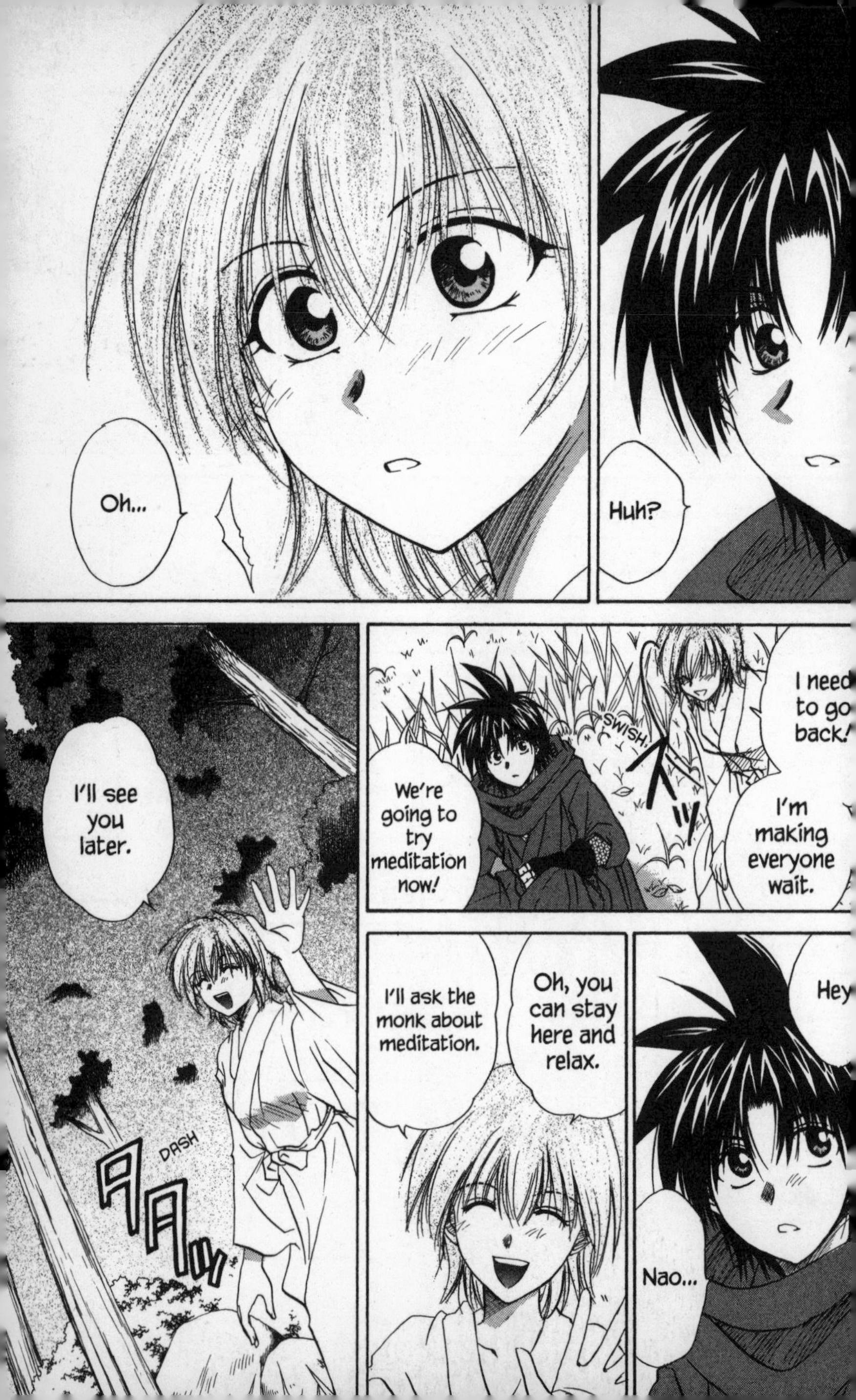
Huh?
Oh...
I need to go back!
I'm making everyone wait.
SWISH
We're going to try meditation now!
Hey
Nao...
Oh, you can stay here and relax.
I'll ask the monk about meditation.
I'll see you later.
DASH

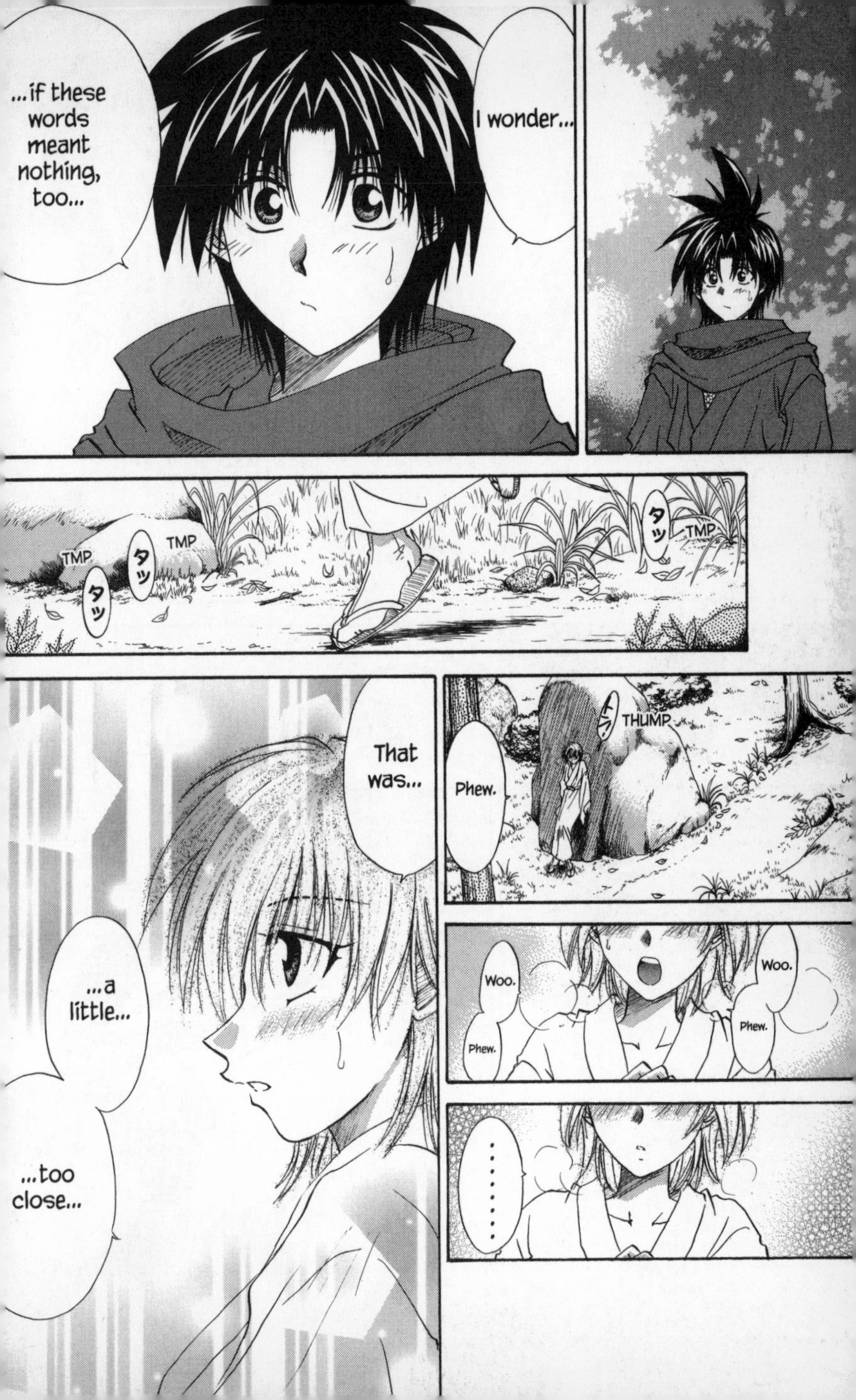
I wonder...
...if these words meant nothing, too...
タッ
TMP
タッ
TMP
タッ
TMP
THUMP
Phew.
Woo.
Phew.
Woo.
Phew.
....
That was...
...a little...
...too close...

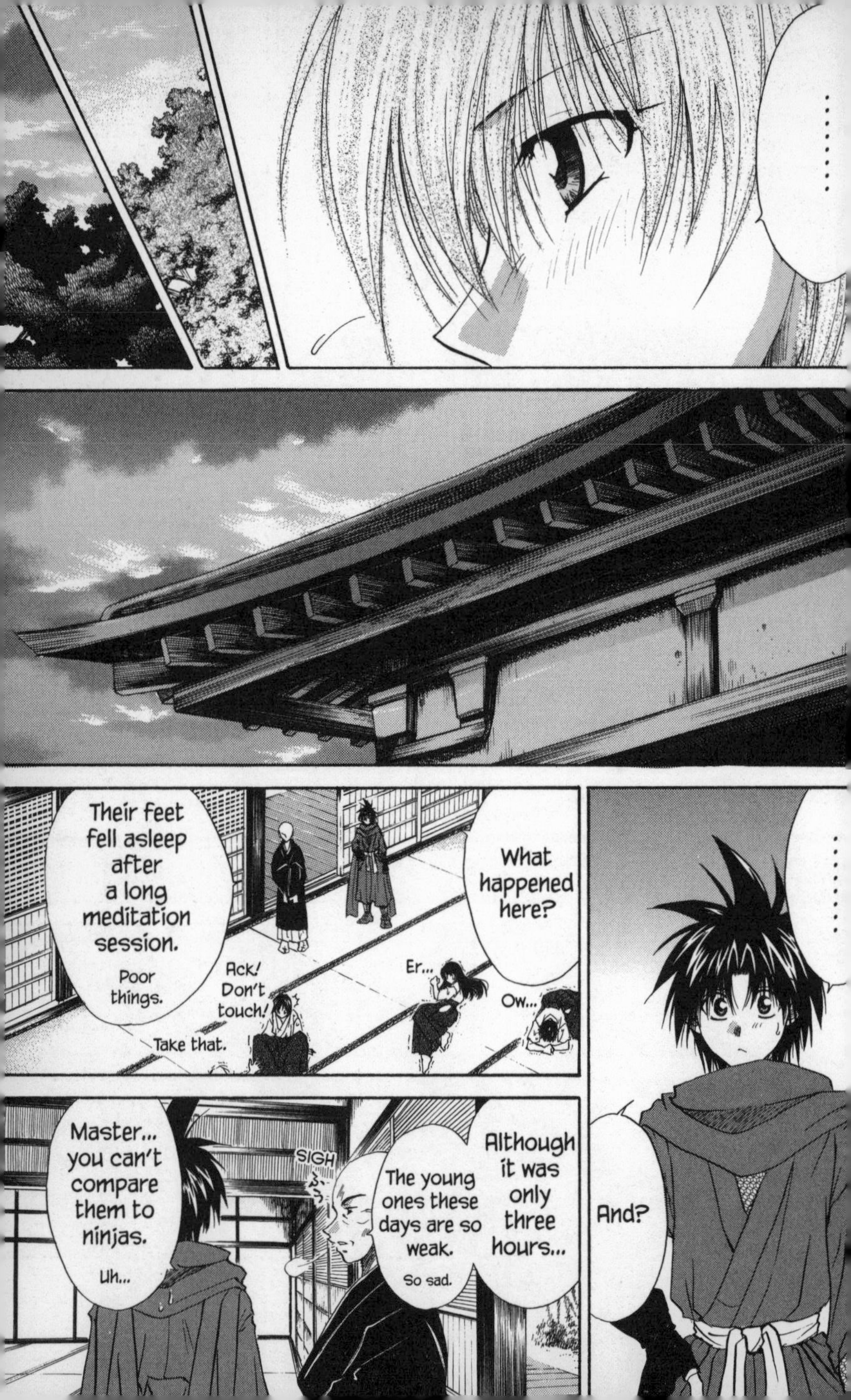
......
......
And?
What happened here?
Their feet fell asleep after a long meditation session.
Ow...
Er...
Ack! Don't touch!
Poor things.
Take that.
Although it was only three hours...
The young ones these days are so weak.
So sad.
SIGH
Master... you can't compare them to ninjas.
Uh...

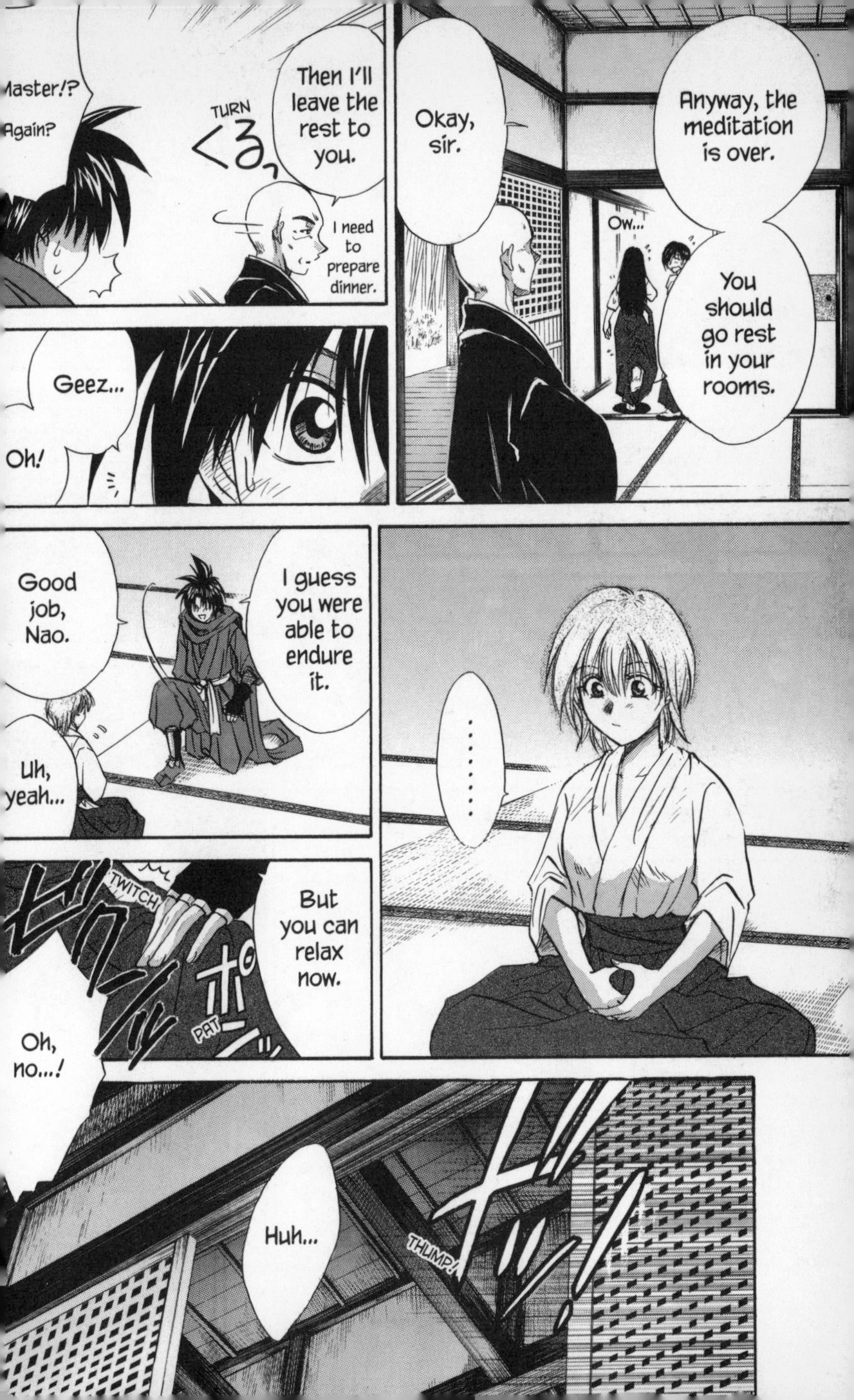
Anyway, the meditation is over.
You should go rest in your rooms.
Ow...
Okay, sir.
Then I'll leave the rest to you.
TURN
I need to prepare dinner.
Master!?
Again?
Geez...
Oh!
......
I guess you were able to endure it.
Good job, Nao.
Uh, yeah...
But you can relax now.
TWITCH
PAT
Oh, no...!
Huh...
THUMP!

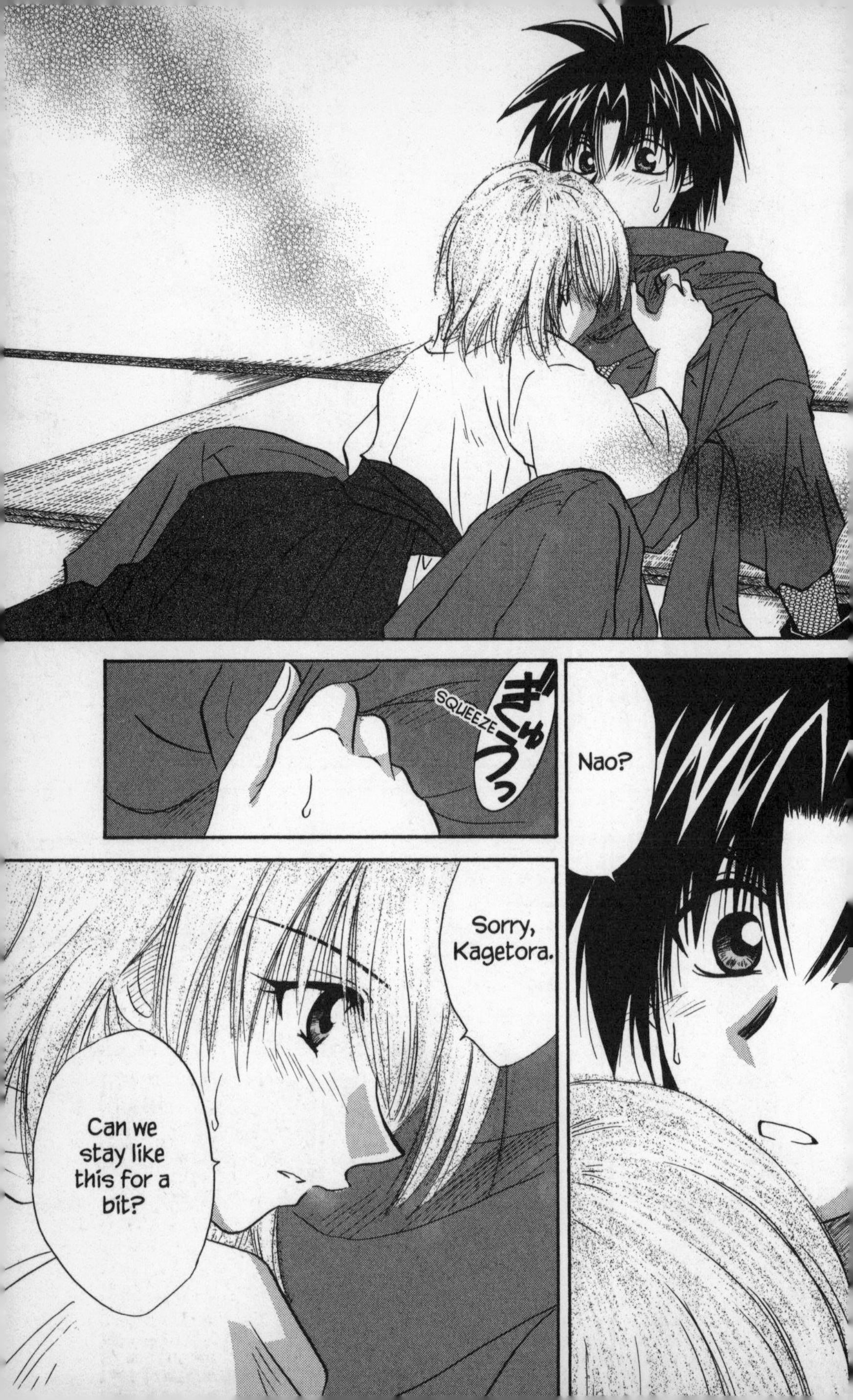
Nao?
ぎゅうっ
SQUEEZE
Sorry, Kagetora.
Can we stay like this for a bit?

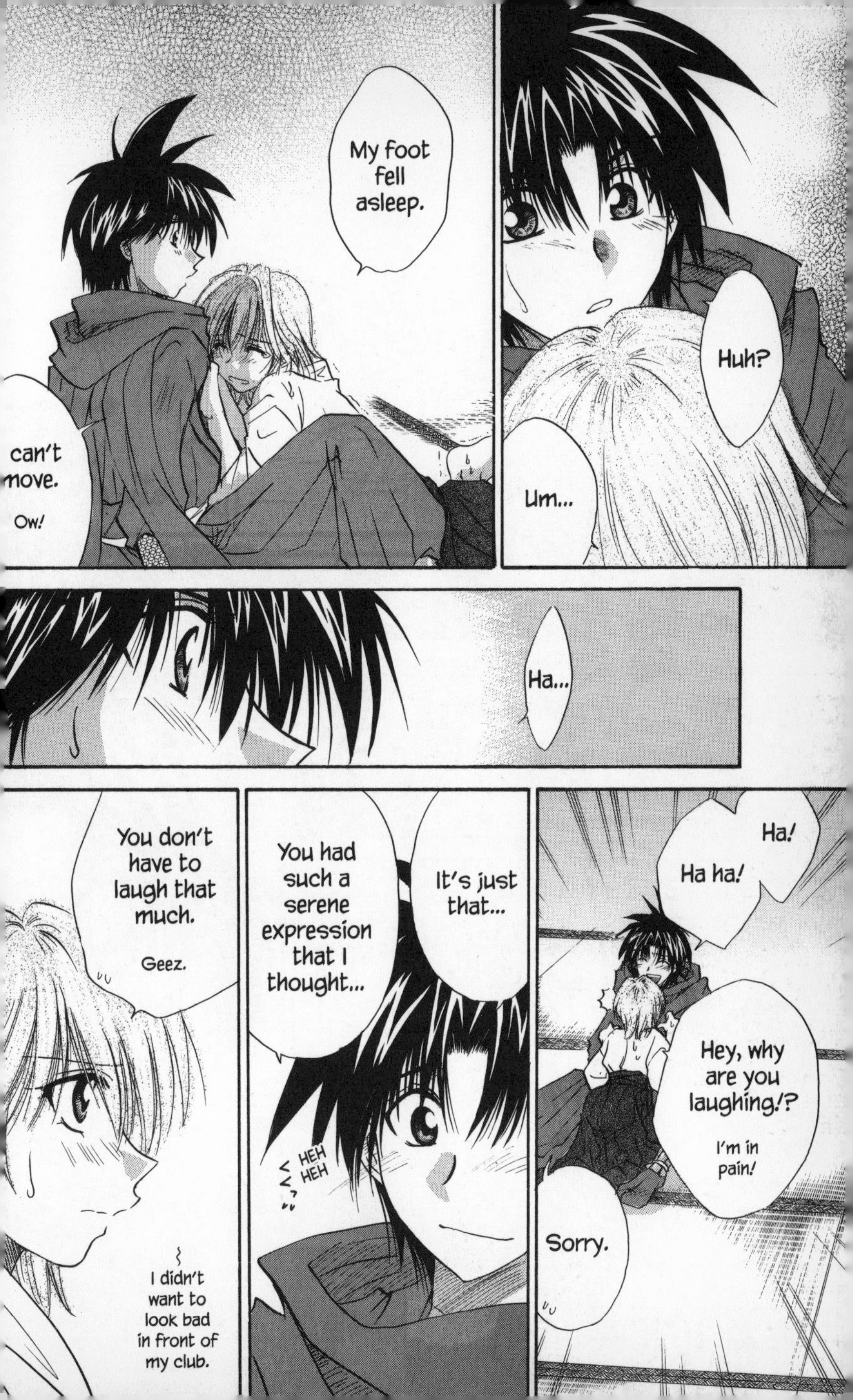
Huh?
Um...
My foot fell asleep.
can't move.
Ow!
Ha...
Ha!
Ha ha!
Hey, why are you laughing!?
I'm in pain!
Sorry.
It's just that...
You had such a serene expression that I thought...
HEH HEH
You don't have to laugh that much.
Geez.
I didn't want to look bad in front of my club.

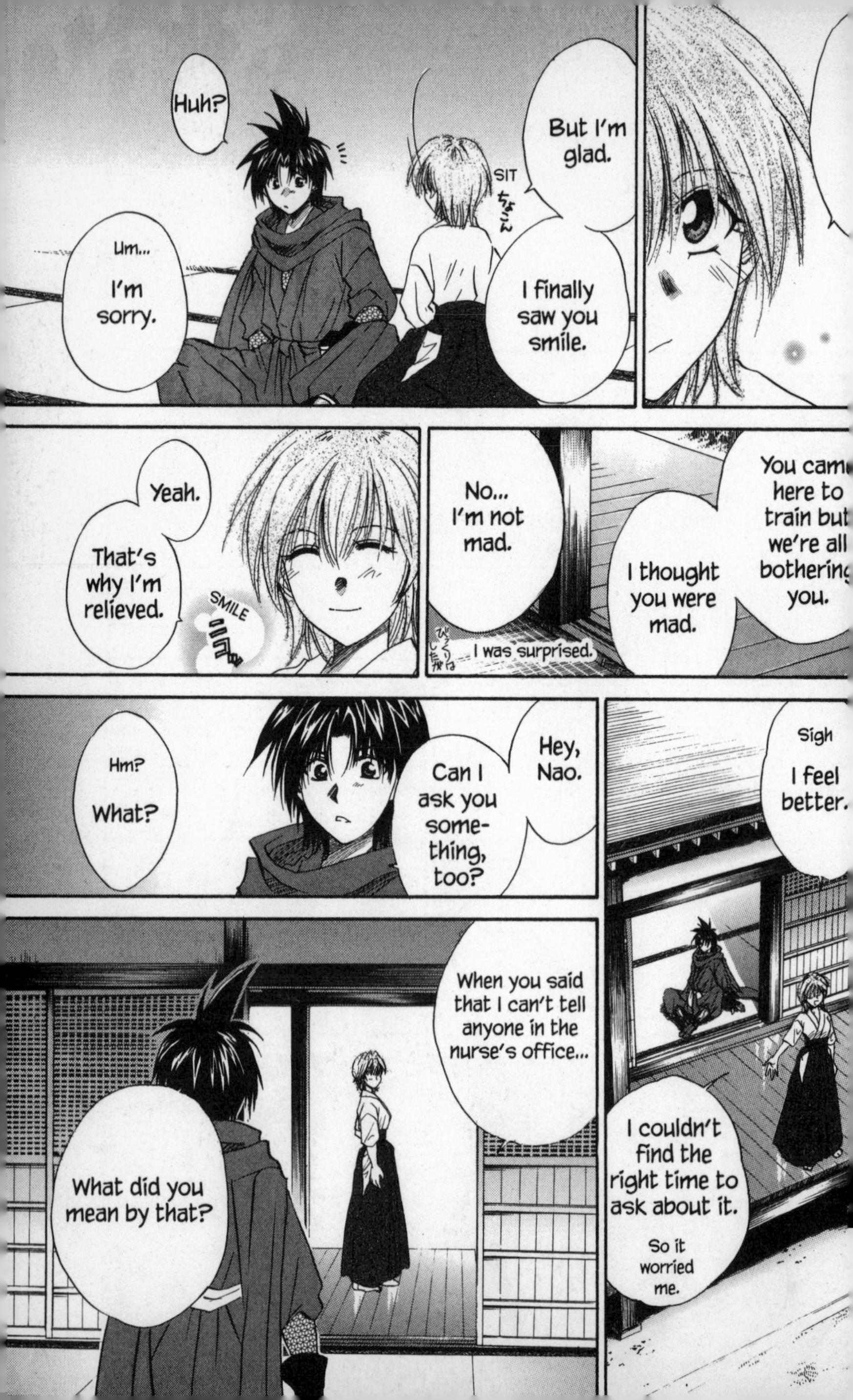

But I'm glad.
SIT
ちょこん
Huh?
I finally saw you smile.
Um... I'm sorry.
You cam here to train bu we're all botherin you.
I thought you were mad.
No... I'm not mad.
I was surprised.
びっくりはしたがね
Yeah.
That's why I'm relieved.
SMILE
Sigh I feel better.
I couldn't find the right time to ask about it.
So it worried me.
Hey, Nao.
Can I ask you some-thing, too?
Hm? What?
When you said that I can't tell anyone in the nurse's office...
What did you mean by that?

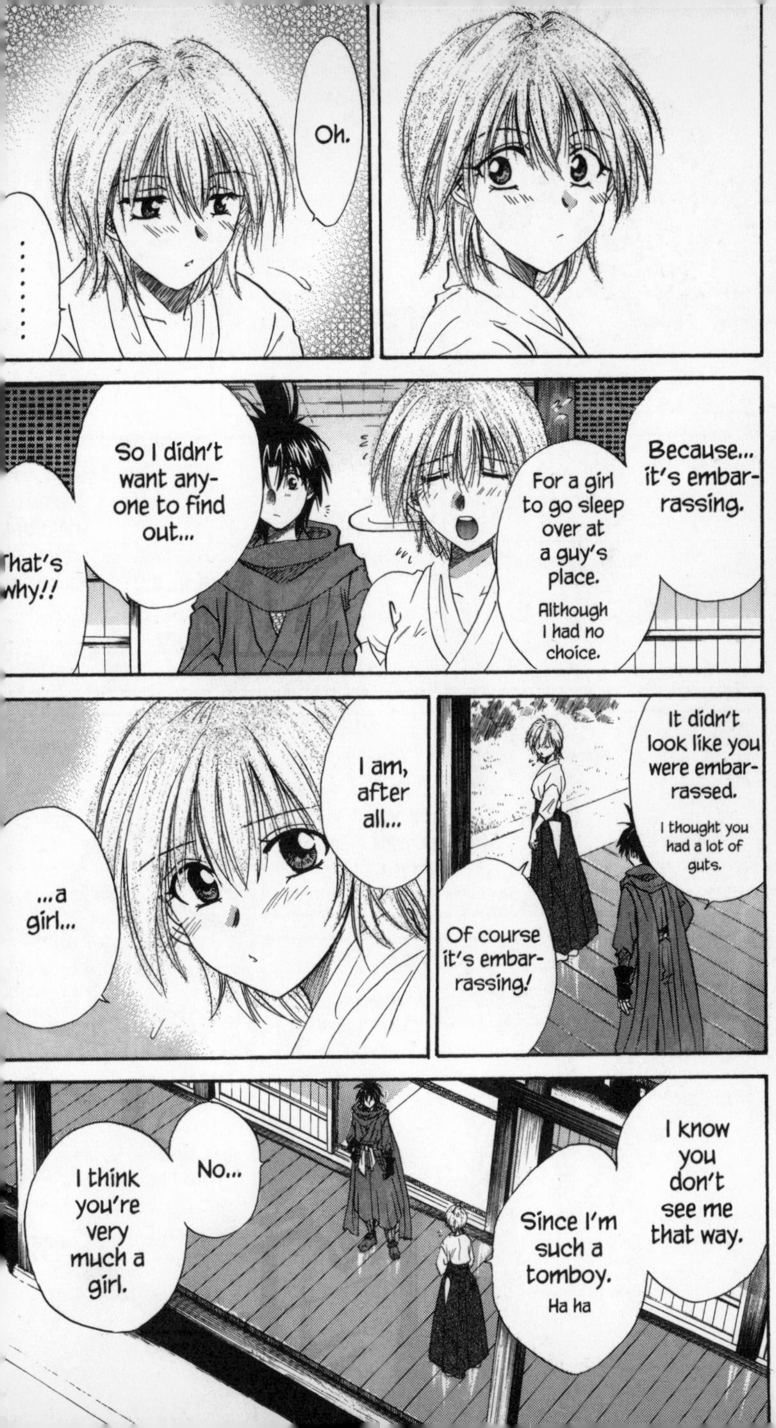
Oh.
......
Because... it's embarrassing.
For a girl to go sleep over at a guy's place.
Although I had no choice.
So I didn't want anyone to find out...
That's why!!
It didn't look like you were embarrassed.
I thought you had a lot of guts.
Of course it's embarrassing!
I am, after all...
...a girl...
I know you don't see me that way.
Since I'm such a tomboy.
Ha ha
No...
I think you're very much a girl.

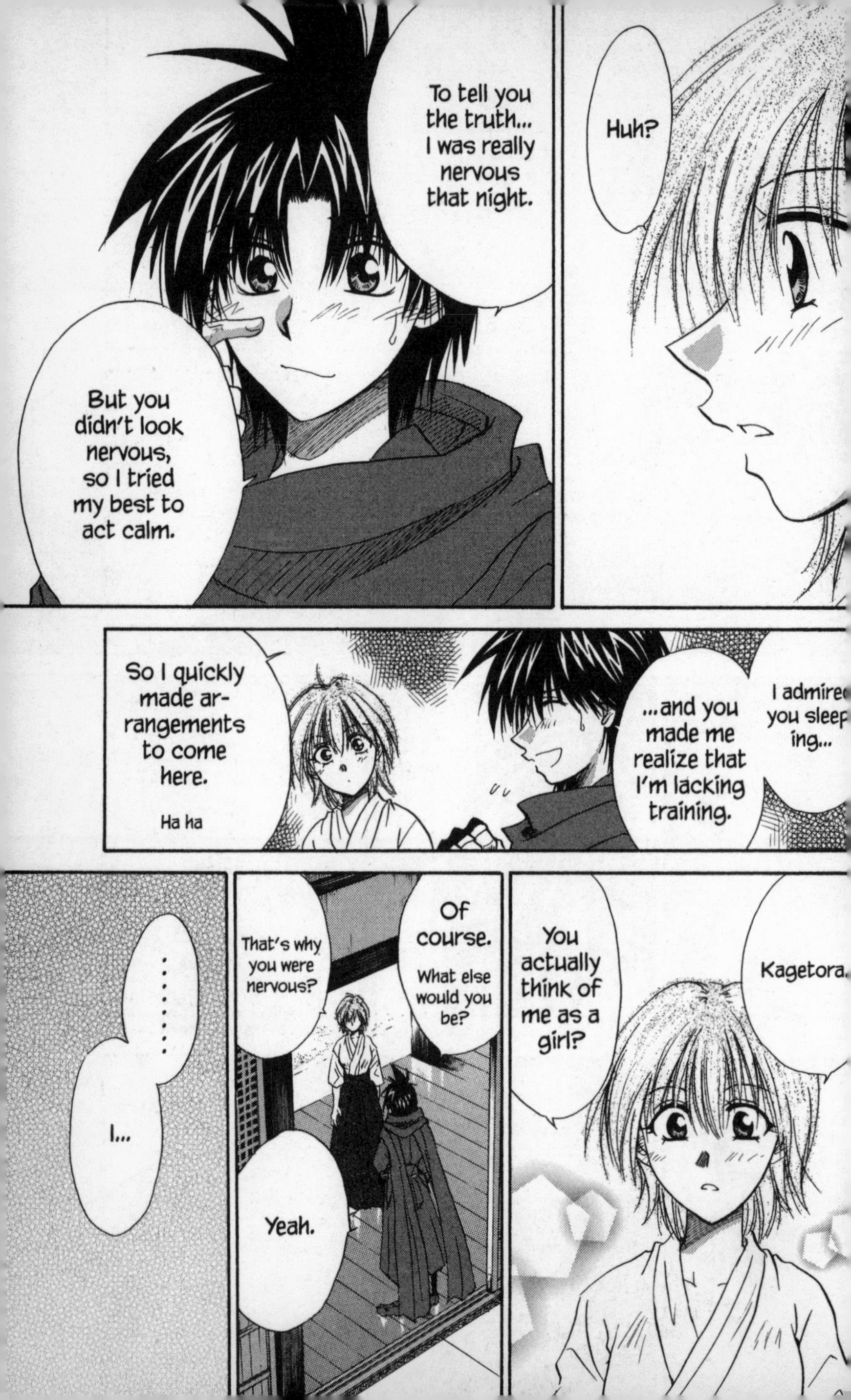
Huh?
To tell you the truth... I was really nervous that night.
But you didn't look nervous, so I tried my best to act calm.
I admire you sleep ing...
...and you made me realize that I'm lacking training.
So I quickly made ar- rangements to come here.
Ha ha
Kagetora.
You actually think of me as a girl?
Of course.
What else would you be?
That's why you were nervous?
Yeah.
......
I...

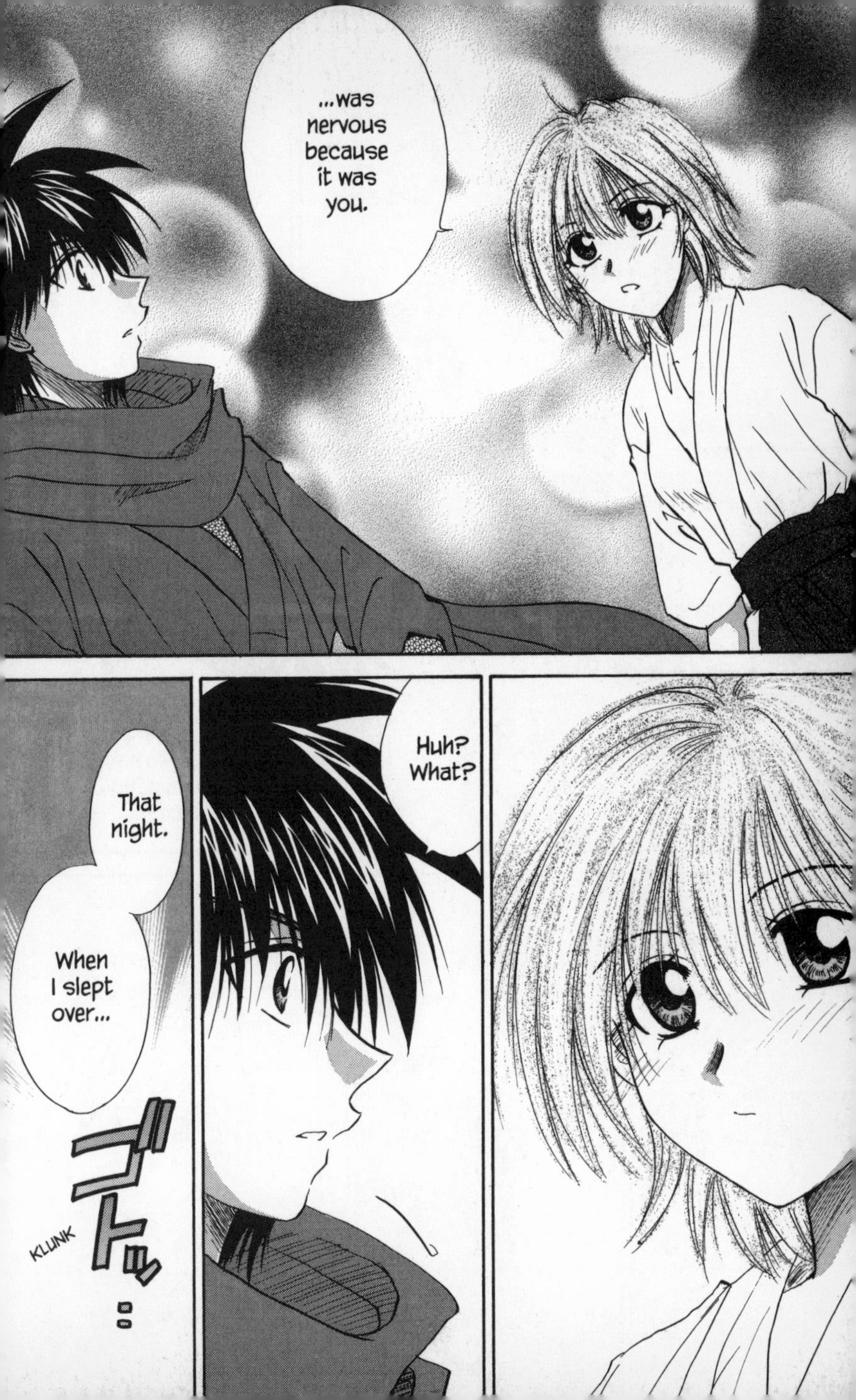
...was nervous because it was you.
Huh? What?
That night.
When I slept over...
ゴトッ
KLUNK

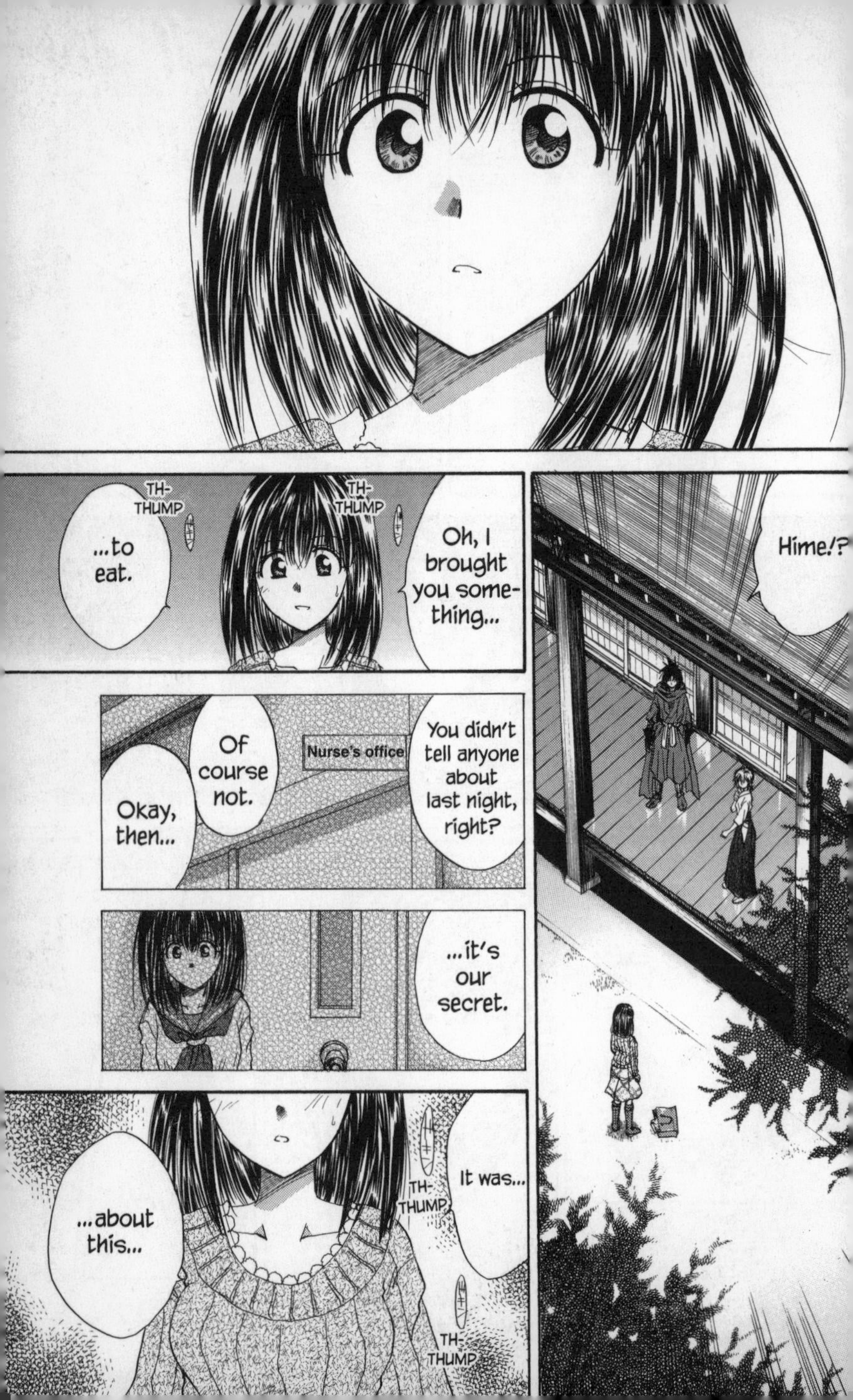
Hime!?
TH-THUMP
Oh, I brought you some-thing...
TH-THUMP
...to eat.
You didn't tell anyone about last night, right?
Nurse's office
Of course not.
Okay, then...
...it's our secret.
It was...
TH-THUMP
...about this...
TH-THUMP

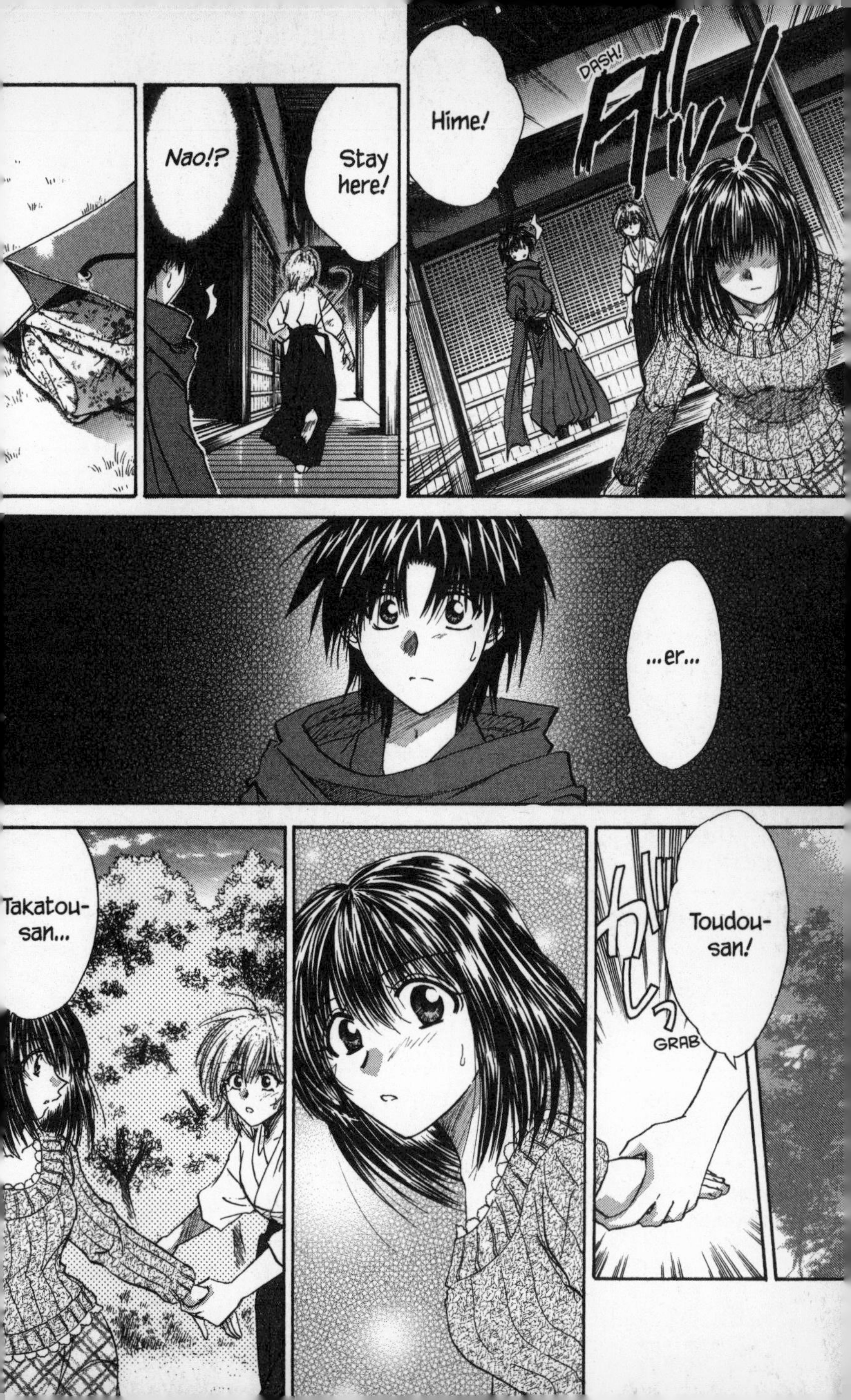
DASH!
Hime!
Stay here!
Nao!?
...er...
Toudou-san!
GRAB
Takatou-san...

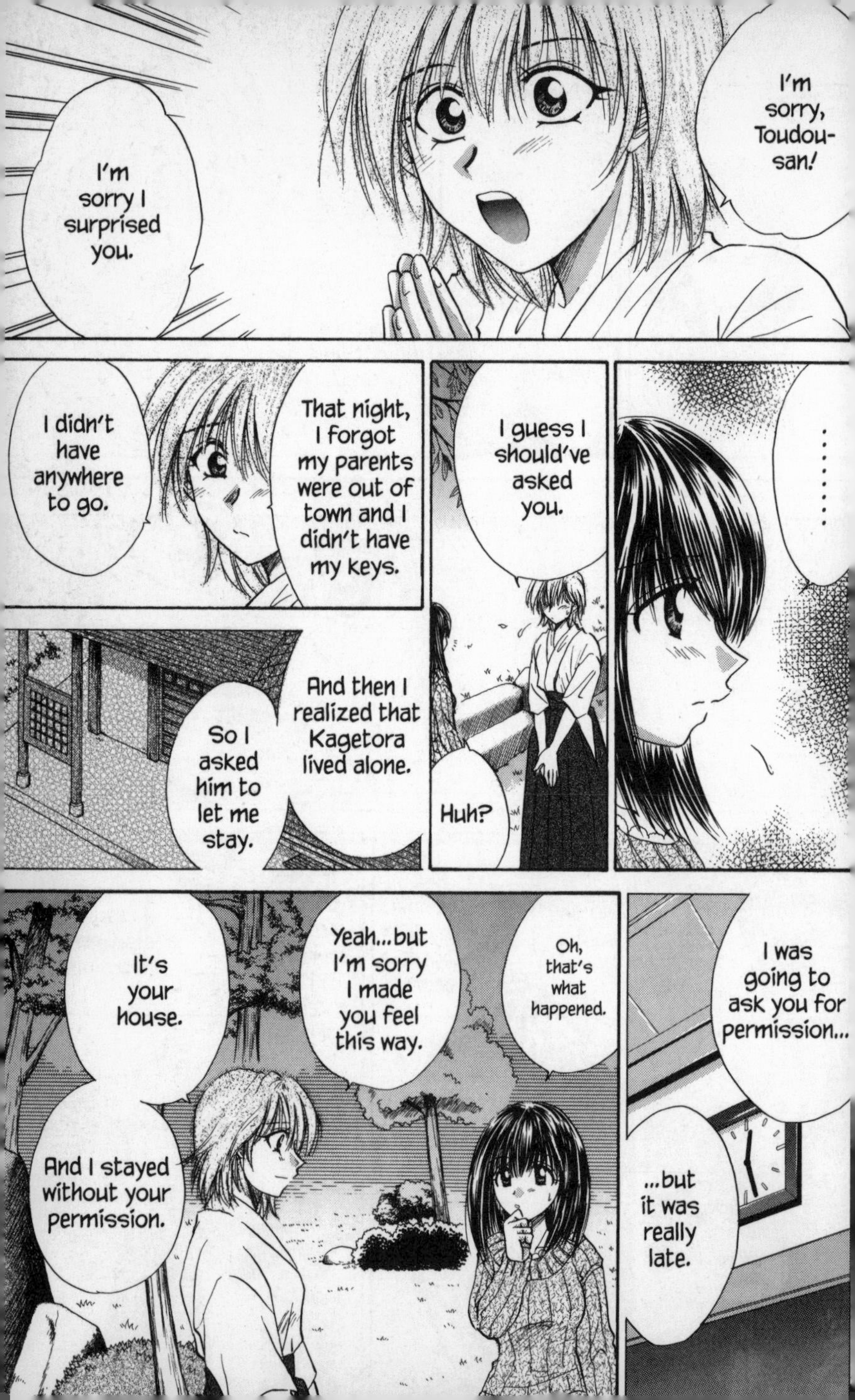
I'm sorry, Toudou-san!
I'm sorry I surprised you.
......
I guess I should've asked you.
Huh?
That night, I forgot my parents were out of town and I didn't have my keys.
I didn't have anywhere to go.
And then I realized that Kagetora lived alone.
So I asked him to let me stay.
I was going to ask you for permission...
...but it was really late.
Oh, that's what happened.
Yeah...but I'm sorry I made you feel this way.
It's your house.
And I stayed without your permission.

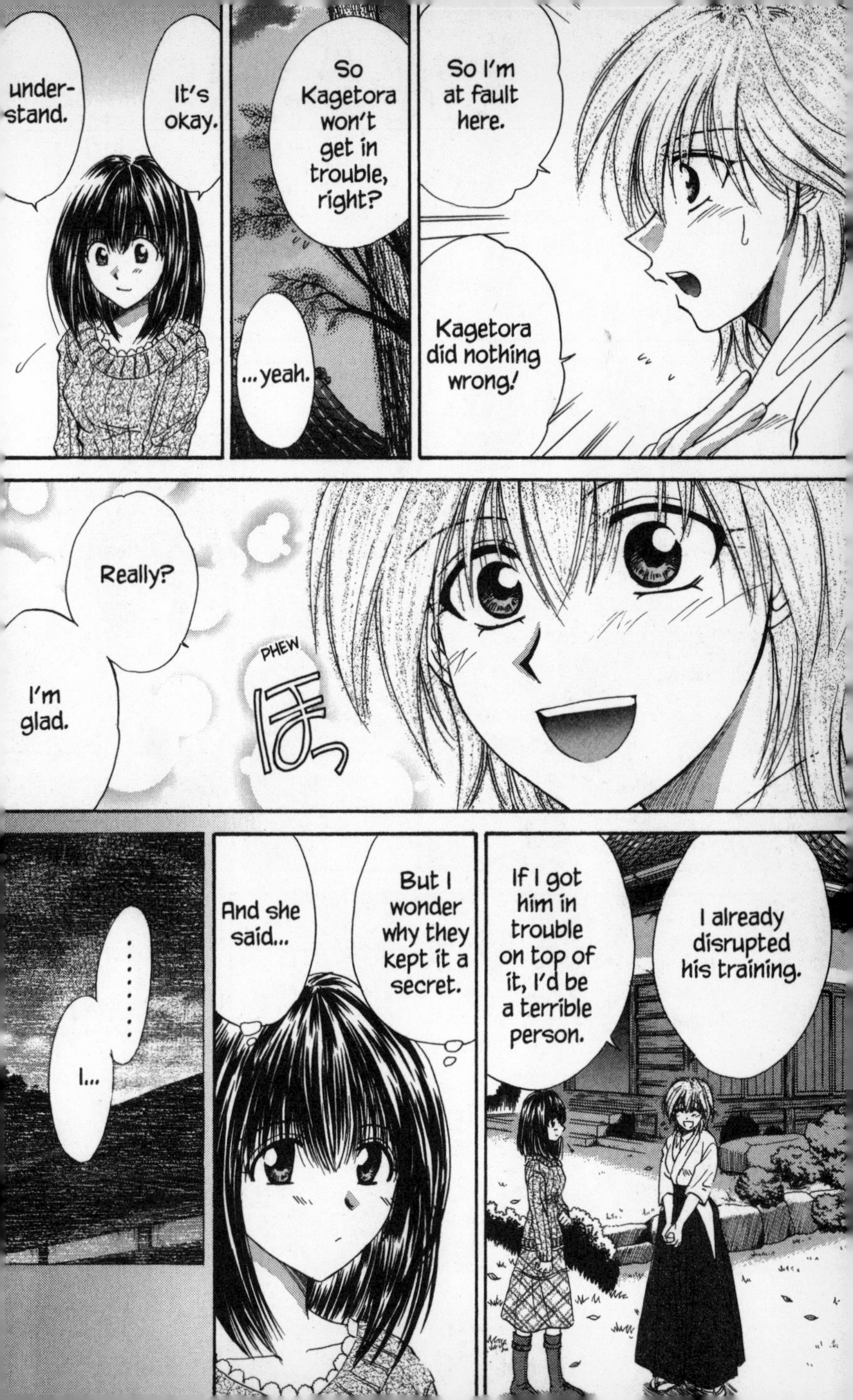
So I'm at fault here.
Kagetora did nothing wrong!
So Kagetora won't get in trouble, right?
...yeah.
It's okay.
under-stand.
Really?
PHEW
ほっ
I'm glad.
I already disrupted his training.
If I got him in trouble on top of it, I'd be a terrible person.
But I wonder why they kept it a secret.
And she said...
......
I...

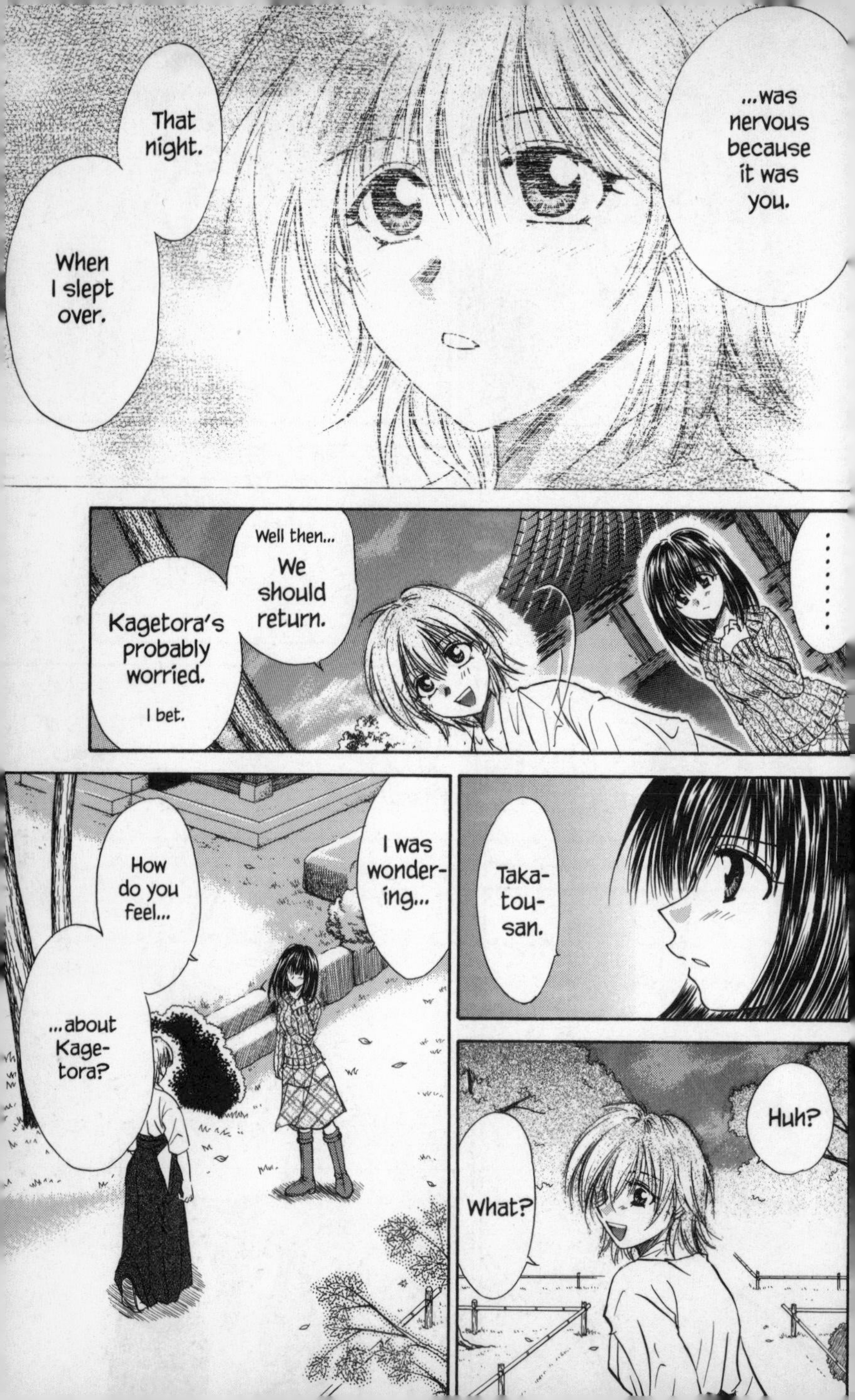
...was nervous because it was you.
That night.
When I slept over.
......
Well then... We should return.
Kagetora's probably worried. I bet.
Taka-tou-san.
Huh?
What?
I was wonder-ing...
How do you feel...
...about Kage-tora?

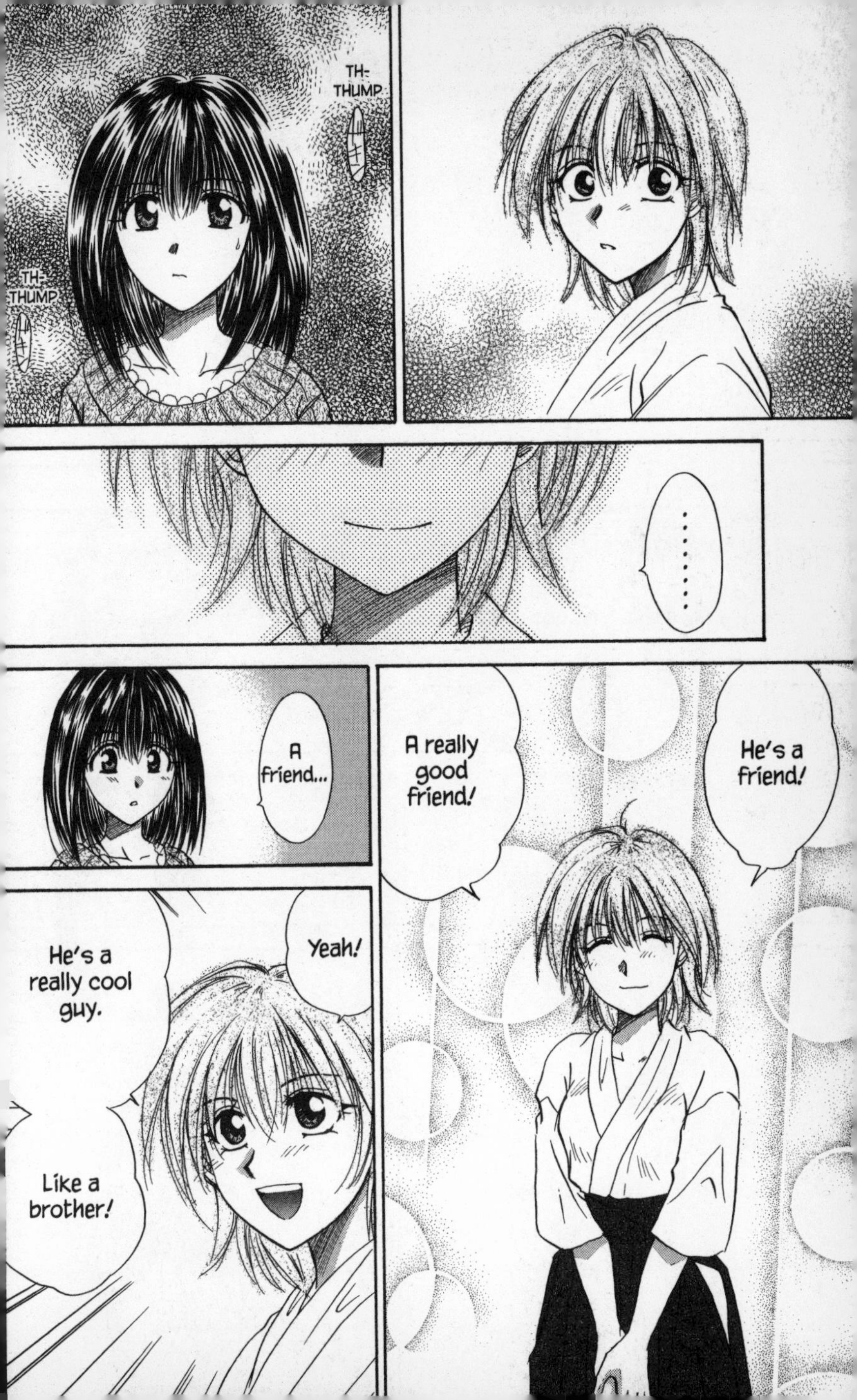
TH-THUMP
TH-THUMP
......
He's a friend!
A really good friend!
A friend...
Yeah!
He's a really cool guy.
Like a brother!

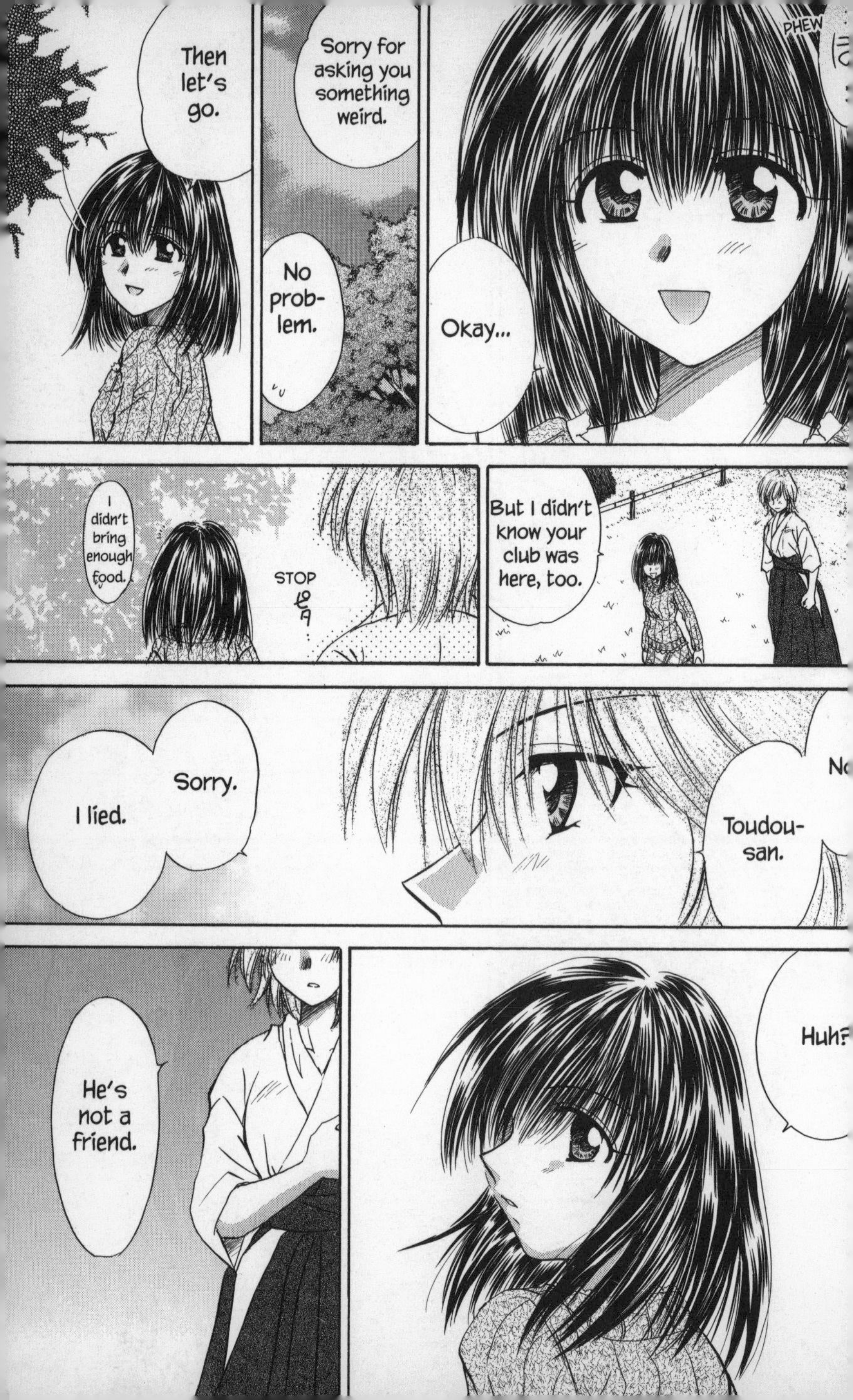
PHEW
Okay...
Sorry for asking you something weird.
No prob-lem.
Then let's go.
But I didn't know your club was here, too.
STOP
I didn't bring enough food.
No
Toudou-san.
Sorry.
I lied.
Huh?
He's not a friend.

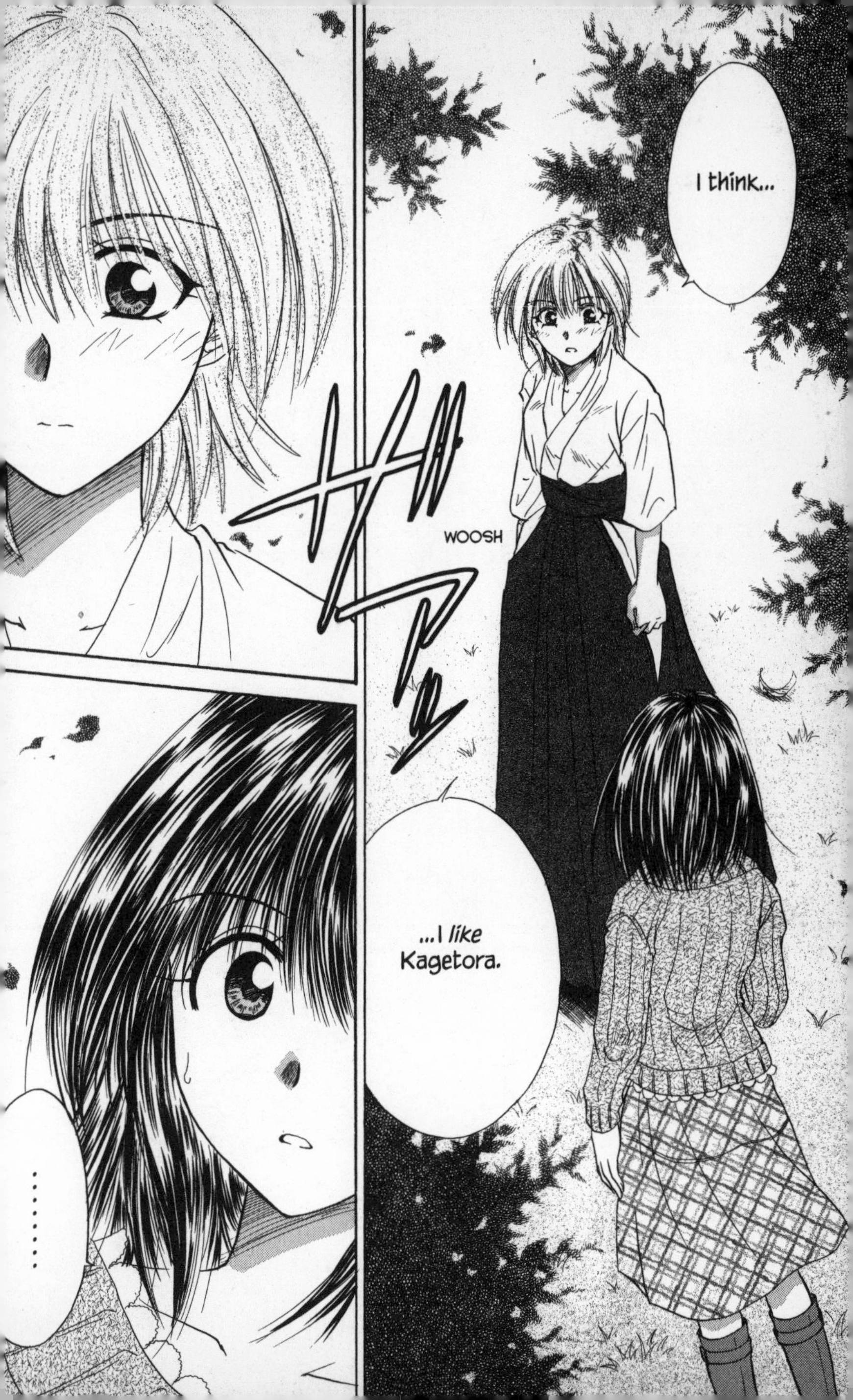

I think...
WOOSH
...I like Kagetora.
....

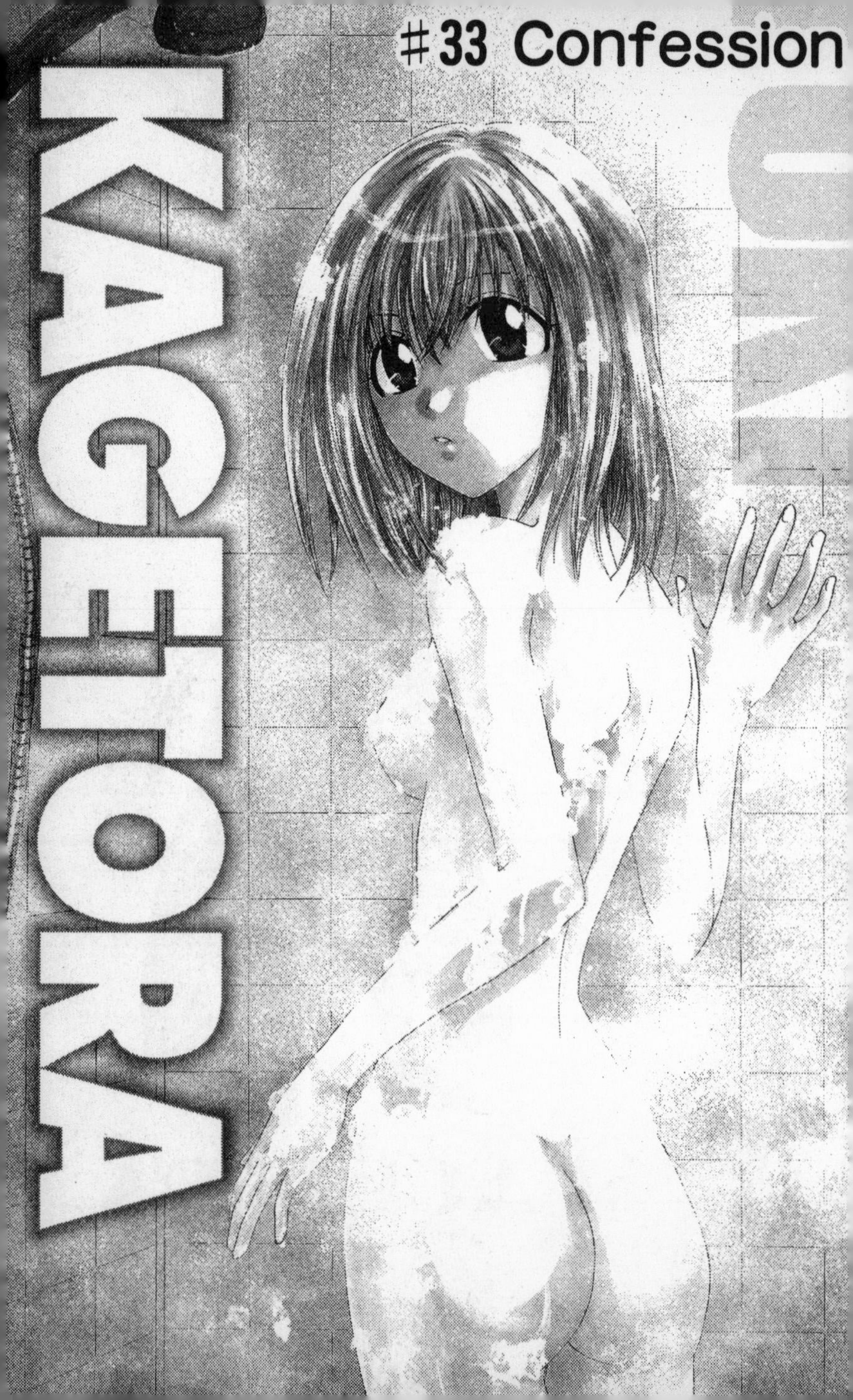
#33 Confession
KAGETORA

Kotetsu

虎鉄

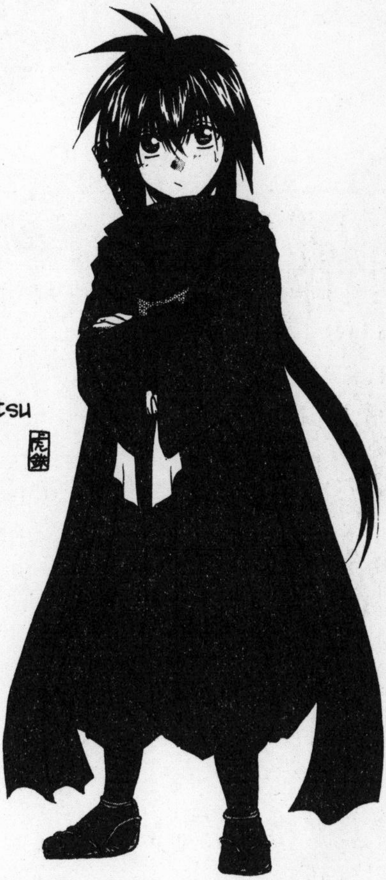

KAGETORA

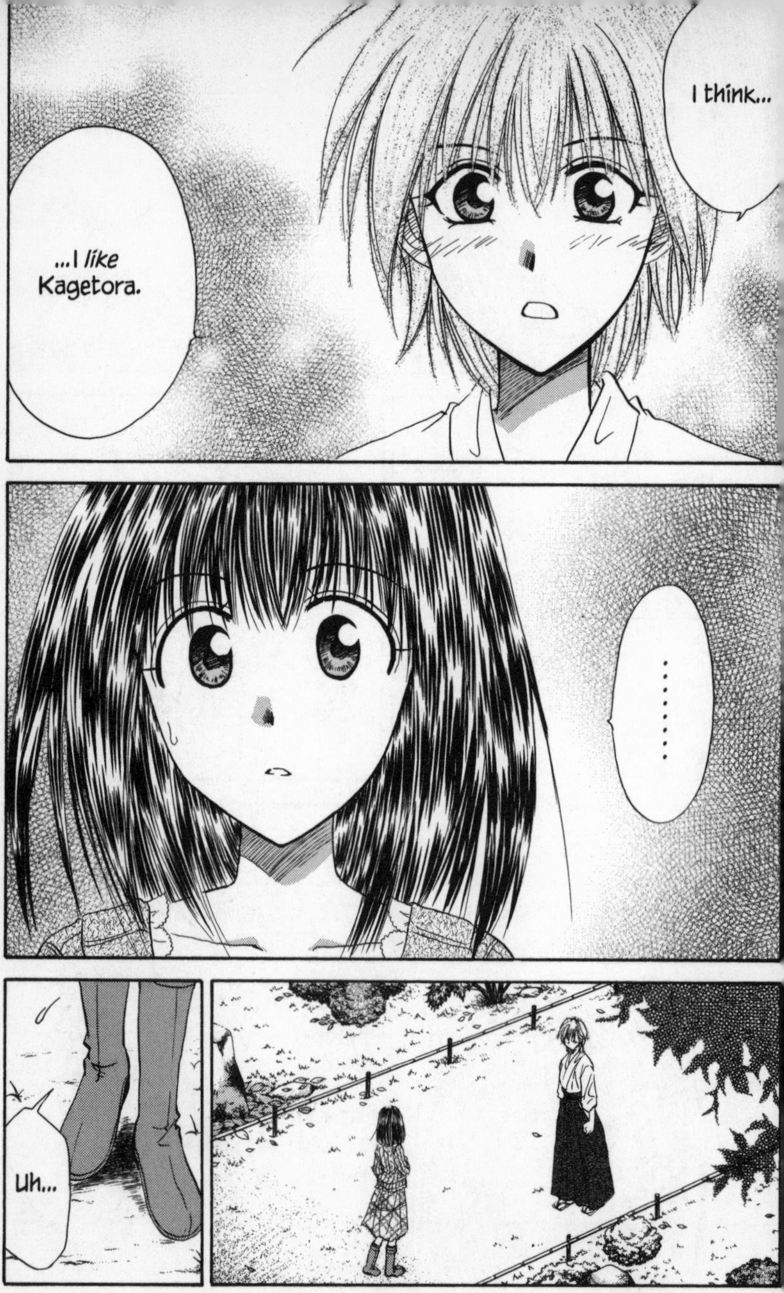
I think...
...I like Kagetora.
......
Uh...

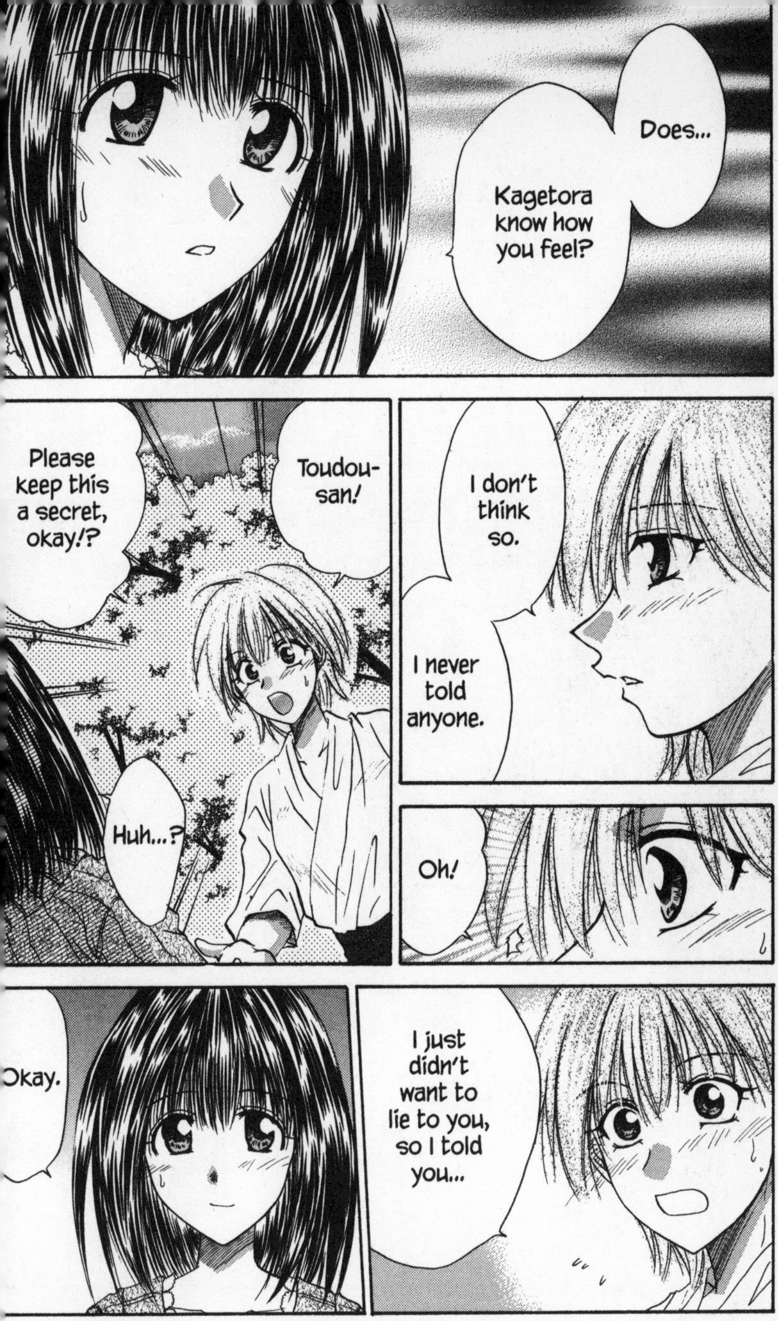
Does...
Kagetora know how you feel?
I don't think so.
I never told anyone.
Oh!
Toudou-san!
Please keep this a secret, okay!?
Huh...?
I just didn't want to lie to you, so I told you...
Okay.

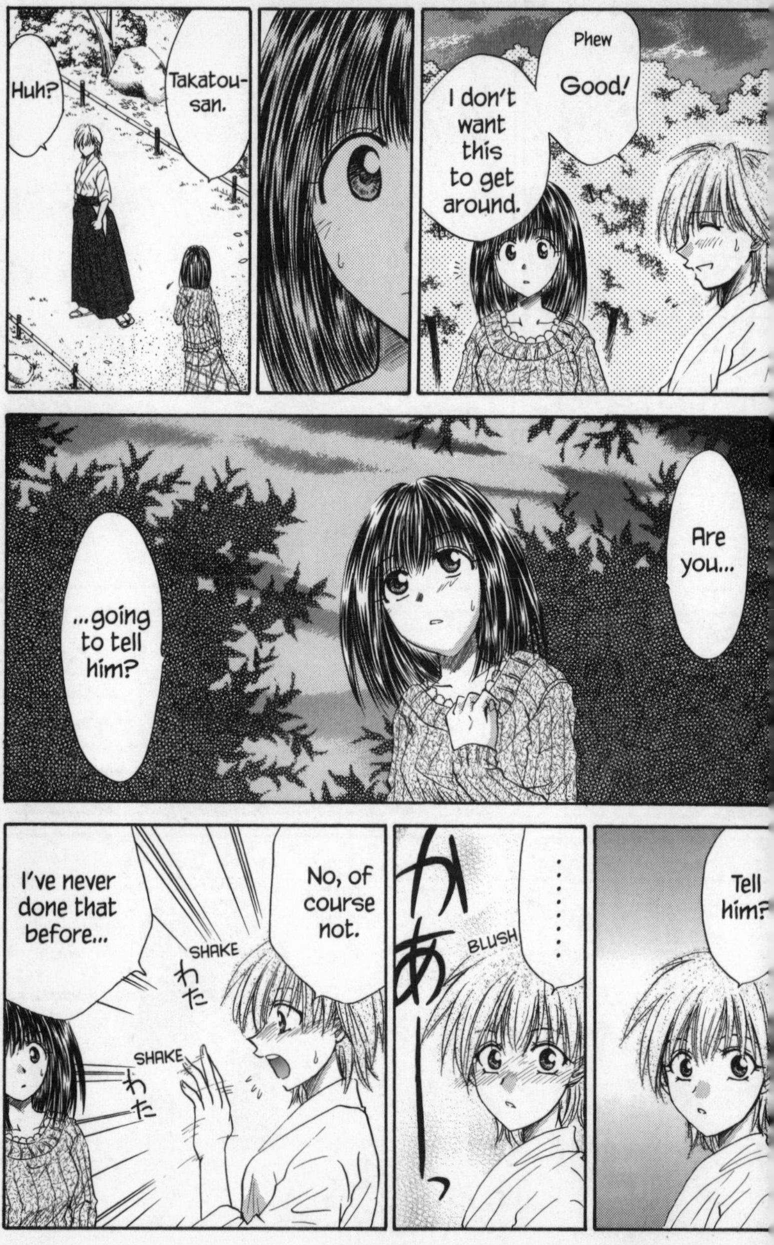
Phew
Good!
I don't want this to get around.
Takatou-san.
Huh?
Are you...
...going to tell him?
Tell him?
......
かあーっ
BLUSH
No, of course not.
SHAKE
わた
SHAKE
わた
I've never done that before...

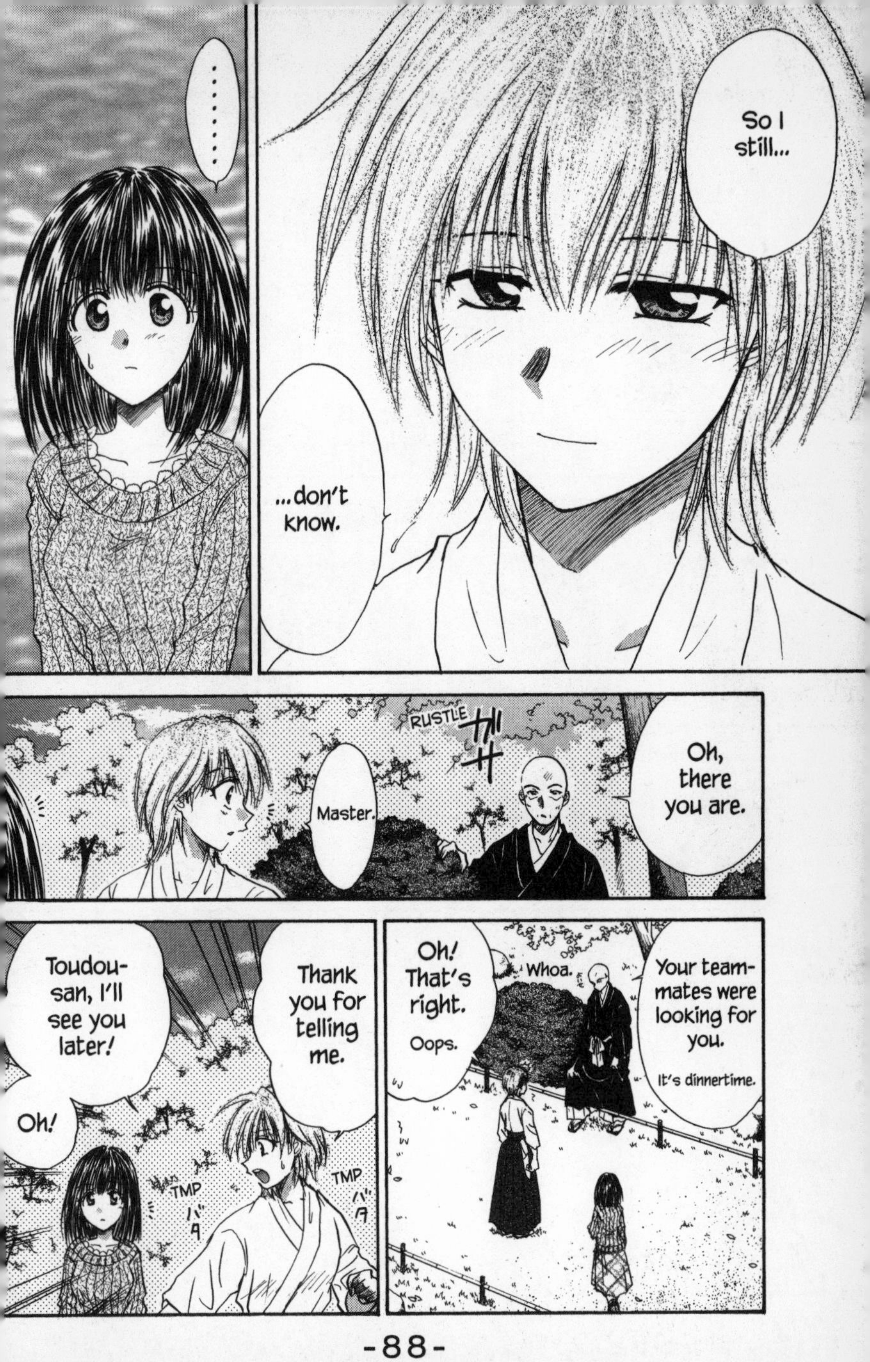
So I still...
...don't know.
......
Oh, there you are.
RUSTLE
Master.
Your team-mates were looking for you.
It's dinnertime.
Whoa.
Oh! That's right.
Oops.
Thank you for telling me.
TMP
Toudou-san, I'll see you later!
TMP
Oh!

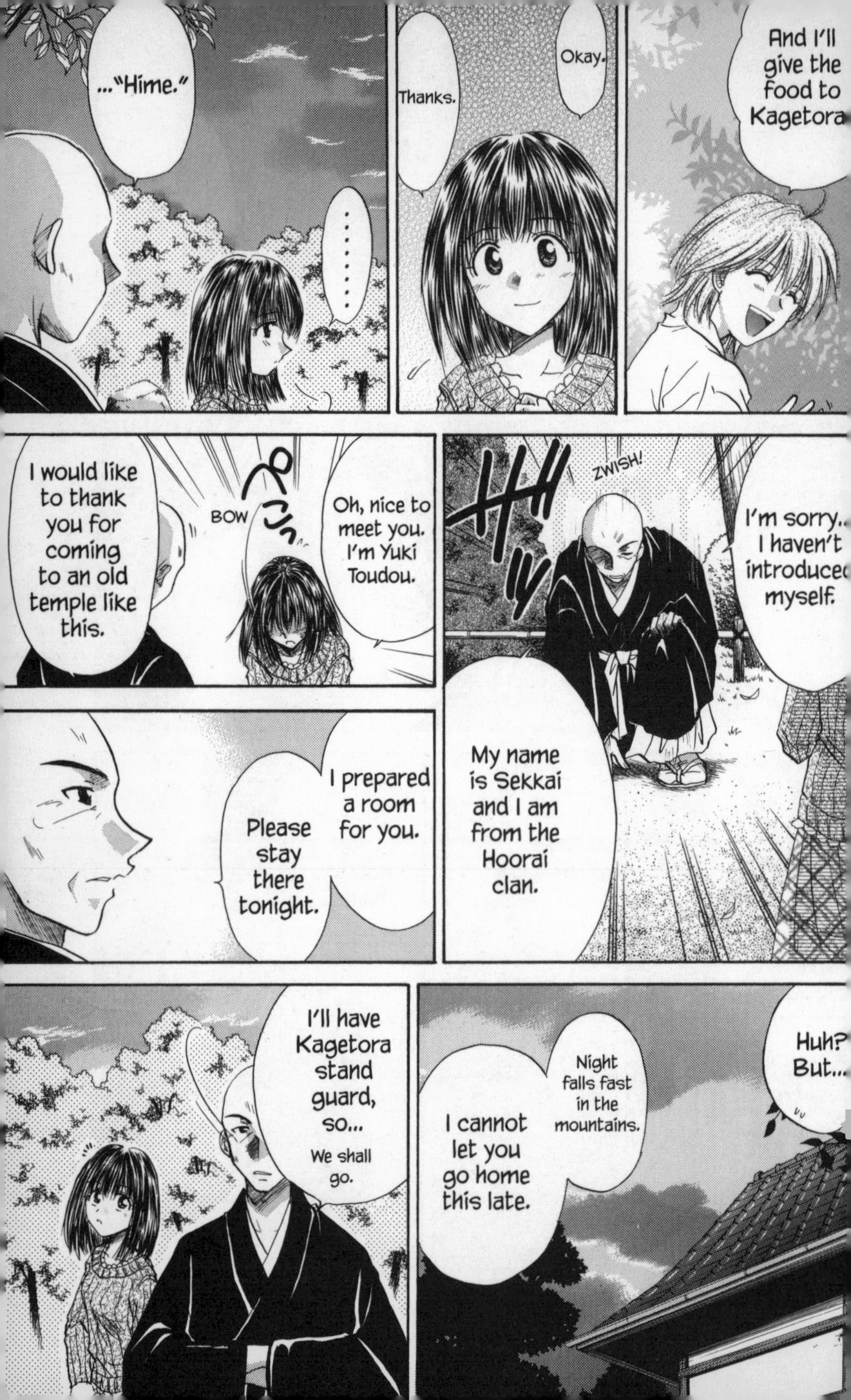
And I'll give the food to Kagetora
Okay.
Thanks.
..."Hime."
......
I'm sorry.. I haven't introduced myself.
ZWISH!
My name is Sekkai and I am from the Hoorai clan.
Oh, nice to meet you. I'm Yuki Toudou.
BOW
I would like to thank you for coming to an old temple like this.
I prepared a room for you.
Please stay there tonight.
Huh? But...
Night falls fast in the mountains.
I cannot let you go home this late.
I'll have Kagetora stand guard, so...
We shall go.

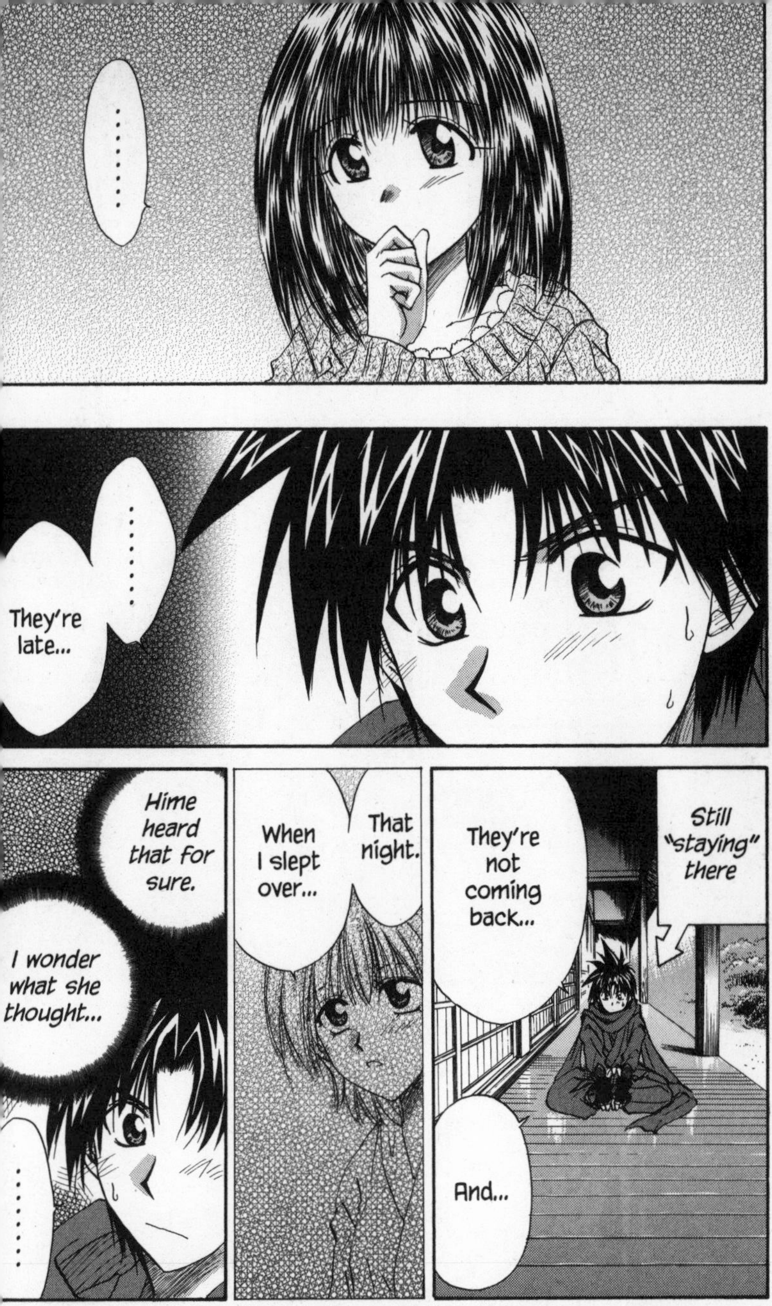
......
......
They're late...
Still "staying" there
They're not coming back...
And...
That night.
When I slept over...
Hime heard that for sure.
I wonder what she thought...
......

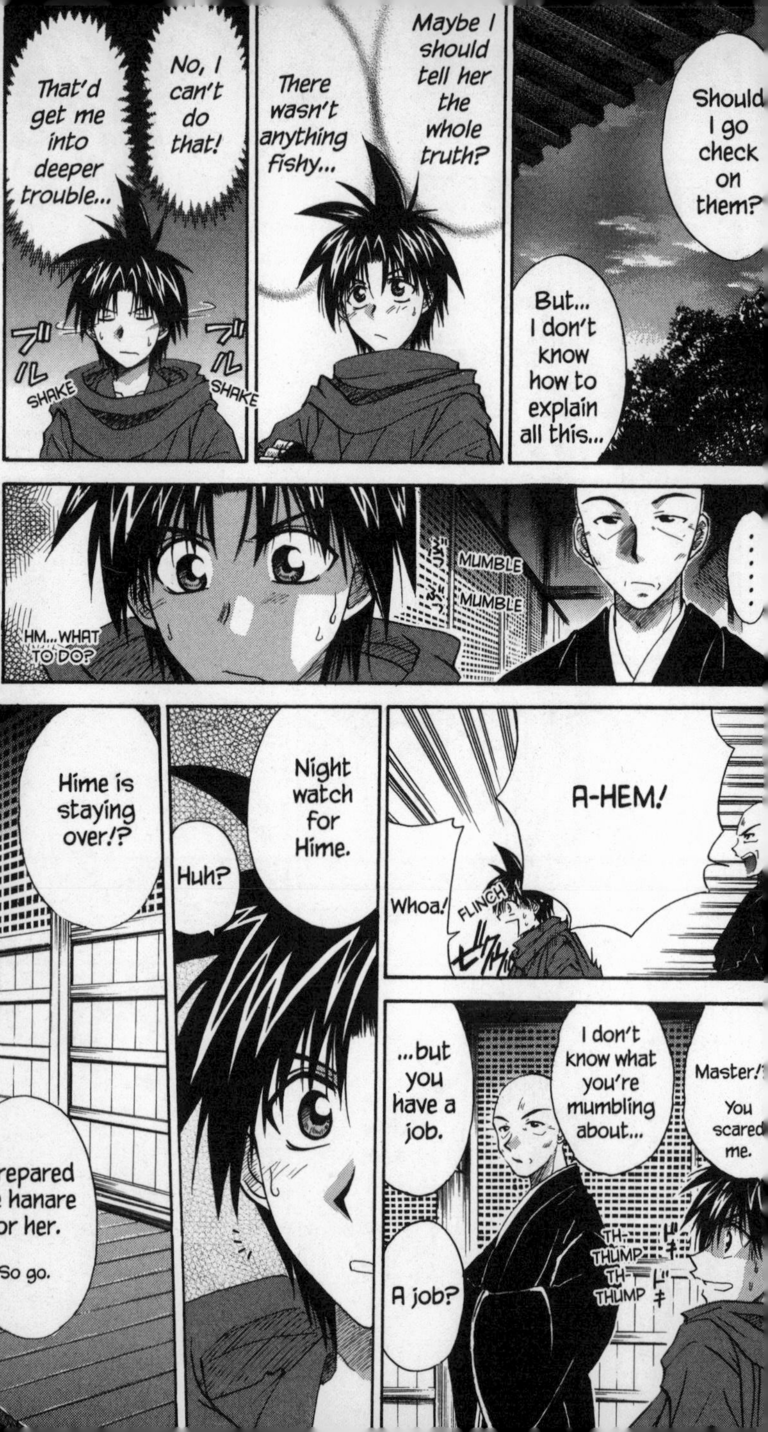
Should I go check on them?
But... I don't know how to explain all this...
Maybe I should tell her the whole truth?
There wasn't anything fishy...
No, I can't do that!
That'd get me into deeper trouble...
SHAKE
SHAKE
.....
MUMBLE
MUMBLE
HM... WHAT TO DO?
A-HEM!
Whoa!
FLINCH
Master!? You scared me.
TH-THUMP
TH-THUMP
I don't know what you're mumbling about...
...but you have a job.
A job?
Night watch for Hime.
Huh?
Hime is staying over!?
I prepared the hanare for her.
So go.

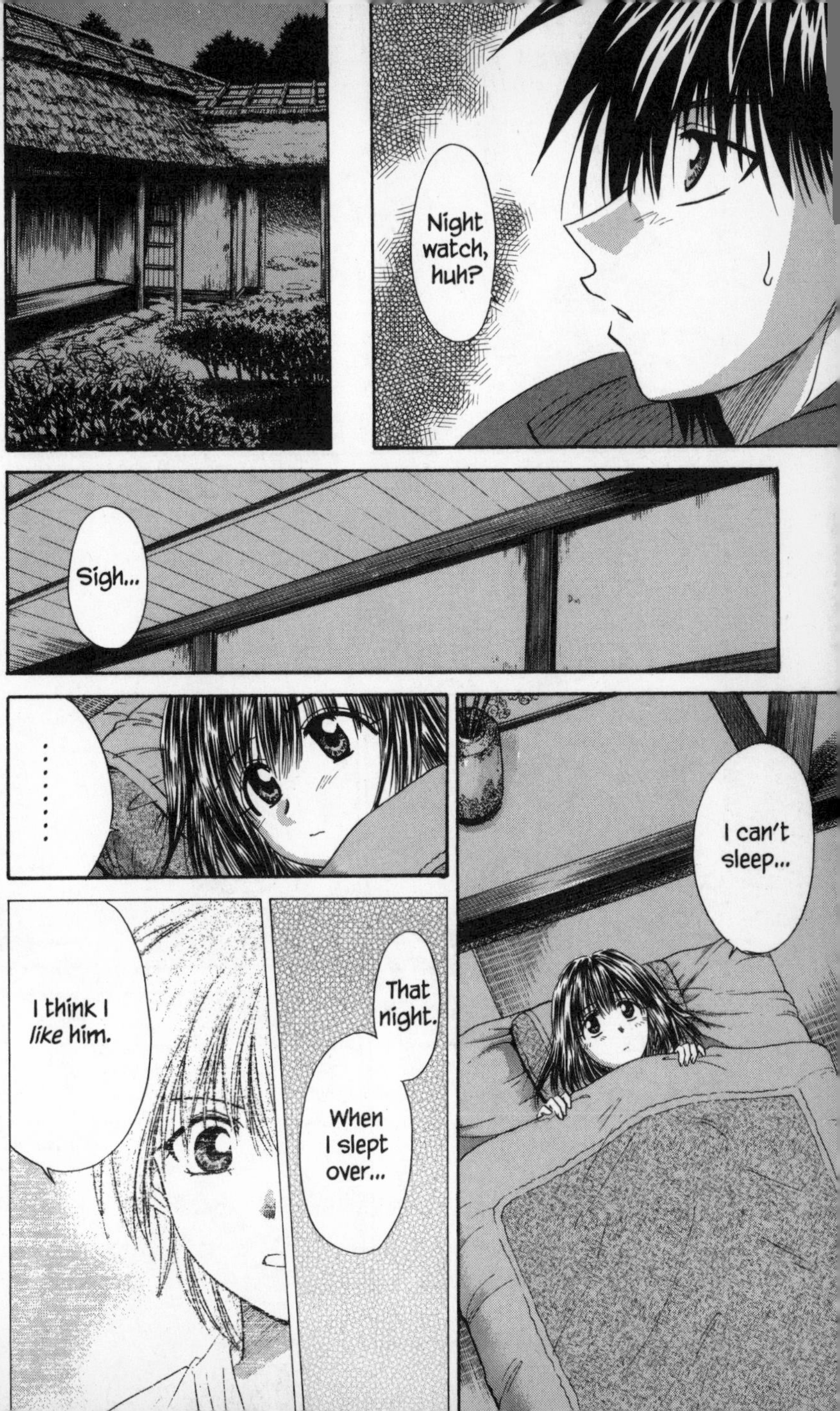
Night watch, huh?
Sigh...
I can't sleep...
....
That night.
When I slept over...
I think I like him.

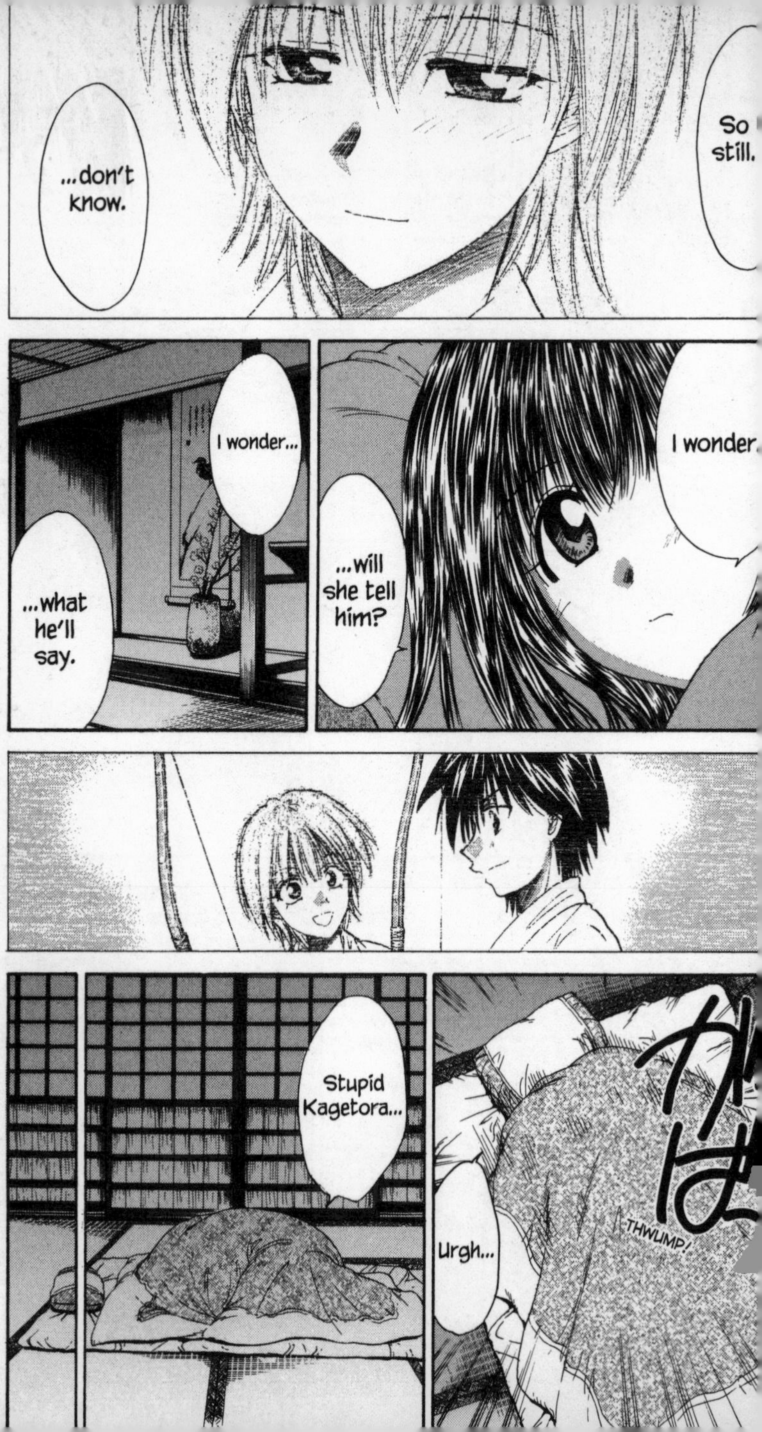

So still.
...don't know.
I wonder.
...will she tell him?
I wonder...
...what he'll say.
THWUMP!
Urgh...
Stupid Kagetora...

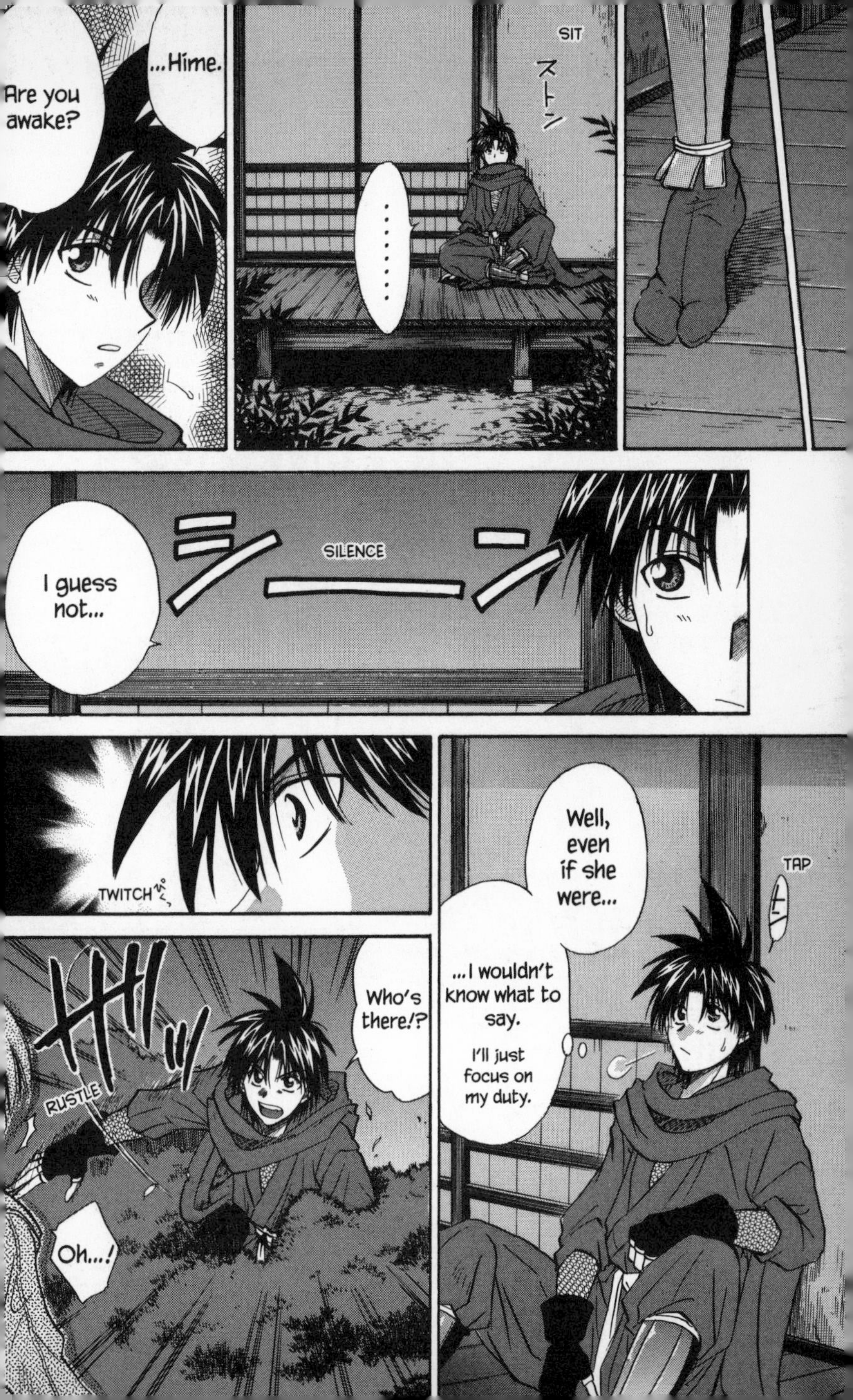

SIT
ストン
……
...Hime.
Are you awake?
SILENCE
シーーン
I guess not...
TAP
Well, even if she were...
...I wouldn't know what to say.
I'll just focus on my duty.
TWITCH
Who's there!?
RUSTLE
Oh...!

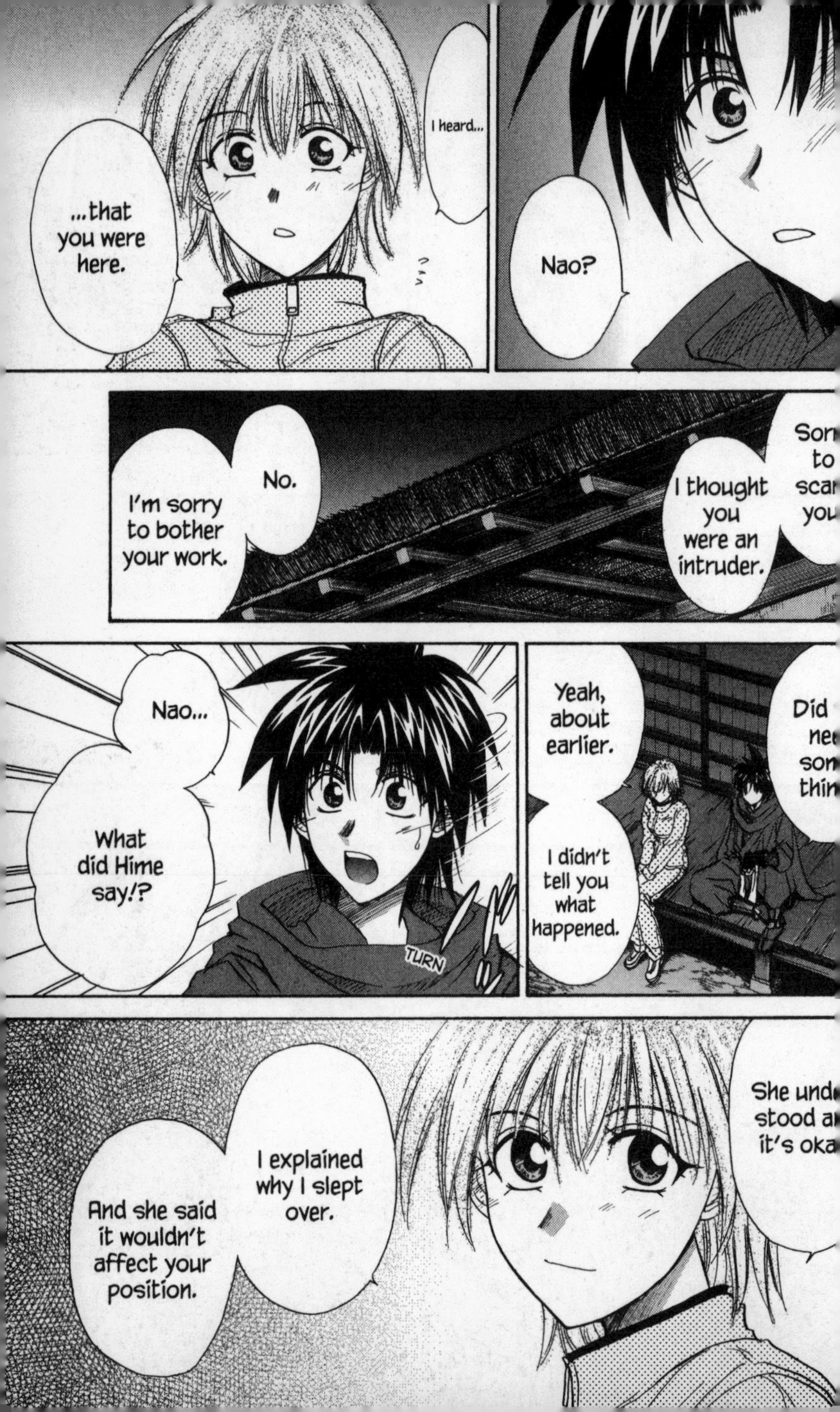
Nao?
I heard...
...that you were here.
Sor to scar you
I thought you were an intruder.
No.
I'm sorry to bother your work.
Did ne son thin
Yeah, about earlier.
I didn't tell you what happened.
Nao...
What did Hime say!?
TURN
She und stood a it's oka
I explained why I slept over.
And she said it wouldn't affect your position.

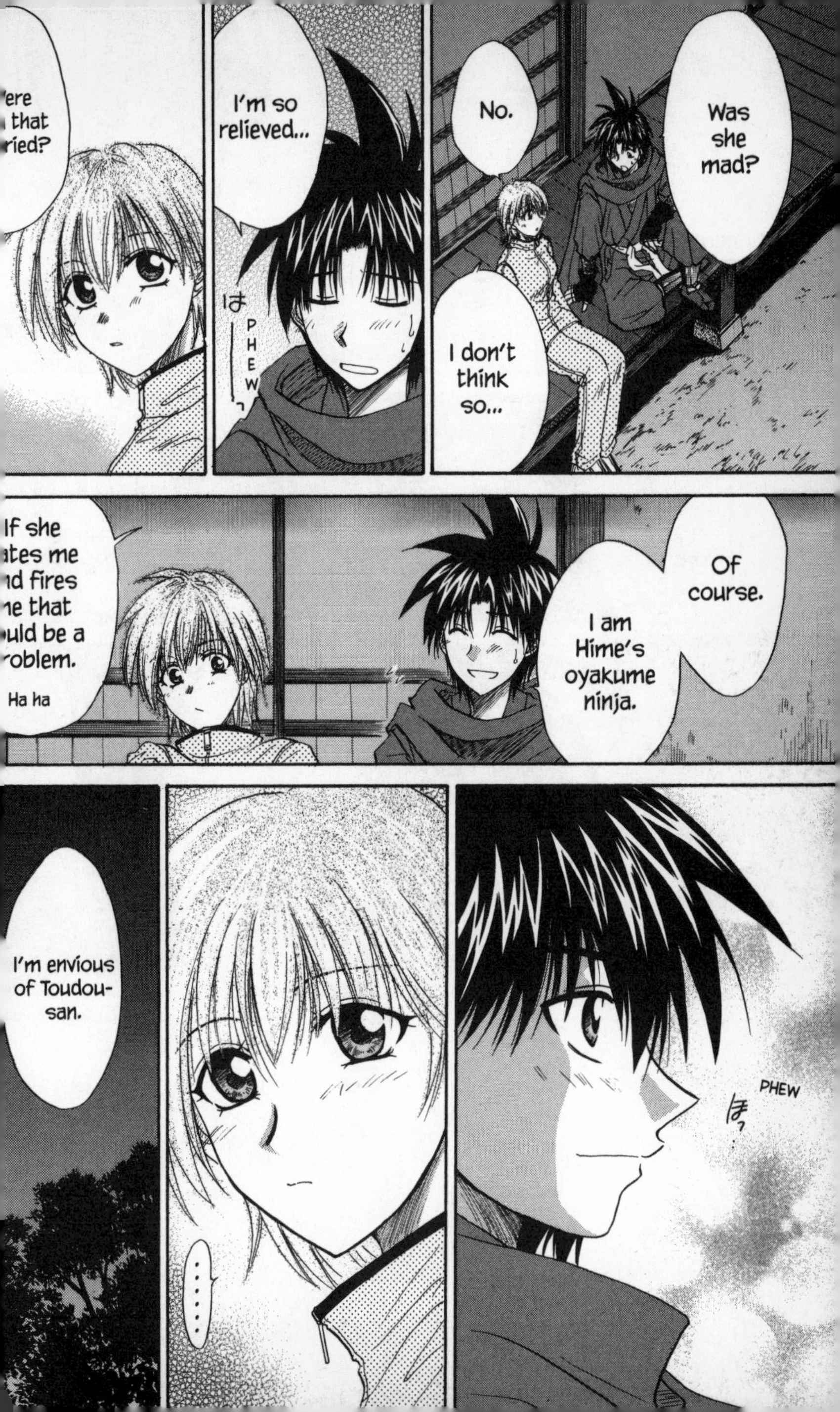
Was she mad?
No.
I don't think so...
I'm so relieved...
は
PHEW
ere
that
ried?
Of course.
I am Hime's oyakume ninja.
If she
ates me
nd fires
ne that
uld be a
roblem.
Ha ha
ほっ
PHEW
......
I'm envious of Toudou-san.

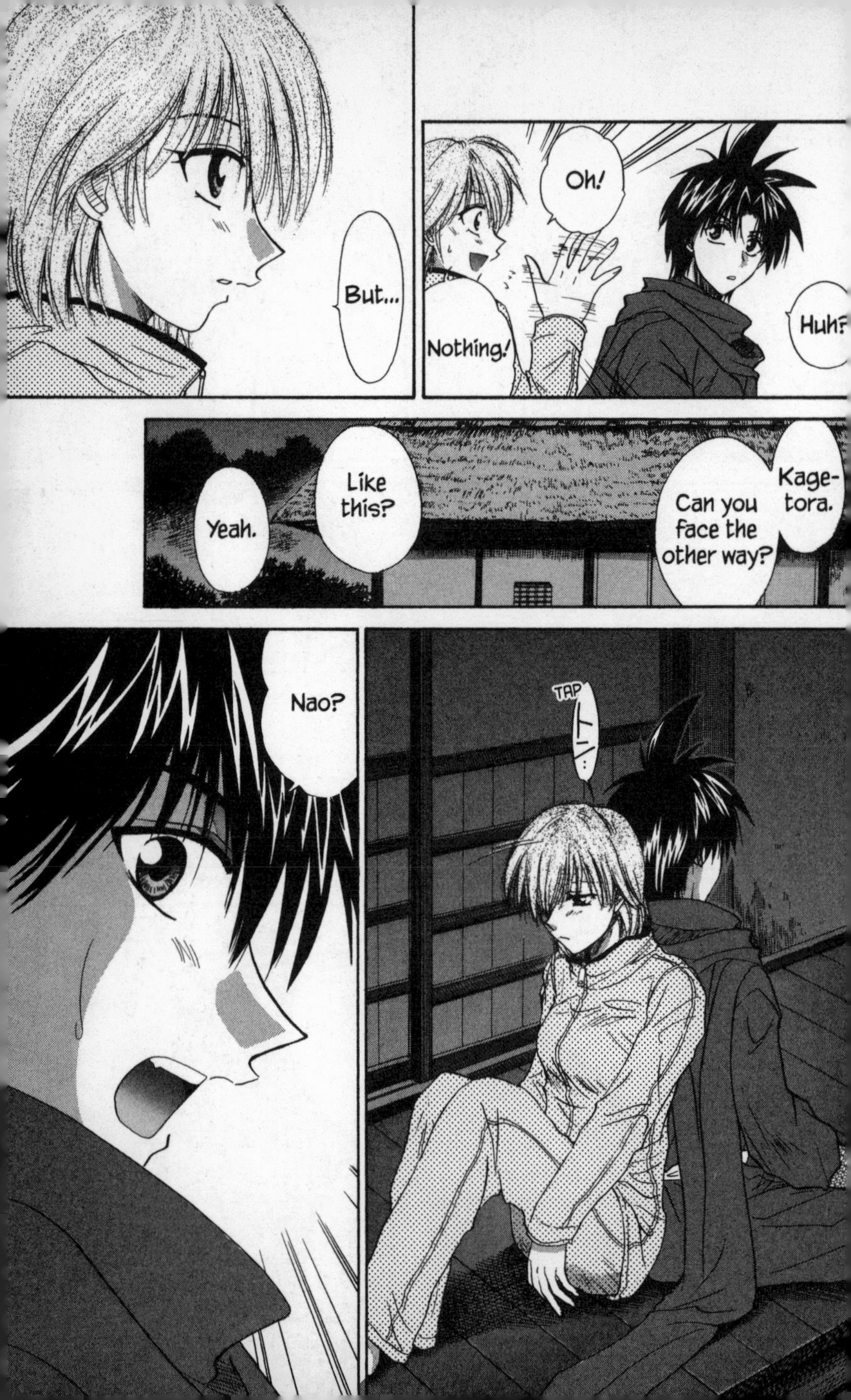
Oh!
Huh?
Nothing!
But...
Kage-tora.
Can you face the other way?
Like this?
Yeah.
TAP
Nao?

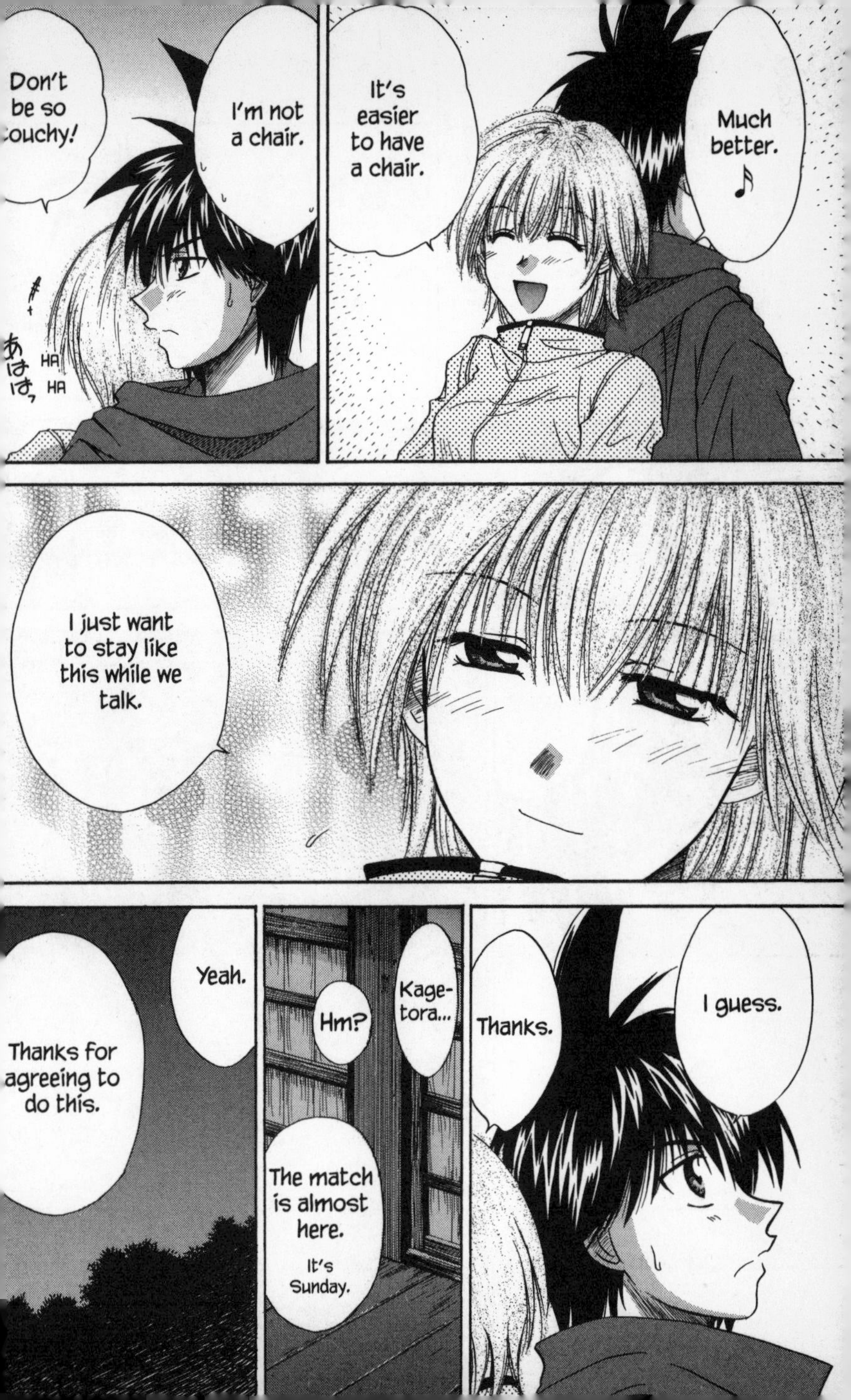
Much better. ♪
It's easier to have a chair.
I'm not a chair.
Don't be so ouchy!
あはは, HA HA
I just want to stay like this while we talk.
I guess.
Thanks.
Kage-tora...
Hm?
The match is almost here.
It's Sunday.
Yeah.
Thanks for agreeing to do this.

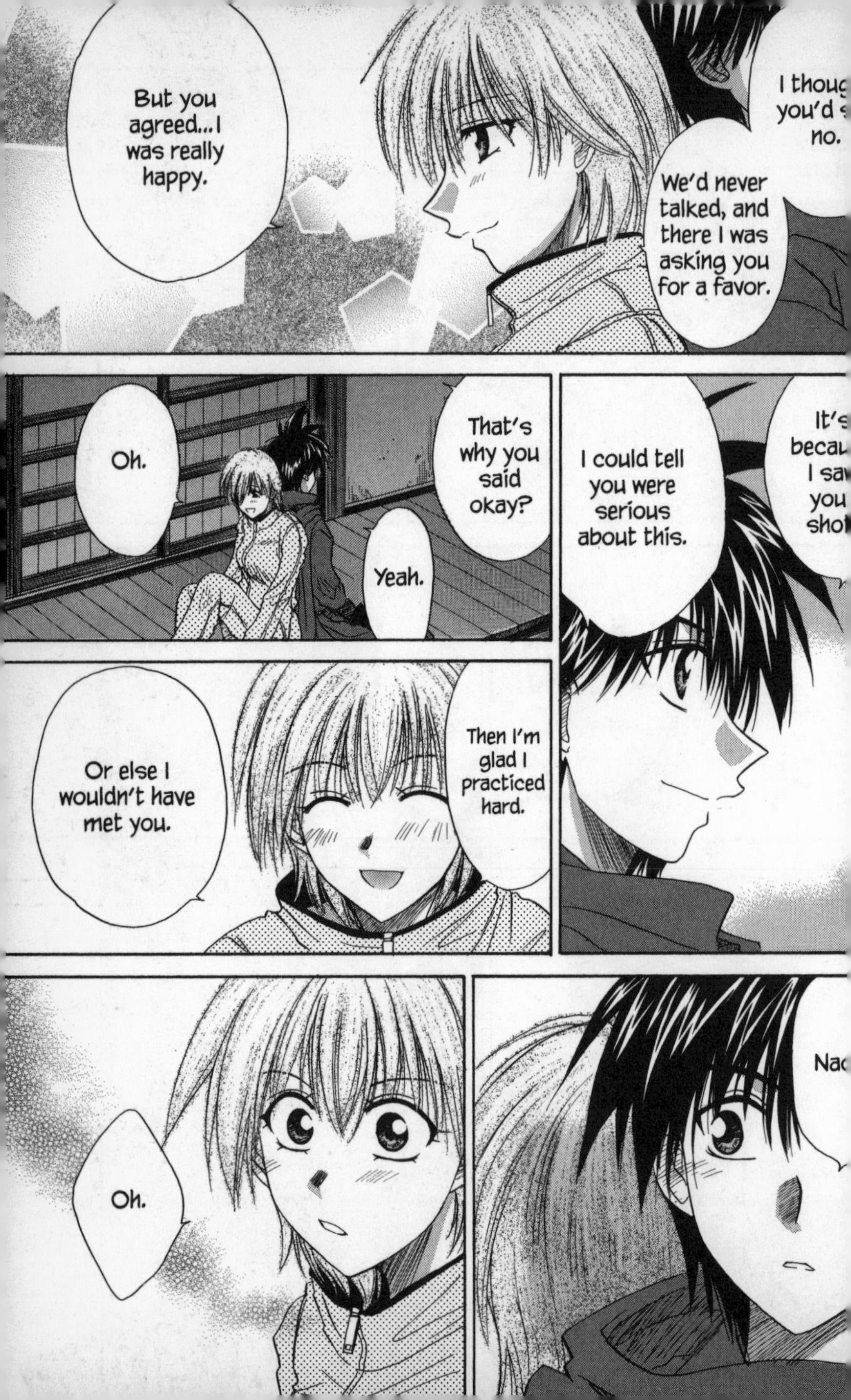
I thoug you'd s no.
We'd never talked, and there I was asking you for a favor.
But you agreed...I was really happy.
It's becau I sa you sho
I could tell you were serious about this.
That's why you said okay?
Yeah.
Oh.
Then I'm glad I practiced hard.
Or else I wouldn't have met you.
Na
Oh.

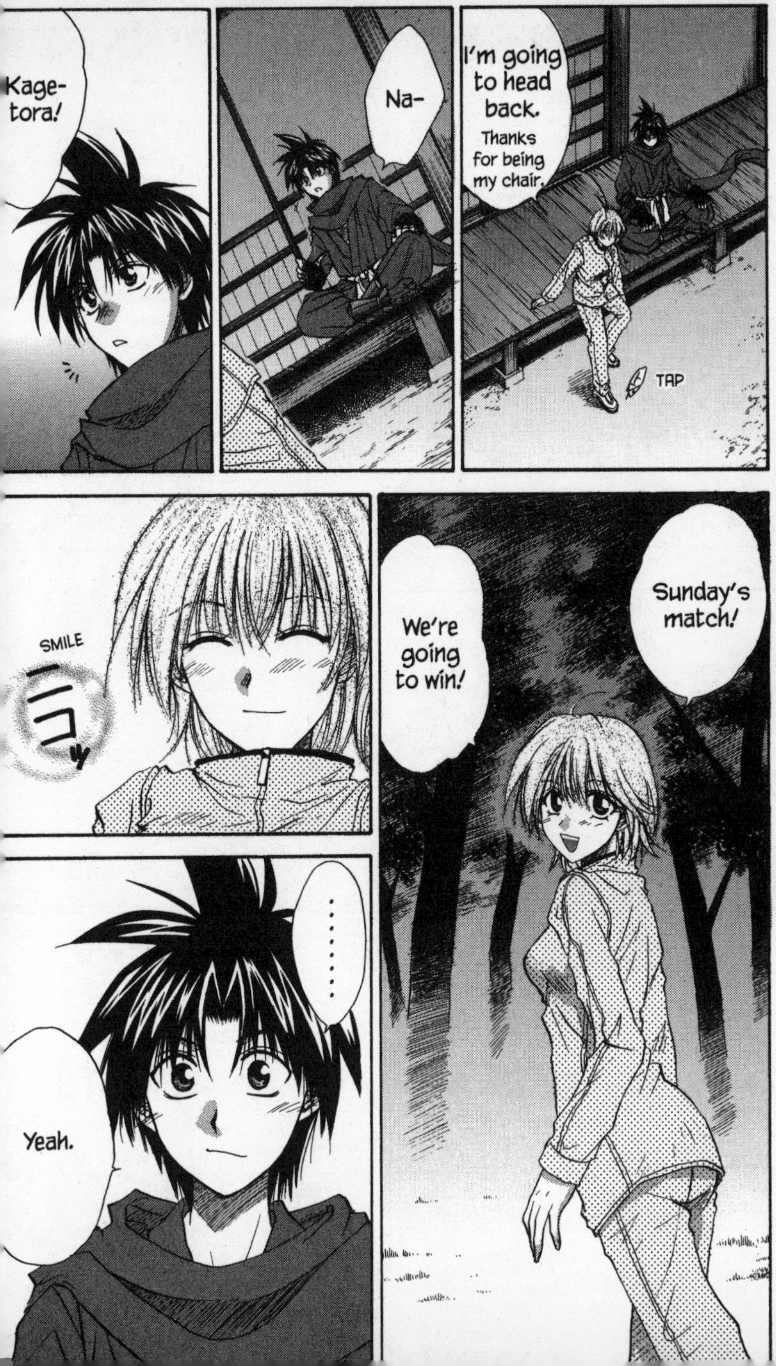
I'm going to head back.
Thanks for being my chair.
TAP
Na-
Kage-tora!
Sunday's match!
We're going to win!
SMILE
ニコッ
......
Yeah.

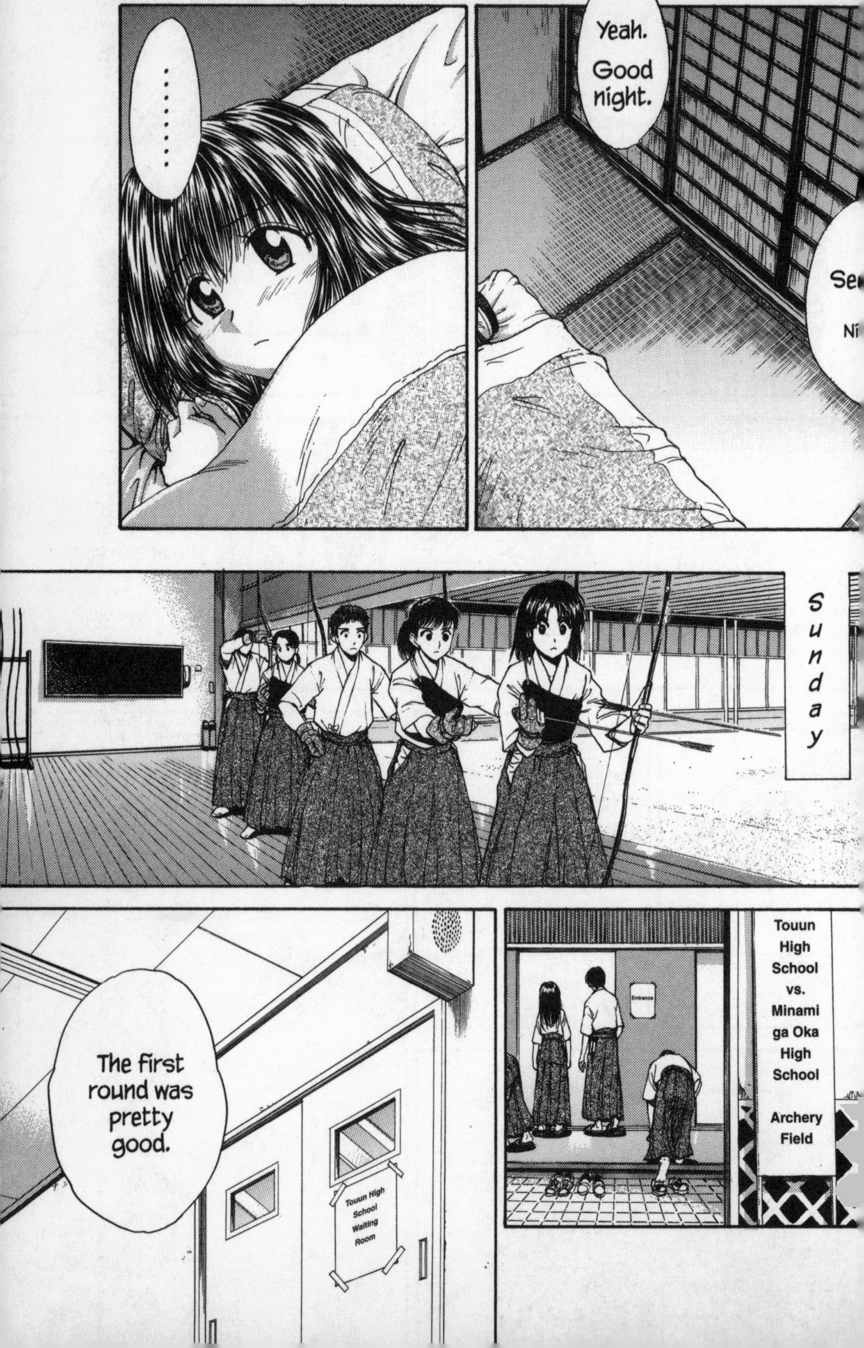
Yeah. Good night.
......
Sunday
Touun High School vs. Minami ga Oka High School Archery Field
Entrance
The first round was pretty good.
Touun High School Waiting Room

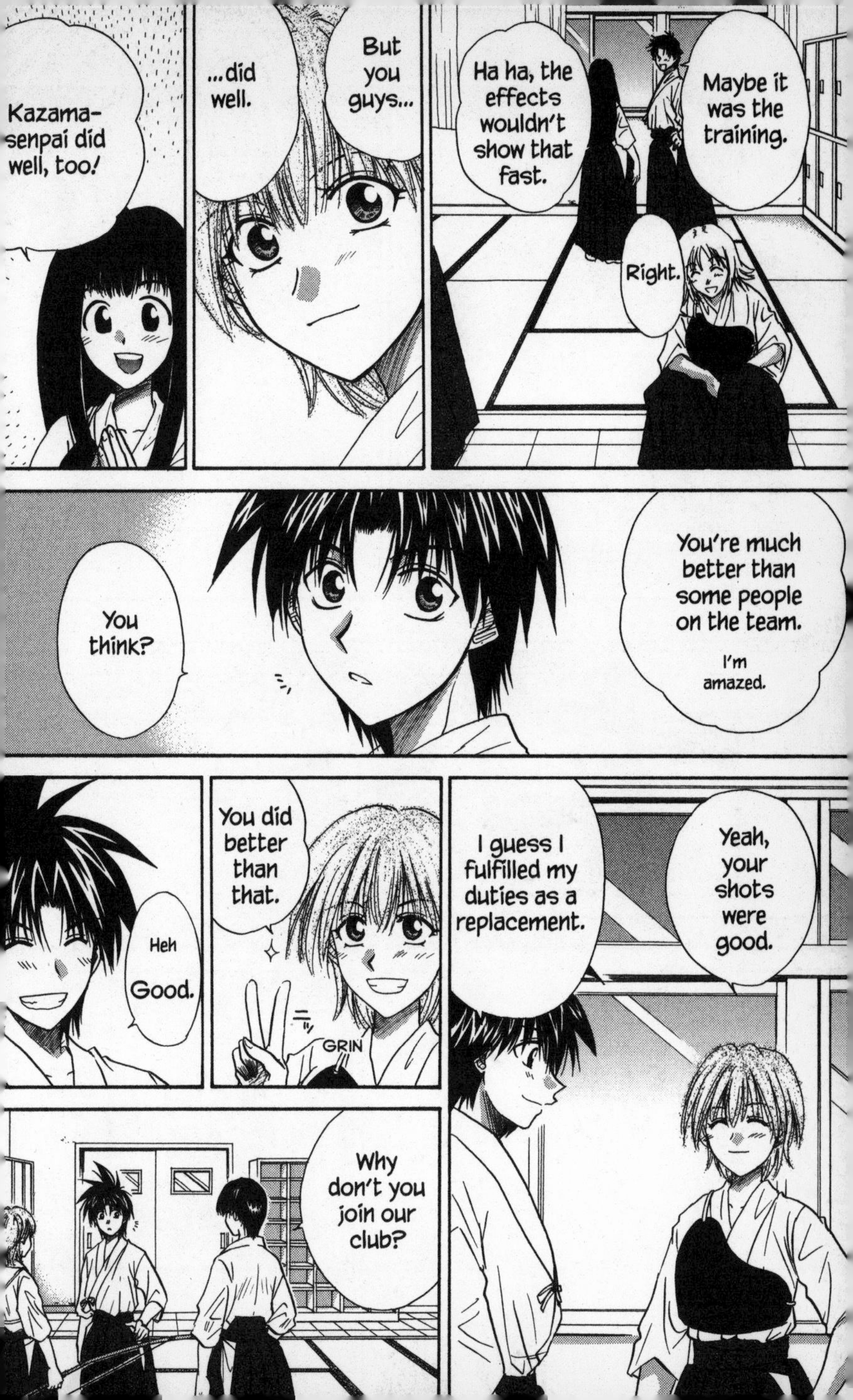
Maybe it was the training.
Ha ha, the effects wouldn't show that fast.
Right.
But you guys...
...did well.
Kazama-senpai did well, too!
You're much better than some people on the team.
I'm amazed.
You think?
Yeah, your shots were good.
I guess I fulfilled my duties as a replacement.
You did better than that.
GRIN
Heh
Good.
Why don't you join our club?

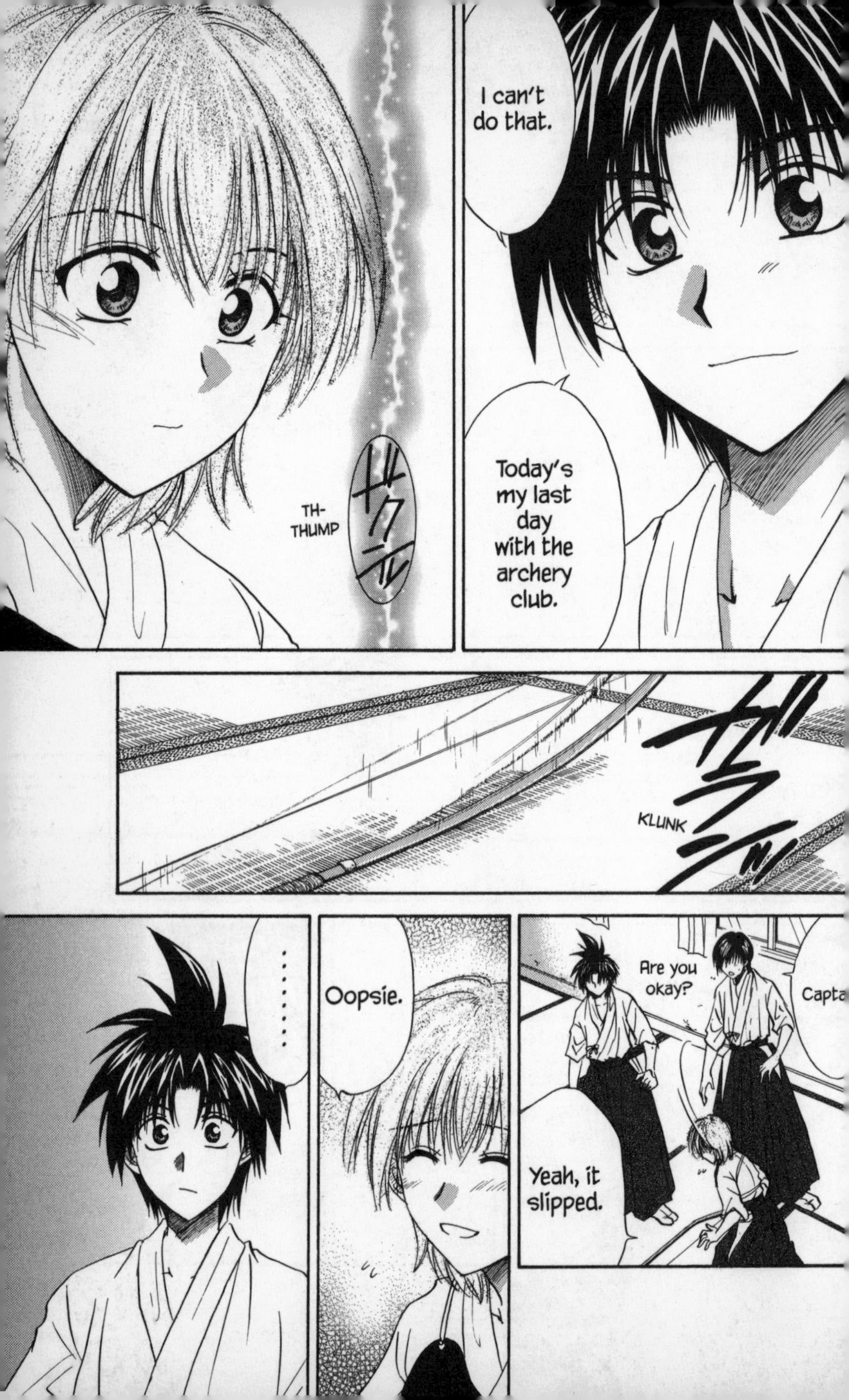
I can't do that.
Today's my last day with the archery club.
TH-THUMP
KLUNK
Capta
Are you okay?
Yeah, it slipped.
Oopsie.
......

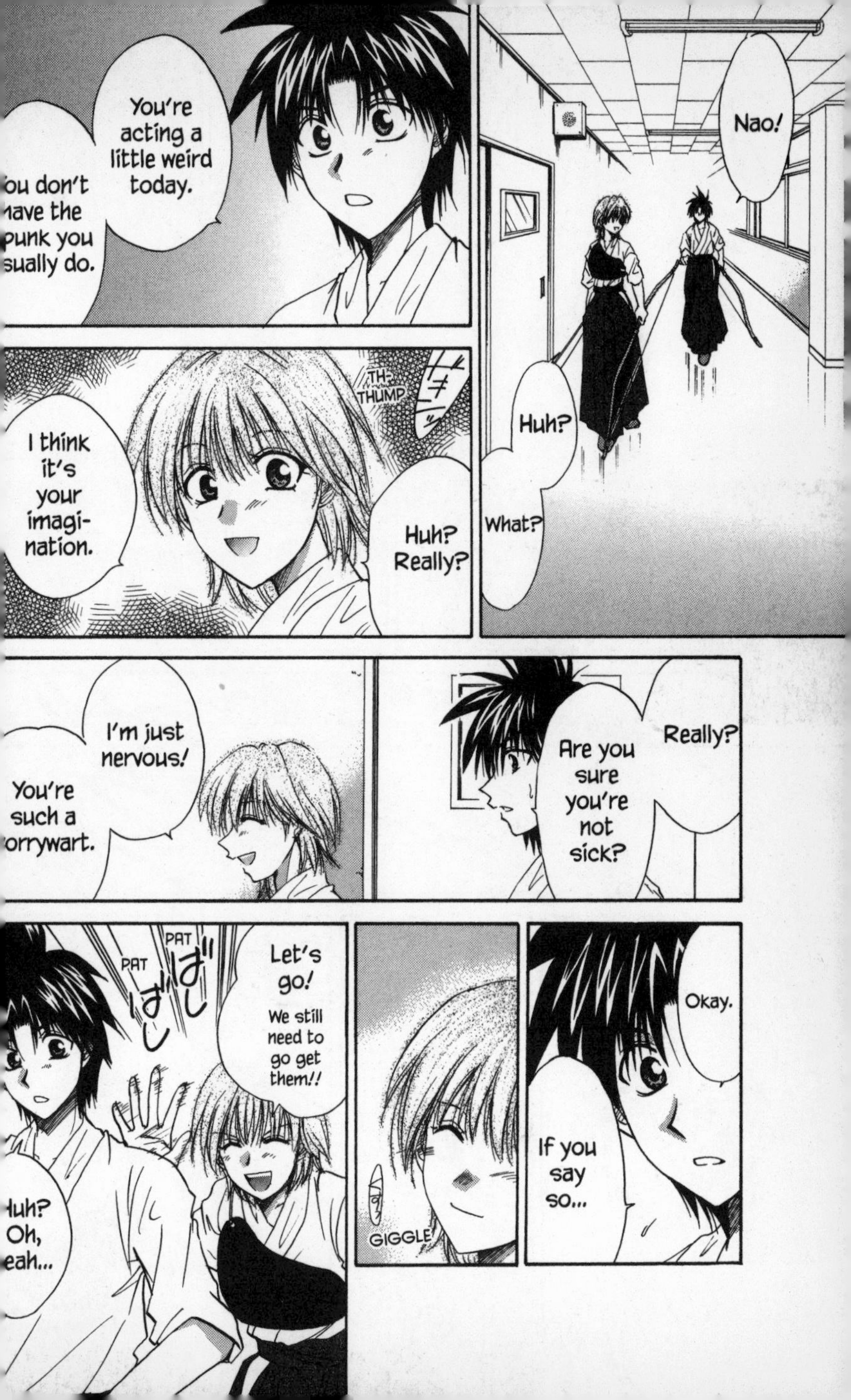

Nao!
Huh?
What?
You're acting a little weird today.
ou don't ave the punk you sually do.
TH-THUMP
Huh? Really?
I think it's your imagi-nation.
Really?
Are you sure you're not sick?
I'm just nervous!
You're such a orrywart.
Okay.
If you say so...
GIGGLE
PAT
PAT
Let's go!
We still need to go get them!!
uh? Oh, eah...

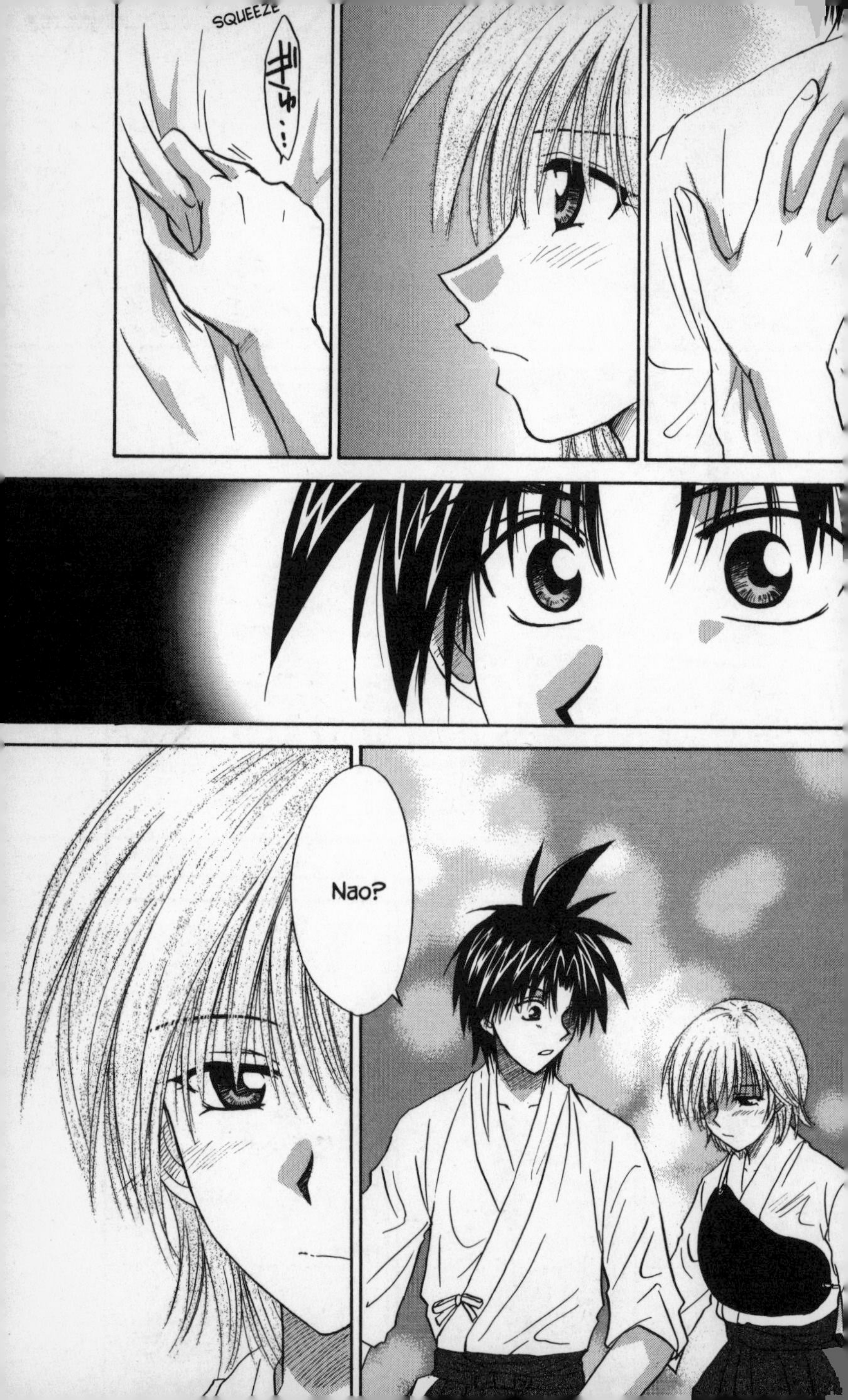
SQUEEZE
ぎゅ…
Nao?

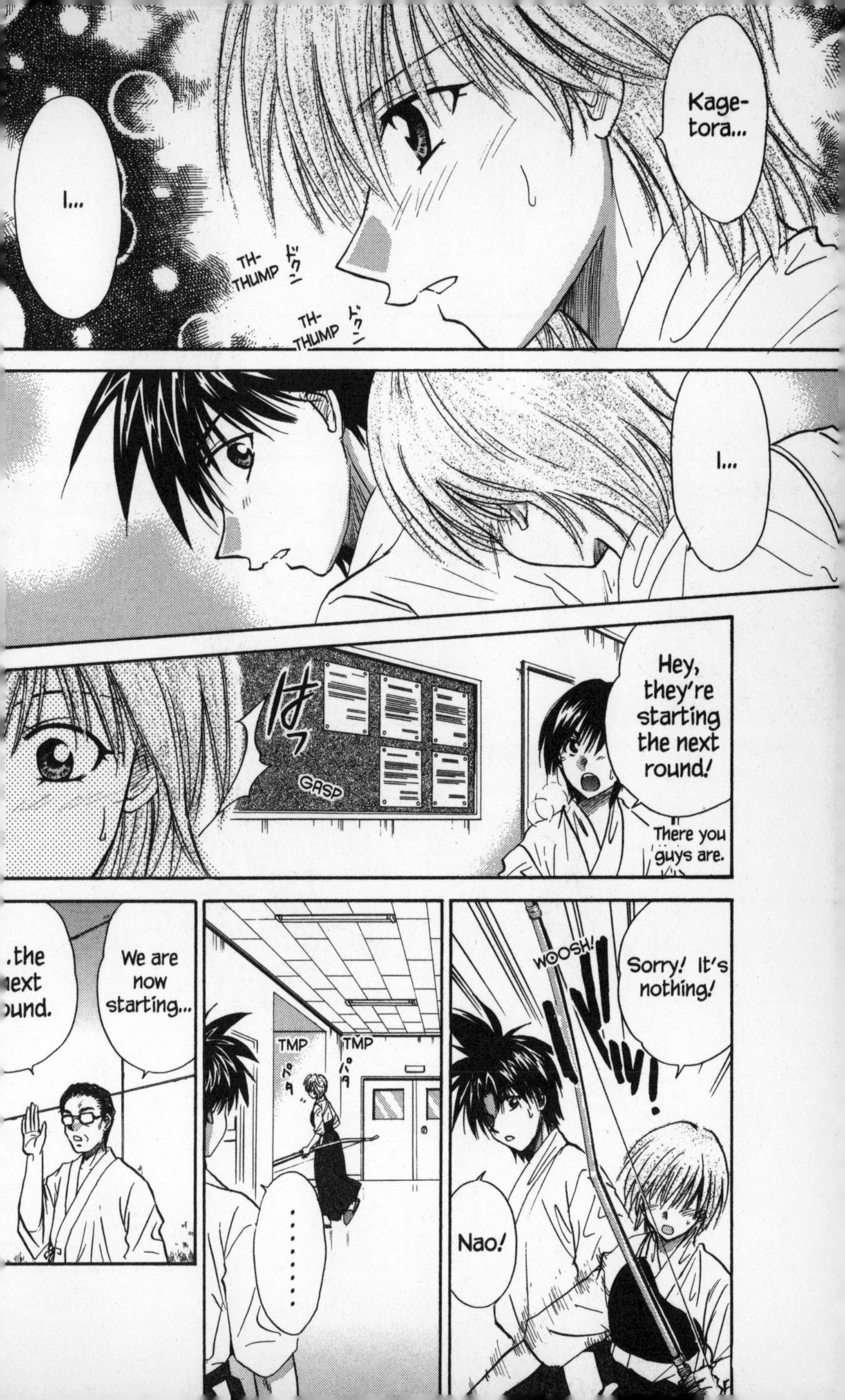
Kage-tora...
I...
TH-THUMP
TH-THUMP
I...
Hey, they're starting the next round!
There you guys are.
GASP
Sorry! It's nothing!
WOOSH!
Nao!
TMP
TMP
......
We are now starting...
.the ext ound.

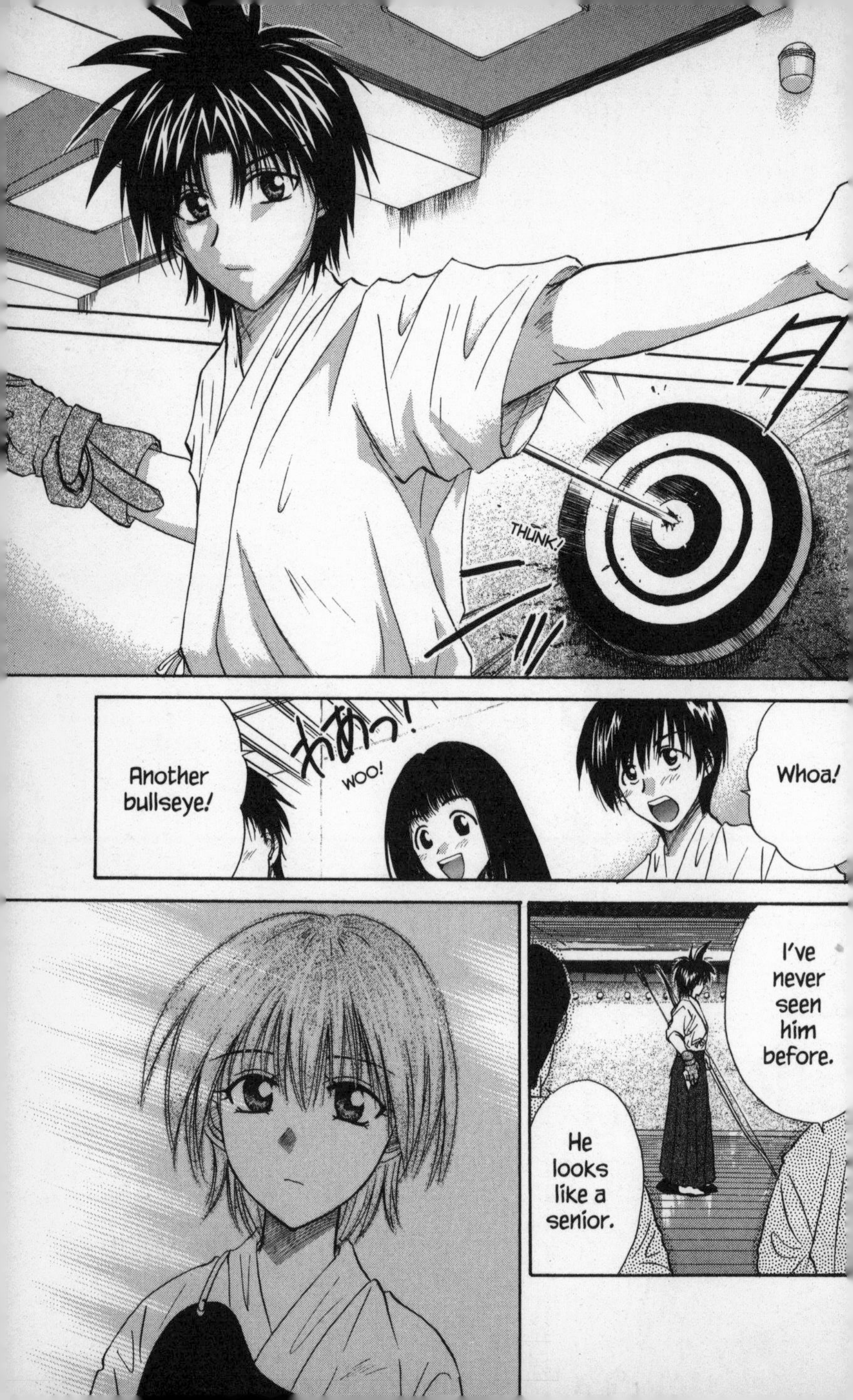
THUNK!
Whoa!
わあっ!
WOO!
Another bullseye!
I've never seen him before.
He looks like a senior.

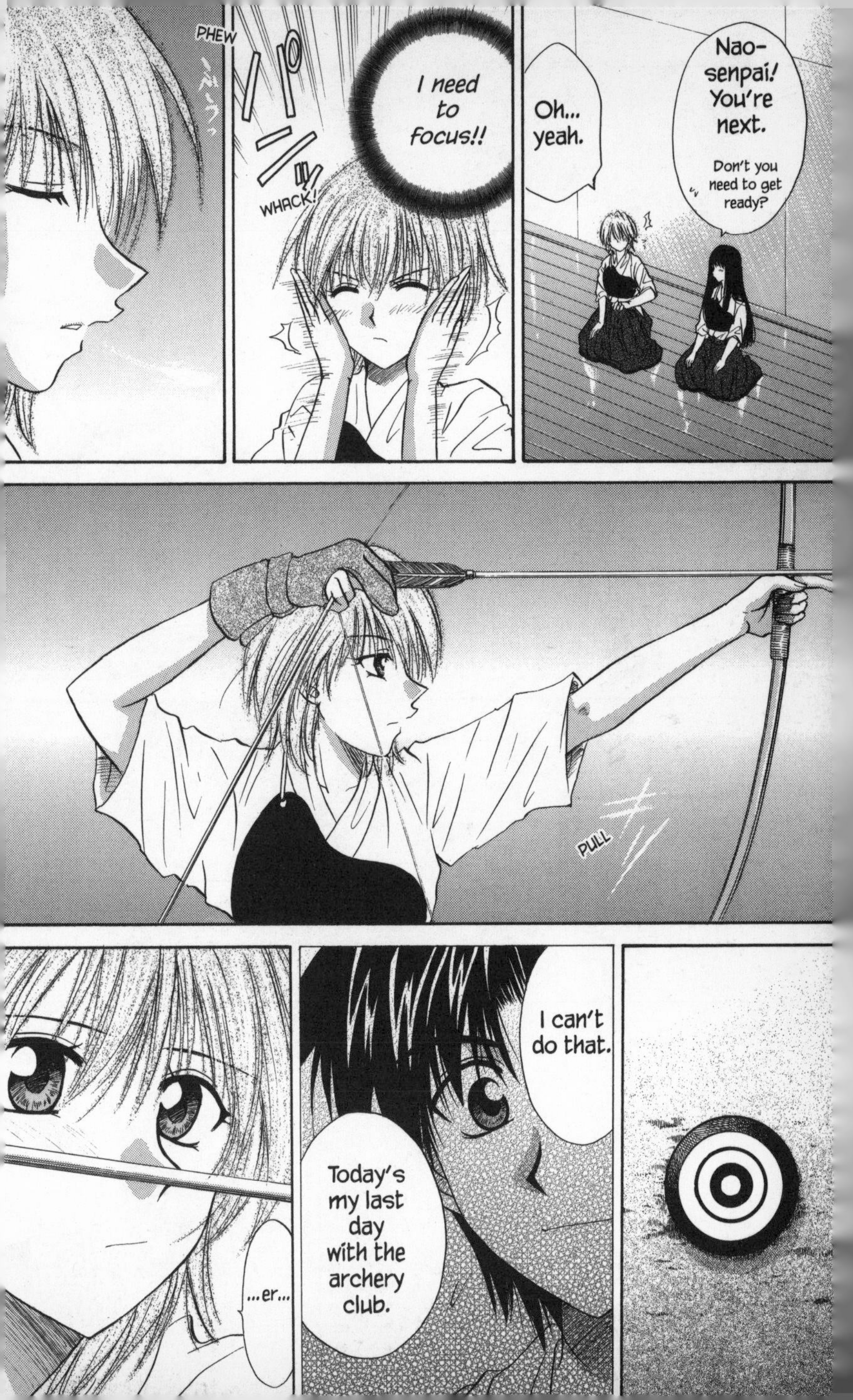
Nao-senpai! You're next.
Don't you need to get ready?
Oh... yeah.
I need to focus!!
WHACK!
PHEW
PULL
I can't do that.
Today's my last day with the archery club.
...er...

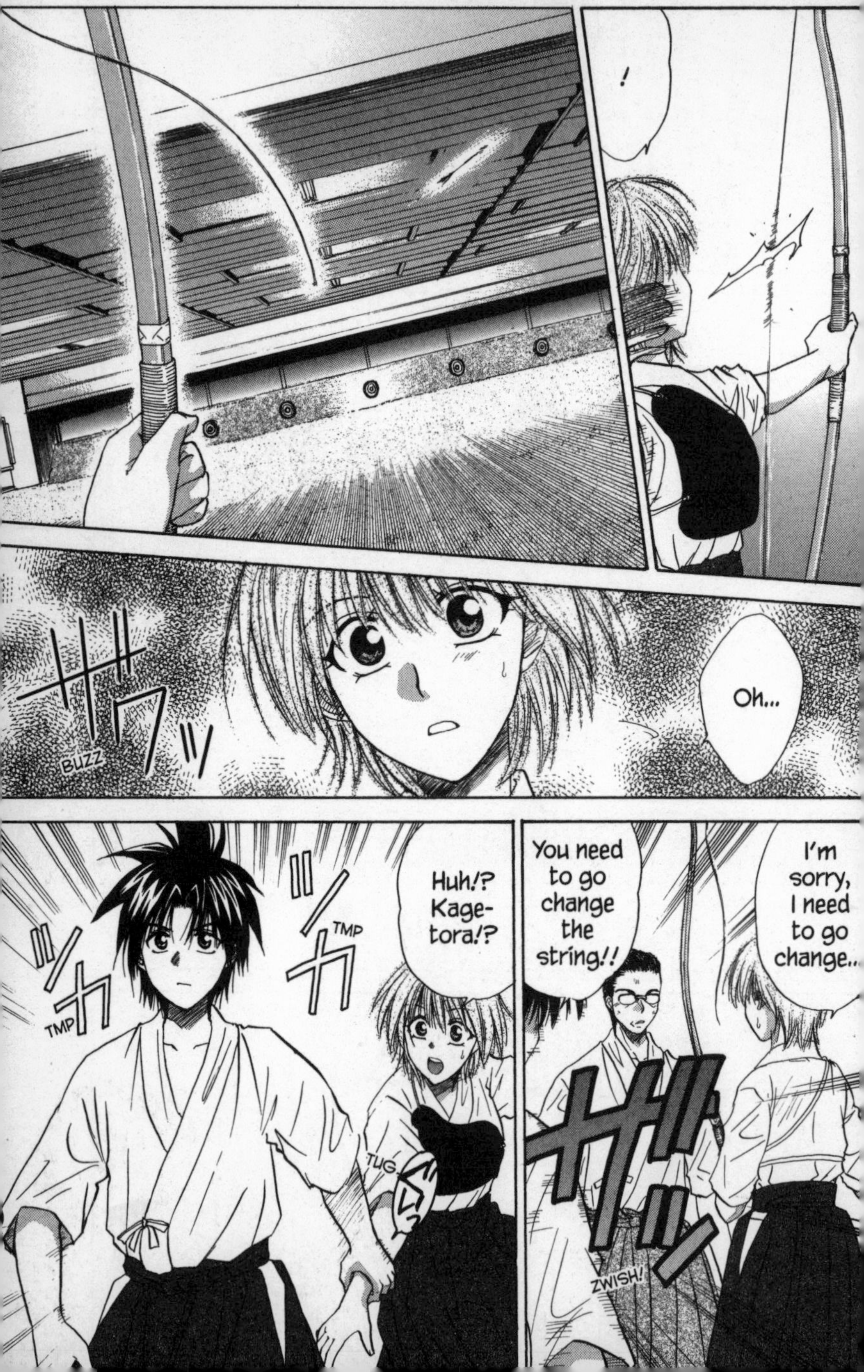
!
Oh...
BUZZ
I'm sorry, I need to go change..
You need to go change the string!!
ZWISH!
Huh!? Kage-tora!?
TMP
TUG
TMP

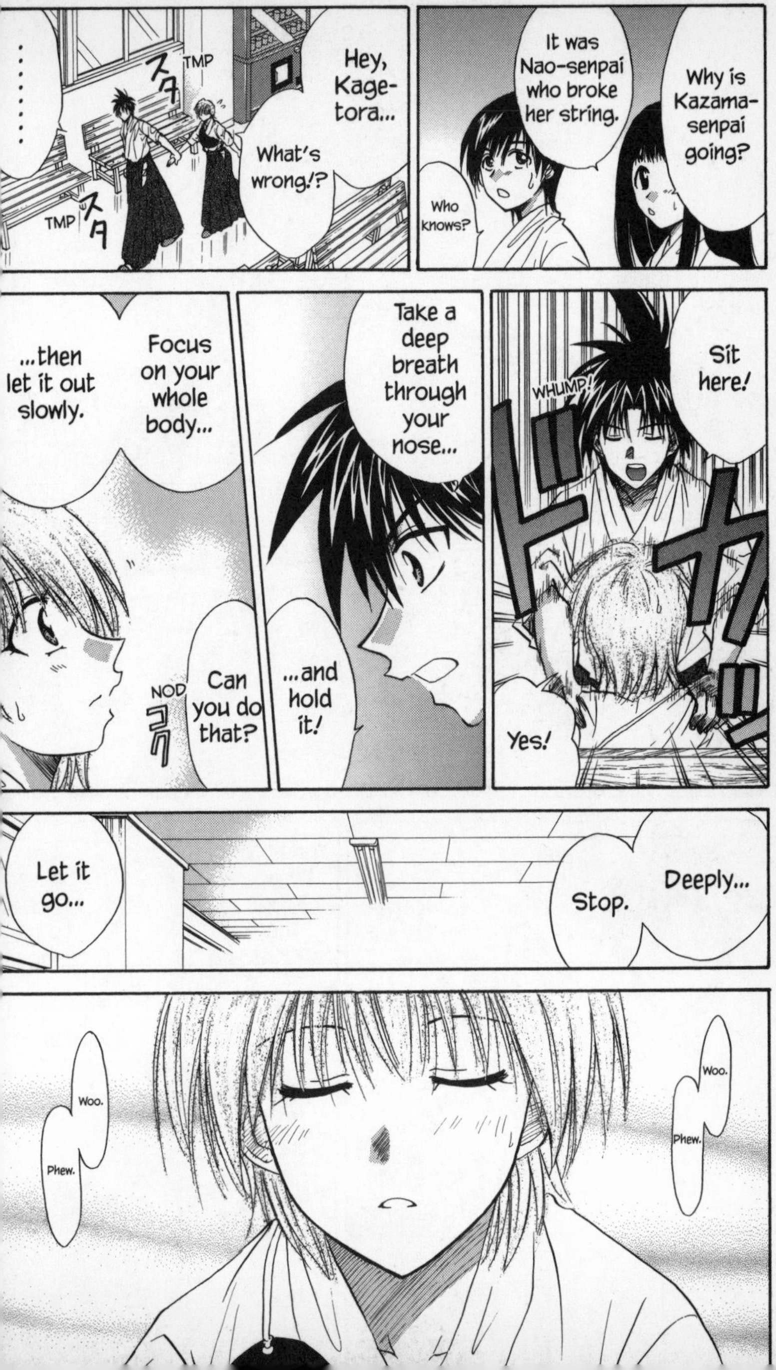
Why is Kazama-senpai going?
It was Nao-senpai who broke her string.
Who knows?
Hey, Kagetora...
TMP スタ
What's wrong!?
TMP スタ
......
Sit here!
WHUMP! ドサッ
Yes!
Take a deep breath through your nose...
...and hold it!
Focus on your whole body...
...then let it out slowly.
Can you do that?
NOD コク
Deeply...
Stop.
Let it go...
Woo.
Phew.
Woo.
Phew.

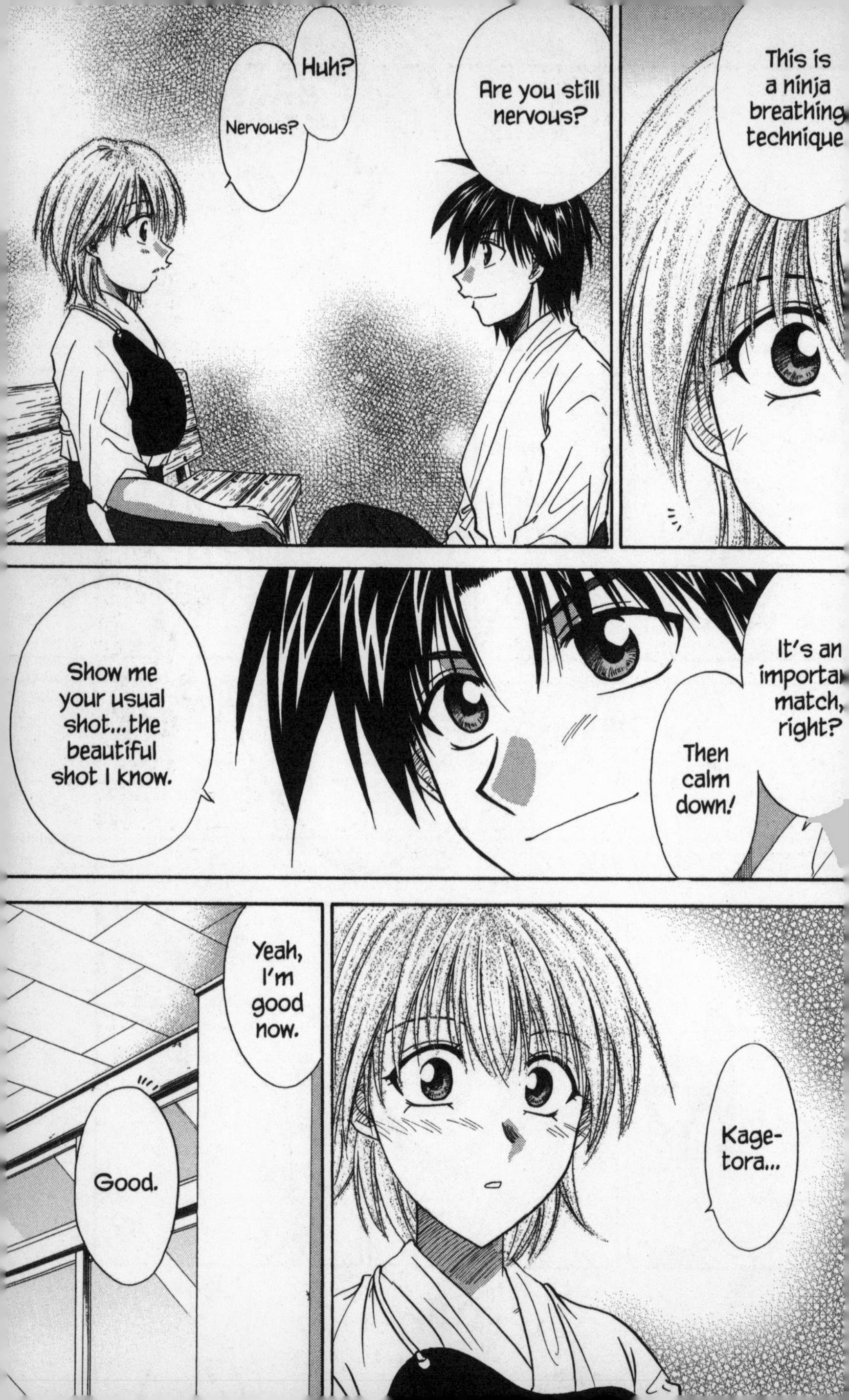
This is a ninja breathing technique
Are you still nervous?
Huh?
Nervous?
It's an importa match, right?
Then calm down!
Show me your usual shot...the beautiful shot I know.
Kage-tora...
Yeah, I'm good now.
Good.

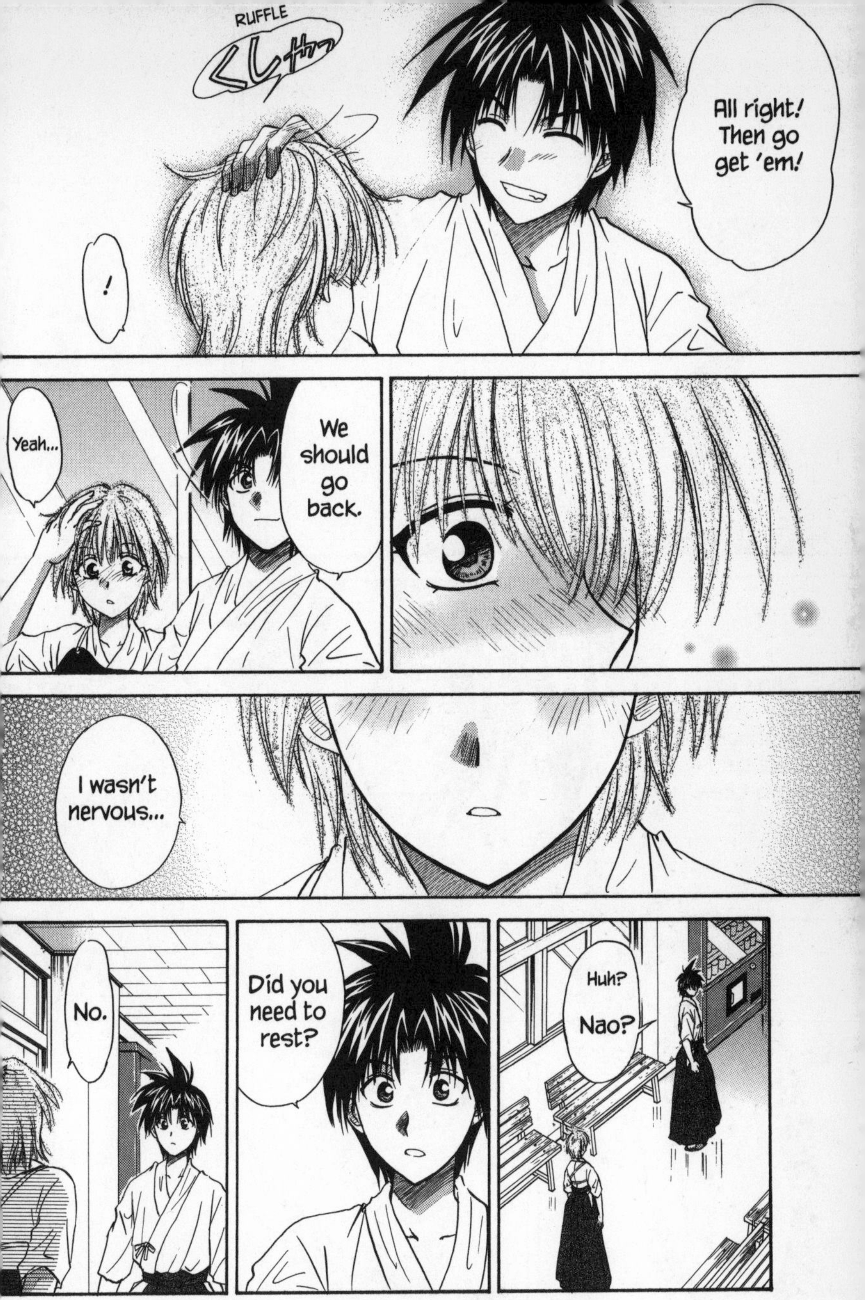
All right! Then go get 'em!
RUFFLE
!
We should go back.
Yeah...
I wasn't nervous...
Huh?
Nao?
Did you need to rest?
No.

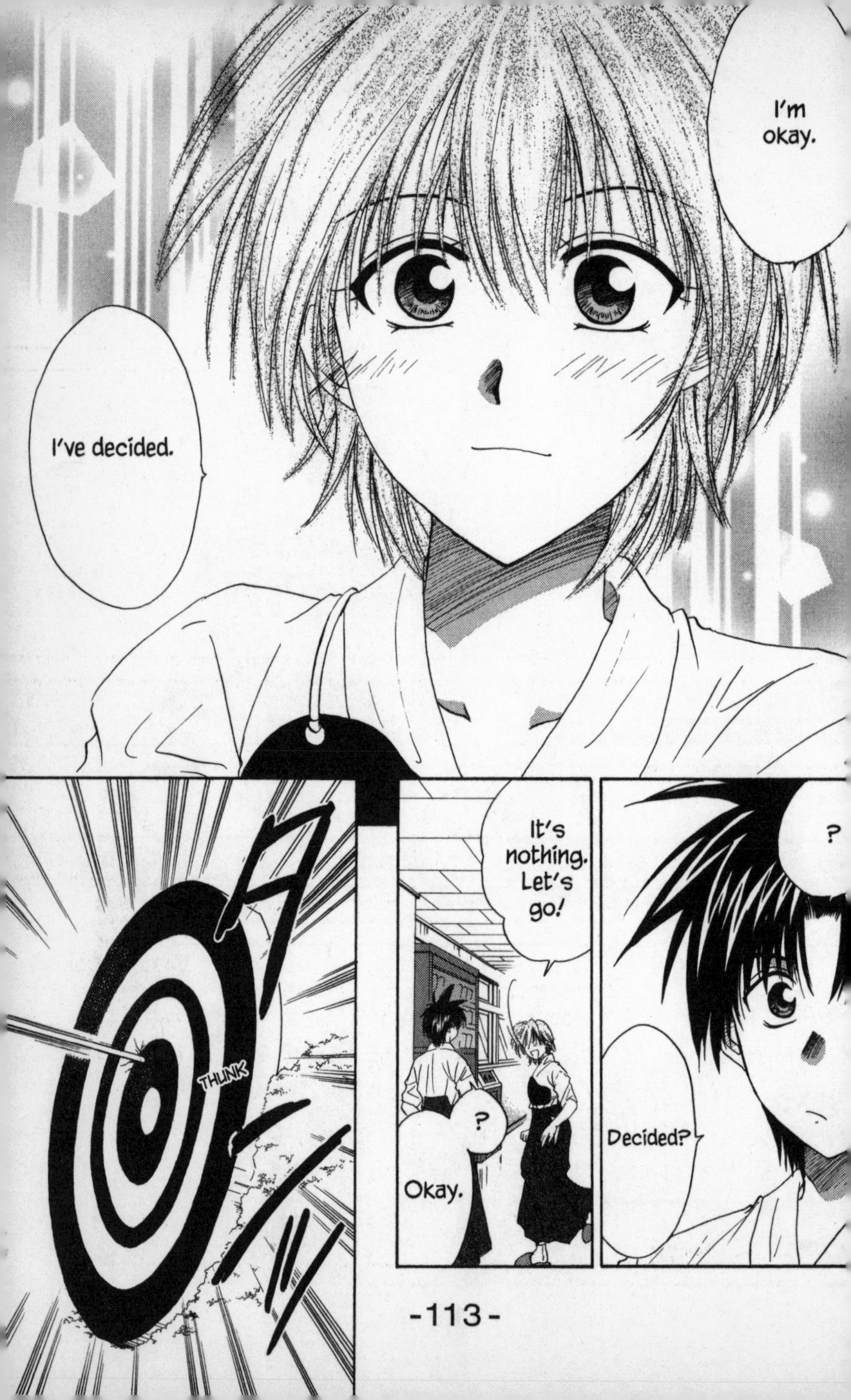
I'm okay.
I've decided.
?
Decided?
It's nothing. Let's go!
?
Okay.
THUNK

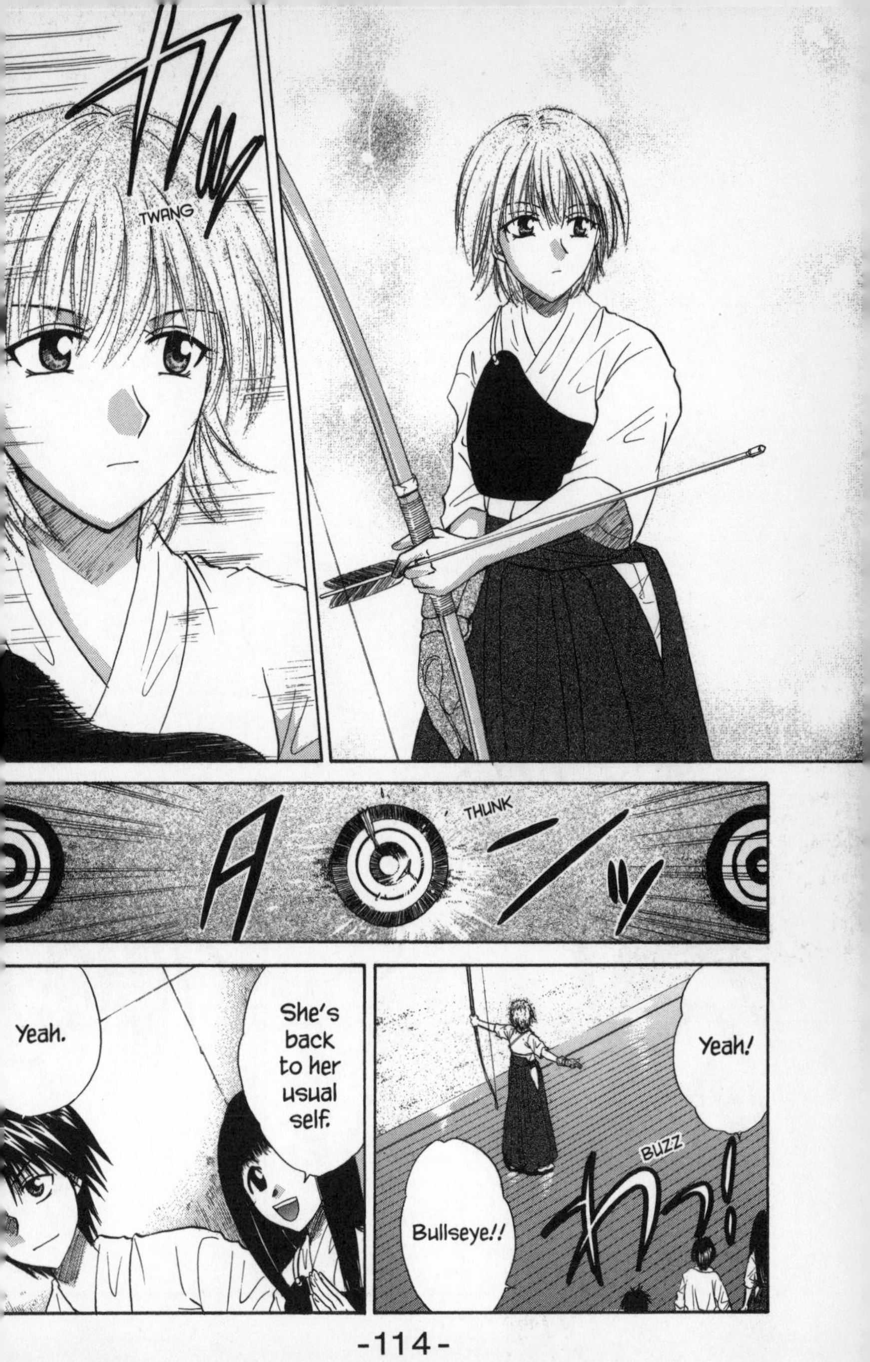
TWANG
THUNK
Yeah!
Bullseye!!
BUZZ
She's back to her usual self.
Yeah.

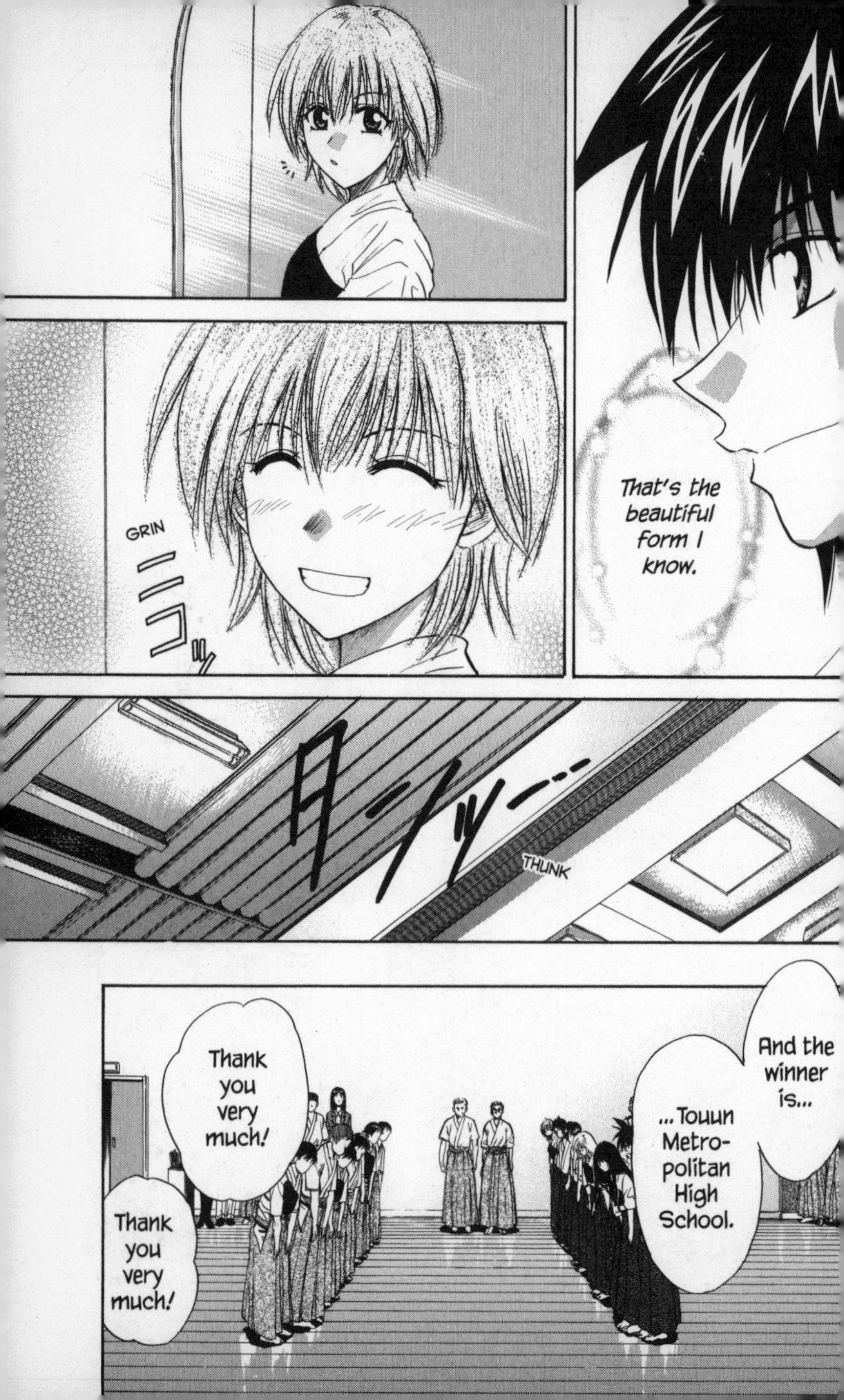
That's the beautiful form I know.
GRIN
THUNK
And the winner is...
...Touun Metropolitan High School.
Thank you very much!
Thank you very much!

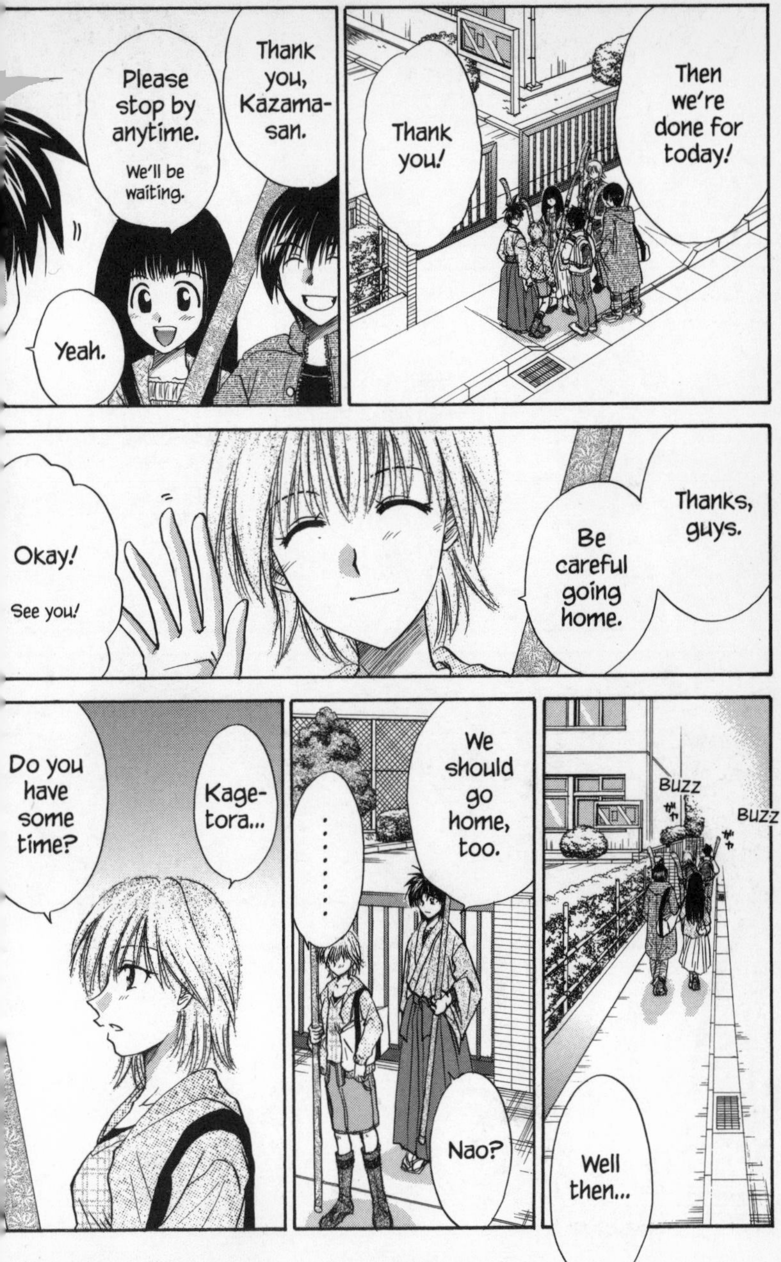
Then we're done for today!
Thank you!
Thank you, Kazama-san.
Please stop by anytime.
We'll be waiting.
Yeah.
Thanks, guys.
Be careful going home.
Okay!
See you!
BUZZ
BUZZ
Well then...
We should go home, too.
....
Nao?
Kage-tora...
Do you have some time?

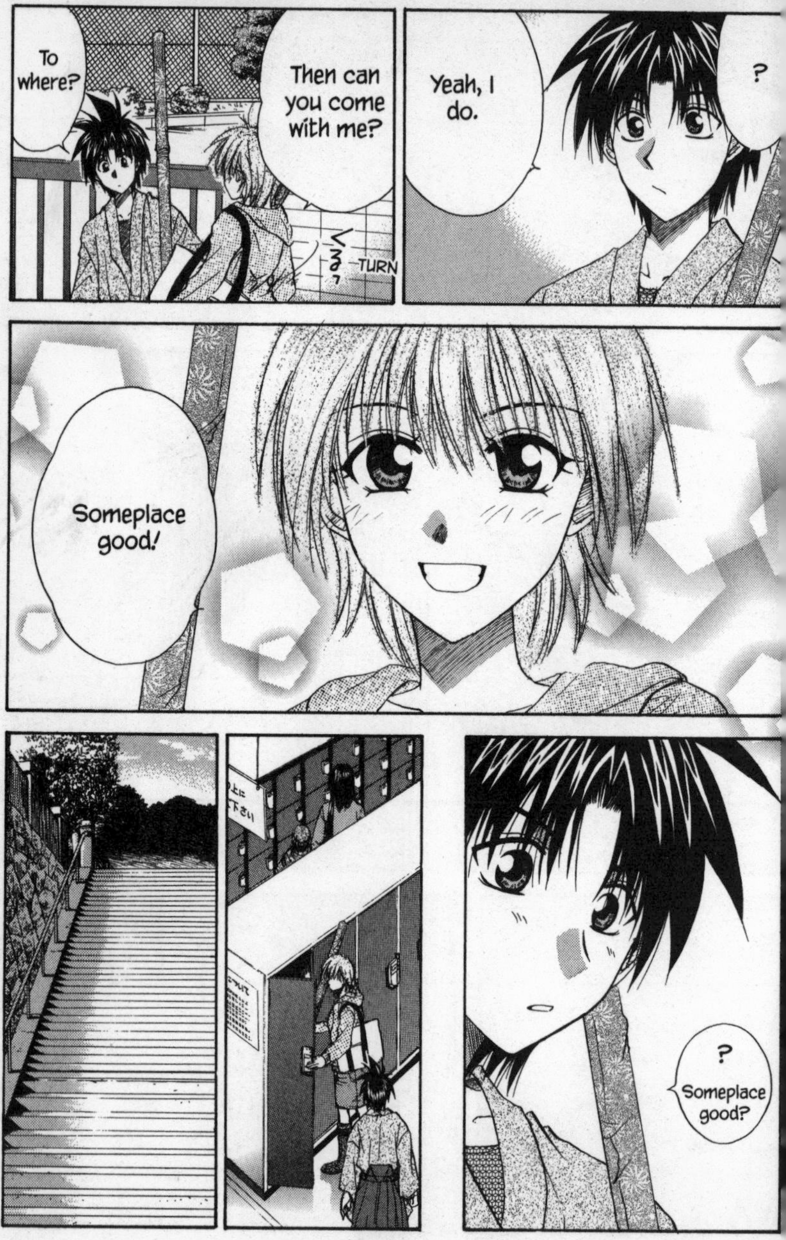
?
Yeah, I do.
Then can you come with me?
TURN
To where?
Someplace good!
?
Someplace good?

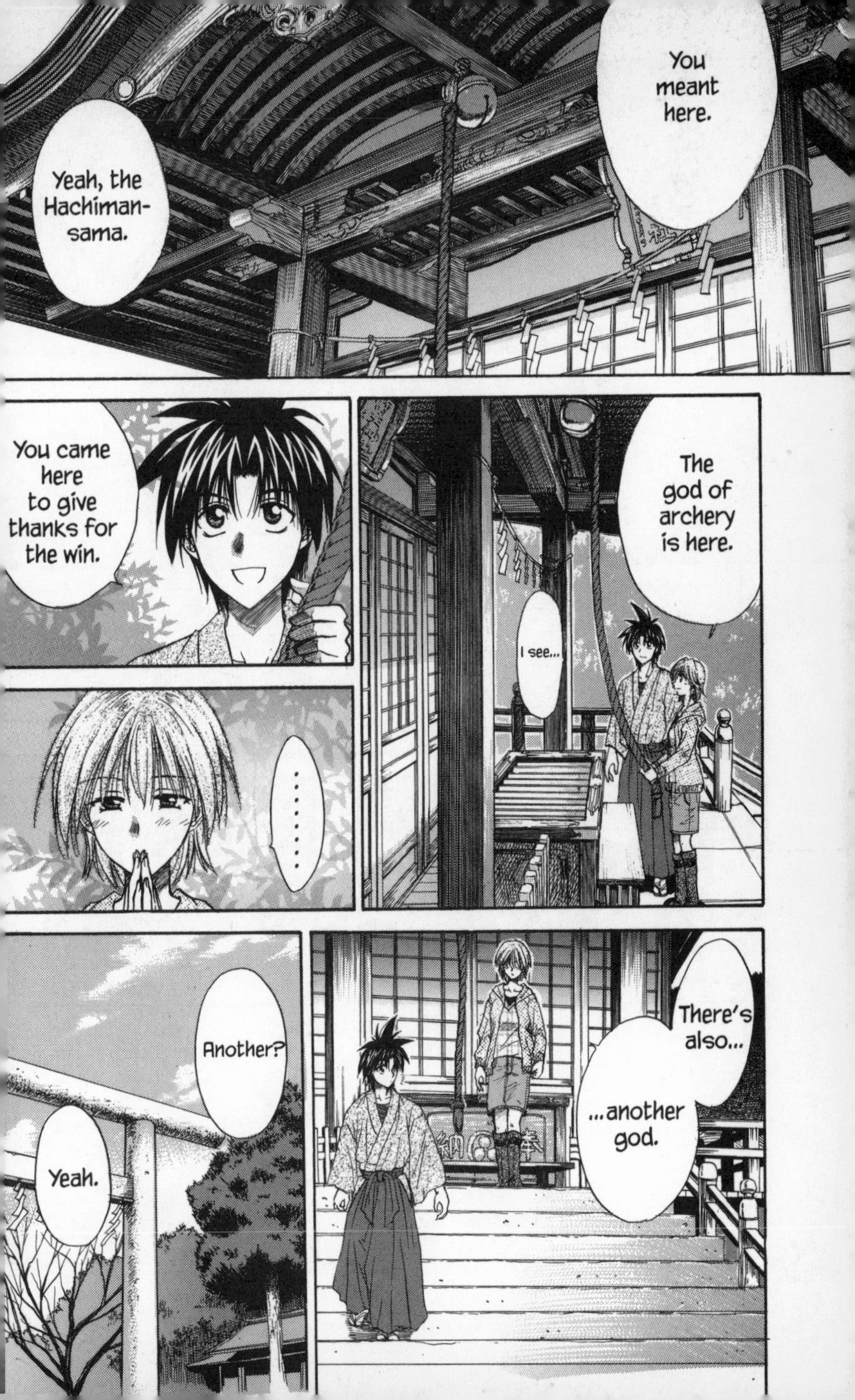
You meant here.
Yeah, the Hachiman-sama.
The god of archery is here.
I see...
You came here to give thanks for the win.
......
There's also...
...another god.
Another?
Yeah.

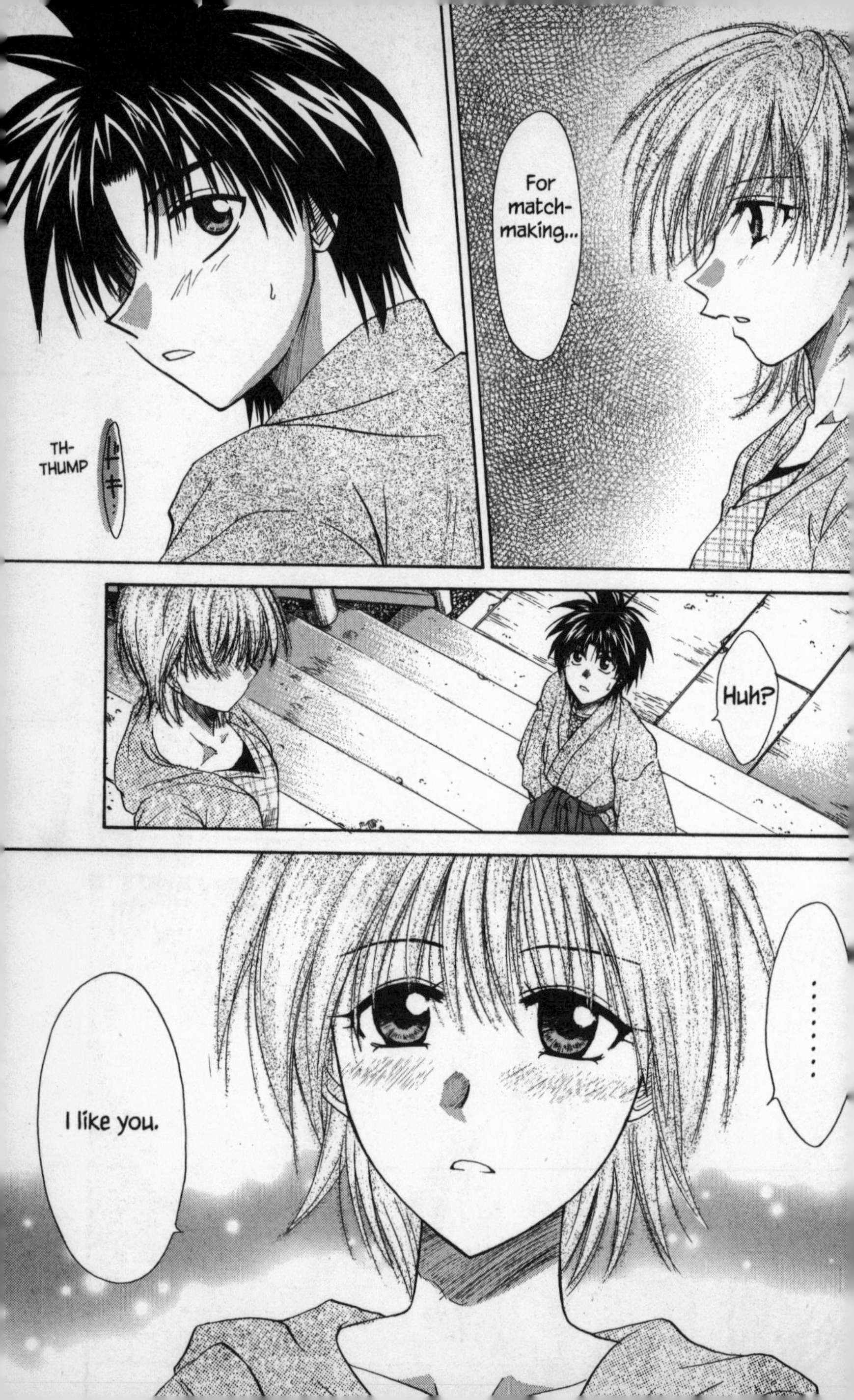
For match-making...
TH-THUMP
Huh?
....
I like you.

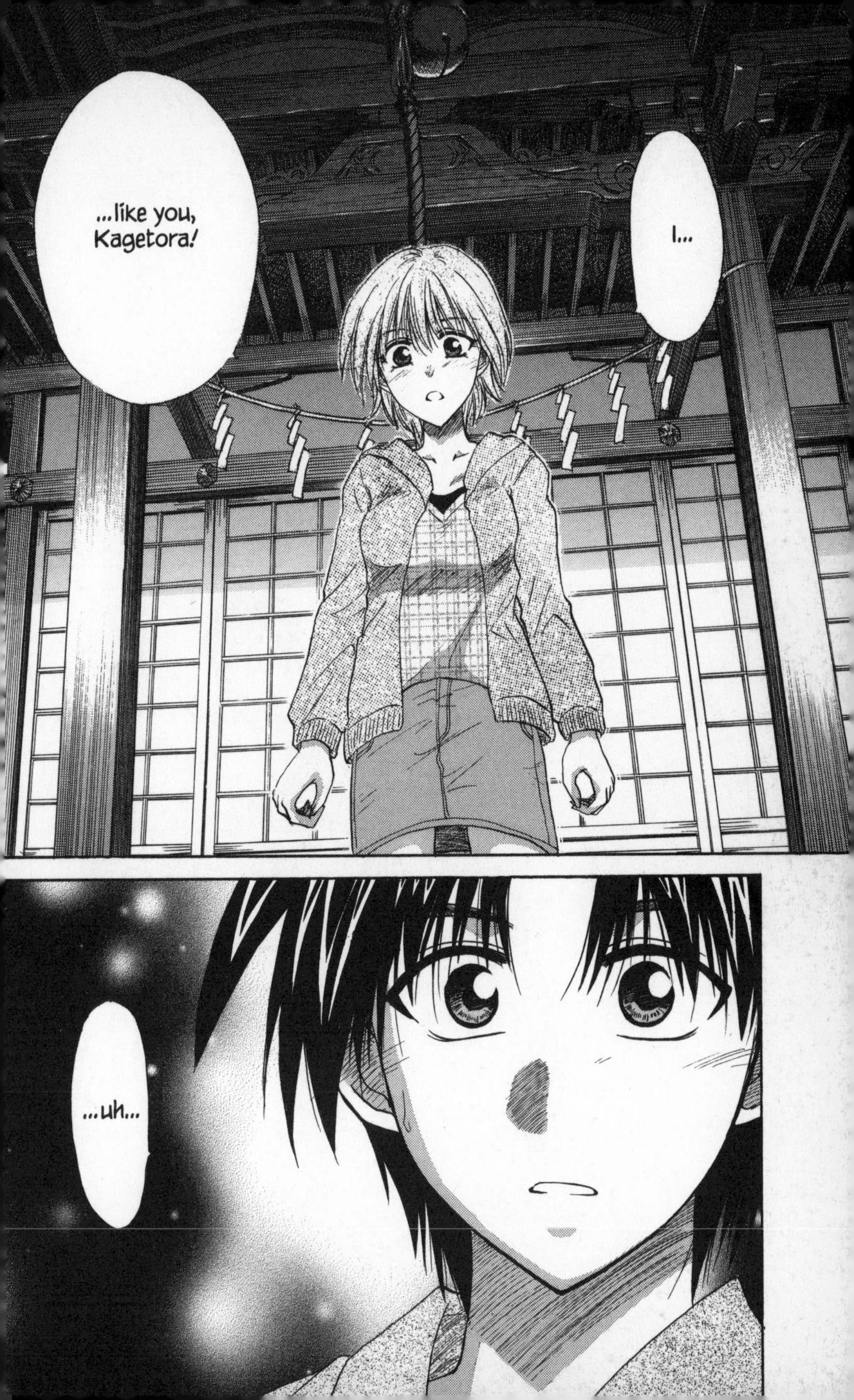
I...
...like you, Kagetora!
...uh...

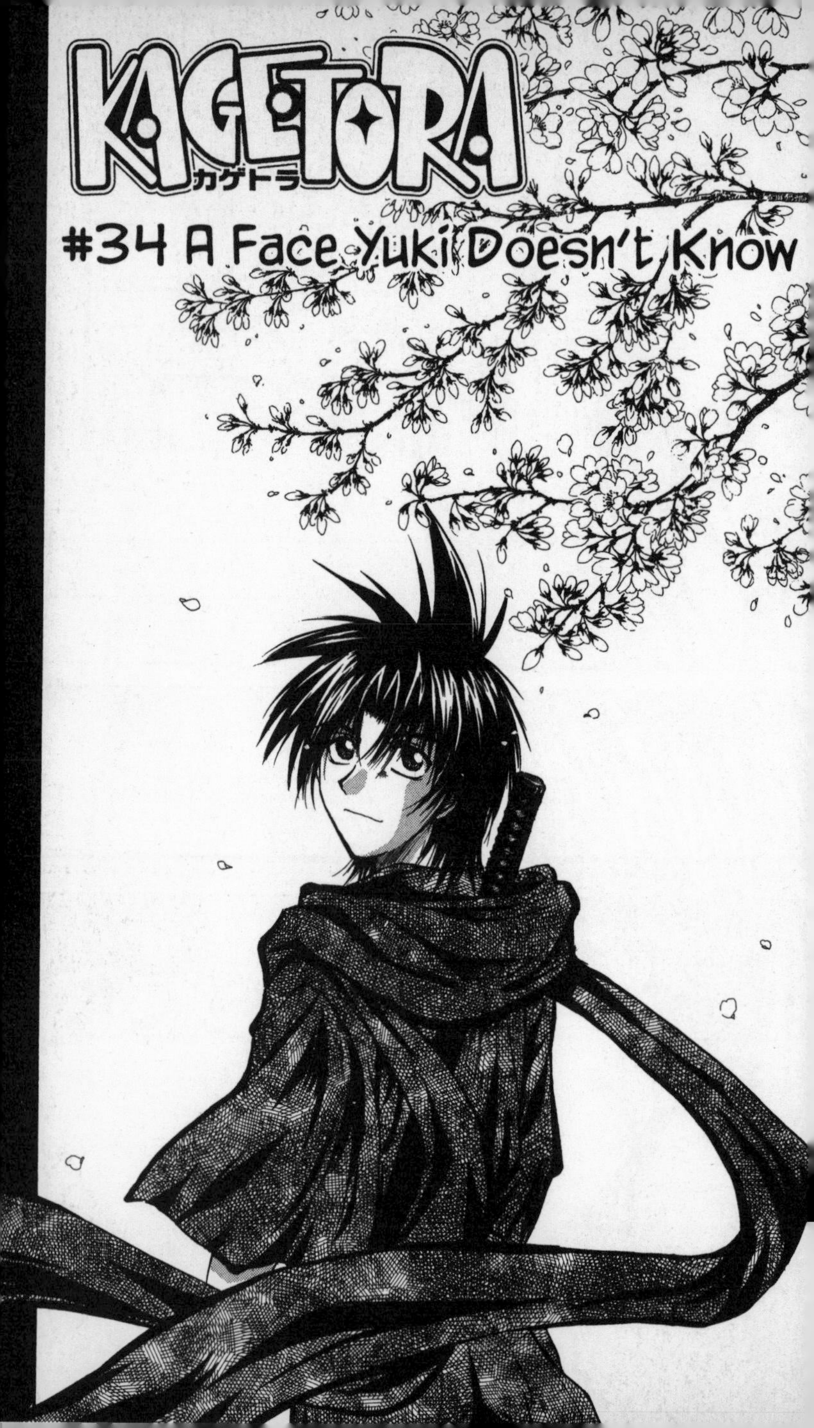
KAGETORA
カゲトラ
#34 A Face Yuki Doesn't Know

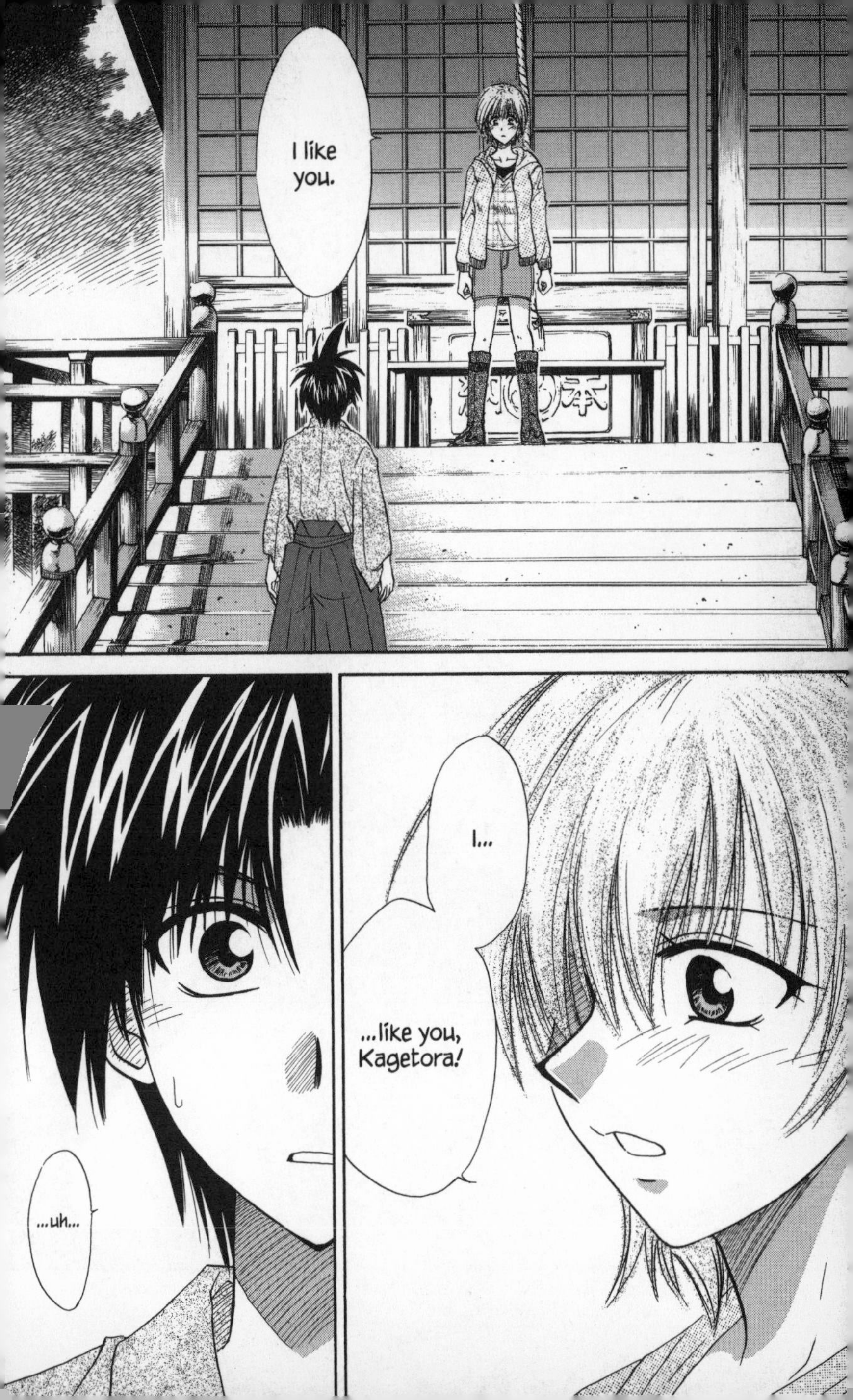
I like you.
I...
...like you, Kagetora!
...uh...

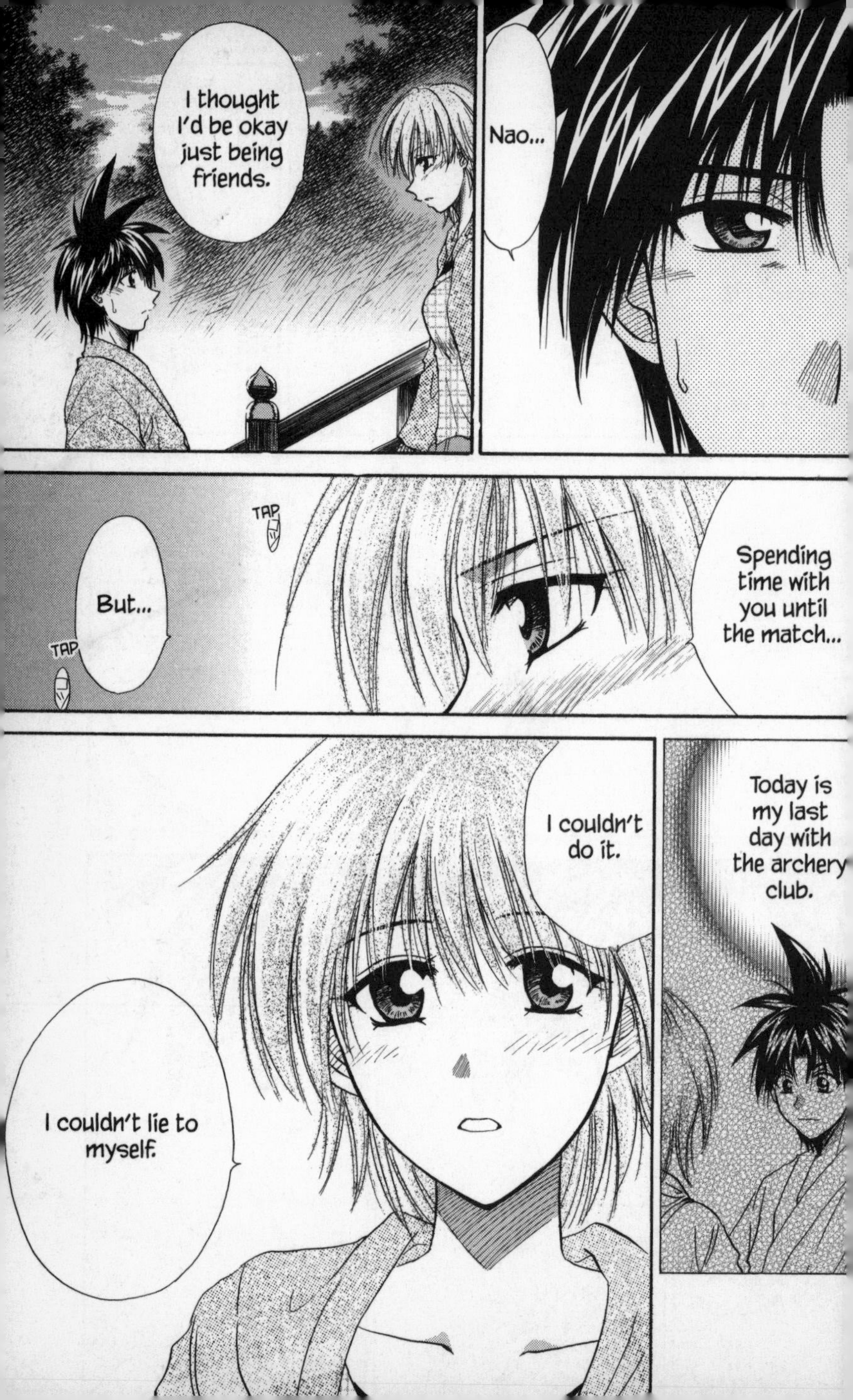
Nao...
I thought I'd be okay just being friends.
Spending time with you until the match...
TAP
But...
TAP
Today is my last day with the archery club.
I couldn't do it.
I couldn't lie to myself.

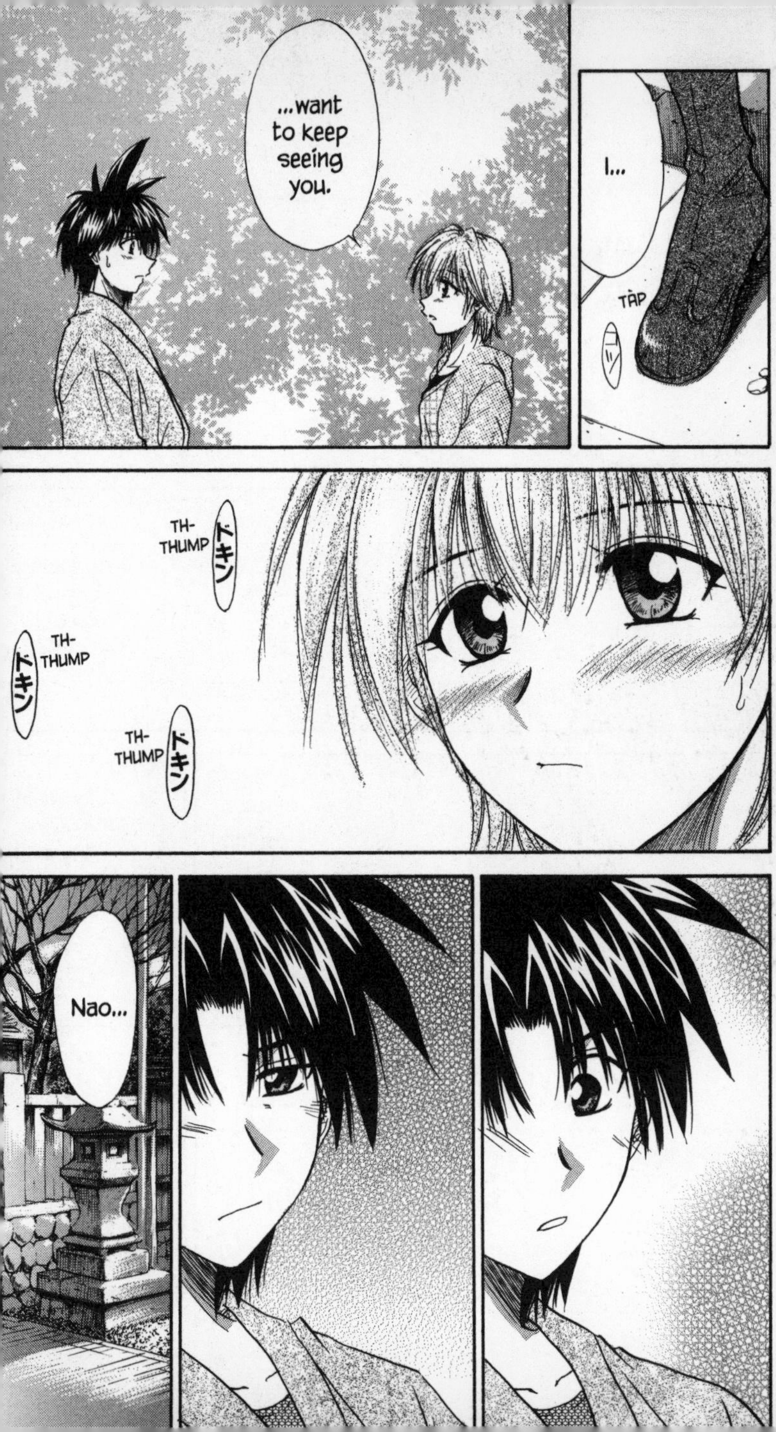
I...
TAP
ゴッ
...want to keep seeing you.
TH-THUMP
ドキン
TH-THUMP
ドキン
TH-THUMP
ドキン
Nao...

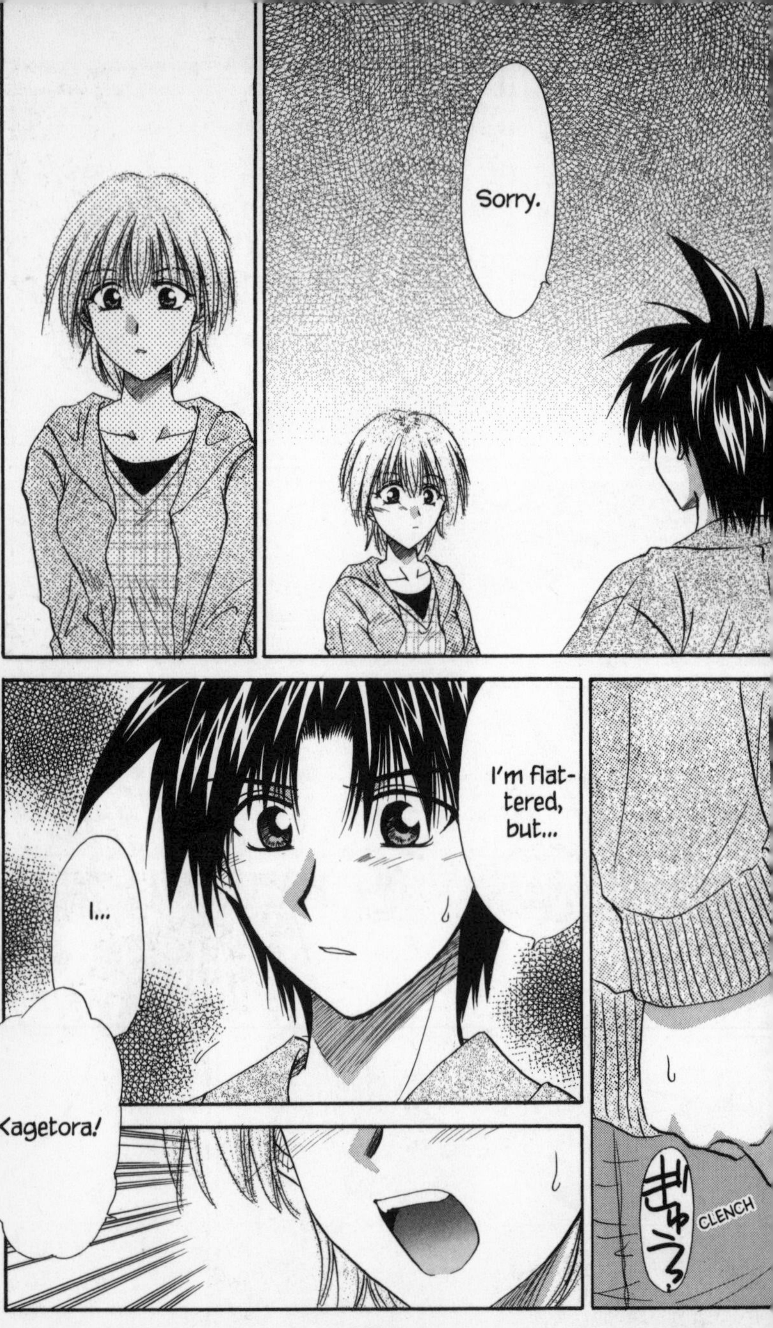
Sorry.
ぎゅう
CLENCH
I'm flat-tered, but...
I...
Kagetora!

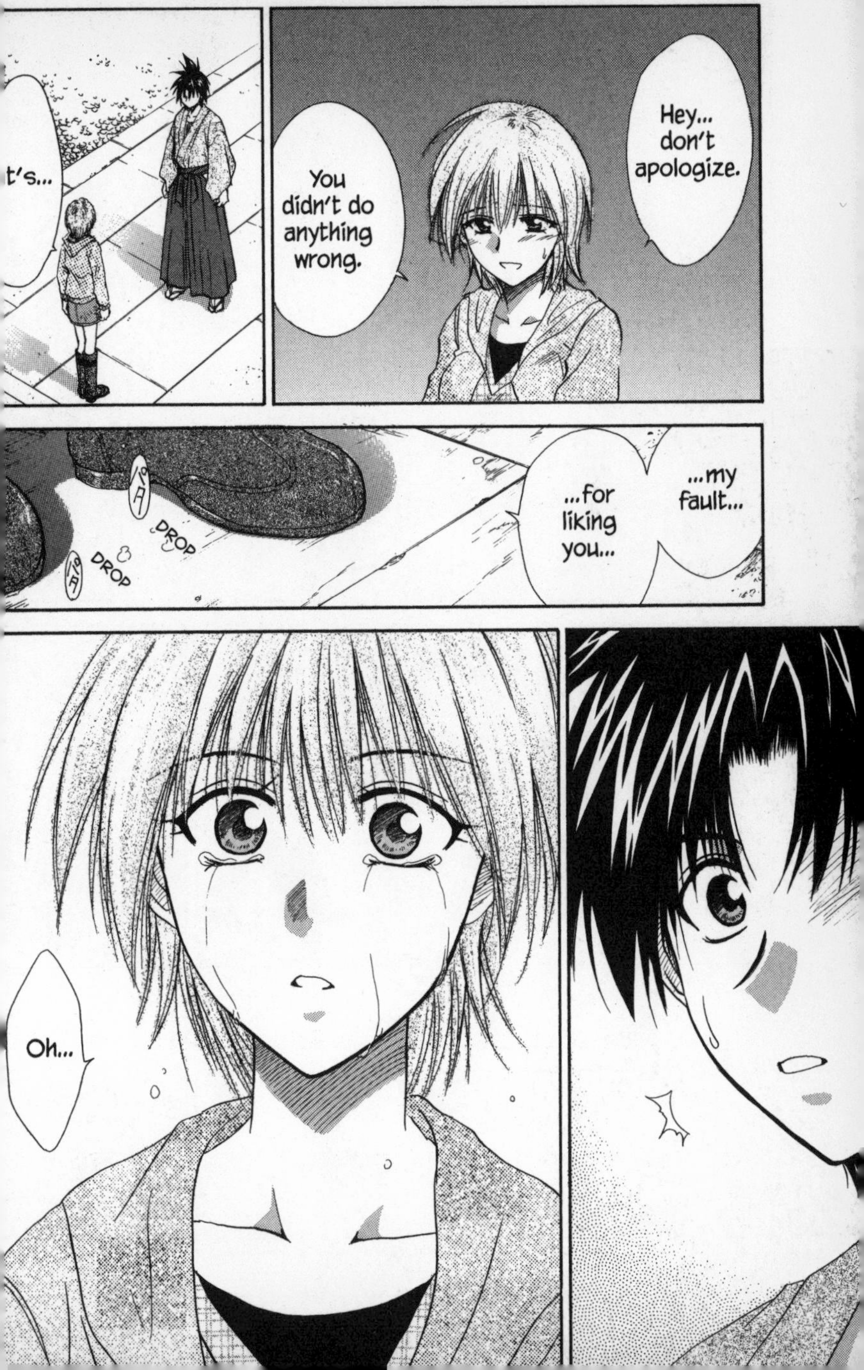
Hey... don't apologize.
You didn't do anything wrong.
t's...
...my fault...
...for liking you...
パタ
DROP
パタ
DROP
Oh...

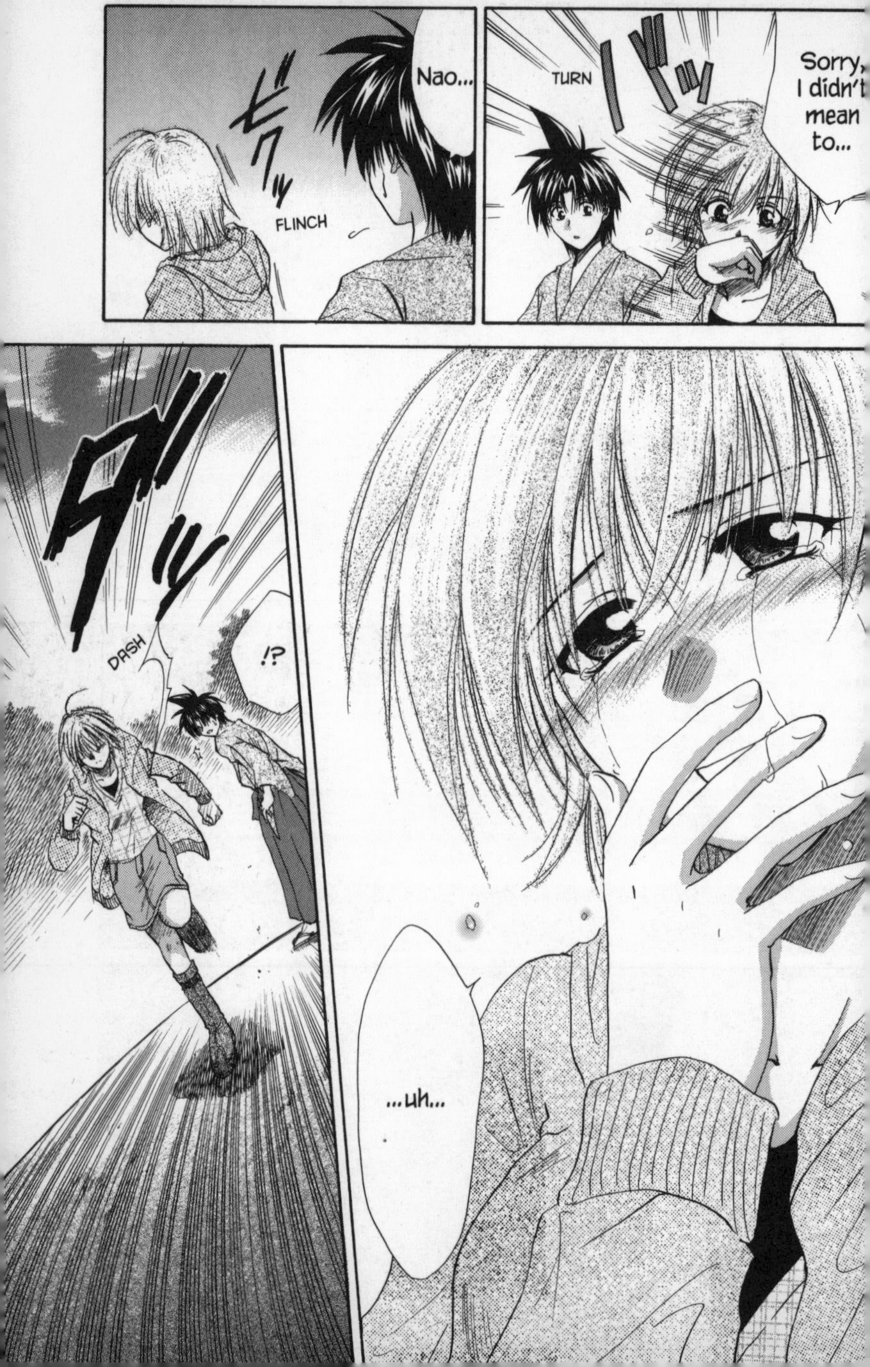
Sorry, I didn't mean to...
TURN
Nao...
FLINCH
...uh...
!?
DASH

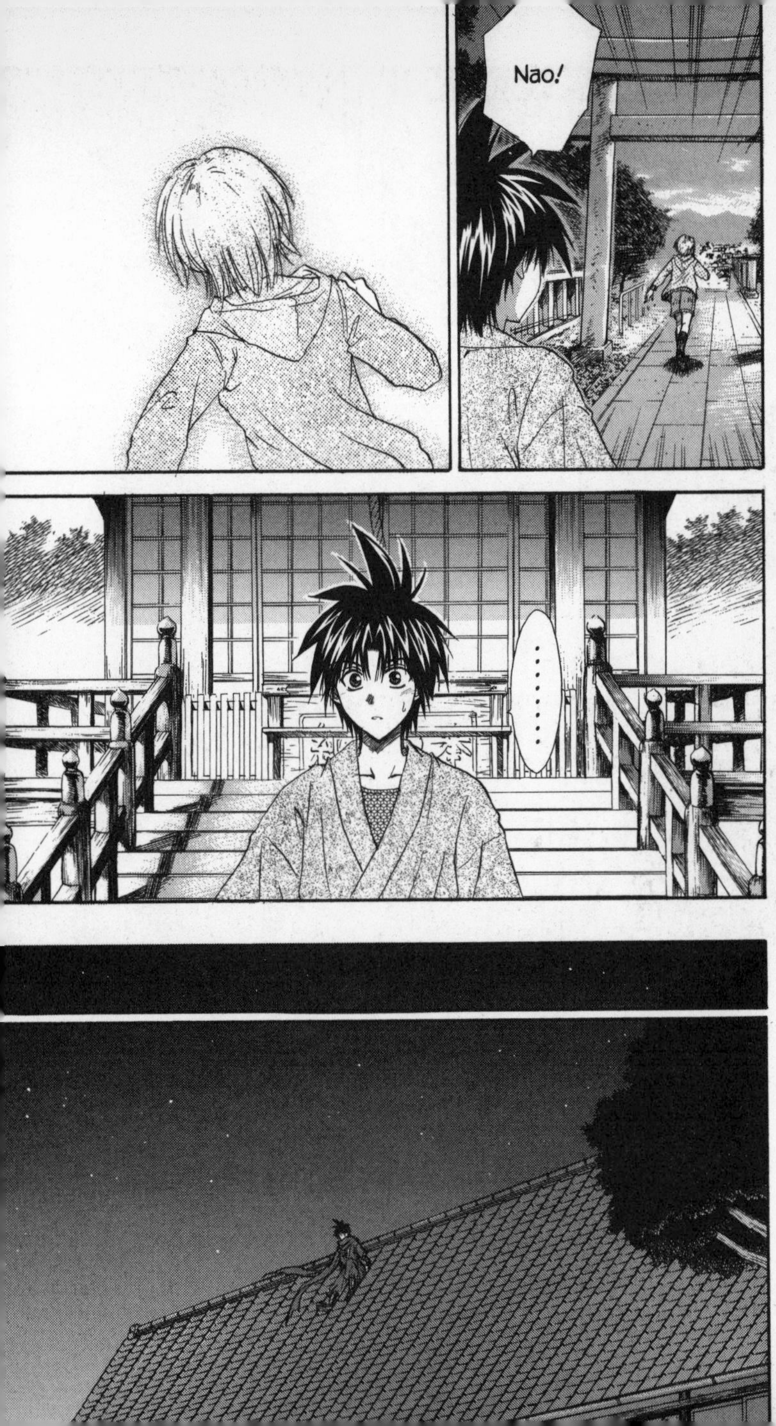
Nao!
......

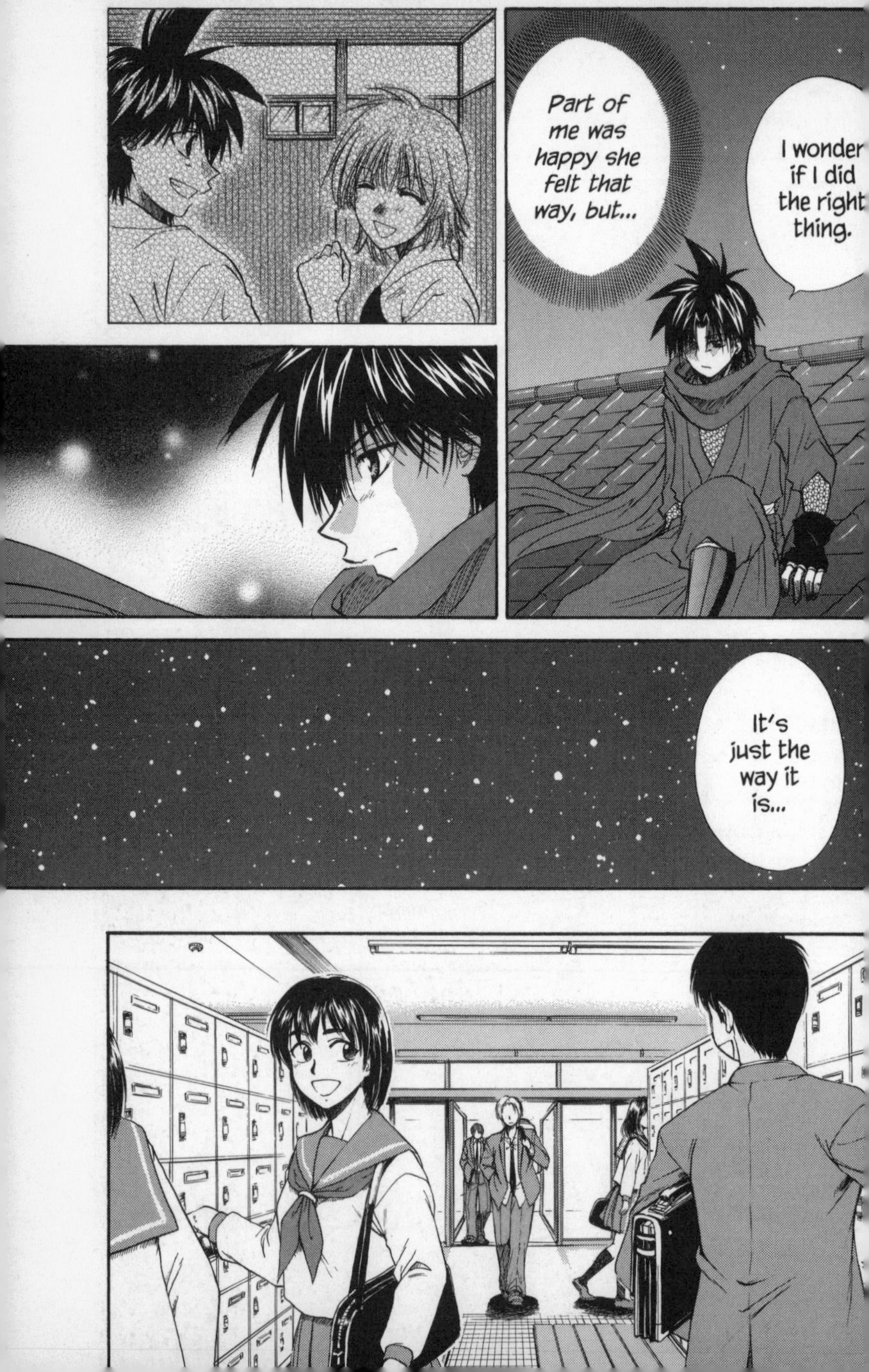
I wonder if I did the right thing.
Part of me was happy she felt that way, but...
It's just the way it is...

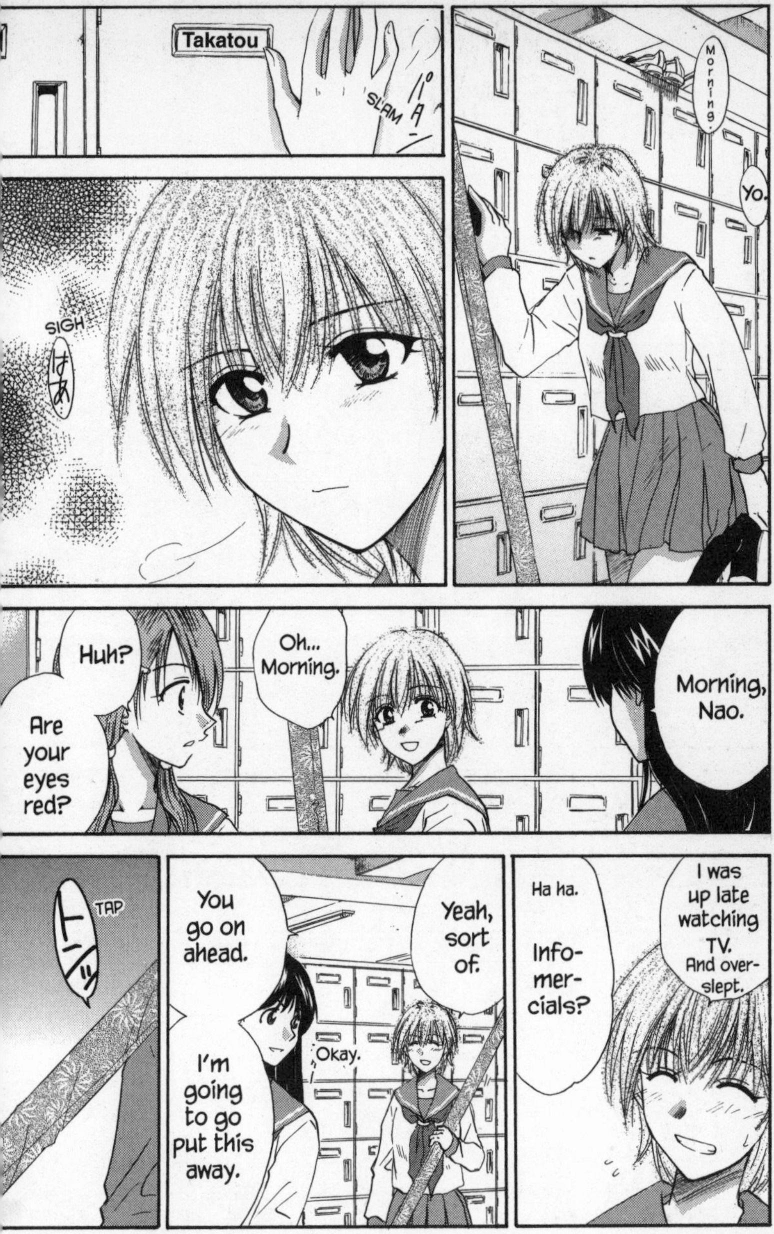

Morning.
Yo.
Takatou
SLAM
SIGH
はあ
Morning, Nao.
Oh... Morning.
Huh?
Are your eyes red?
I was up late watching TV. And over-slept.
Ha ha.
Info-mer-cials?
Yeah, sort of.
You go on ahead.
I'm going to go put this away.
Okay.
TAP

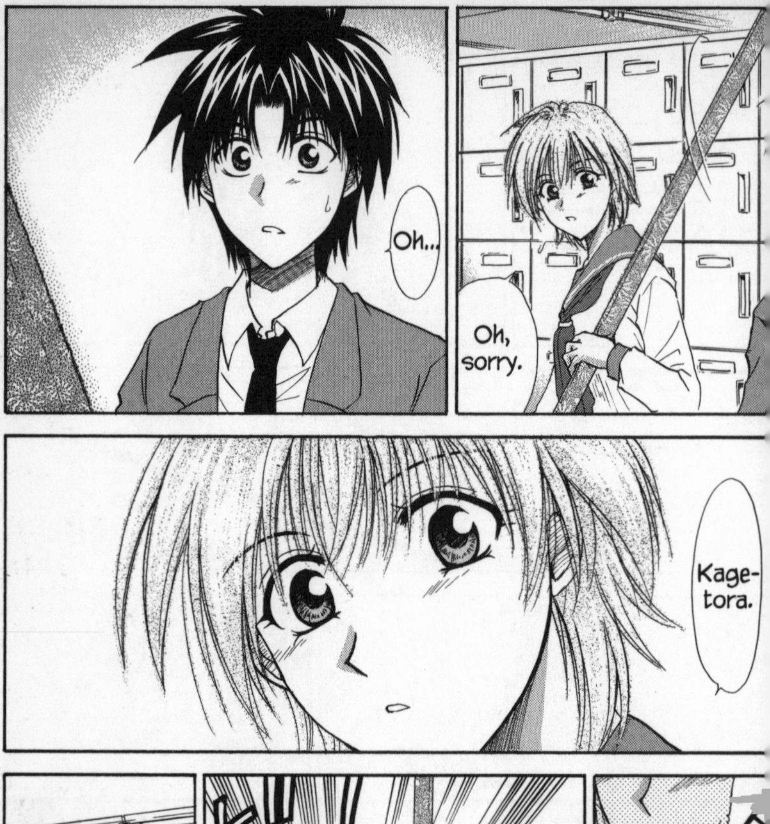
Oh, sorry.
Oh...
Kage-tora.
STING
DASH!

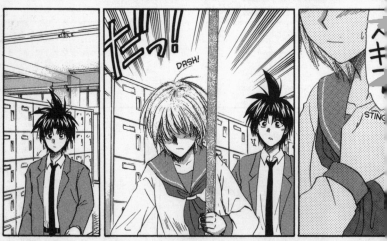

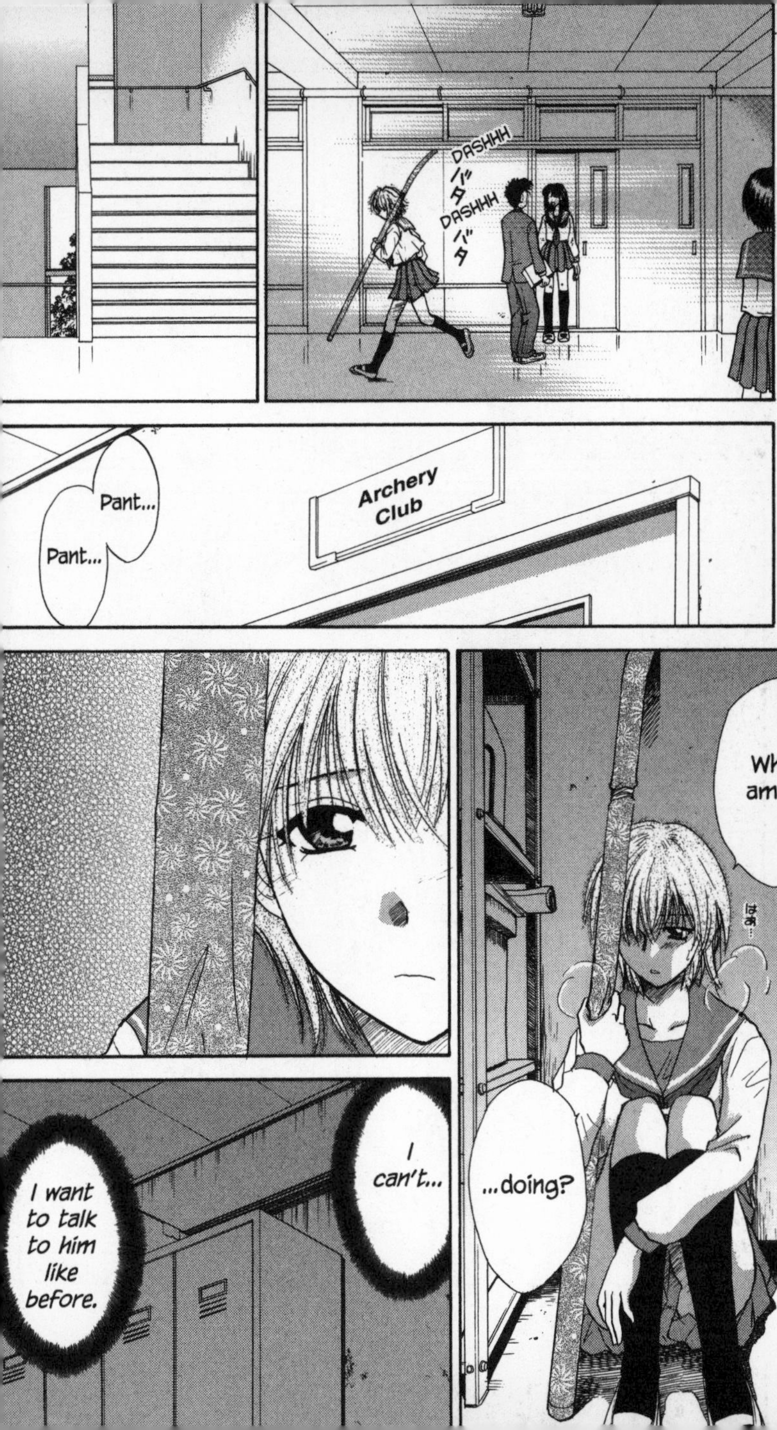
DASHHH
バタ
DASHHH
バタ
Archery Club
Pant...
Pant...
What am I...
はぁ…
PANT...
...doing?
I can't...
I want to talk to him like before.

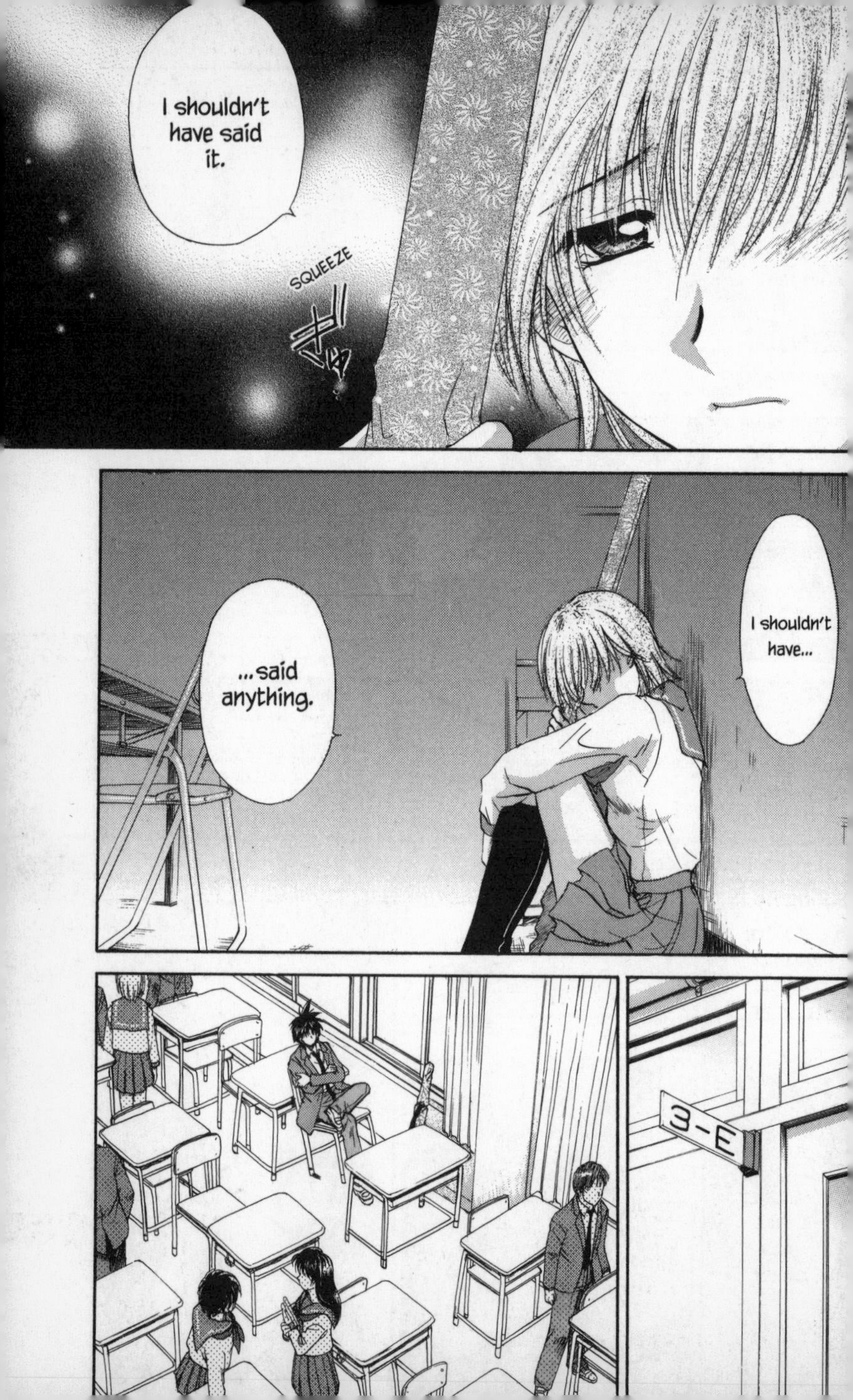
I shouldn't have said it.
SQUEEZE
I shouldn't have...
...said anything.
3-E

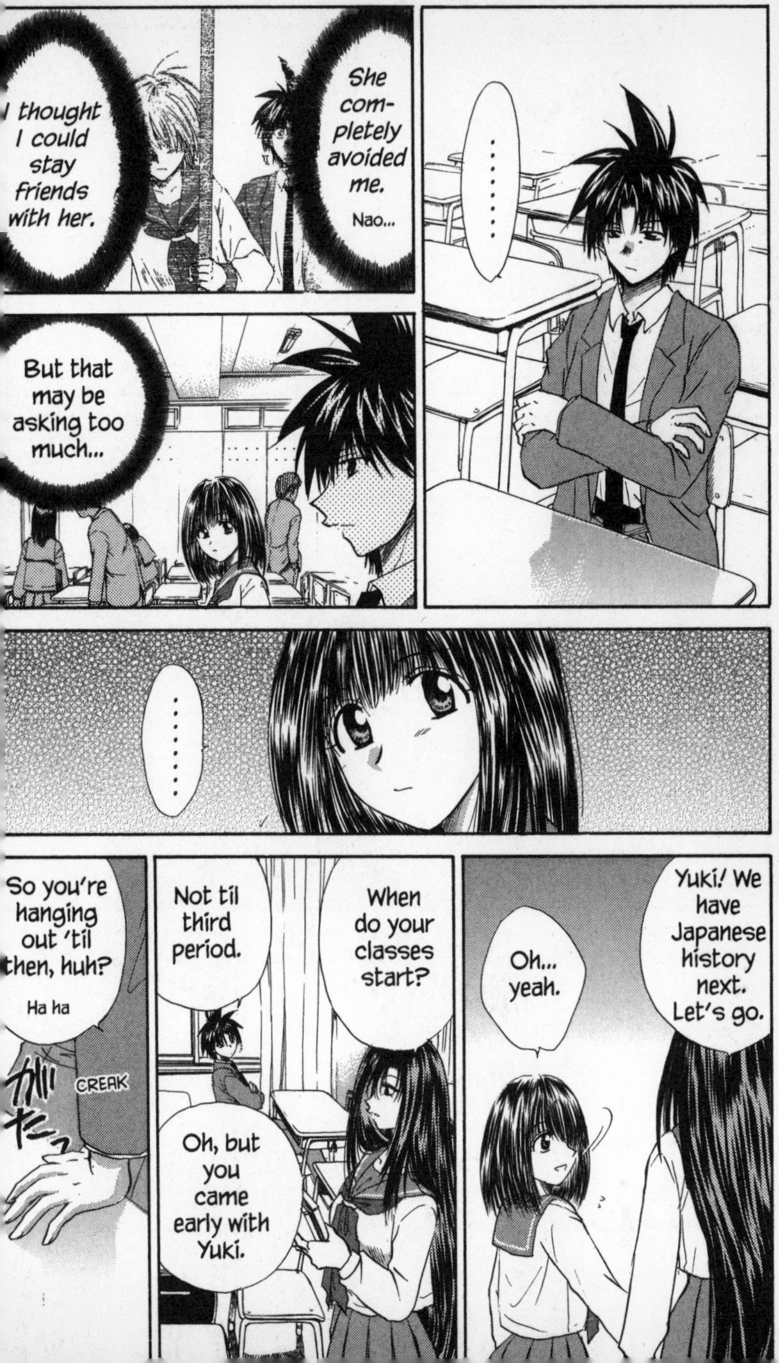
......
She completely avoided me.
Nao...
I thought I could stay friends with her.
But that may be asking too much...
......
Yuki! We have Japanese history next. Let's go.
Oh... yeah.
When do your classes start?
Not til third period.
Oh, but you came early with Yuki.
So you're hanging out 'til then, huh?
Ha ha
CREAK

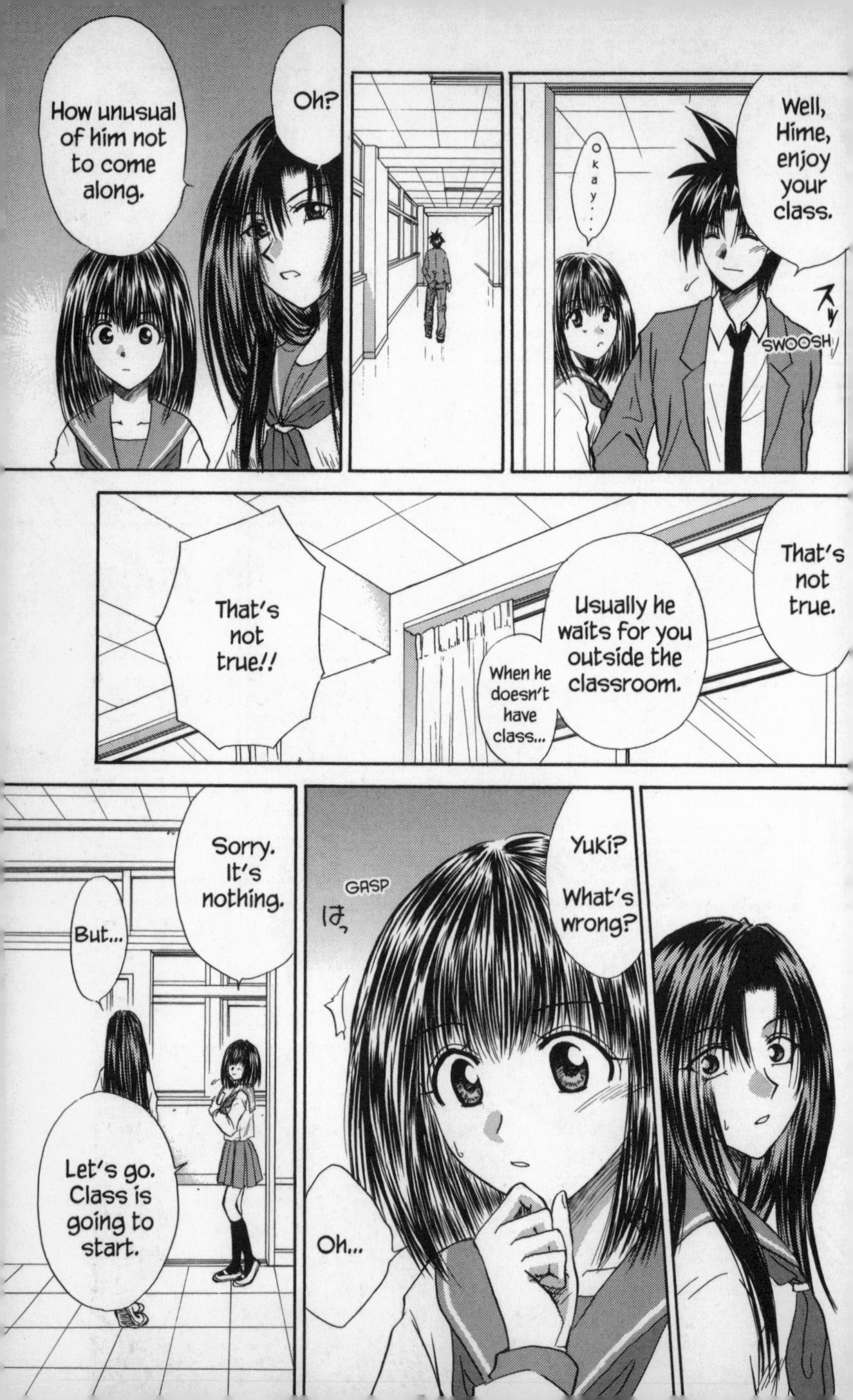
Well, Hime, enjoy your class.
Okay...
スッ
SWOOSH
Oh?
How unusual of him not to come along.
That's not true.
Usually he waits for you outside the classroom.
When he doesn't have class...
That's not true!!
Yuki? What's wrong?
GASP
はっ
Oh...
Sorry. It's nothing.
But...
Let's go. Class is going to start.

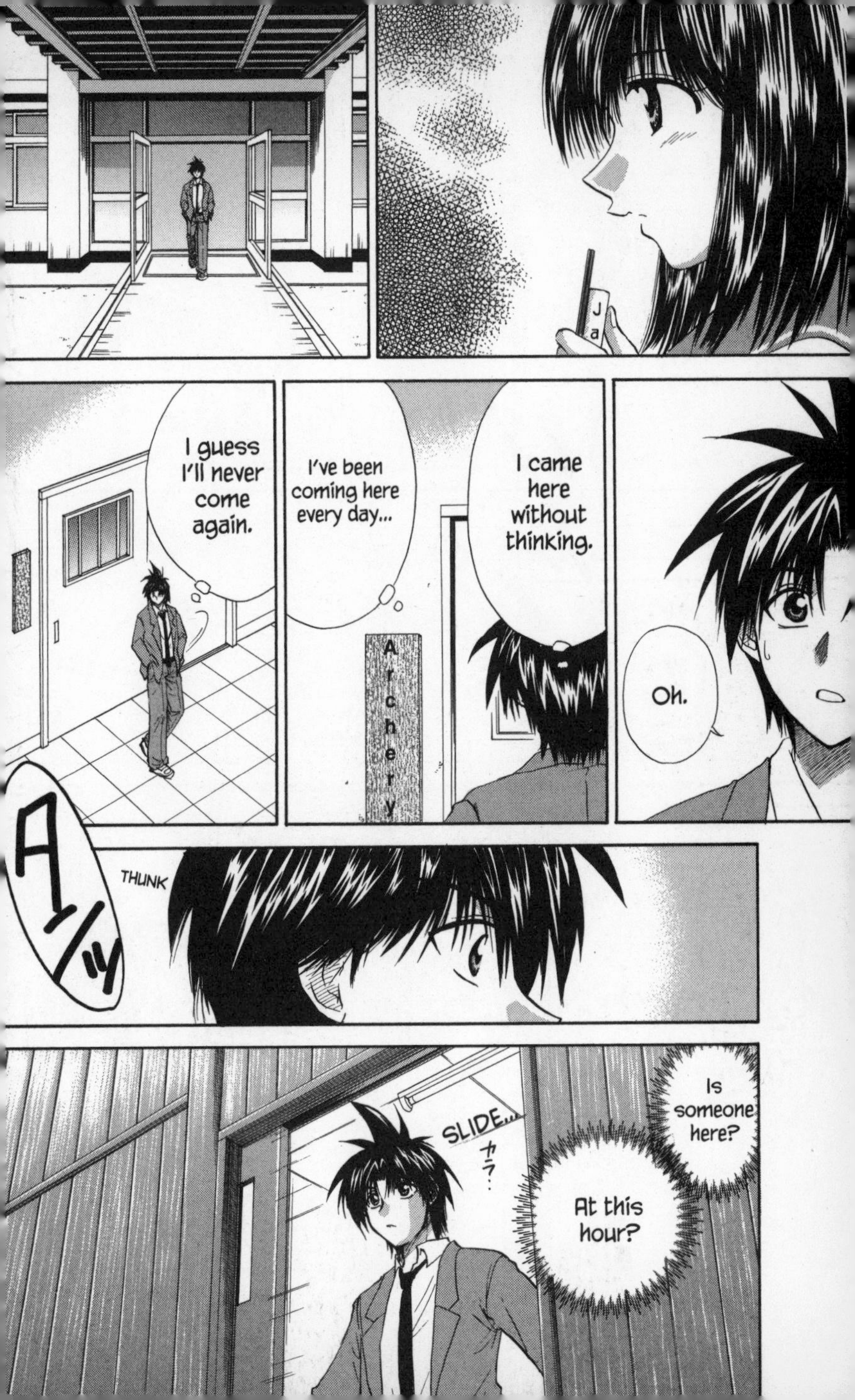
Ja
Oh.
I came here without thinking.
I've been coming here every day...
Archery
I guess I'll never come again.
THUNK
Is someone here?
At this hour?
SLIDE...
カラ…

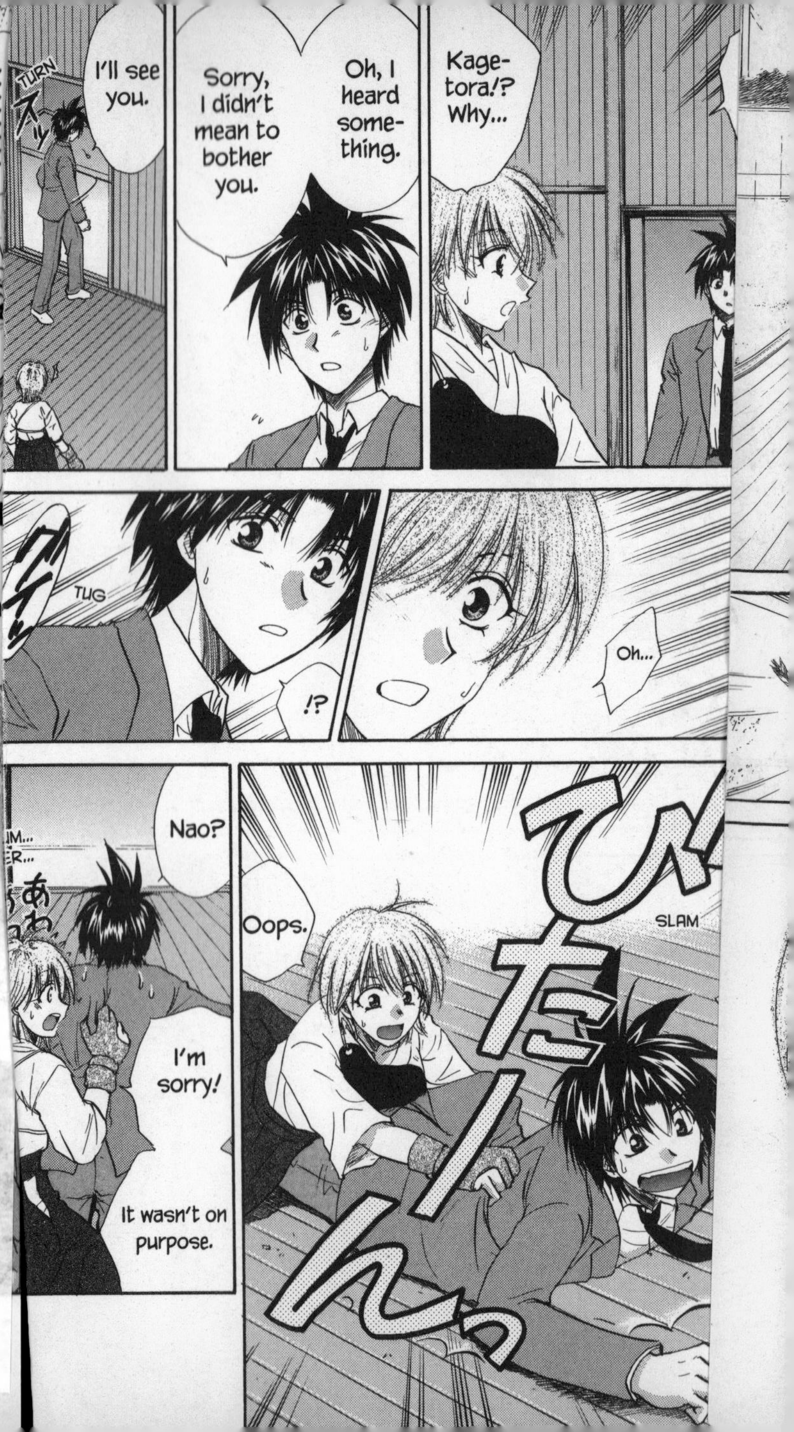
Kage-tora!? Why...
Oh, I heard some-thing.
Sorry, I didn't mean to bother you.
I'll see you.
TURN
Oh...
TUG
!?
SLAM
ひたーんっ
Oops.
Nao?
UM... ER...
I'm sorry!
It wasn't on purpose.
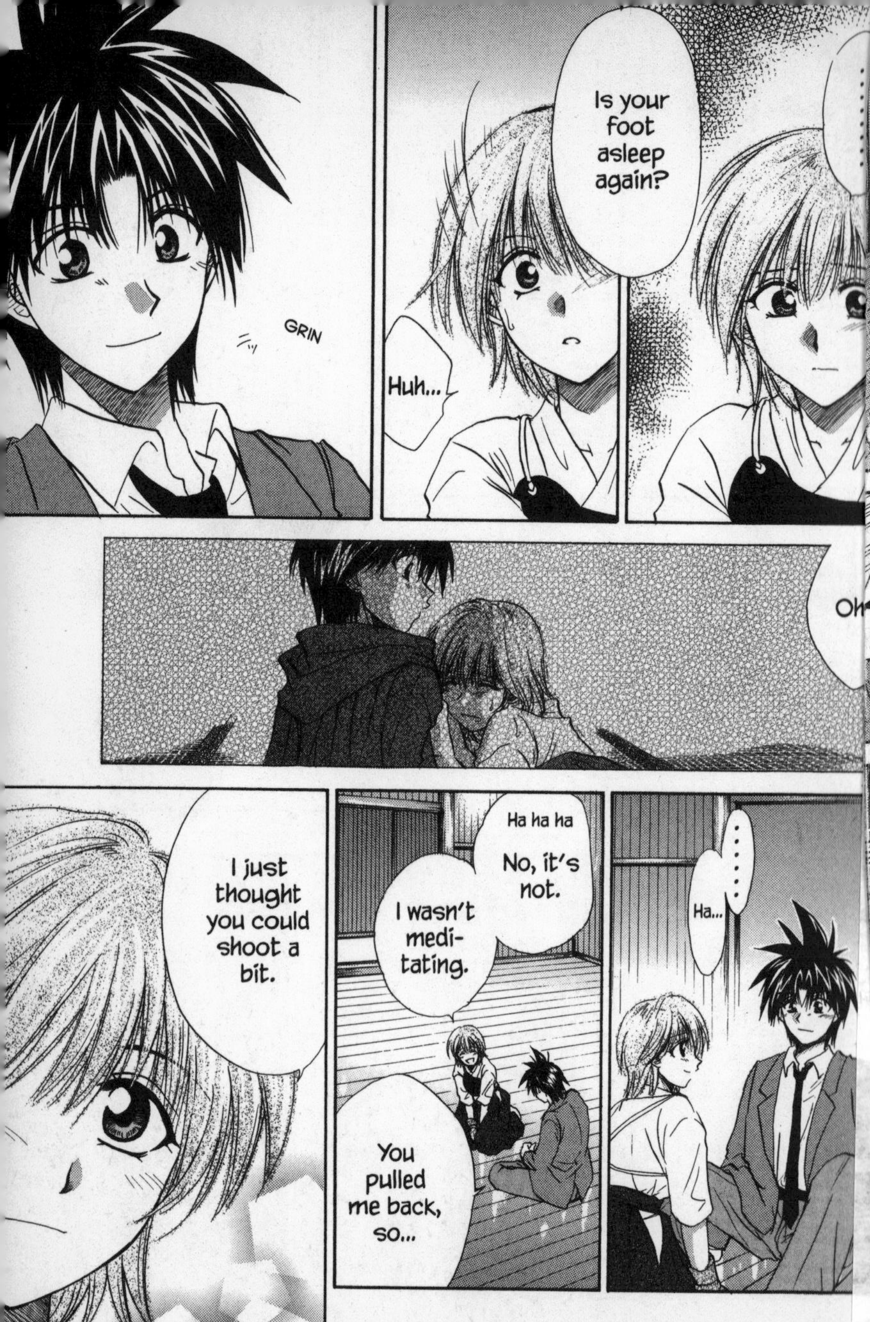
Is your foot asleep again?
Huh...
GRIN
Oh
......
Ha...
Ha ha ha
No, it's not.
I wasn't medi-tating.
You pulled me back, so...
I just thought you could shoot a bit.

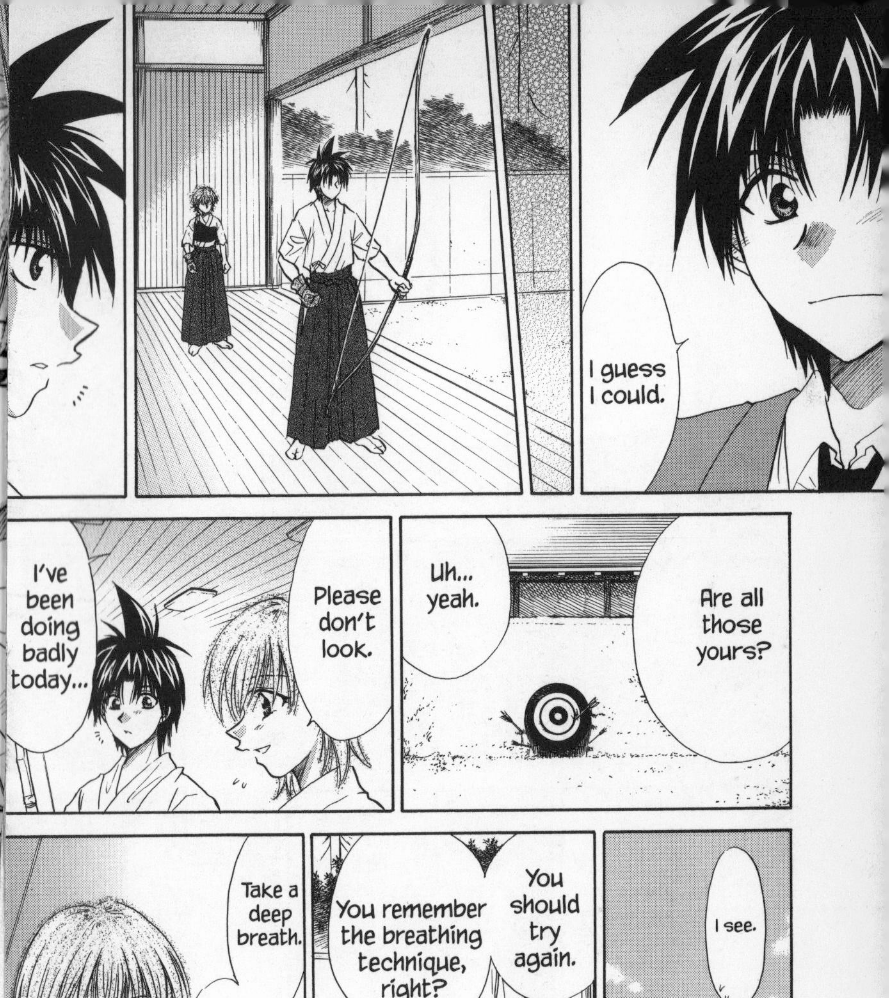
I guess I could.
Are all those yours?
Uh... yeah.
Please don't look.
I've been doing badly today...
I see.
......
You should try again.
You remember the breathing technique, right?
Yeah.
Take a deep breath.
Hold it.
Let it out.

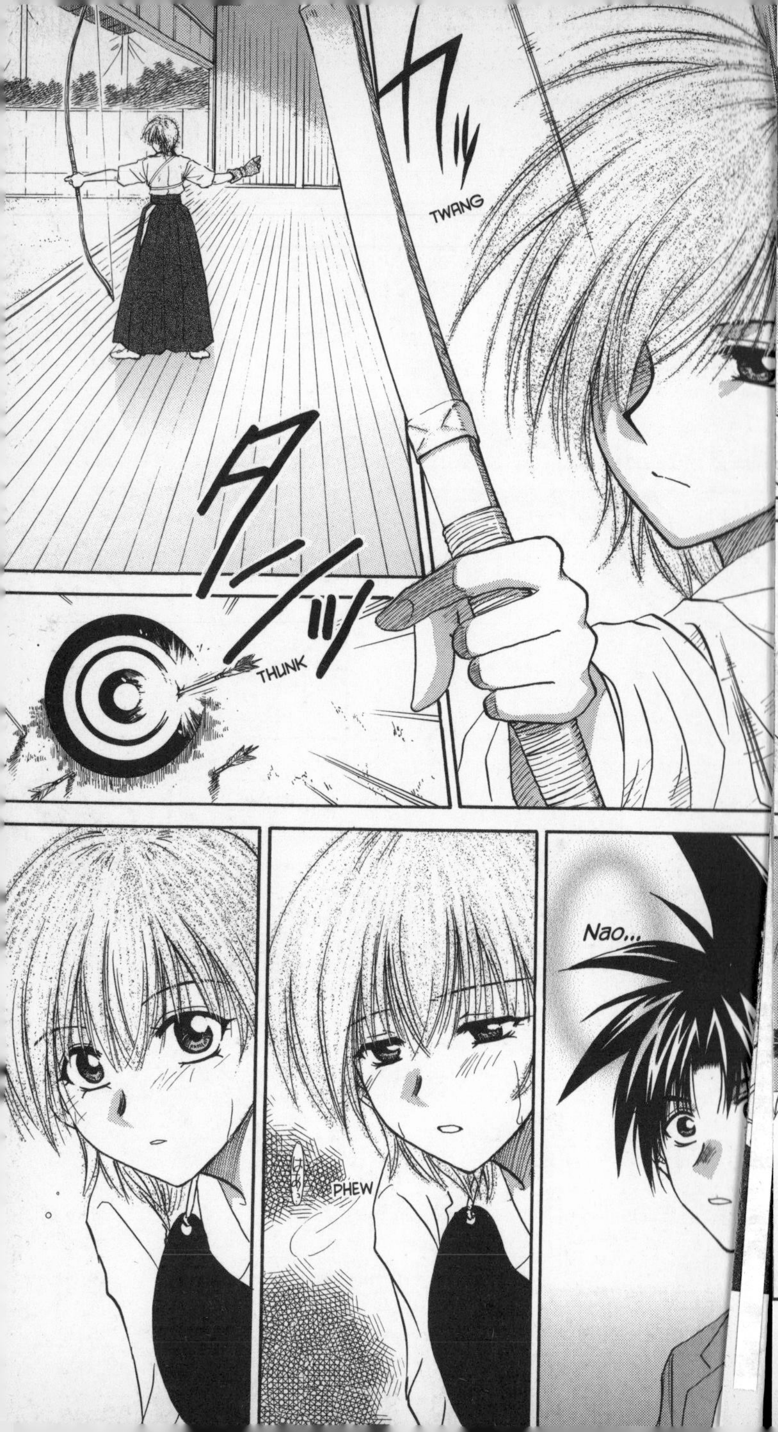
TWANG
THUNK
Nao...
PHEW

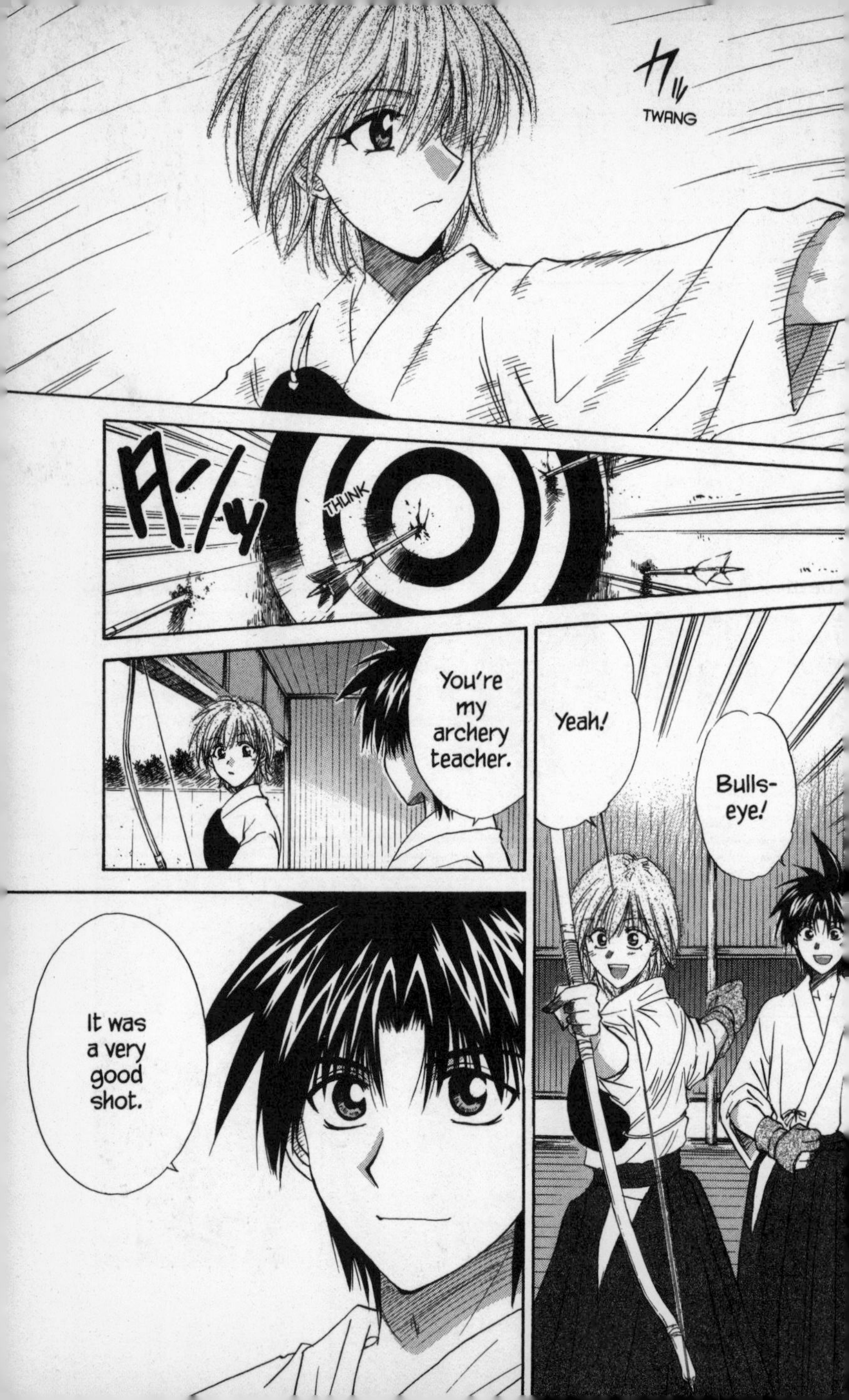
カッ
TWANG
タンッ
THUNK
Bulls-eye!
Yeah!
You're my archery teacher.
It was a very good shot.

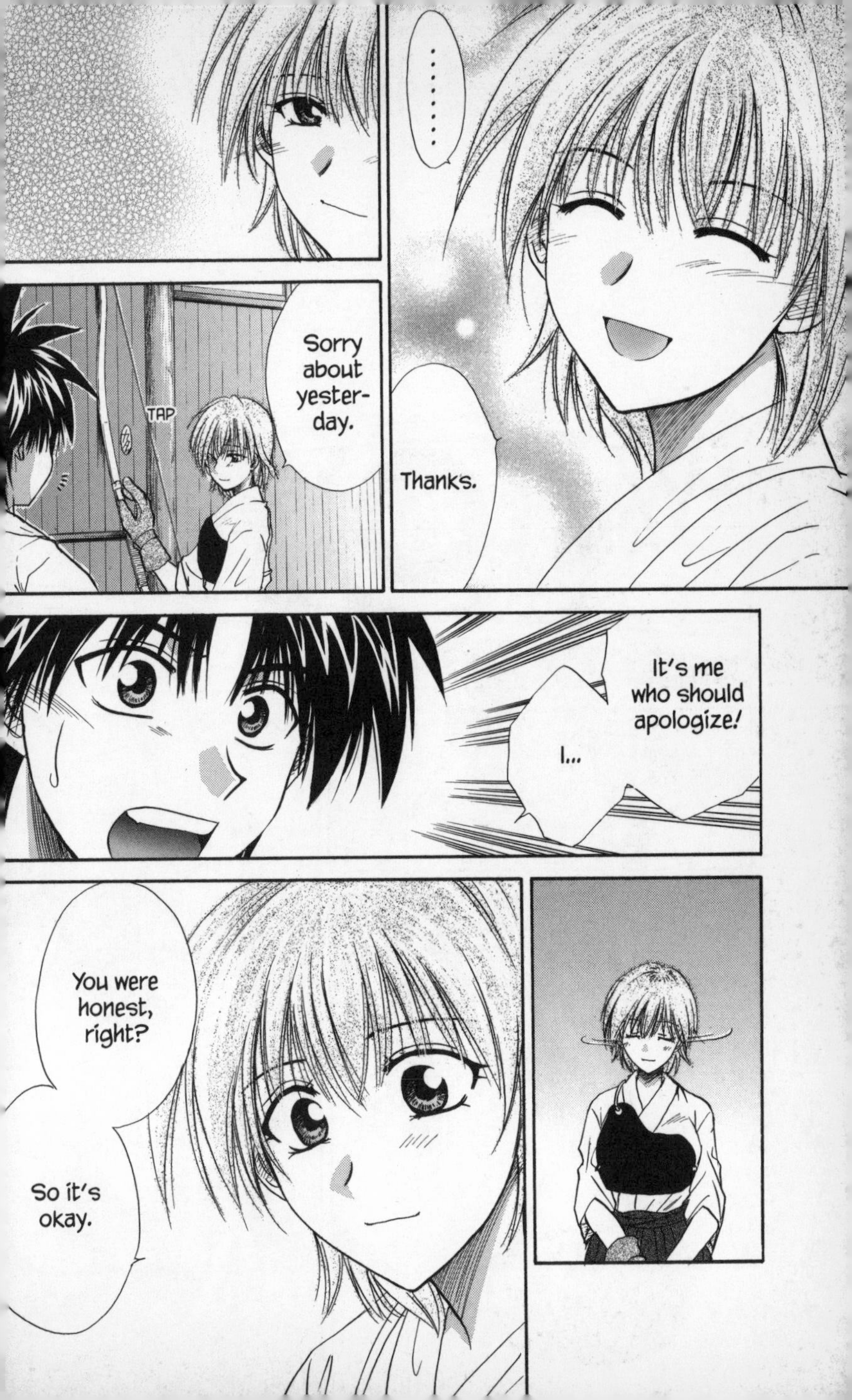
......
Thanks.
Sorry about yester-day.
TAP
It's me who should apologize!
I...
You were honest, right?
So it's okay.

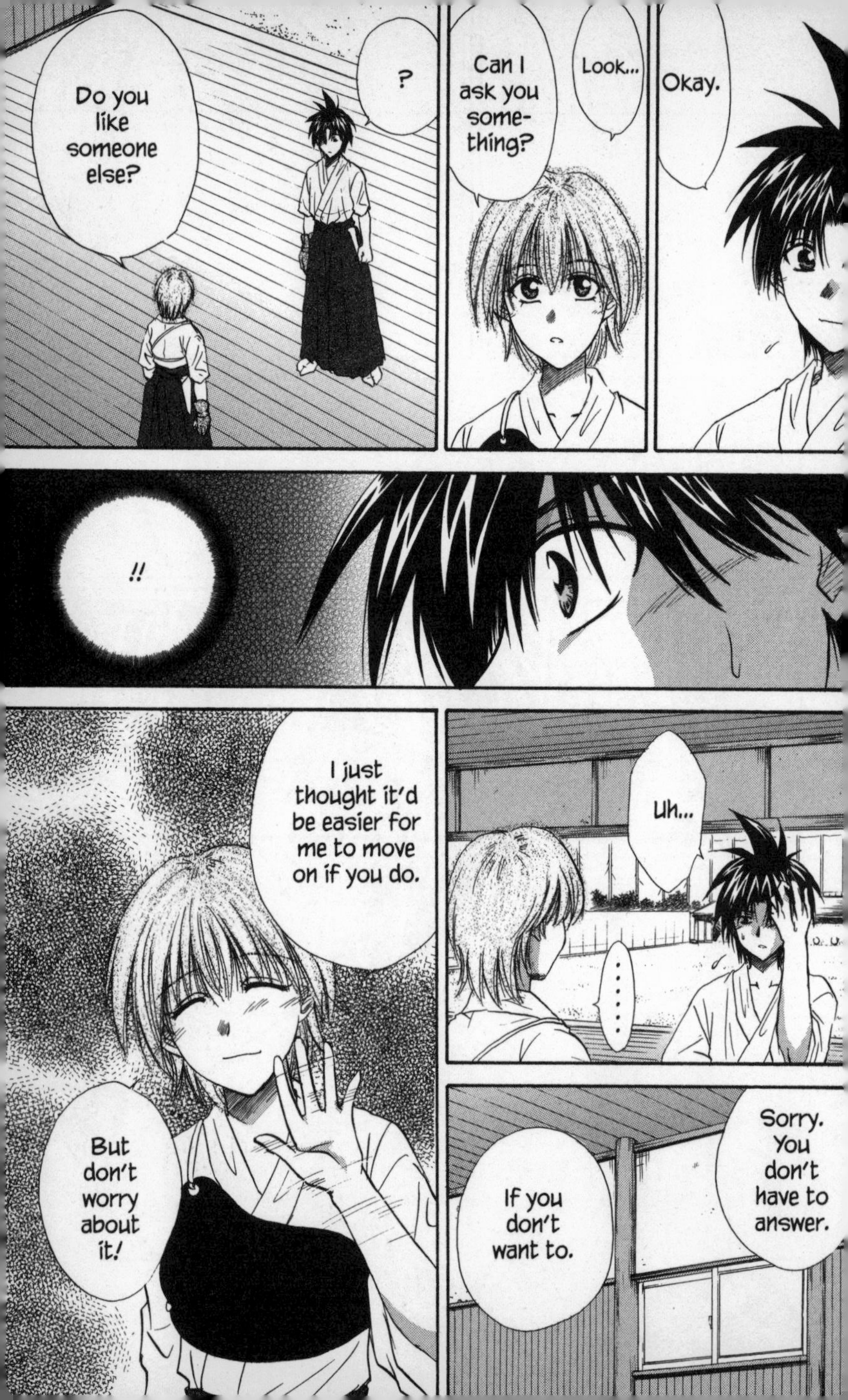

Okay.
Look...
Can I ask you something?
?
Do you like someone else?
!!
Uh...
......
Sorry. You don't have to answer.
If you don't want to.
I just thought it'd be easier for me to move on if you do.
But don't worry about it!

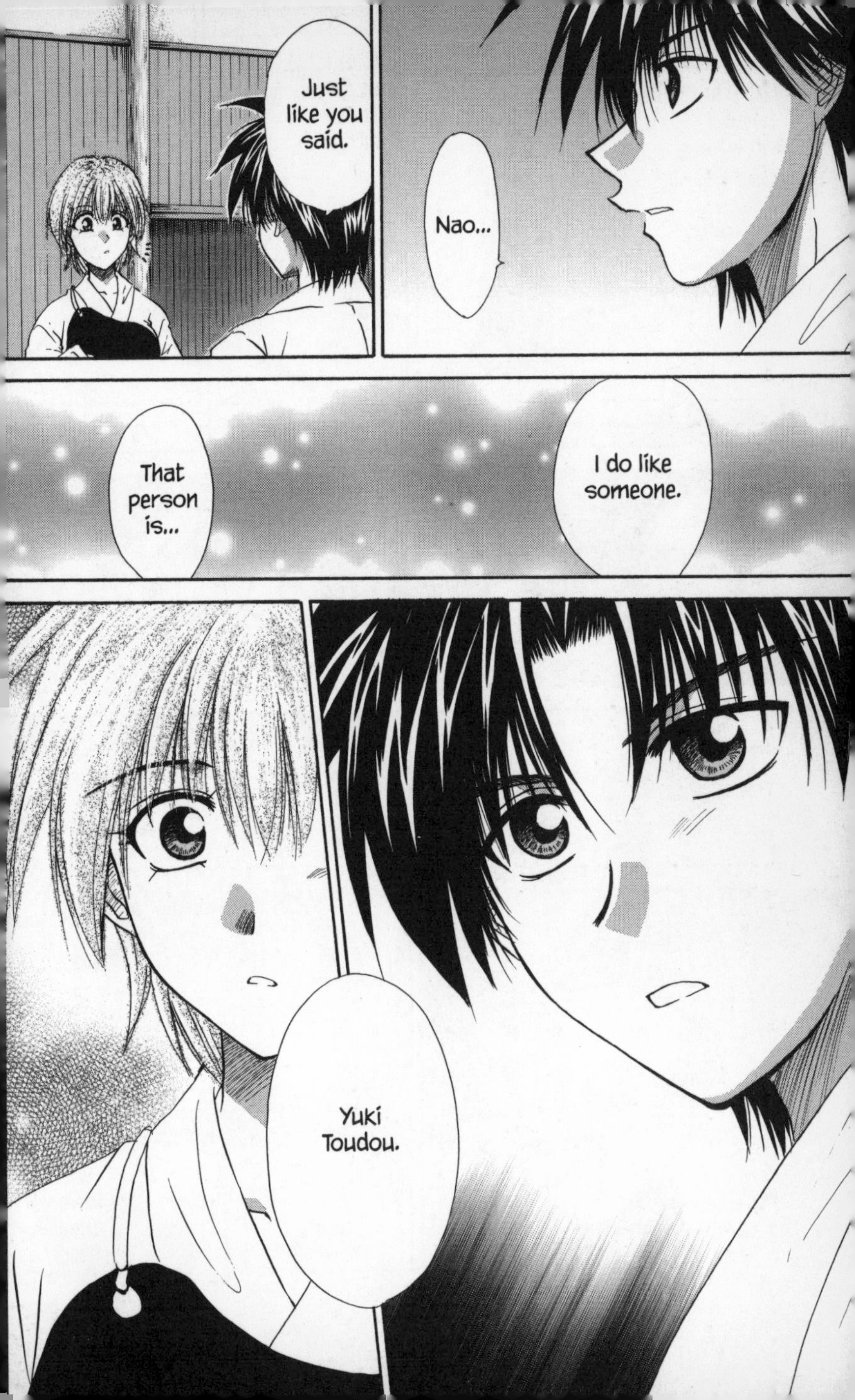
Nao...
Just like you said.
I do like someone.
That person is...
Yuki Toudou.

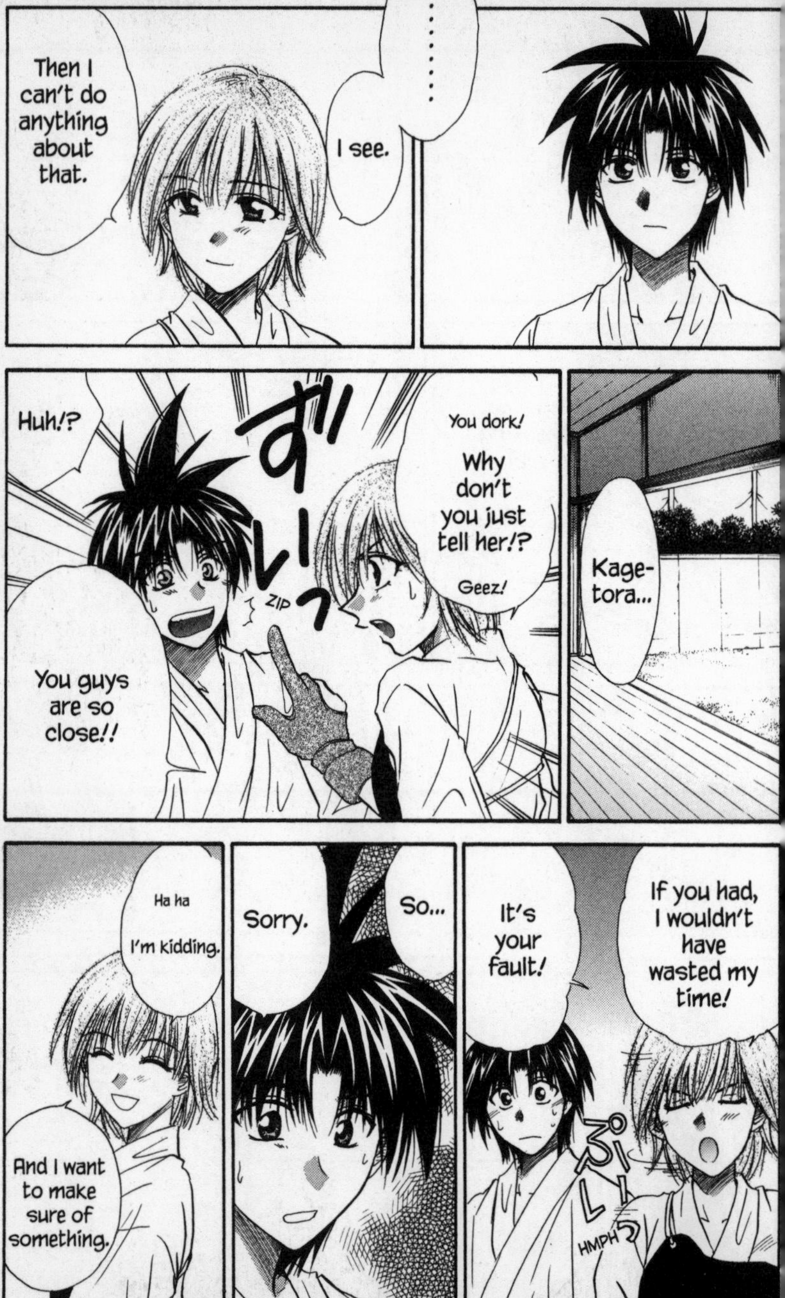
......
I see.
Then I can't do anything about that.
Kage-tora...
You dork!
Why don't you just tell her!?
Geez!
ずいっ
ZIP
Huh!?
You guys are so close!!
If you had, I wouldn't have wasted my time!
It's your fault!
ぷいっ
HMPH
So...
Sorry.
Ha ha
I'm kidding.
And I want to make sure of something.

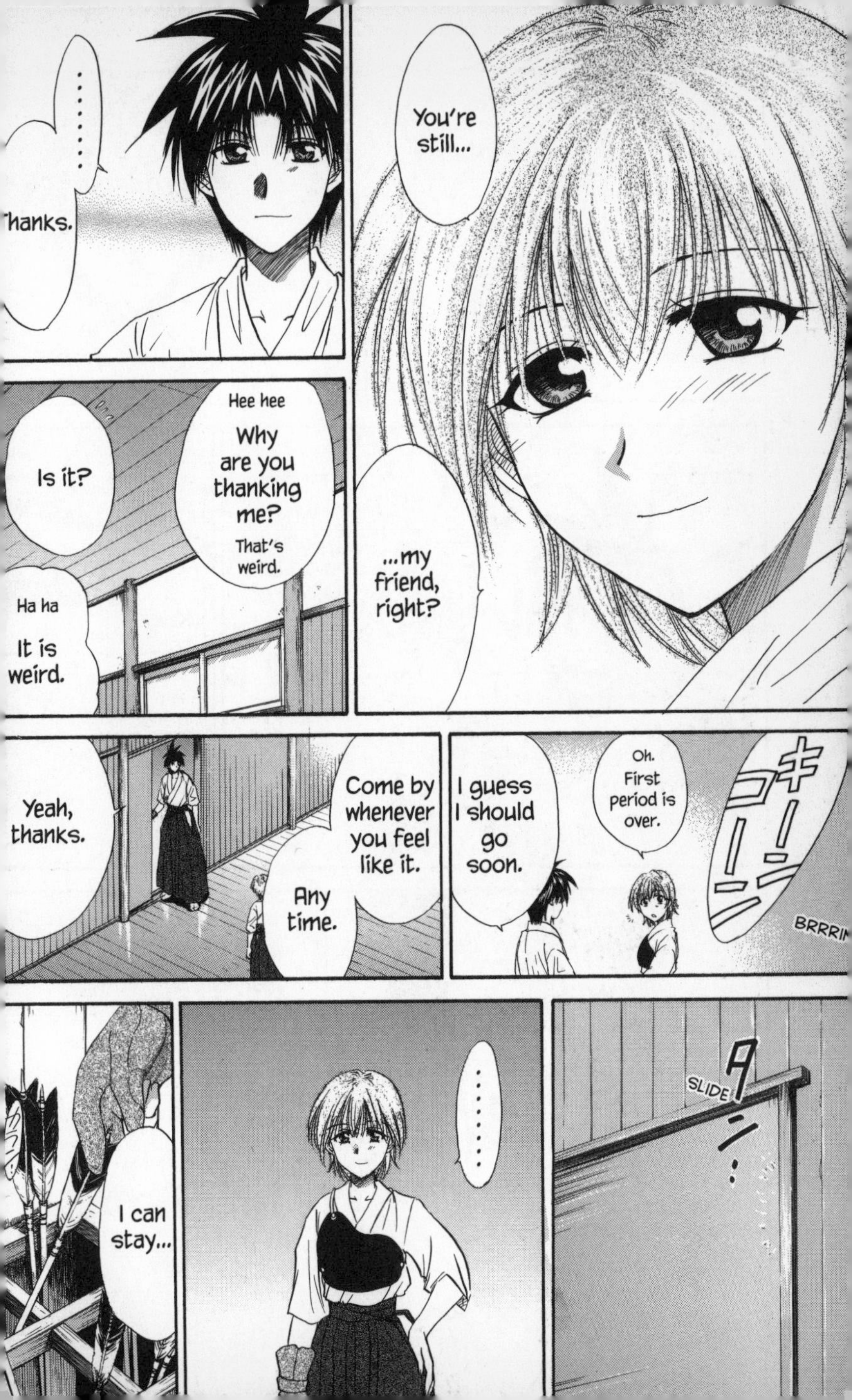
You're still...
...my friend, right?
......
Thanks.
Hee hee
Why are you thanking me?
That's weird.
Is it?
Ha ha
It is weird.
BRRRIN
Oh. First period is over.
I guess I should go soon.
Come by whenever you feel like it.
Any time.
Yeah, thanks.
SLIDE
......
I can stay...

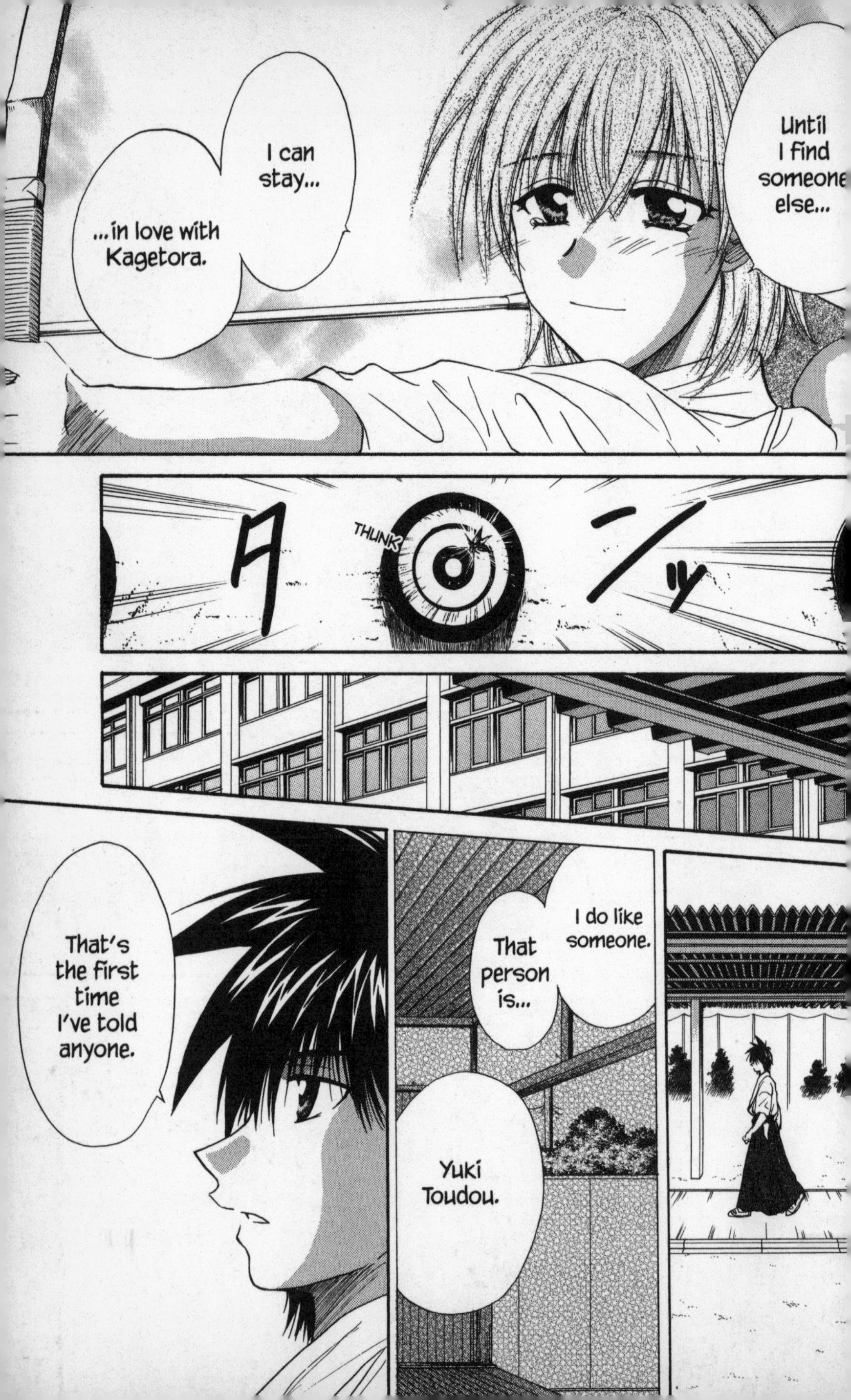
Until I find someone else...
I can stay...
...in love with Kagetora.
タンッ
THUNK
I do like someone.
That person is...
Yuki Toudou.
That's the first time I've told anyone.

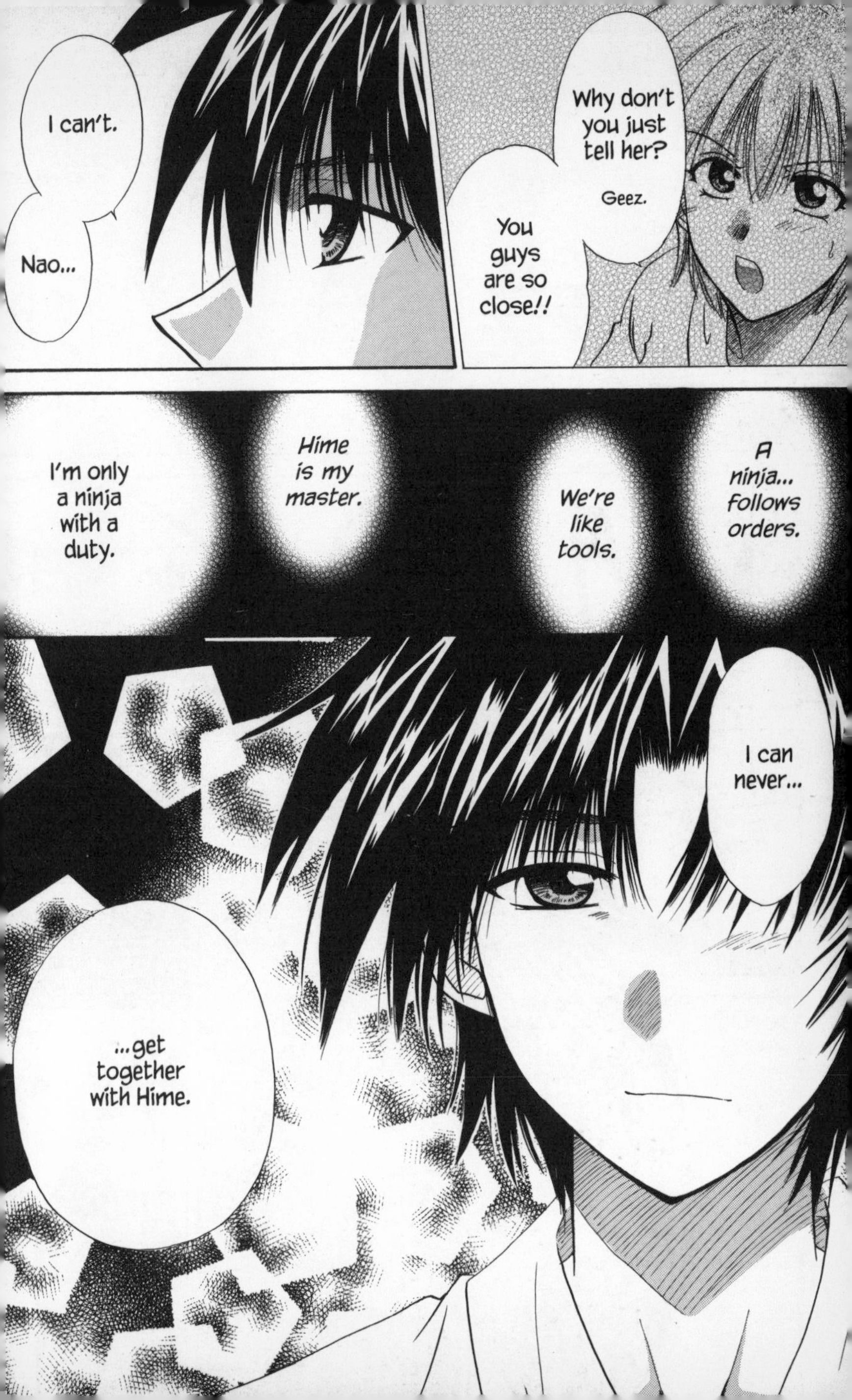
Why don't you just tell her?
Geez.
You guys are so close!!
I can't.
Nao...
A ninja... follows orders.
We're like tools.
Hime is my master.
I'm only a ninja with a duty.
I can never...
...get together with Hime.

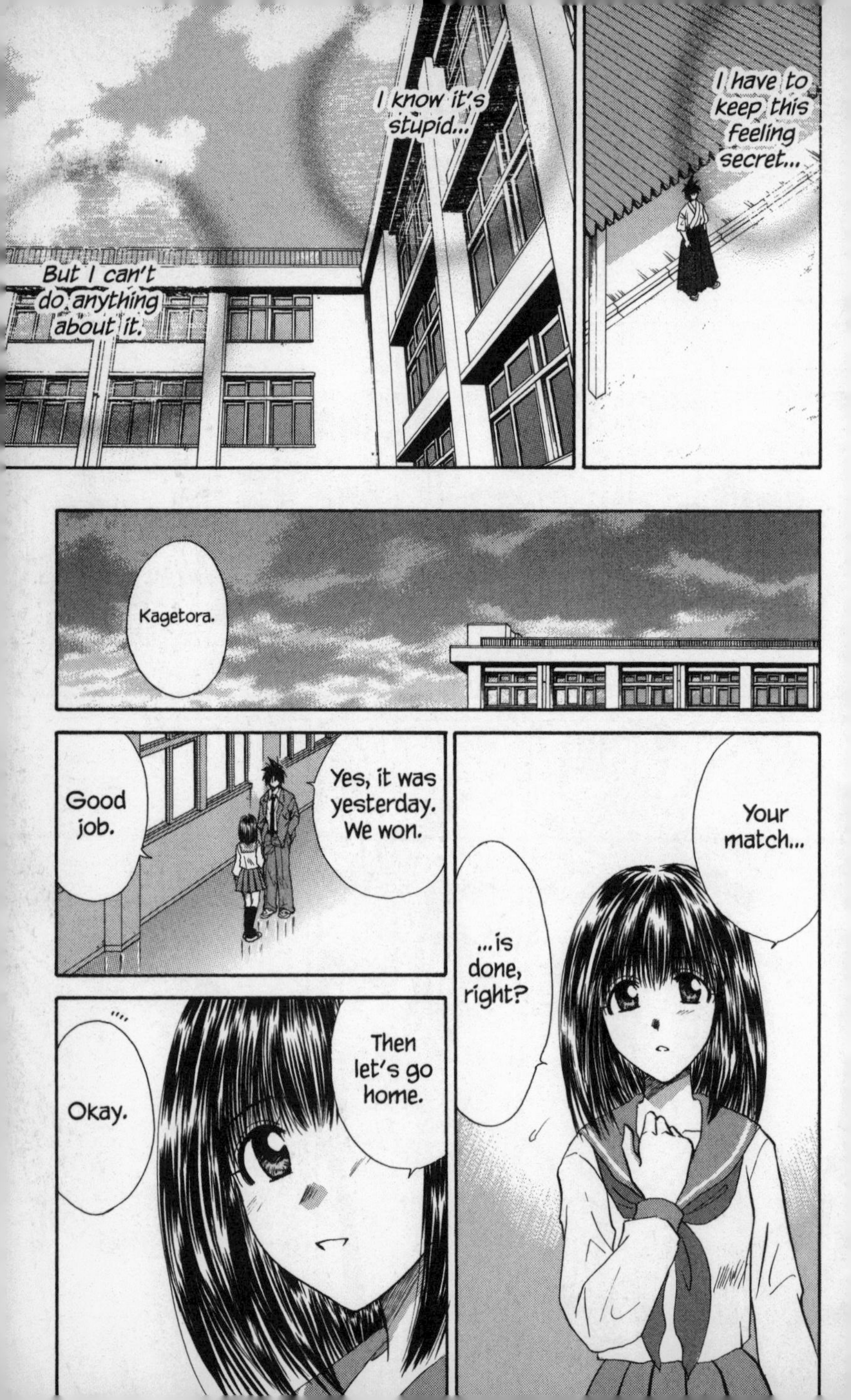
I have to keep this feeling secret...
I know it's stupid...
But I can't do anything about it.
Kagetora.
Your match...
...is done, right?
Yes, it was yesterday. We won.
Good job.
Then let's go home.
...
Okay.

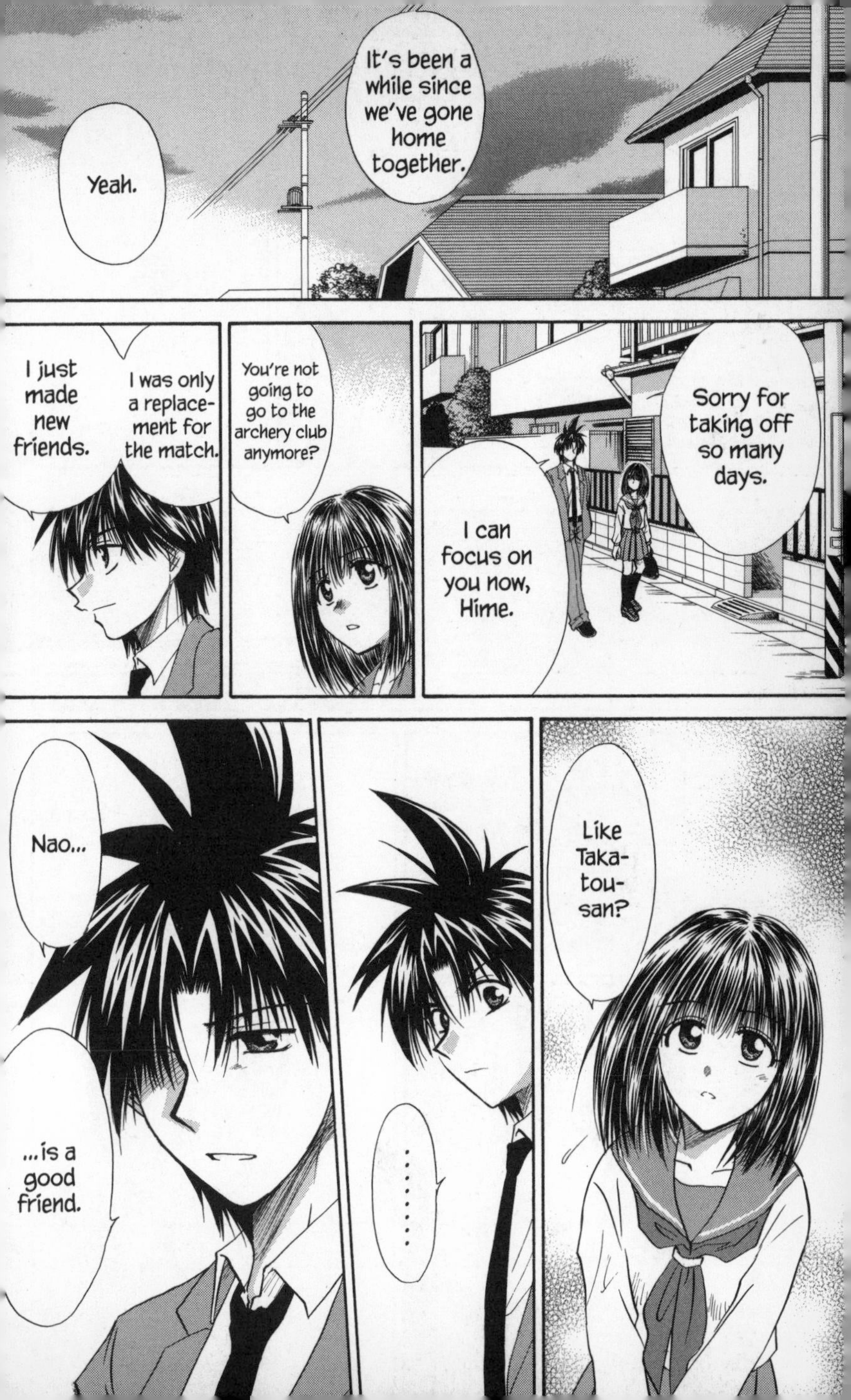
It's been a while since we've gone home together.
Yeah.
Sorry for taking off so many days.
I can focus on you now, Hime.
You're not going to go to the archery club anymore?
I was only a replacement for the match.
I just made new friends.
Like Taka-tou-san?
......
Nao...
...is a good friend.

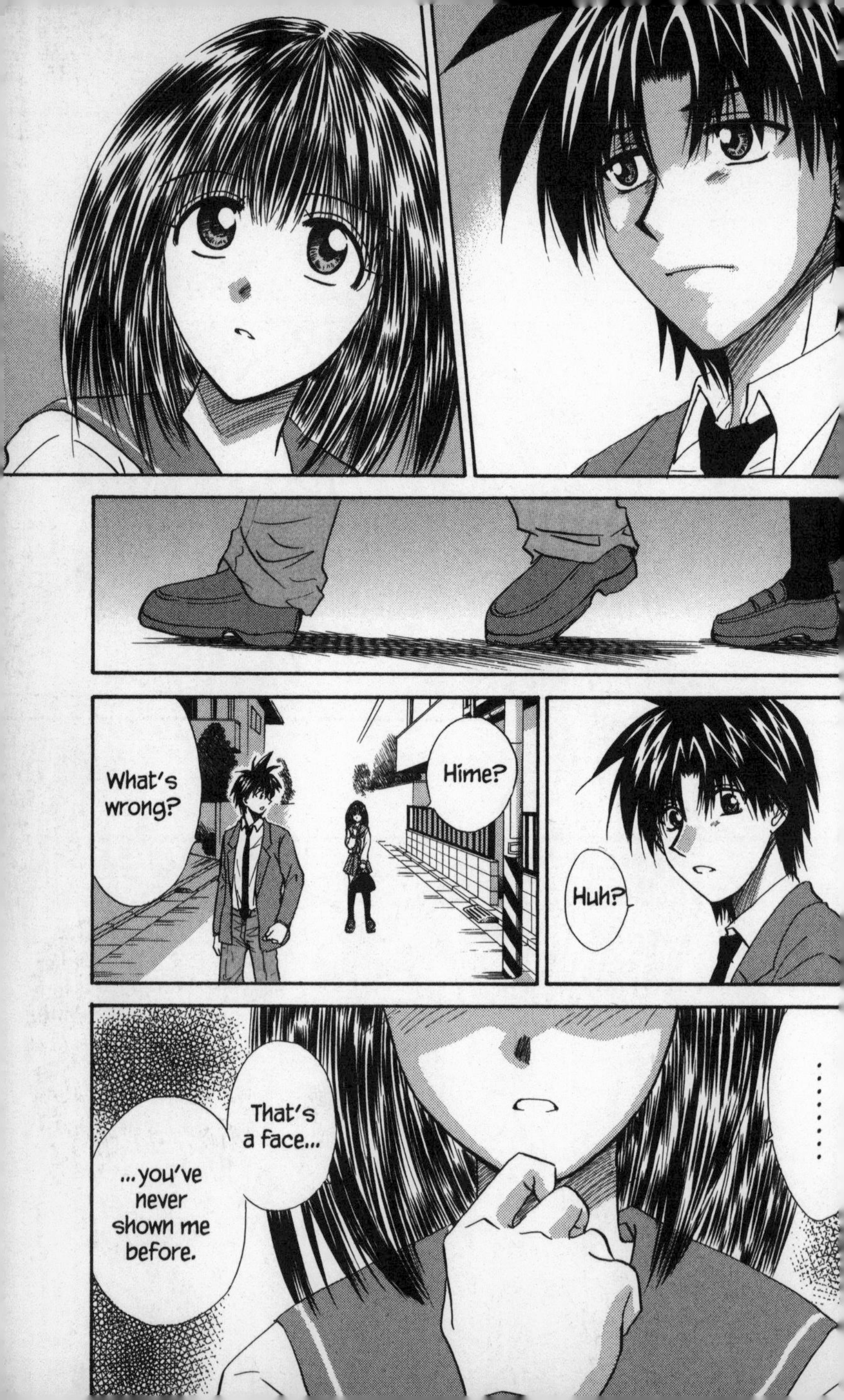
Huh?
Hime?
What's wrong?
......
That's a face...
...you've never shown me before.

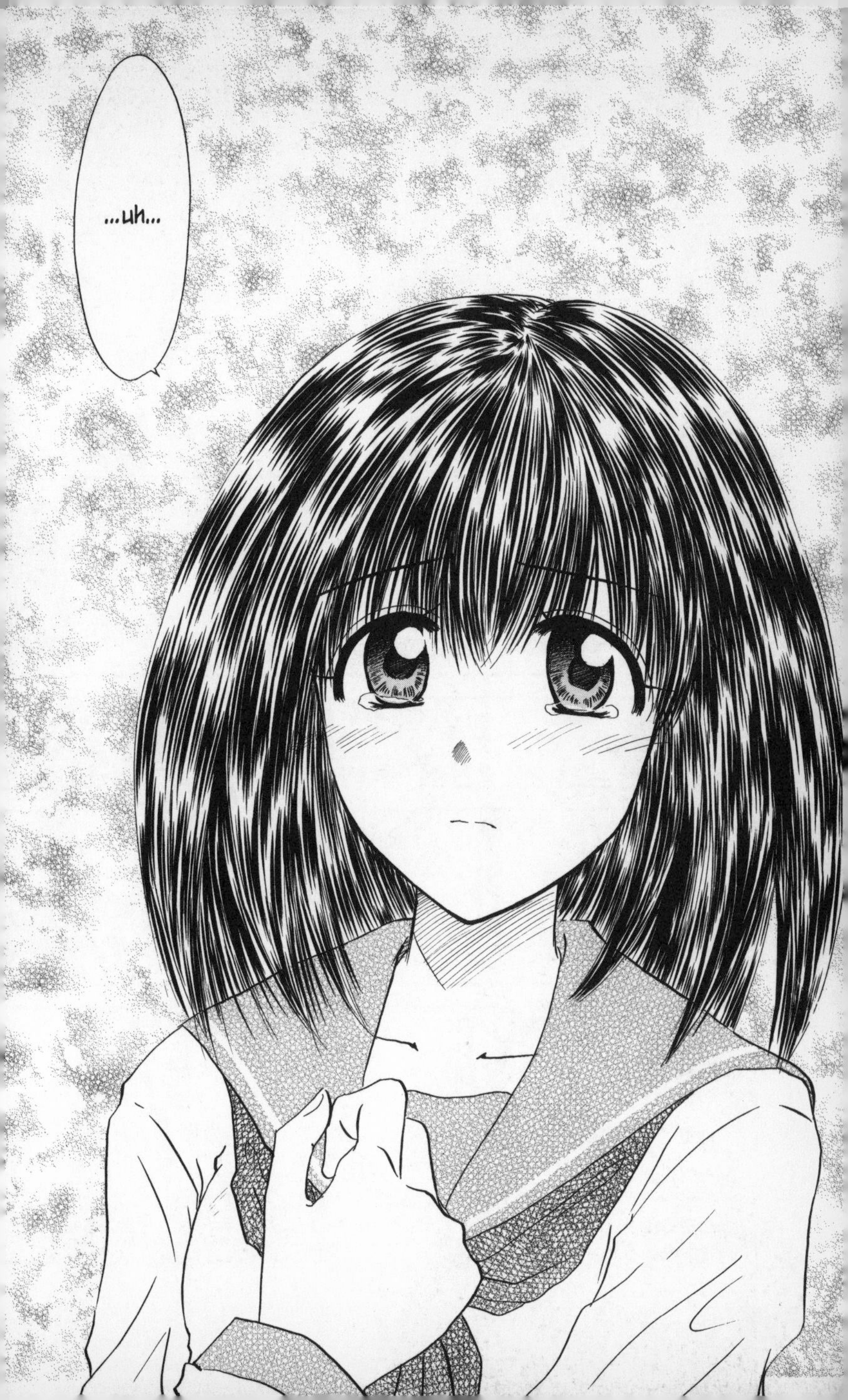
...uh...

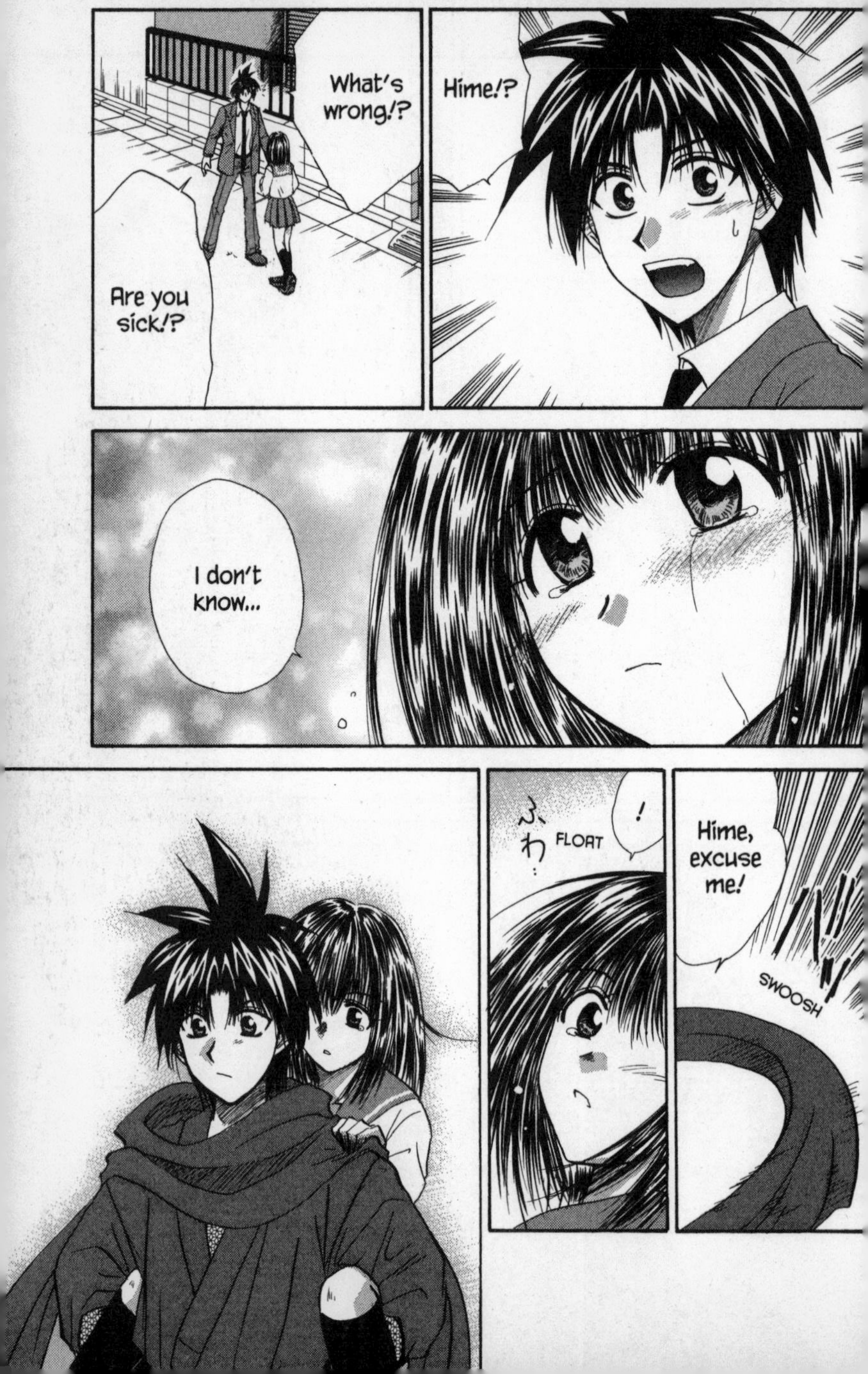
Hime!?
What's wrong!?
Are you sick!?
I don't know...
Hime, excuse me!
SWOOSH
!
ふわ
FLOAT

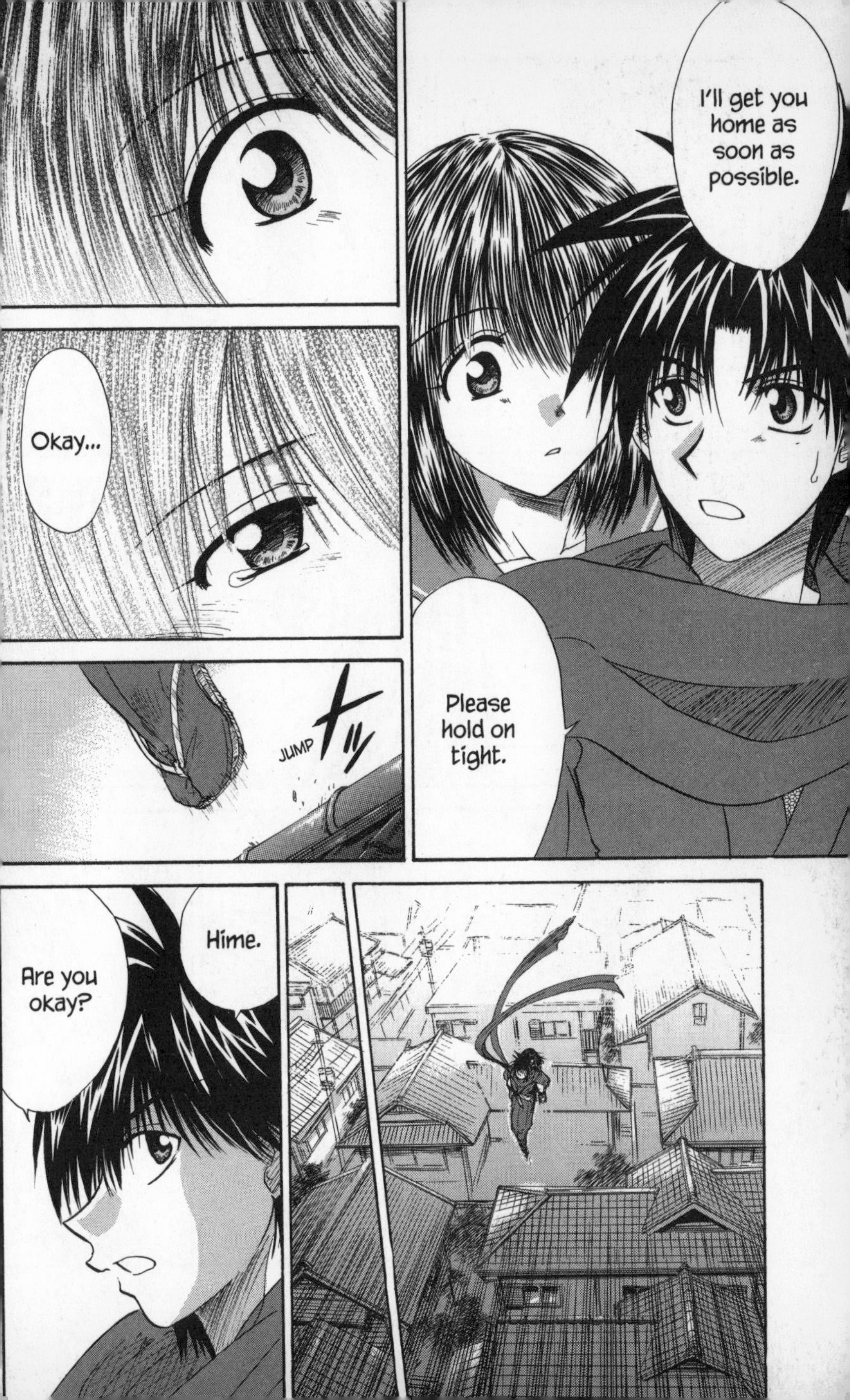
I'll get you home as soon as possible.
Please hold on tight.
Okay...
JUMP
Hime.
Are you okay?

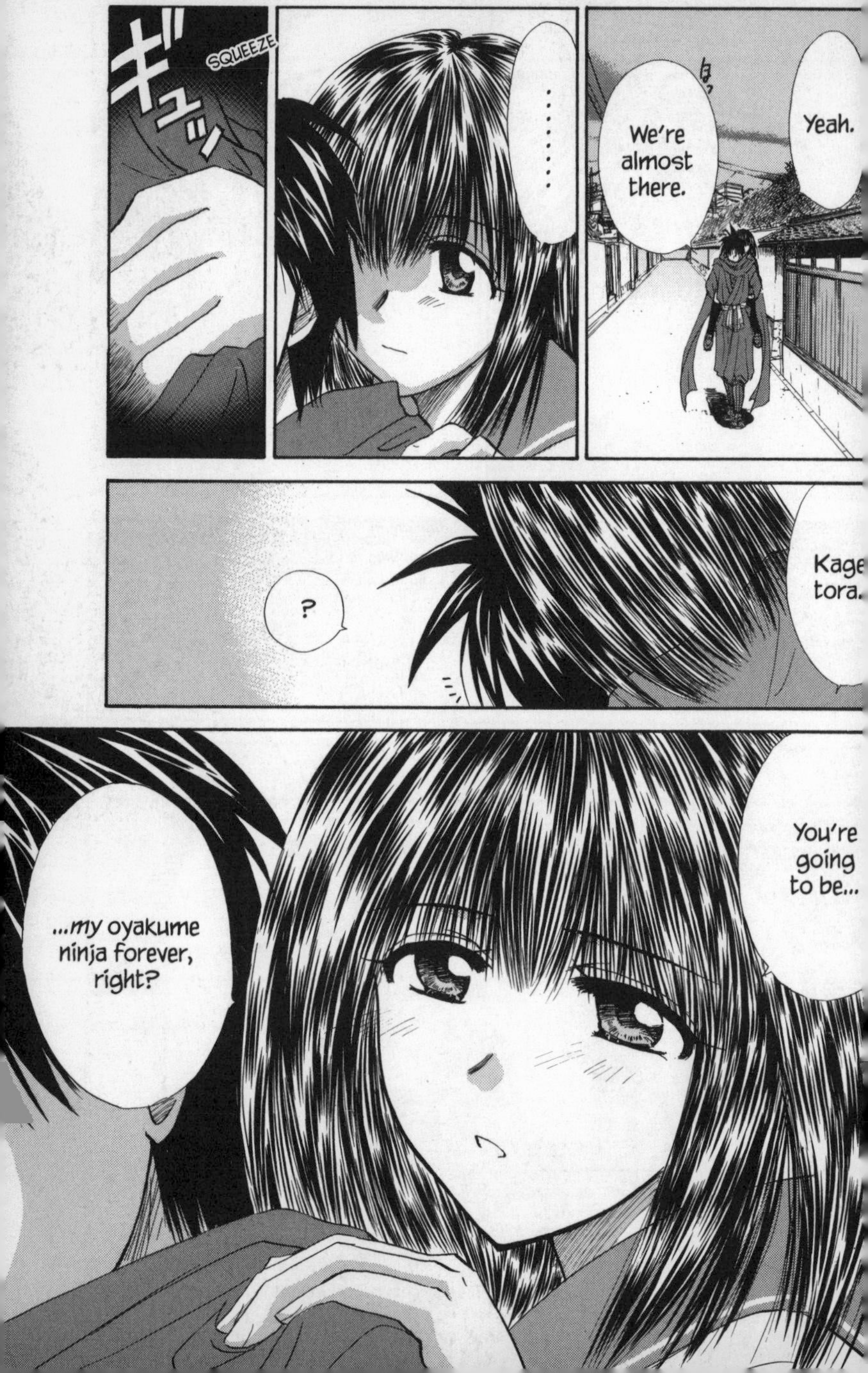
Yeah.
We're almost there.
......
ギュッ
SQUEEZE
Kage tora.
?
You're going to be...
...my oyakume ninja forever, right?

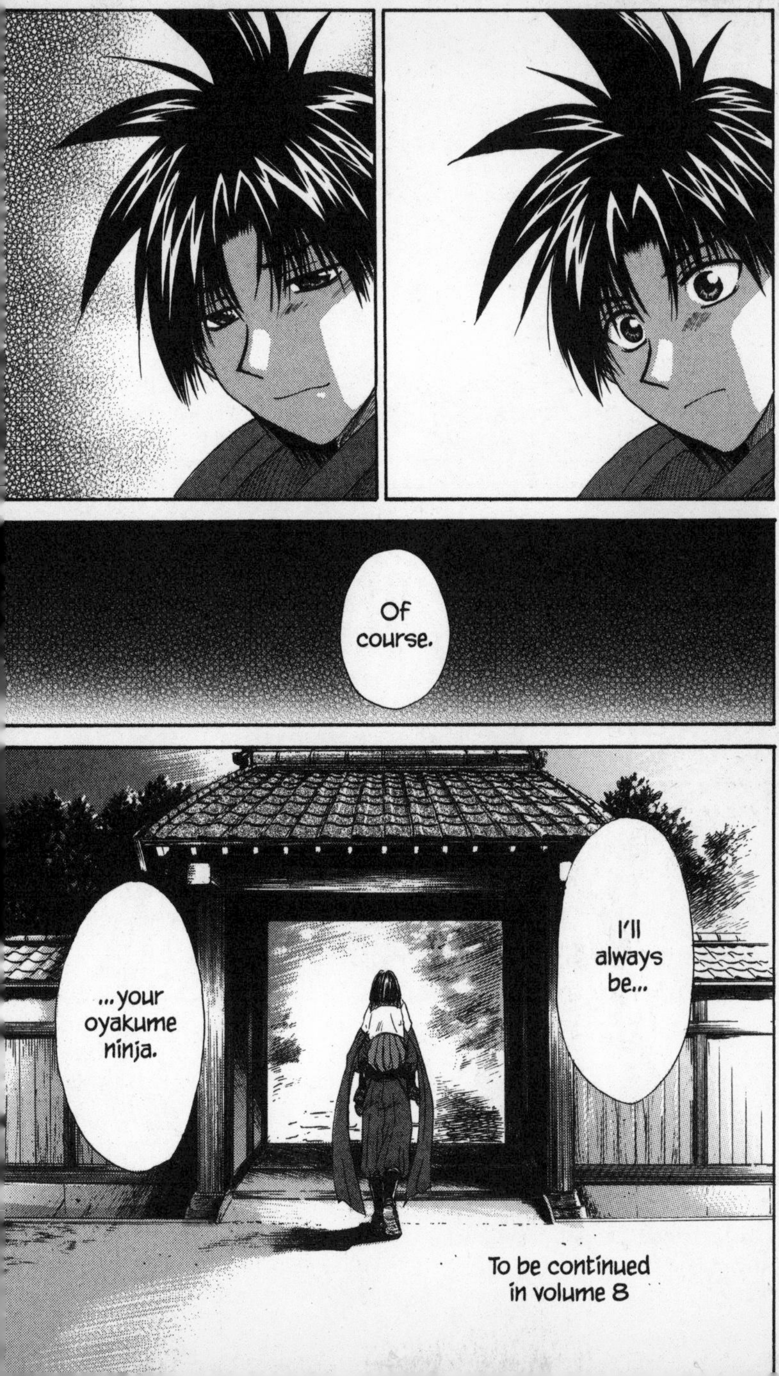
Of course.
I'll always be...
...your oyakume ninja.
To be continued in volume 8

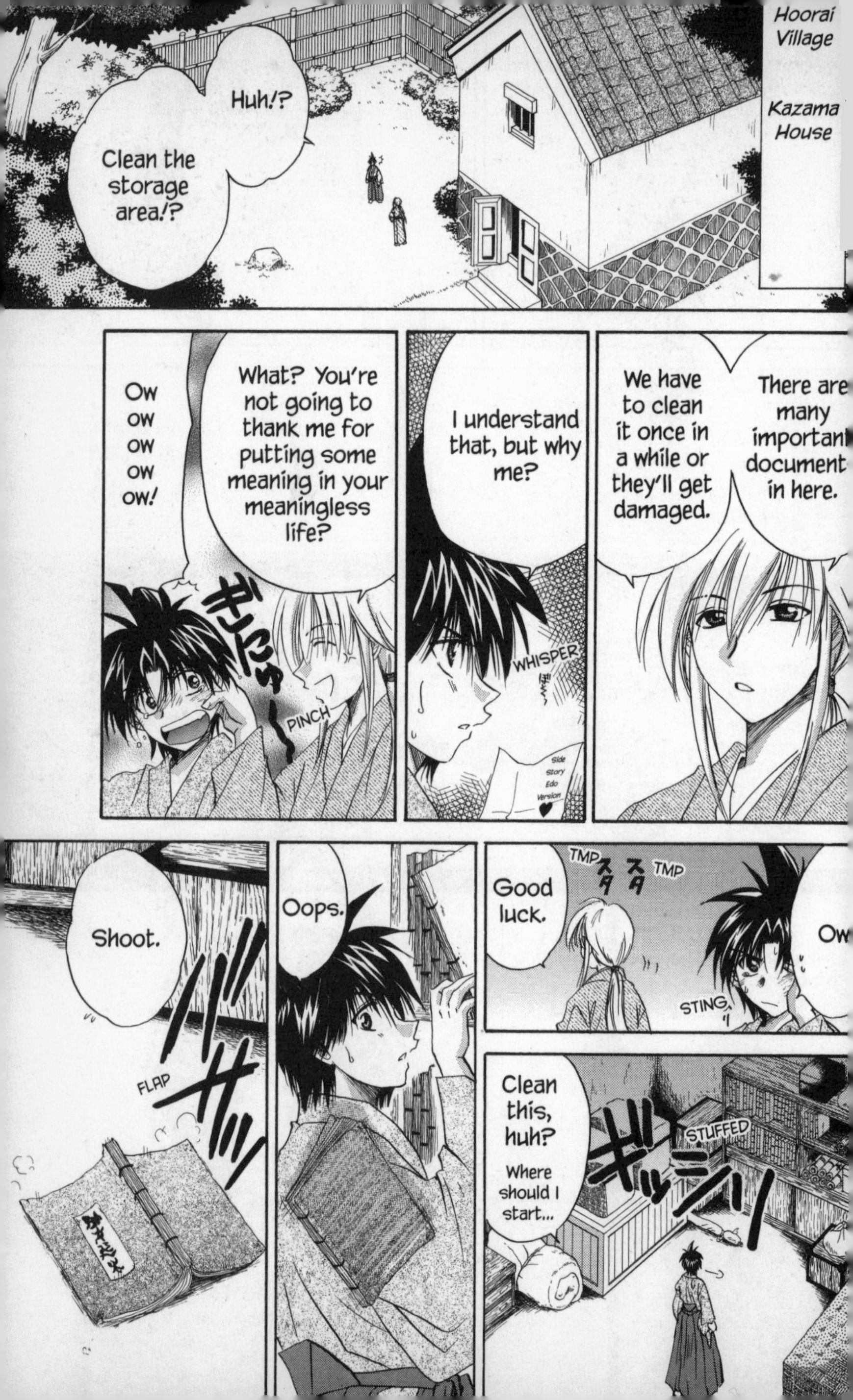

Hoorai Village
Kazama House
Huh!?
Clean the storage area!?
There are many importan document in here.
We have to clean it once in a while or they'll get damaged.
I understand that, but why me?
WHISPER
Side Story Edo Version
What? You're not going to thank me for putting some meaning in your meaningless life?
Ow ow ow ow ow!
PINCH
Ow
TMP TMP
Good luck.
STING
Clean this, huh?
Where should I start...
STUFFED
Oops.
Shoot.
FLAP

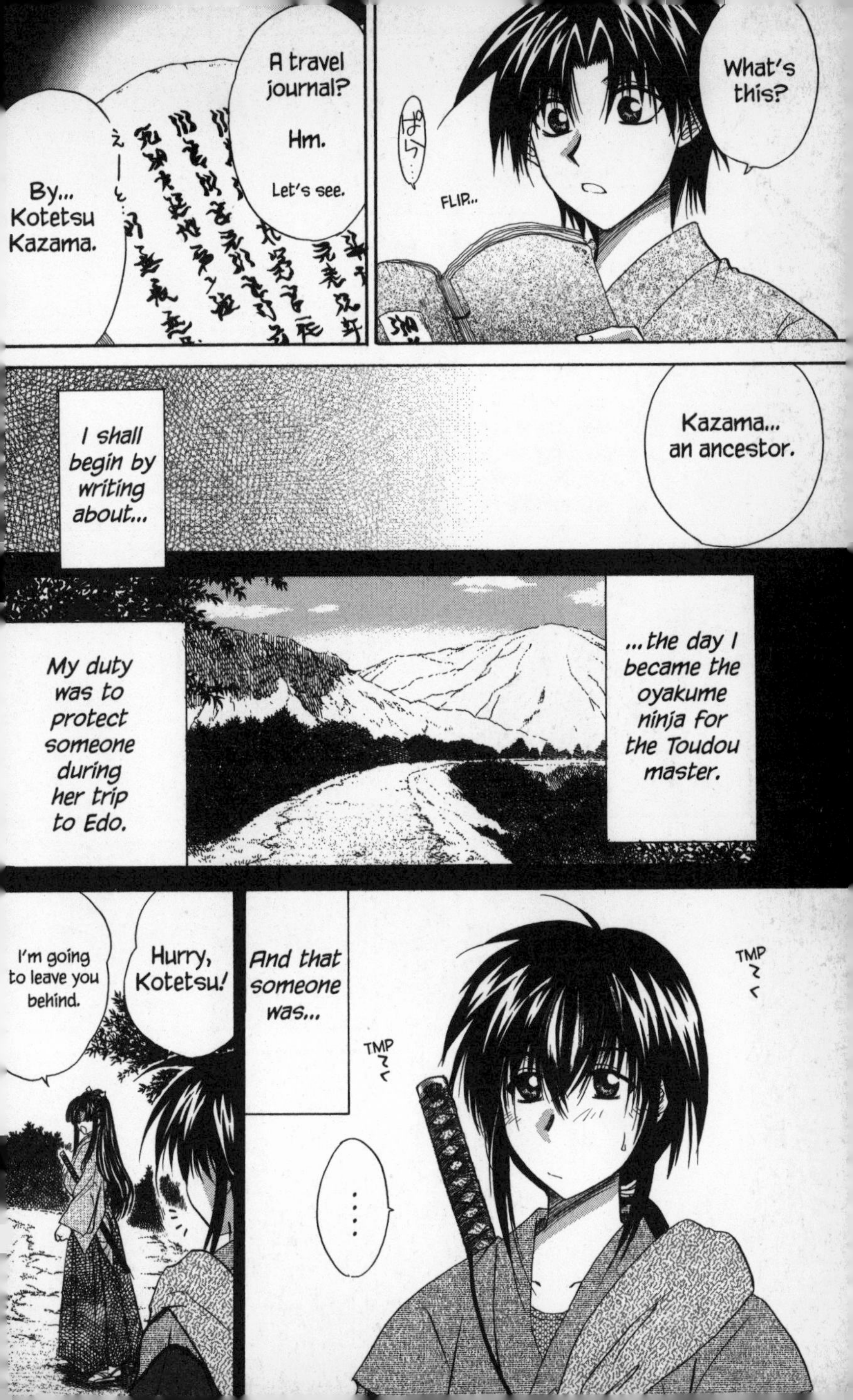
What's this?
ぱら…
FLIP...
A travel journal?
Hm.
Let's see.
えーと…
By... Kotetsu Kazama.
Kazama... an ancestor.
I shall begin by writing about...
...the day I became the oyakume ninja for the Toudou master.
My duty was to protect someone during her trip to Edo.
TMP
TMP
....
And that someone was...
Hurry, Kotetsu!
I'm going to leave you behind.

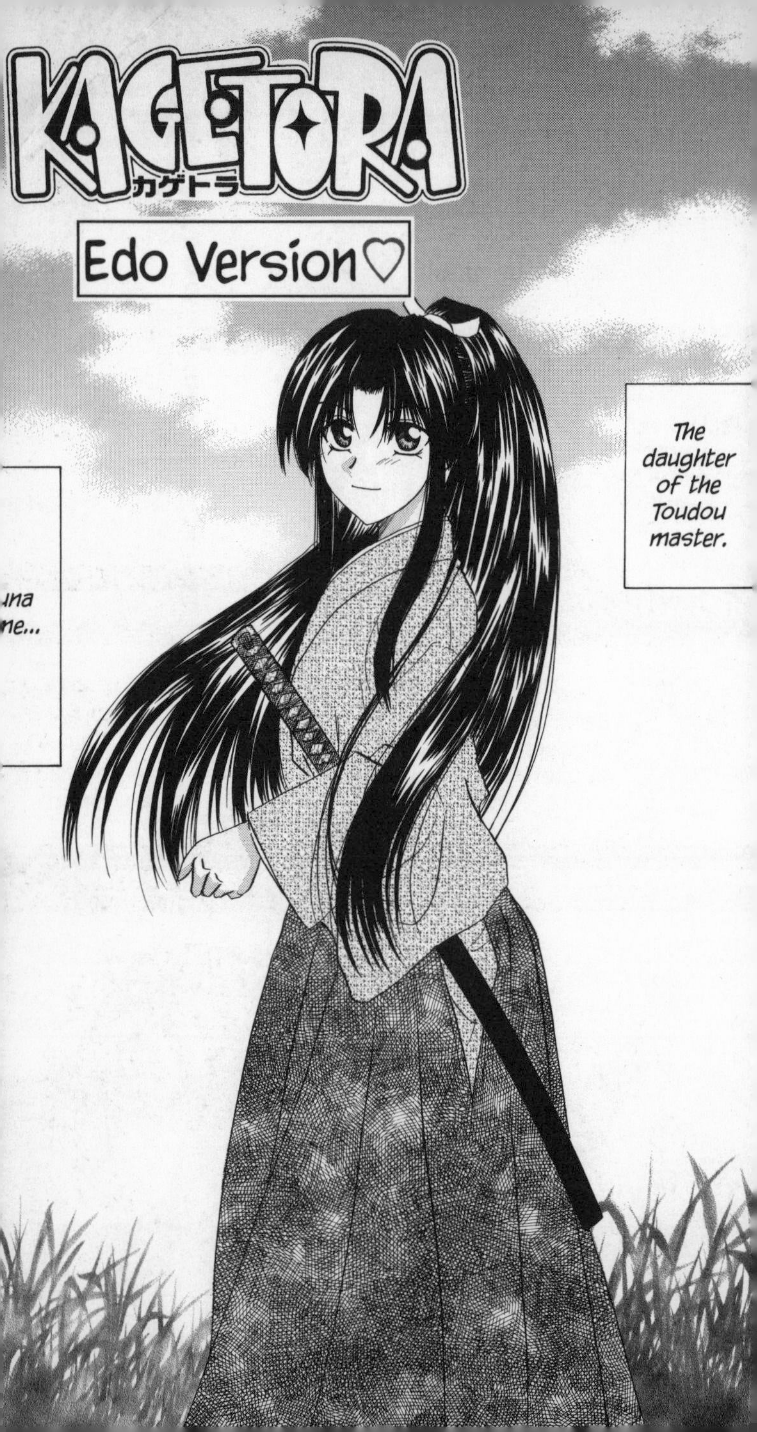
KAGETORA
カゲトラ
Edo Version♡
The daughter of the Toudou master.

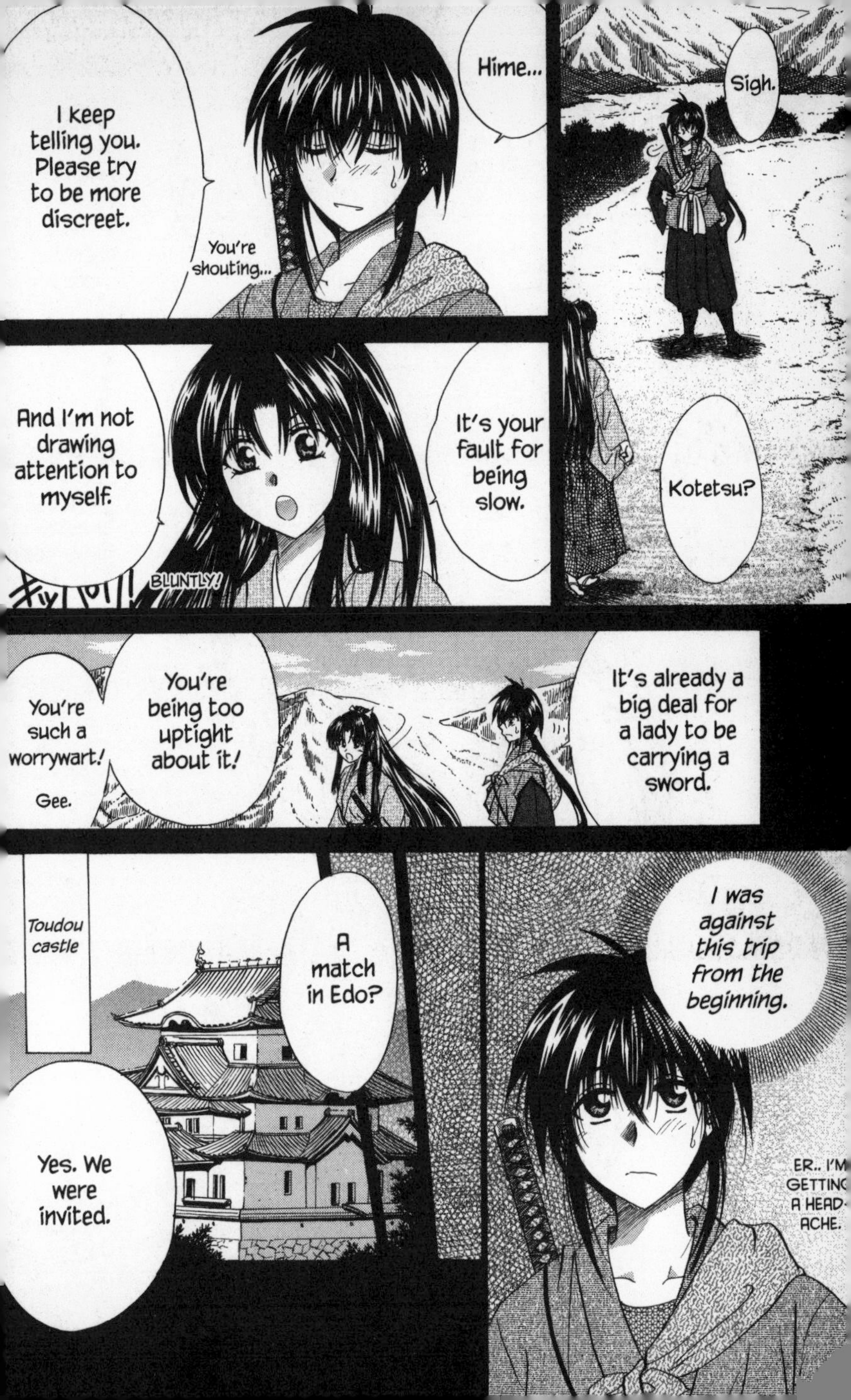
Sigh.
Kotetsu?
Hime...
I keep telling you. Please try to be more discreet.
You're shouting...
It's your fault for being slow.
And I'm not drawing attention to myself.
BLUNTLY!
It's already a big deal for a lady to be carrying a sword.
You're being too uptight about it!
You're such a worrywart!
Gee.
I was against this trip from the beginning.
ER.. I'M GETTING A HEAD-ACHE.
Toudou castle
A match in Edo?
Yes. We were invited.

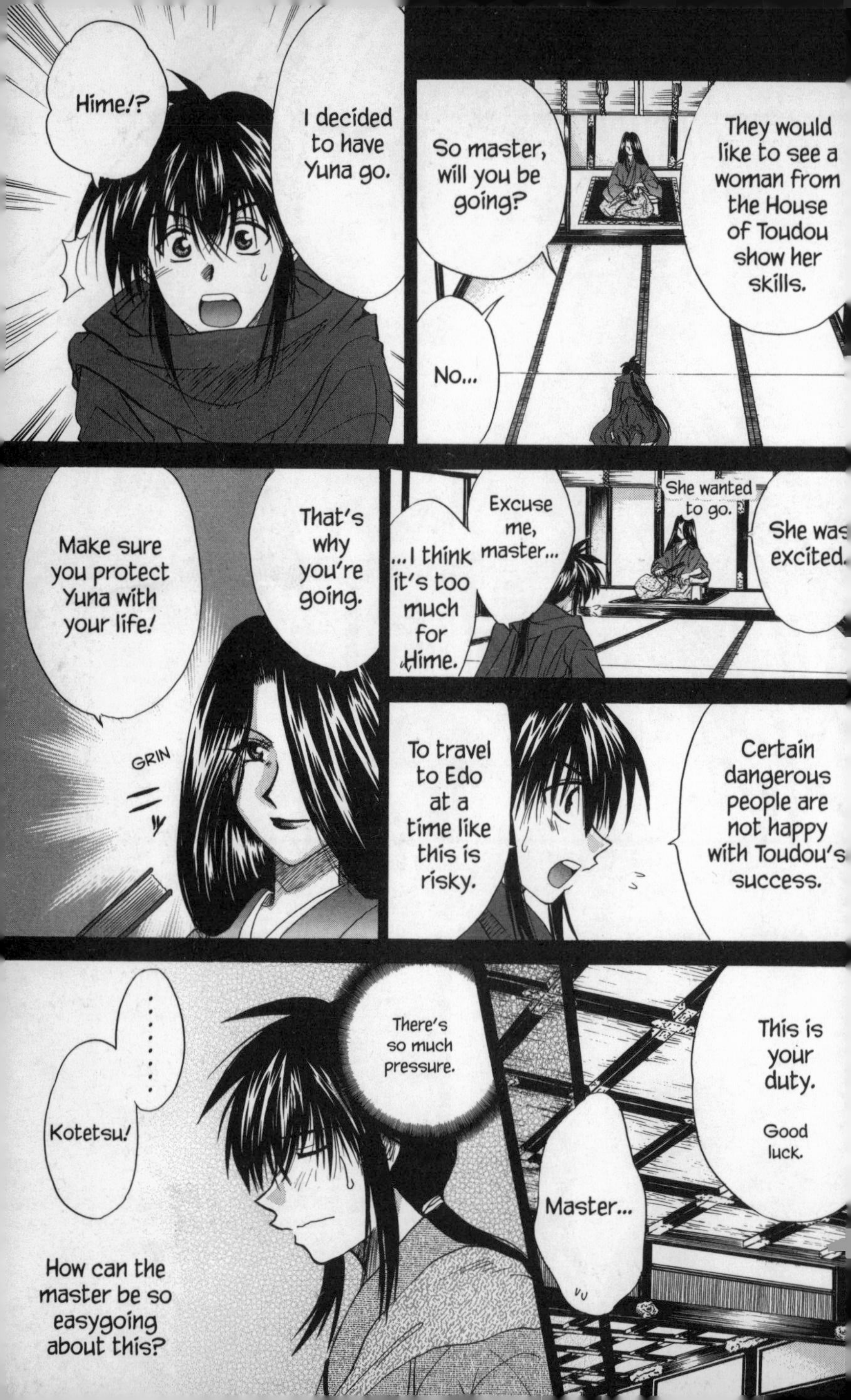
They would like to see a woman from the House of Toudou show her skills.
So master, will you be going?
No...
I decided to have Yuna go.
Hime!?
She was excited.
She wanted to go.
Excuse me, master...
...I think it's too much for Hime.
Certain dangerous people are not happy with Toudou's success.
To travel to Edo at a time like this is risky.
That's why you're going.
Make sure you protect Yuna with your life!
GRIN
This is your duty.
Good luck.
Master...
There's so much pressure.
......
Kotetsu!
How can the master be so easygoing about this?

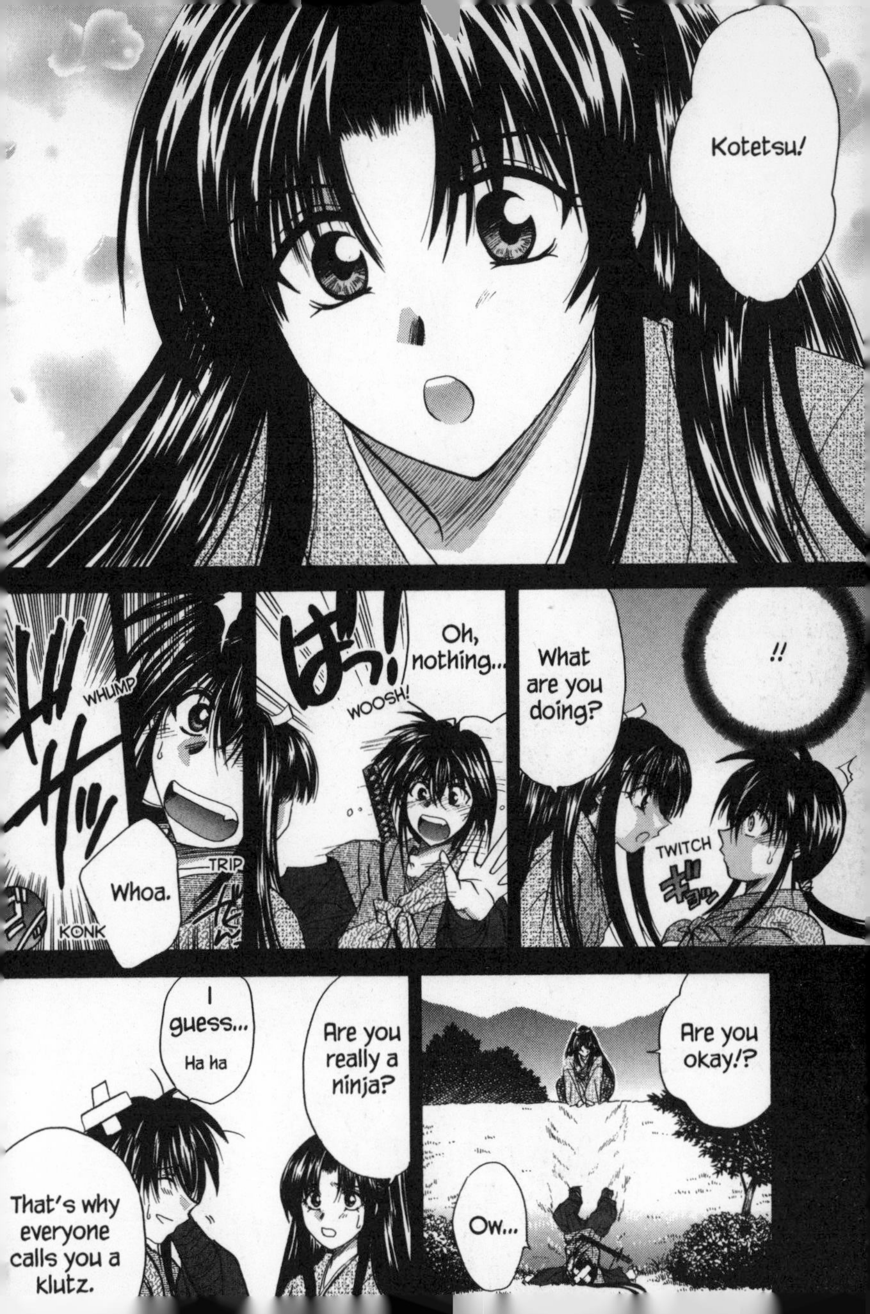
Kotetsu!
!!
What are you doing?
TWITCH
Oh, nothing...
ばっ!
WOOSH!
WHUMP
Whoa.
TRIP
KONK
Are you okay!?
Ow...
Are you really a ninja?
I guess...
Ha ha
That's why everyone calls you a klutz.

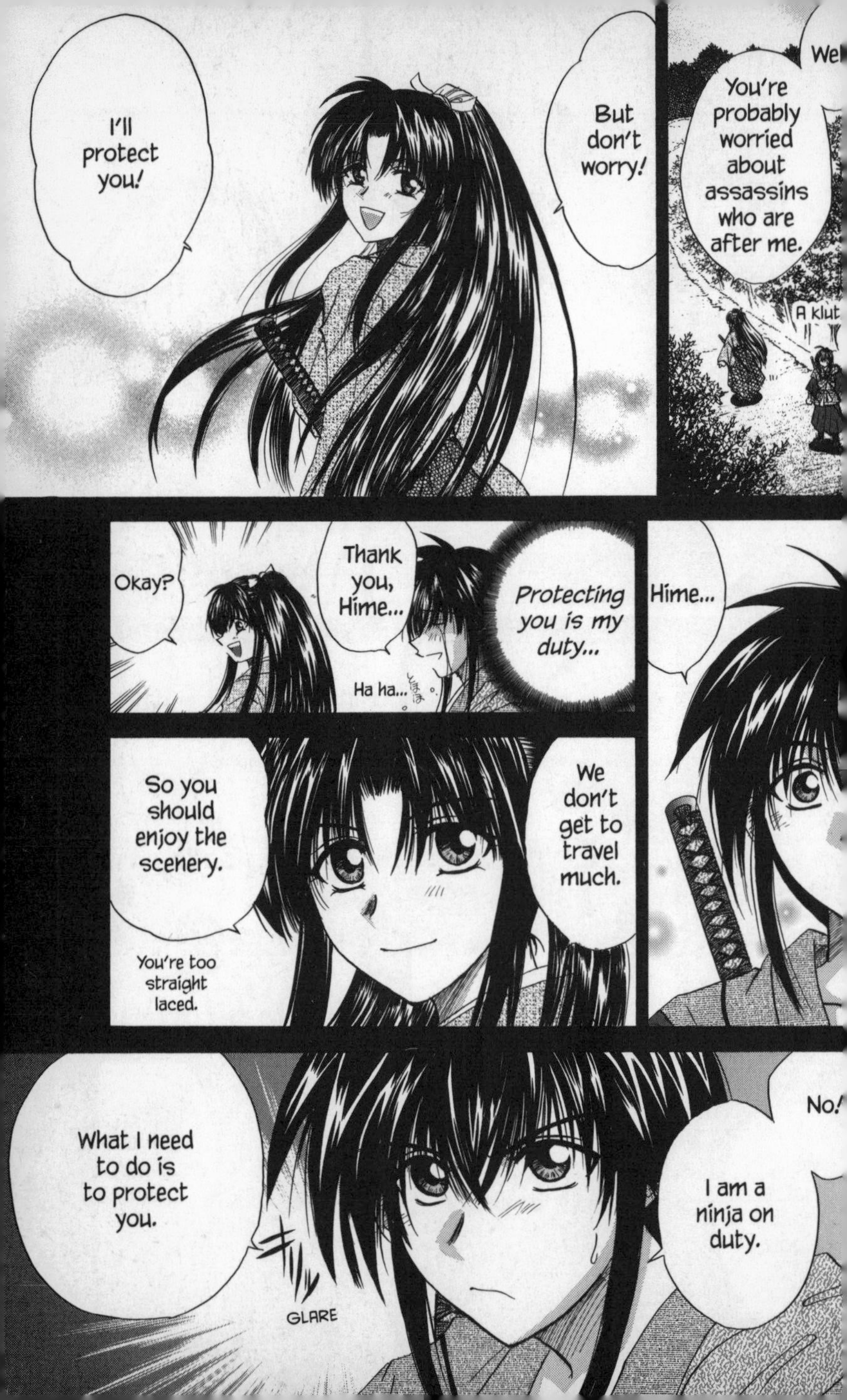

We
You're probably worried about assassins who are after me.
A klut
But don't worry!
I'll protect you!
Hime...
Protecting you is my duty...
Thank you, Hime...
Ha ha...
Okay?
We don't get to travel much.
So you should enjoy the scenery.
You're too straight laced.
No!
I am a ninja on duty.
What I need to do is to protect you.
GLARE

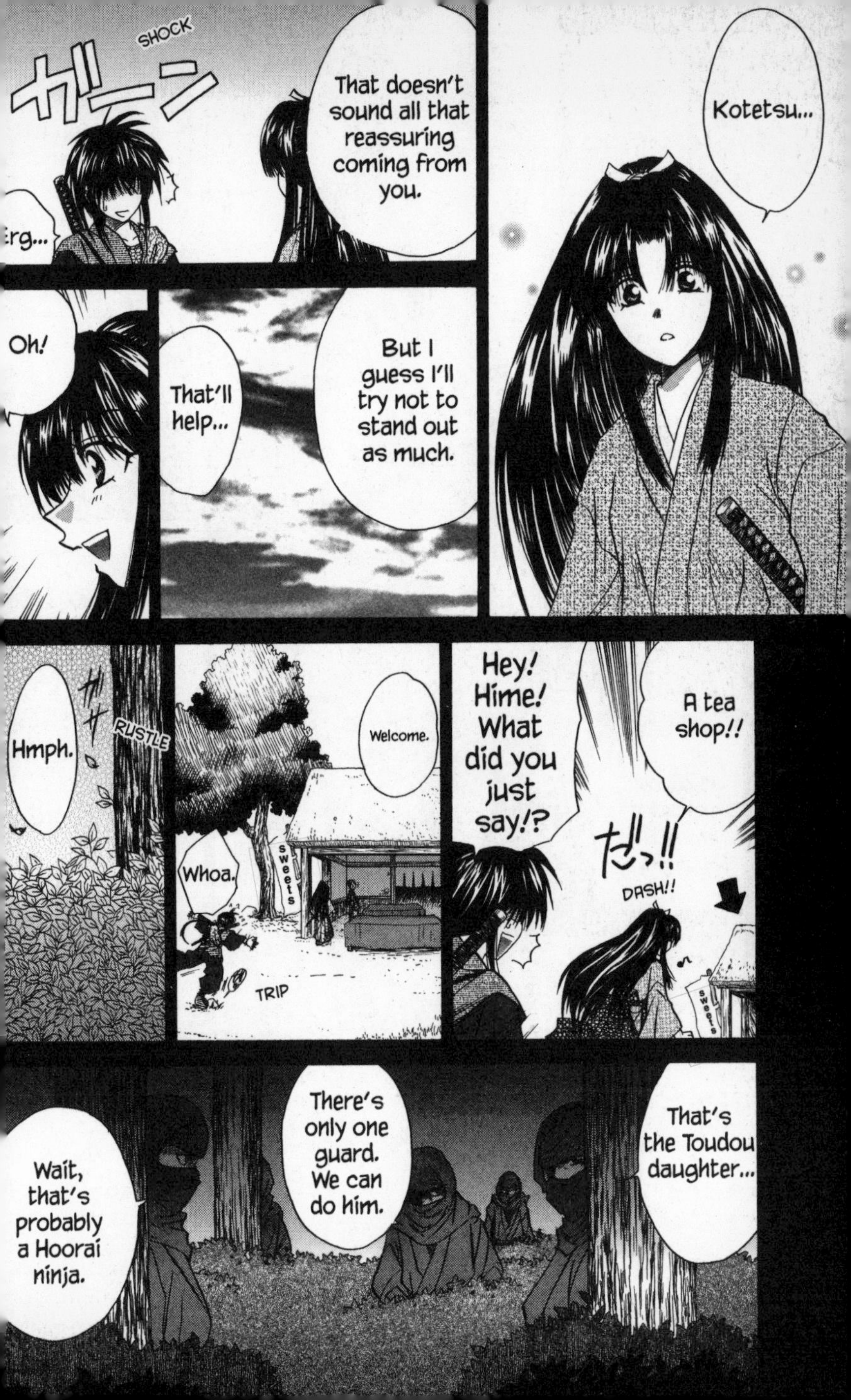
Kotetsu...
That doesn't sound all that reassuring coming from you.
ガーン
SHOCK
rg...
But I guess I'll try not to stand out as much.
That'll help...
Oh!
A tea shop!!
Hey! Hime! What did you just say!?
だっ!!
DASH!!
sweets
Welcome.
sweets
Whoa.
TRIP
Hmph.
ガサ
RUSTLE
That's the Toudou daughter...
There's only one guard. We can do him.
Wait, that's probably a Hoorai ninja.

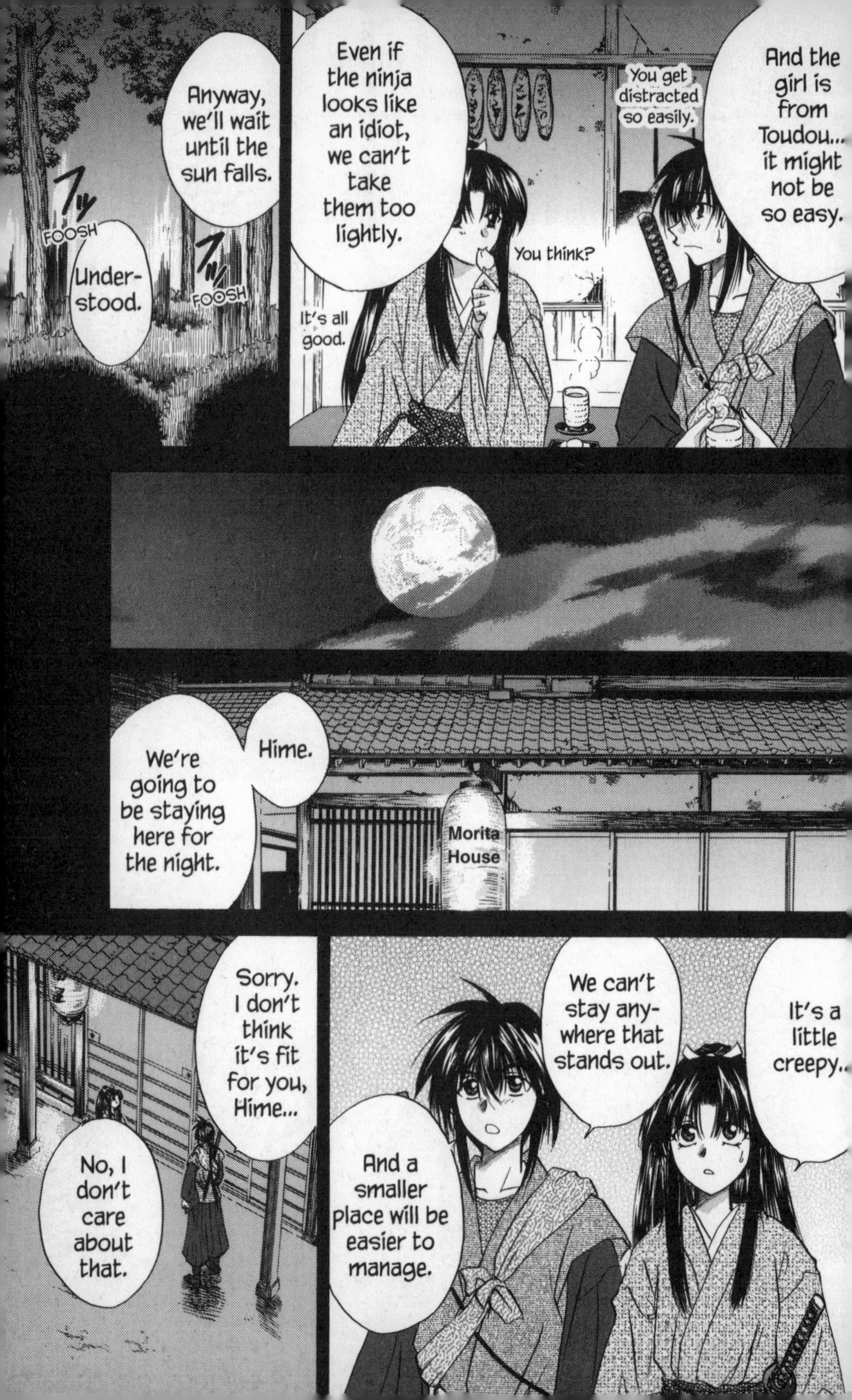
And the girl is from Toudou... it might not be so easy.
You get distracted so easily.
Even if the ninja looks like an idiot, we can't take them too lightly.
You think?
It's all good.
Anyway, we'll wait until the sun falls.
FOOSH
FOOSH
Under-stood.
Hime.
We're going to be staying here for the night.
Morita House
It's a little creepy...
We can't stay any-where that stands out.
And a smaller place will be easier to manage.
Sorry. I don't think it's fit for you, Hime...
No, I don't care about that.

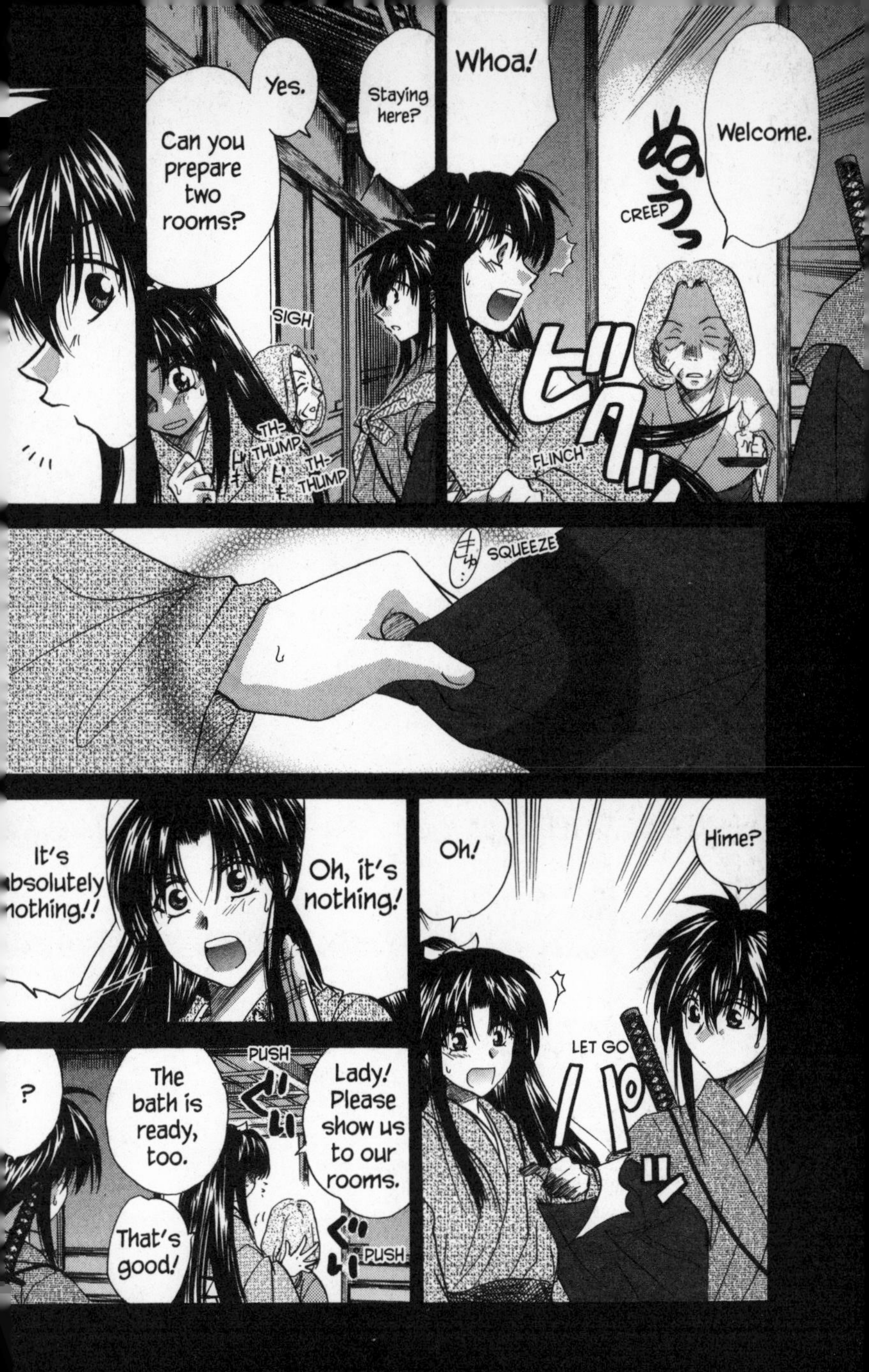
Welcome.
CREEP
FLINCH
Whoa!
Staying here?
Yes.
Can you prepare two rooms?
SIGH
TH-THUMP
TH-THUMP
SQUEEZE
Hime?
Oh!
LET GO
Oh, it's nothing!
It's bsolutely nothing!!
Lady! Please show us to our rooms.
PUSH
The bath is ready, too.
PUSH
That's good!
?

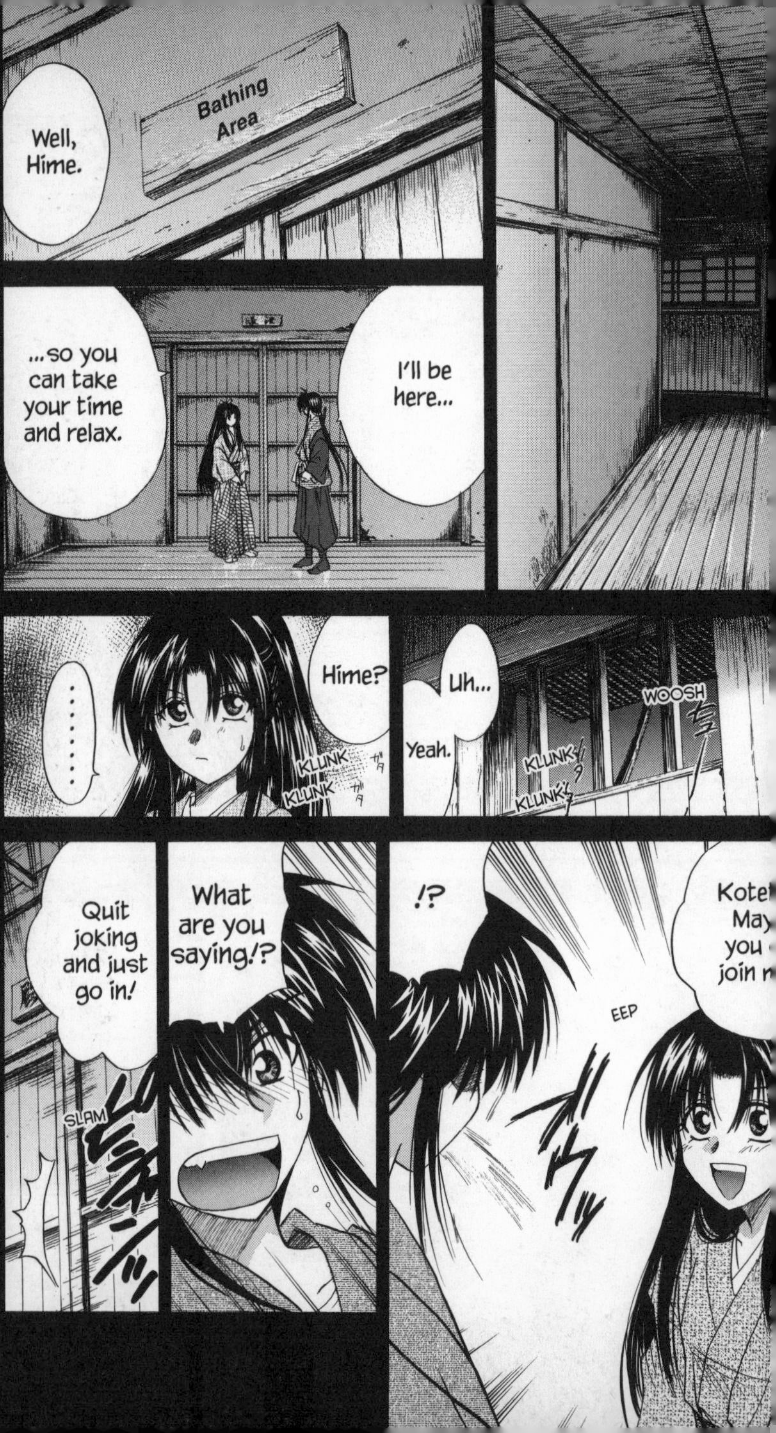
Bathing Area
Well, Hime.
I'll be here...
...so you can take your time and relax.
Uh...
Yeah.
WOOSH
KLUNK
KLUNK
Hime?
......
KLUNK
KLUNK
Kote
May
you
join
EEP
!?
What are you saying!?
Quit joking and just go in!
SLAM

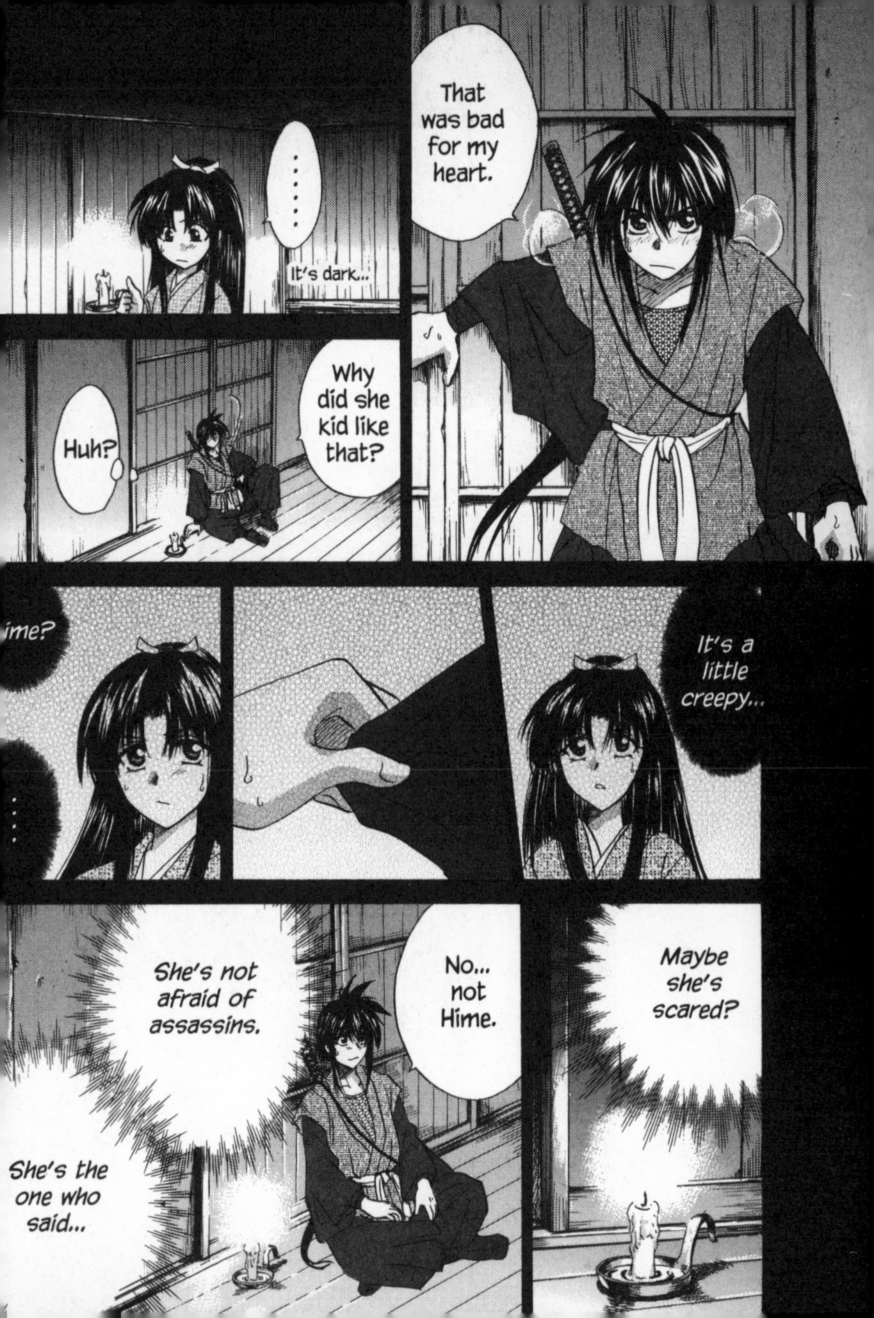
That was bad for my heart.
......
It's dark...
Why did she kid like that?
Huh?
It's a little creepy...
ime?
....
Maybe she's scared?
No... not Hime.
She's not afraid of assassins.
She's the one who said...

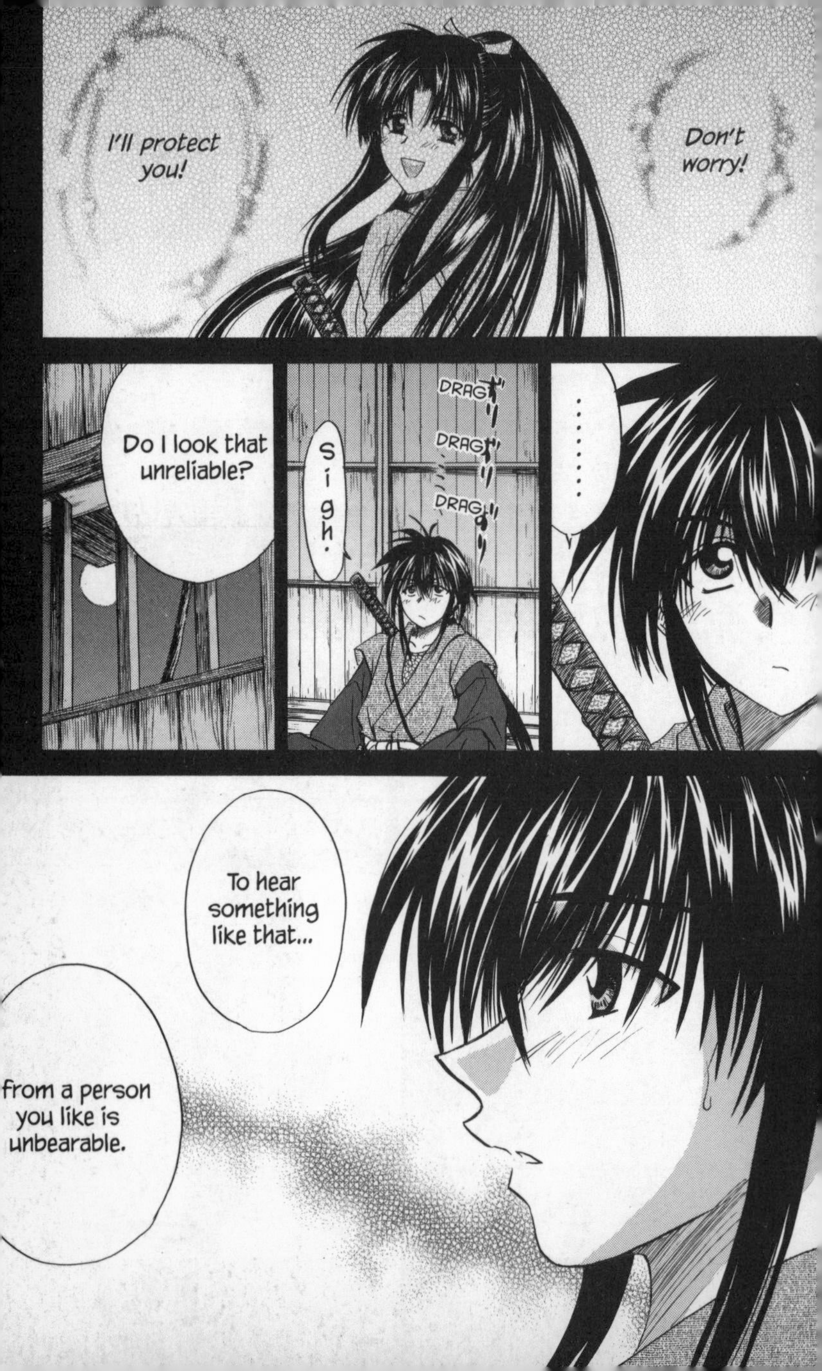
Don't worry!
I'll protect you!
......
DRAG
DRAG
DRAG
Sigh.
Do I look that unreliable?
To hear something like that...
from a person you like is unbearable.

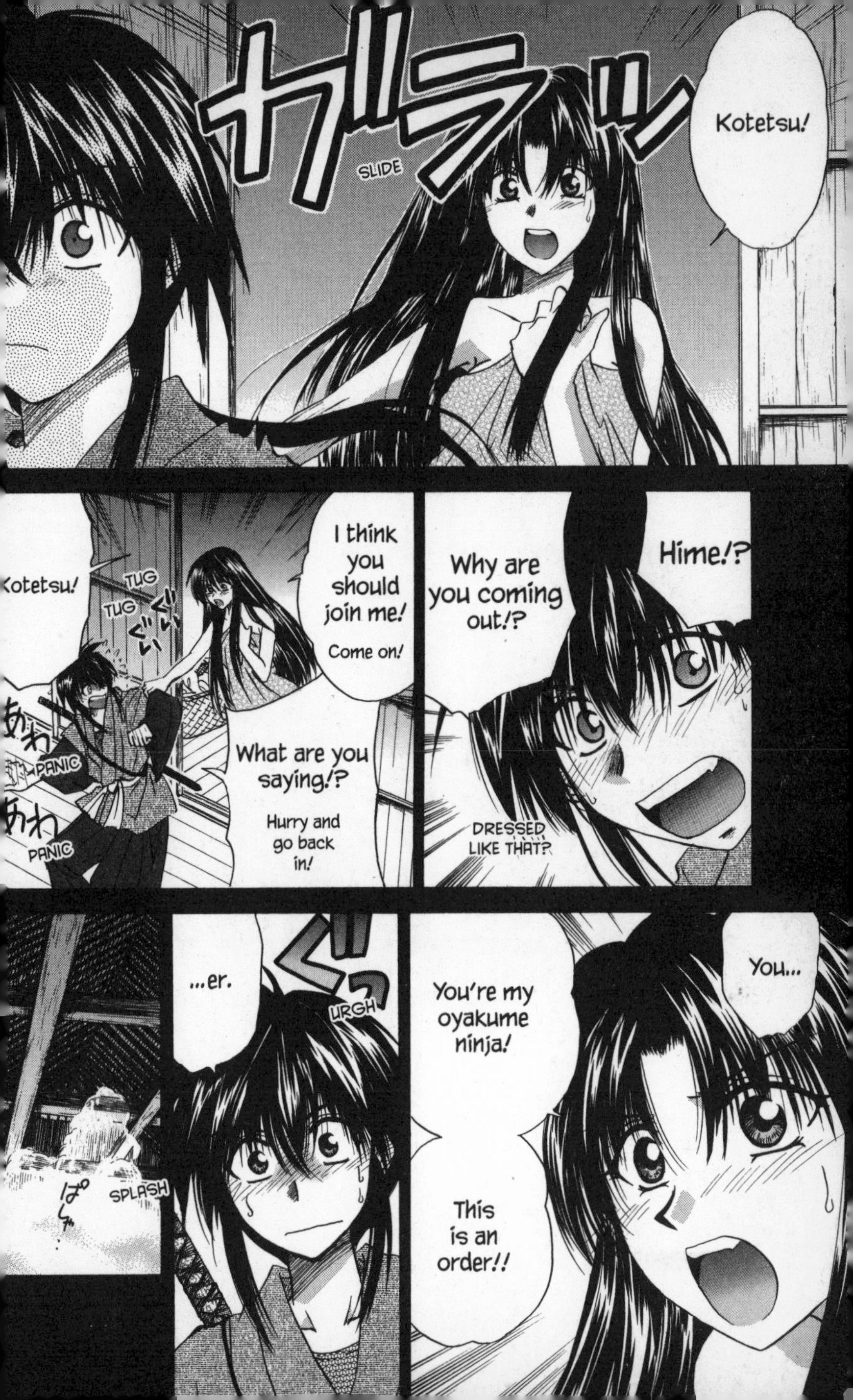
ガラッ
SLIDE
Kotetsu!
Hime!?
Why are you coming out!?
DRESSED LIKE THAT?
I think you should join me!
Come on!
What are you saying!?
Hurry and go back in!
Kotetsu!
ぐいぐい
TUG
TUG
あわ
PANIC
あわ
PANIC
You...
You're my oyakume ninja!
This is an order!!
...er.
ぐっ
URGH
ぱしゃ
SPLASH

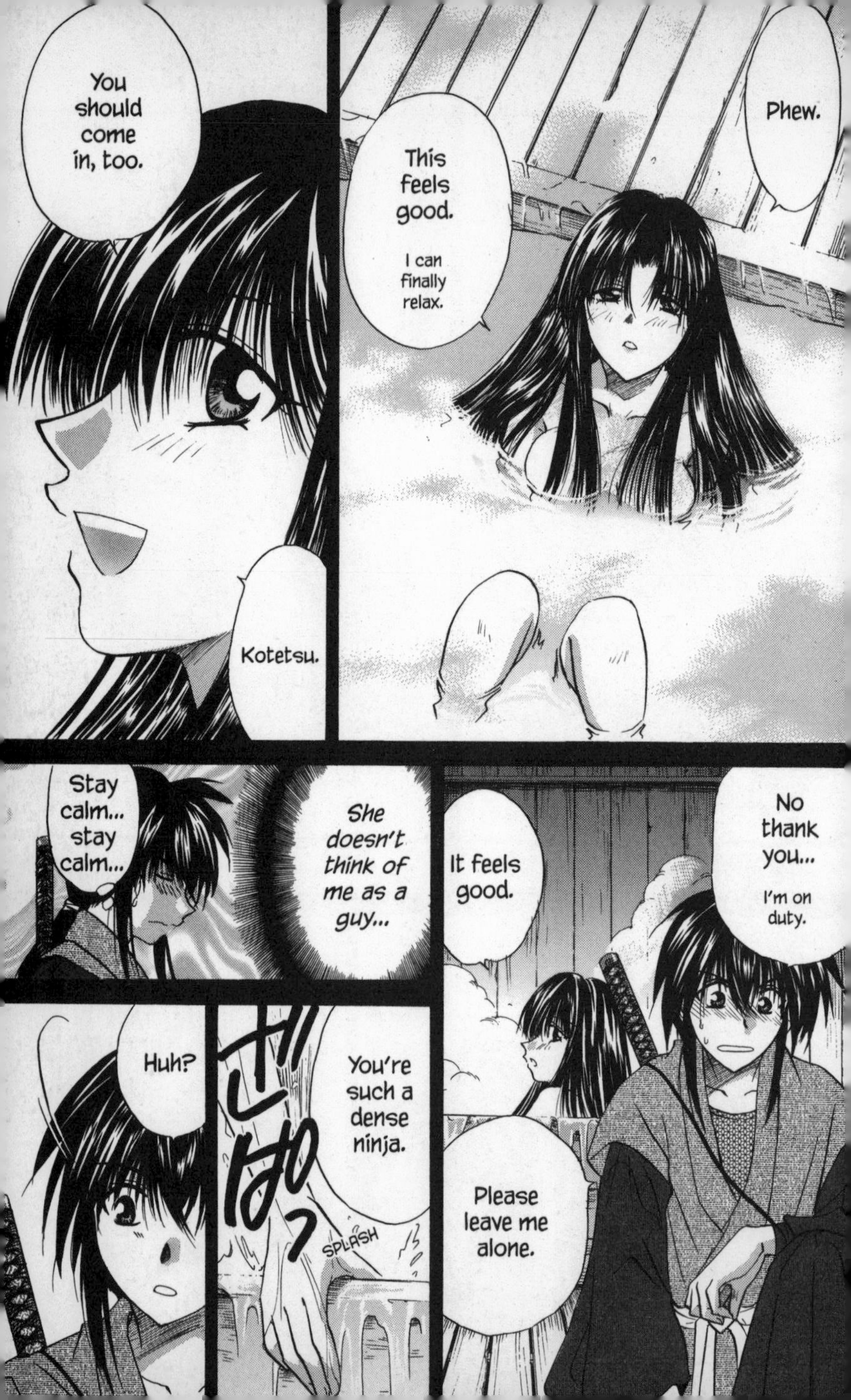
Phew.
This feels good.
I can finally relax.
You should come in, too.
Kotetsu.
No thank you...
I'm on duty.
It feels good.
Please leave me alone.
She doesn't think of me as a guy...
Stay calm... stay calm...
You're such a dense ninja.
SPLASH
Huh?

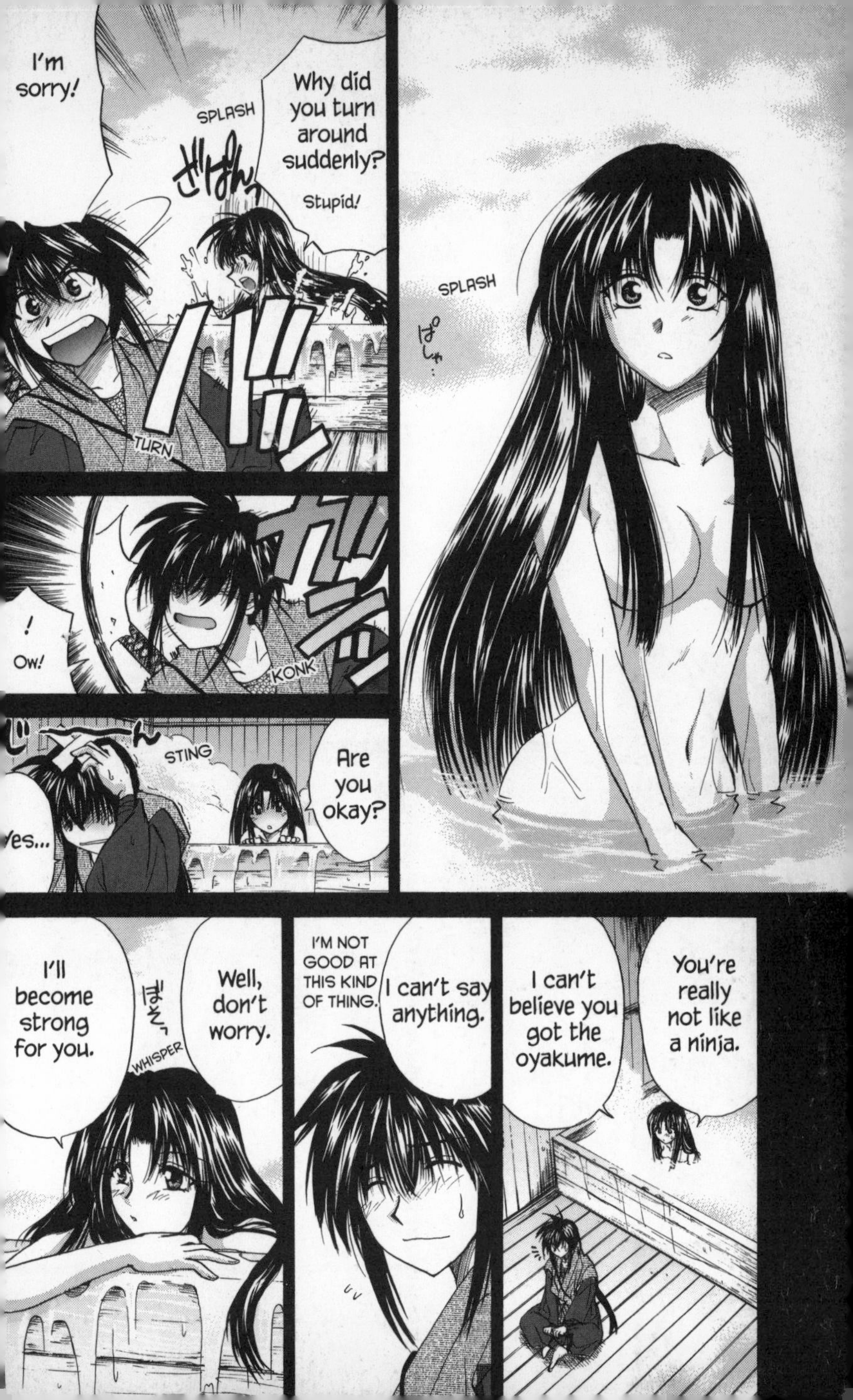
SPLASH
ぱしゃ
Why did you turn around suddenly?
I'm sorry!
SPLASH
ざばんっ
Stupid!
TURN
!
Ow!
KONK
Are you okay?
STING
じーーん
Yes...
You're really not like a ninja.
I can't believe you got the oyakume.
I can't say anything.
I'M NOT GOOD AT THIS KIND OF THING.
Well, don't worry.
ぼそっ
WHISPER
I'll become strong for you.

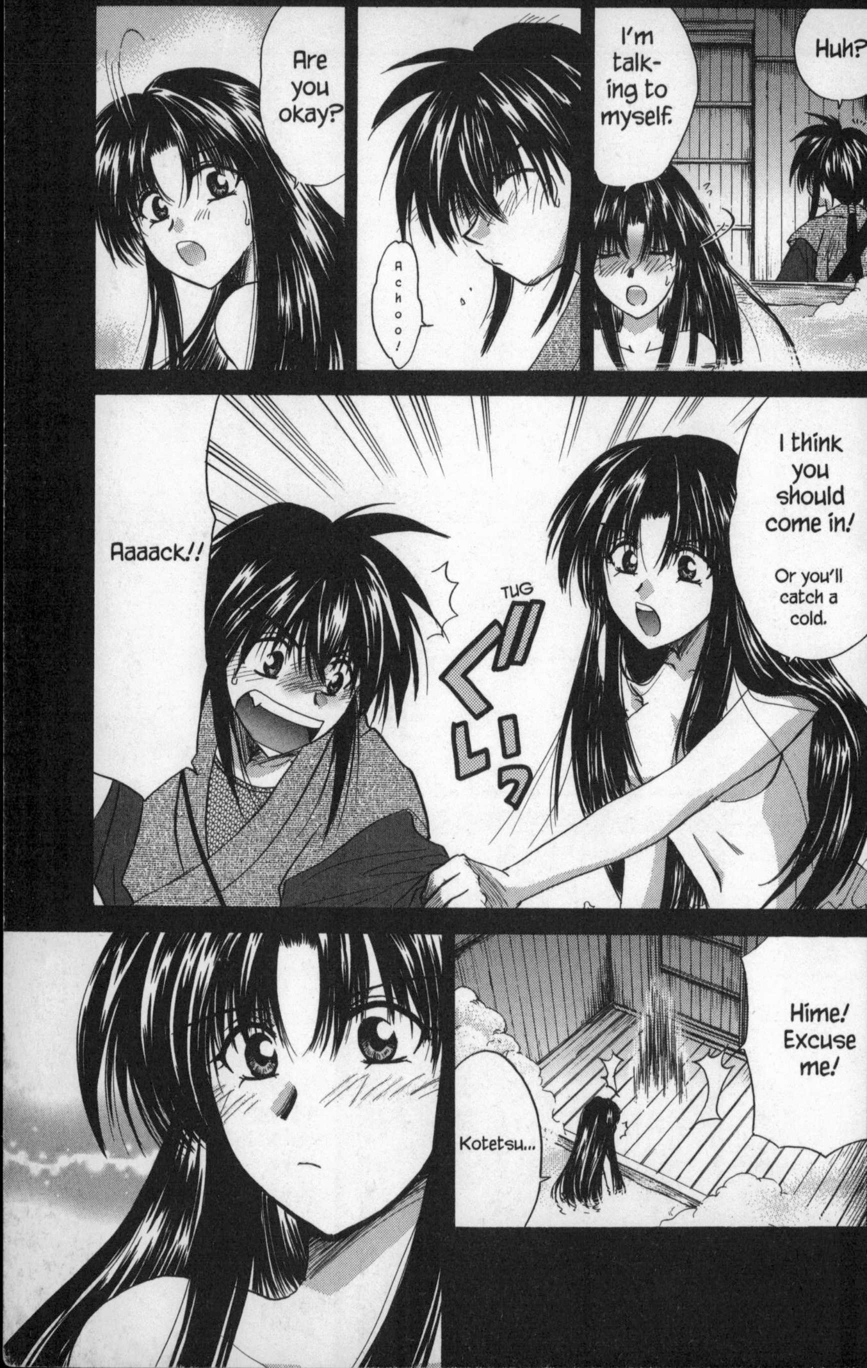
Huh?
I'm talking to myself.
Achoo!
Are you okay?
I think you should come in!
Or you'll catch a cold.
TUG
Aaaack!!
Hime! Excuse me!
Kotetsu...

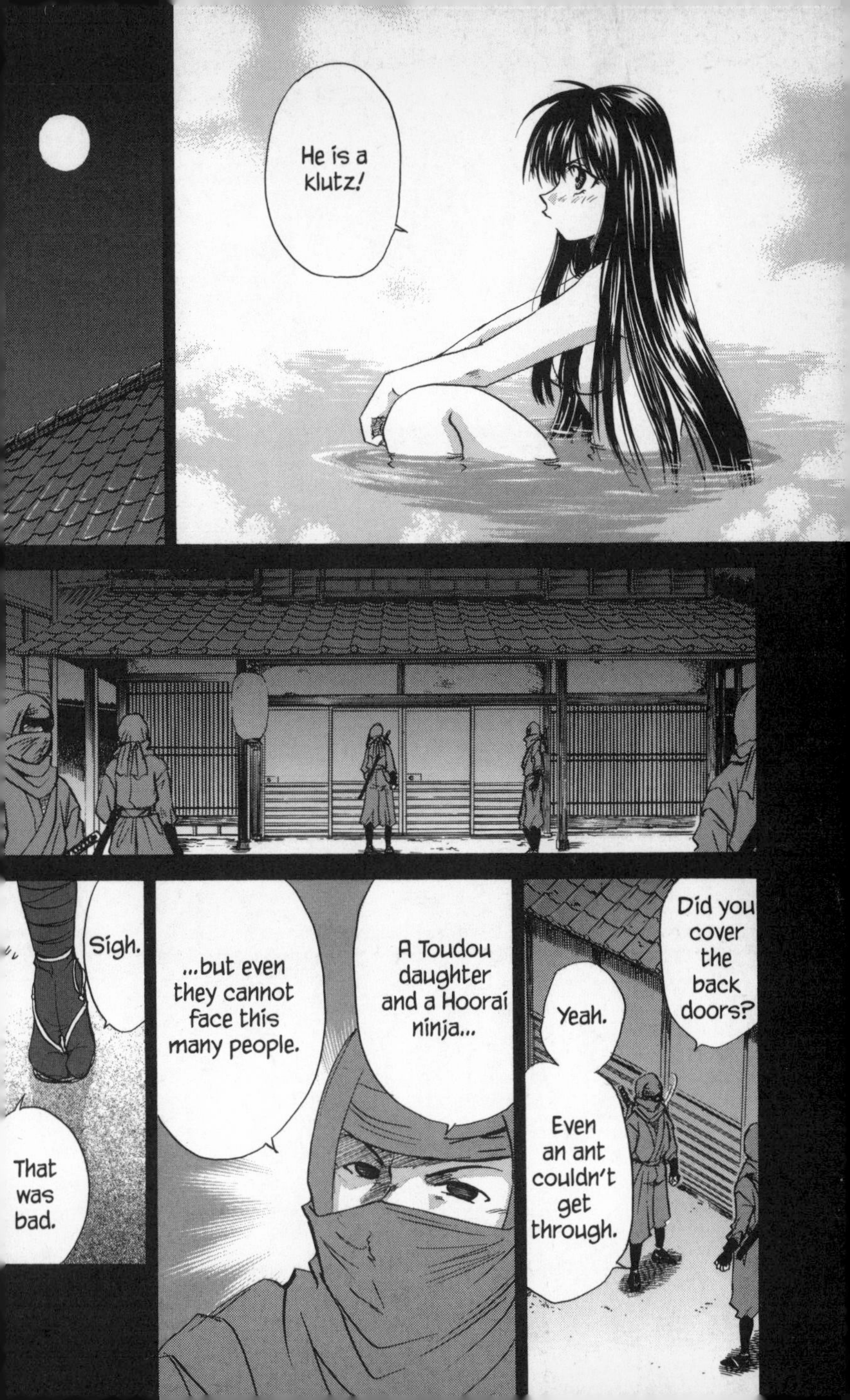
He is a klutz!
Did you cover the back doors?
Yeah.
Even an ant couldn't get through.
A Toudou daughter and a Hoorai ninja...
...but even they cannot face this many people.
Sigh.
That was bad.

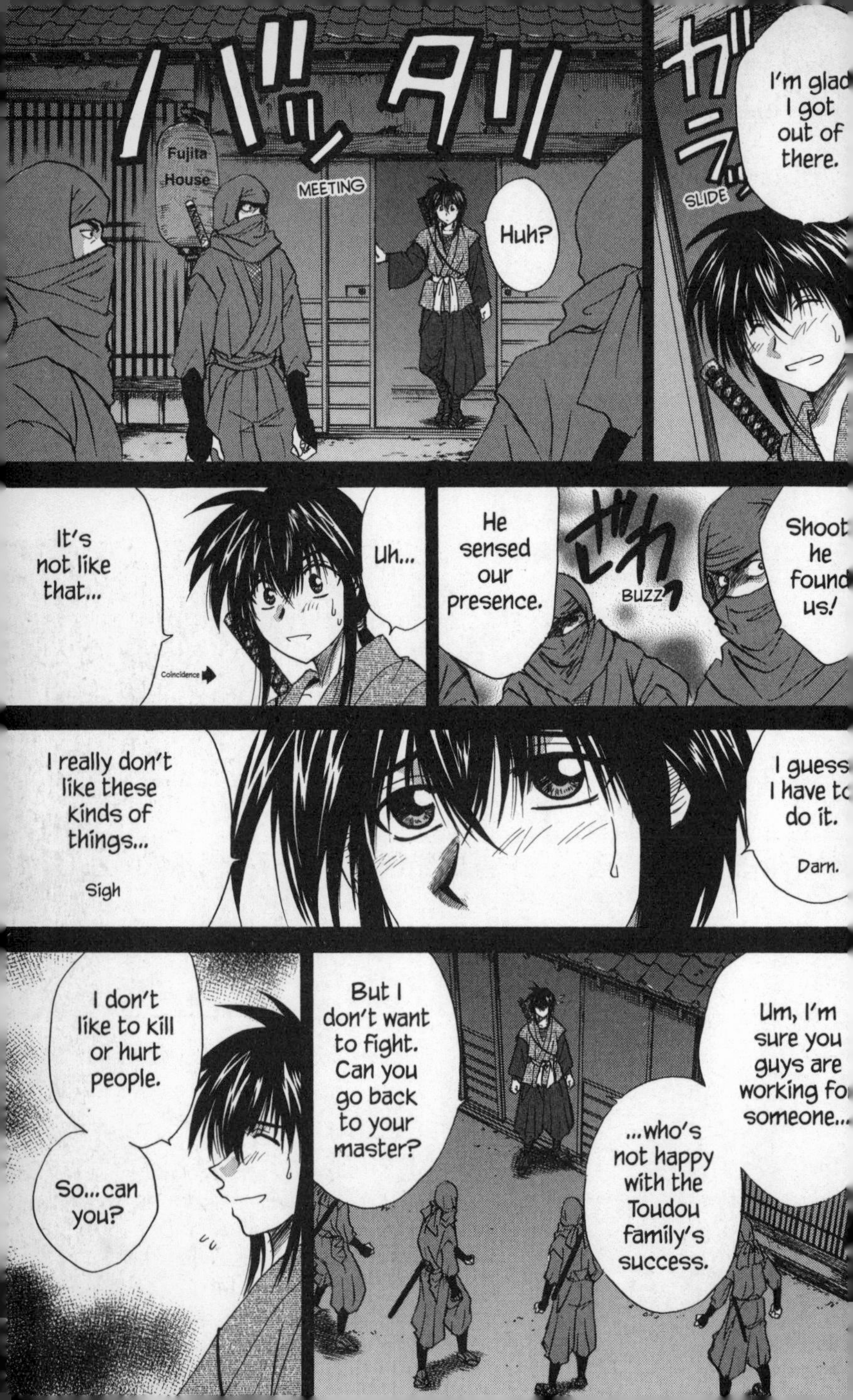
I'm glad I got out of there.
SLIDE
Huh?
MEETING
Fujita House
Shoot he found us!
BUZZ
He sensed our presence.
Uh...
Coincidence
It's not like that...
I guess I have to do it.
Darn.
I really don't like these kinds of things...
Sigh
Um, I'm sure you guys are working for someone...
...who's not happy with the Toudou family's success.
But I don't want to fight. Can you go back to your master?
I don't like to kill or hurt people.
So...can you?

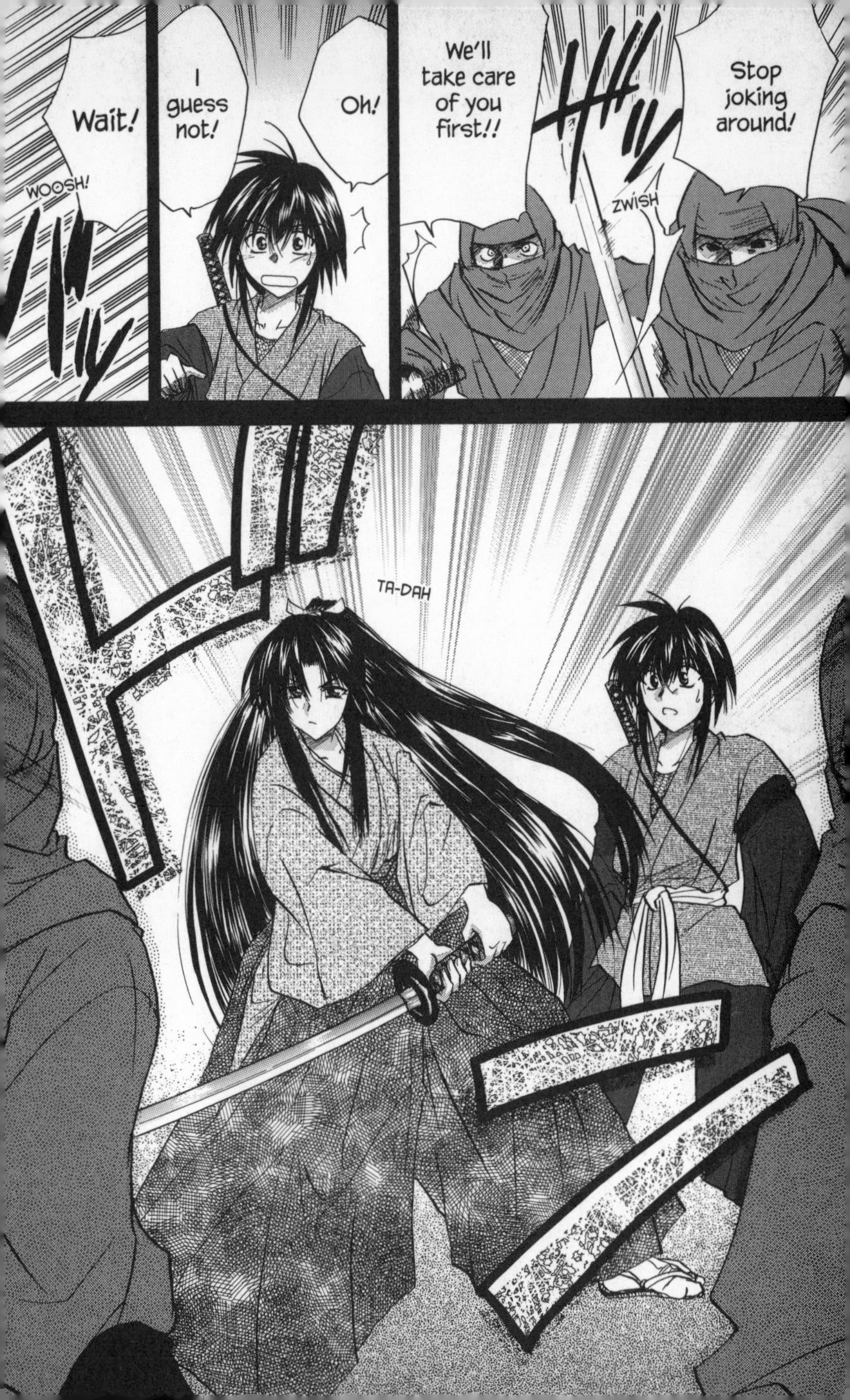
Stop joking around!
We'll take care of you first!!
ZWISH
Oh!
I guess not!
Wait!
WOOSH!
TA-DAH

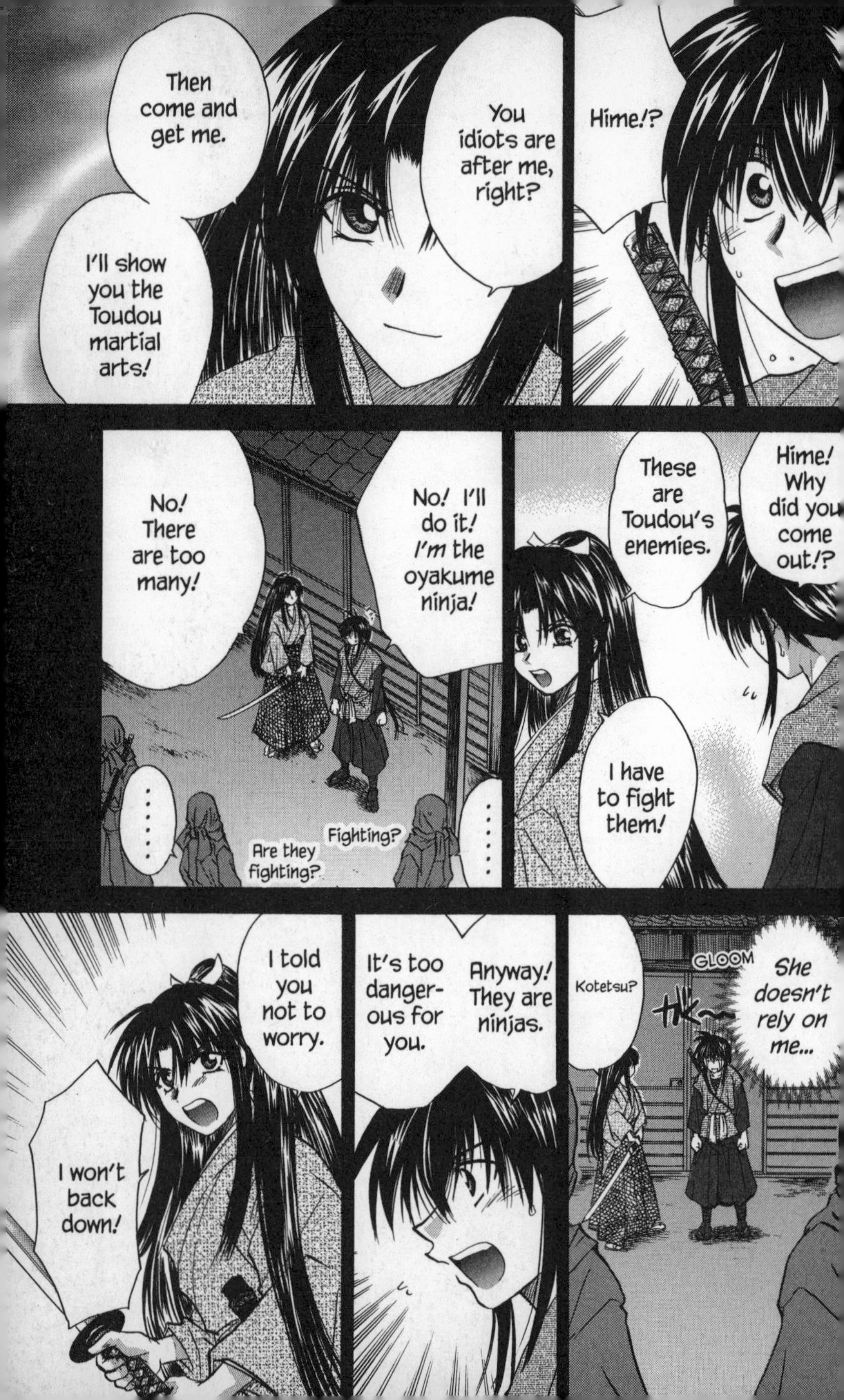

Hime!?
You idiots are after me, right?
Then come and get me.
I'll show you the Toudou martial arts!
Hime! Why did you come out!?
These are Toudou's enemies.
I have to fight them!
No! I'll do it! *I'm* the oyakume ninja!
No! There are too many!
......
Fighting?
Are they fighting?
......
She doesn't rely on me...
GLOOM
Kotetsu?
Anyway! They are ninjas.
It's too danger-ous for you.
I told you not to worry.
I won't back down!

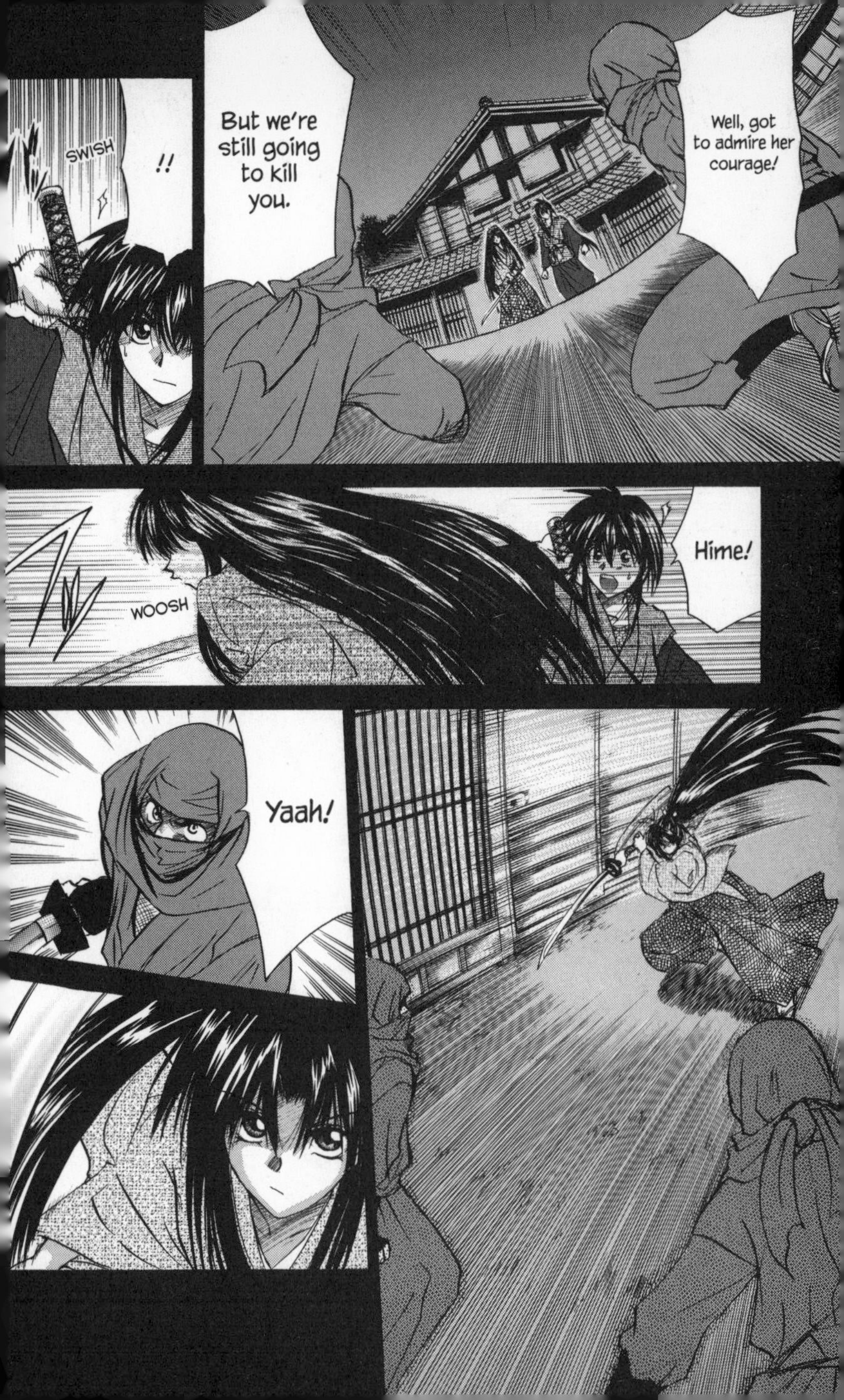
Well, got to admire her courage!
But we're still going to kill you.
SWISH
!!
Hime!
WOOSH
Yaah!

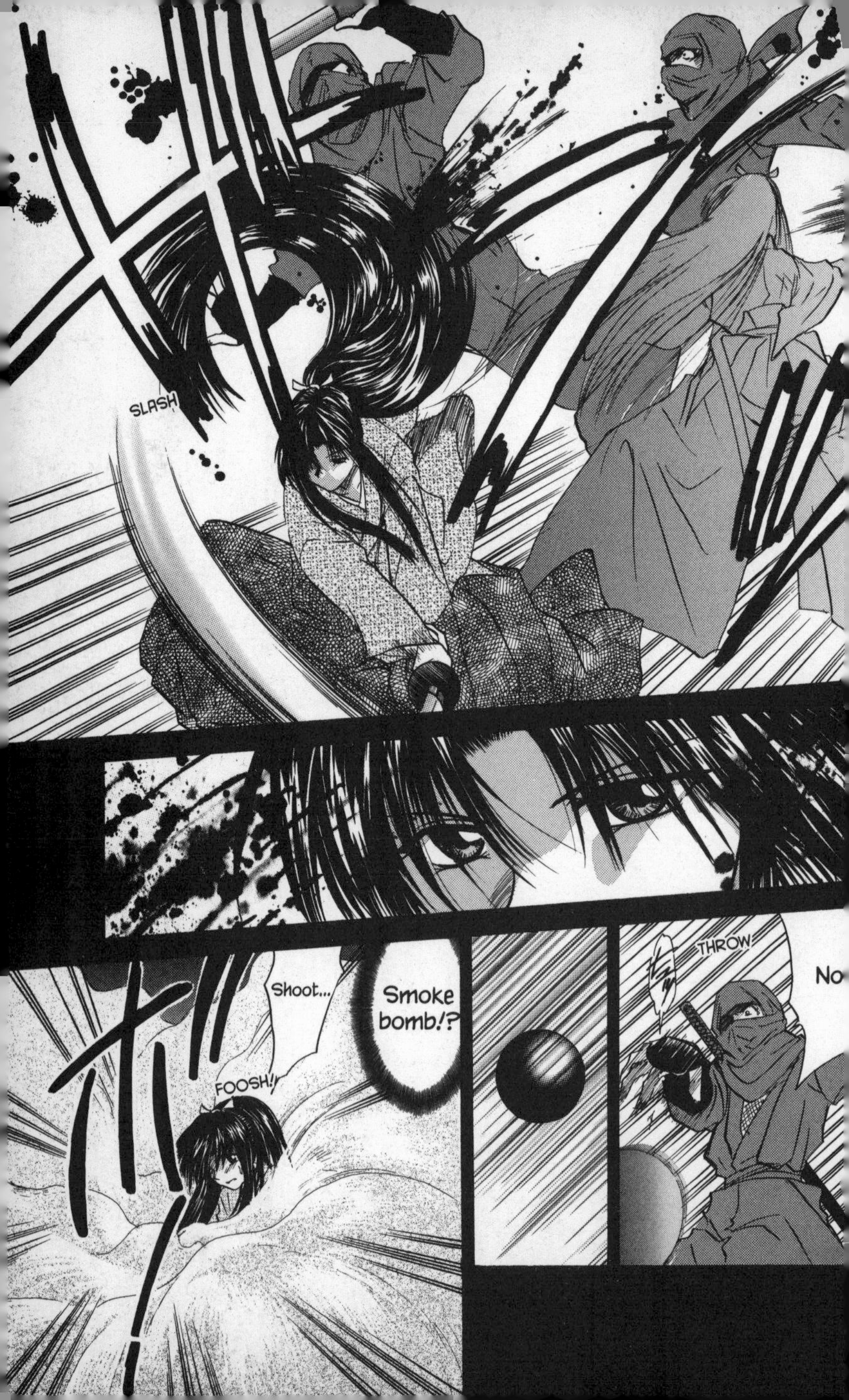
SLASH
THROW
No
Smoke bomb!?
Shoot...
FOOSH!

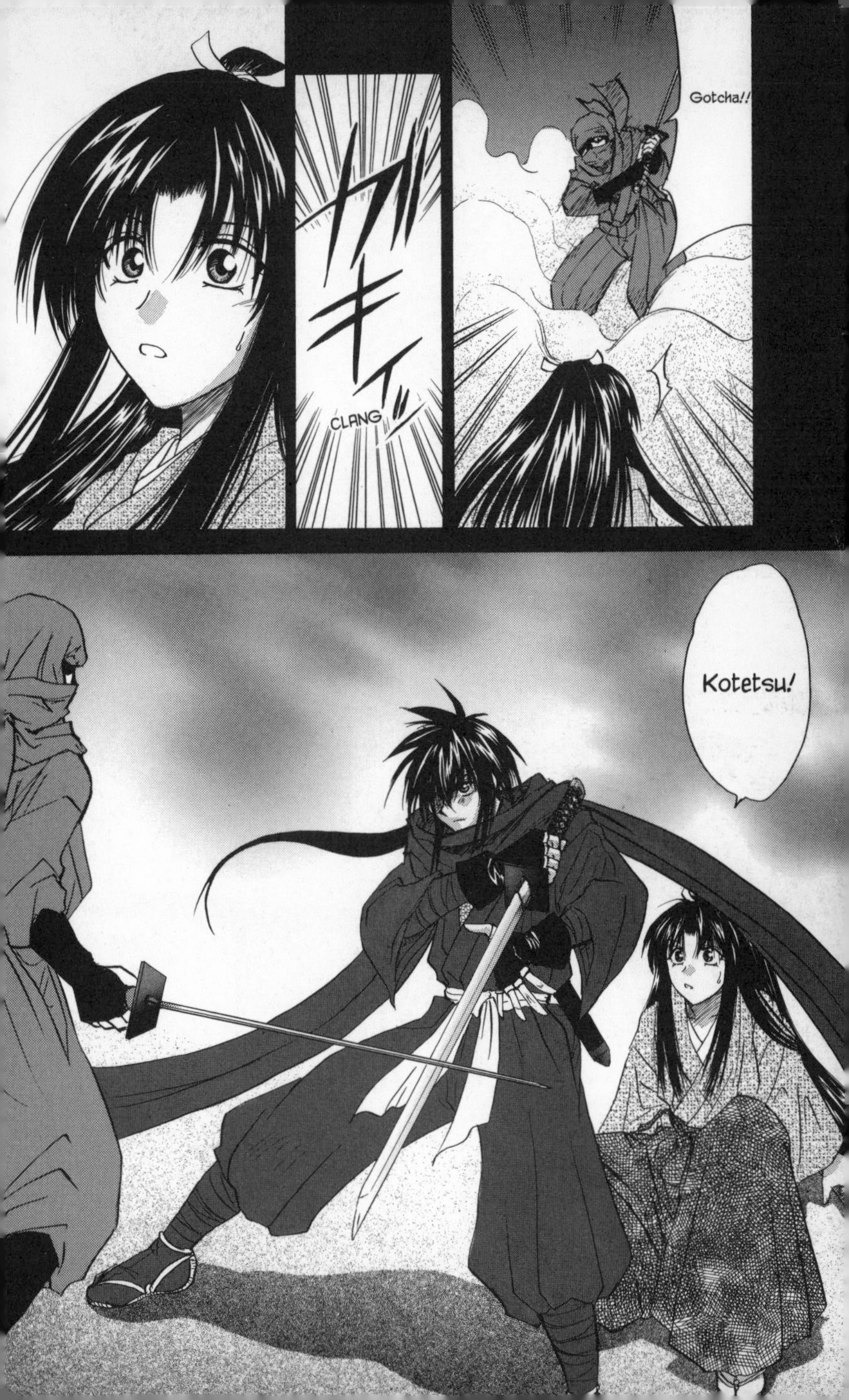
Gotcha!!
CLANG
Kotetsu!

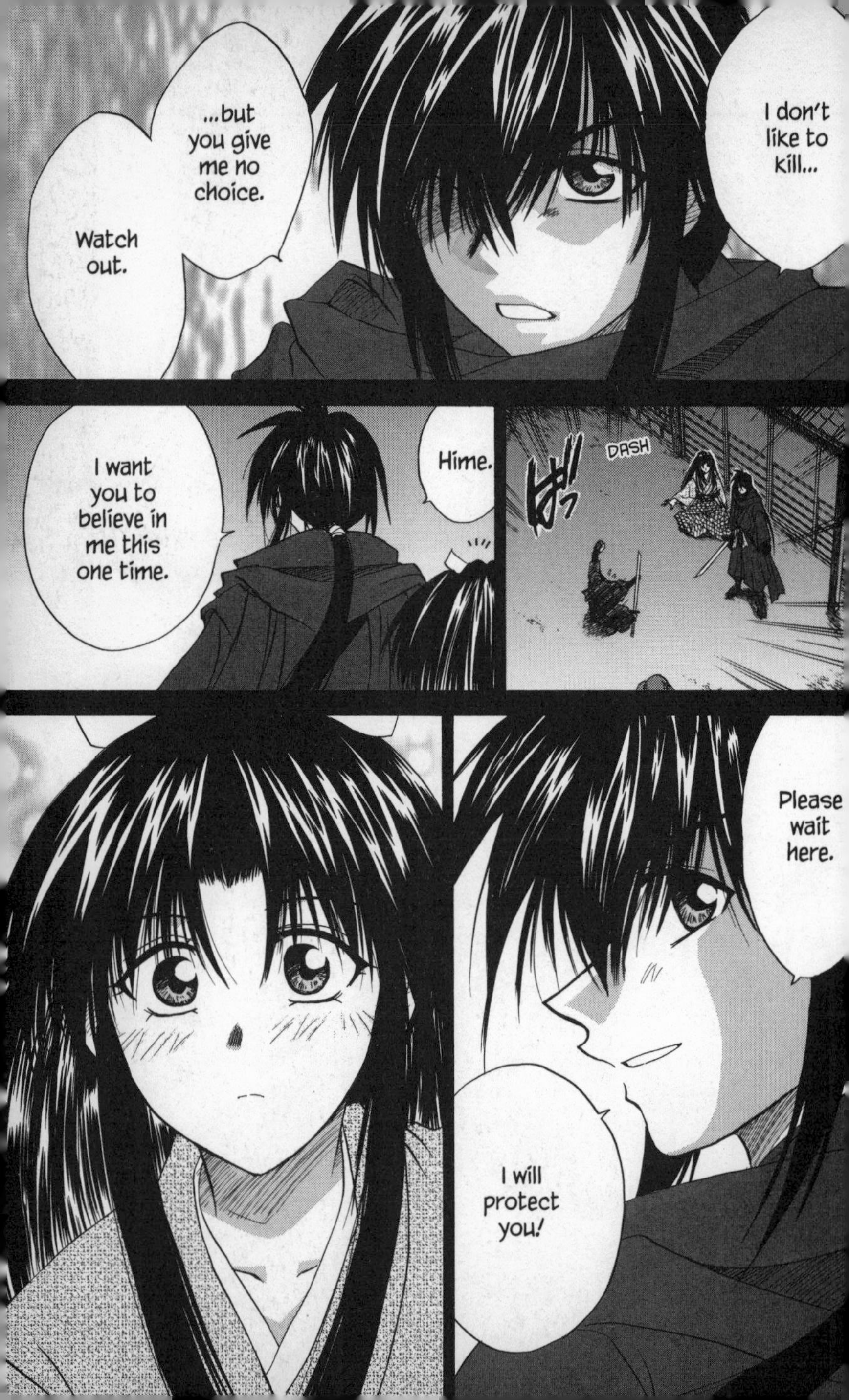
I don't like to kill...
...but you give me no choice.
Watch out.
DASH
Hime.
I want you to believe in me this one time.
Please wait here.
I will protect you!

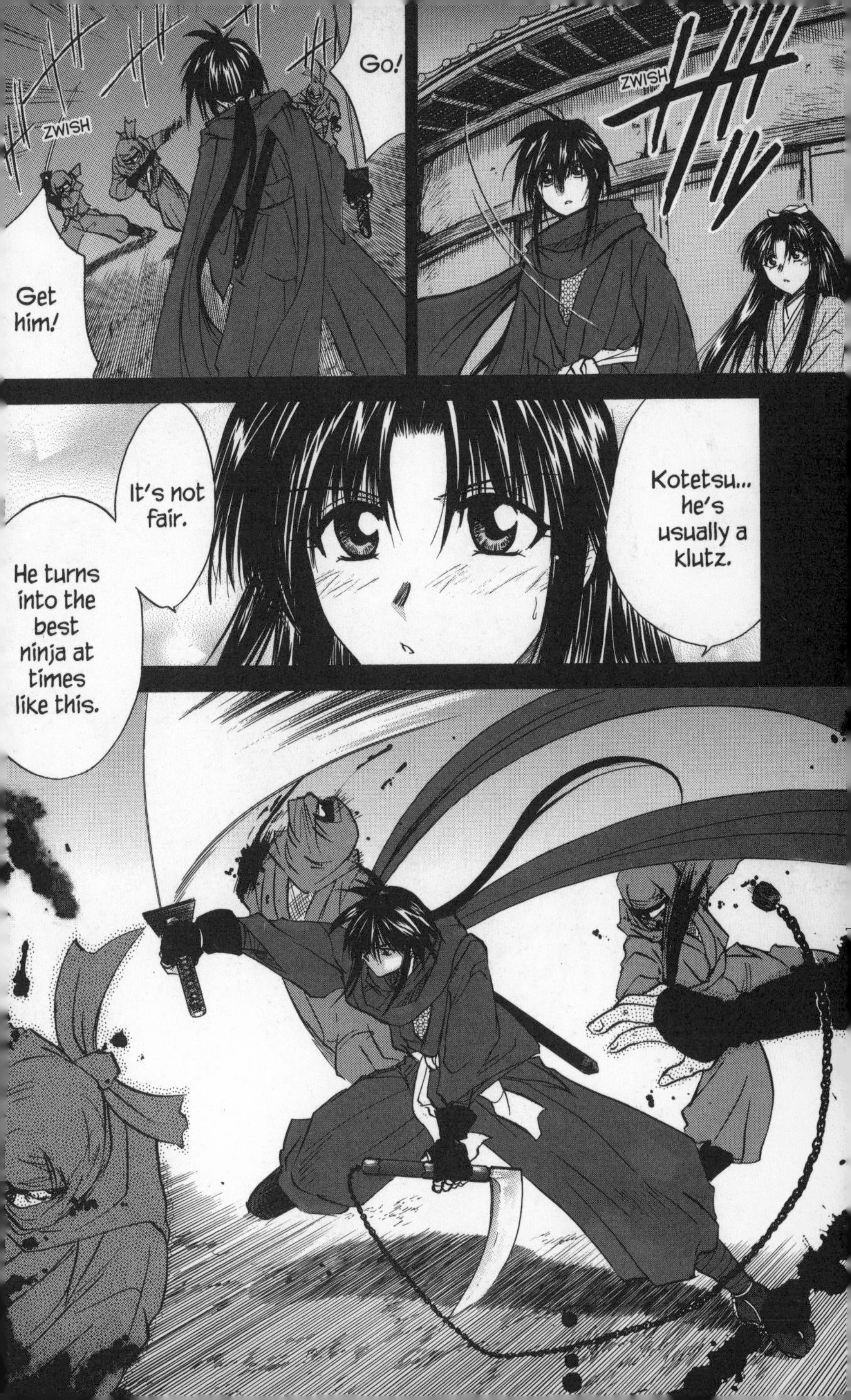
ZWISH
Go!
ZWISH
Get him!
Kotetsu... he's usually a klutz.
It's not fair.
He turns into the best ninja at times like this.

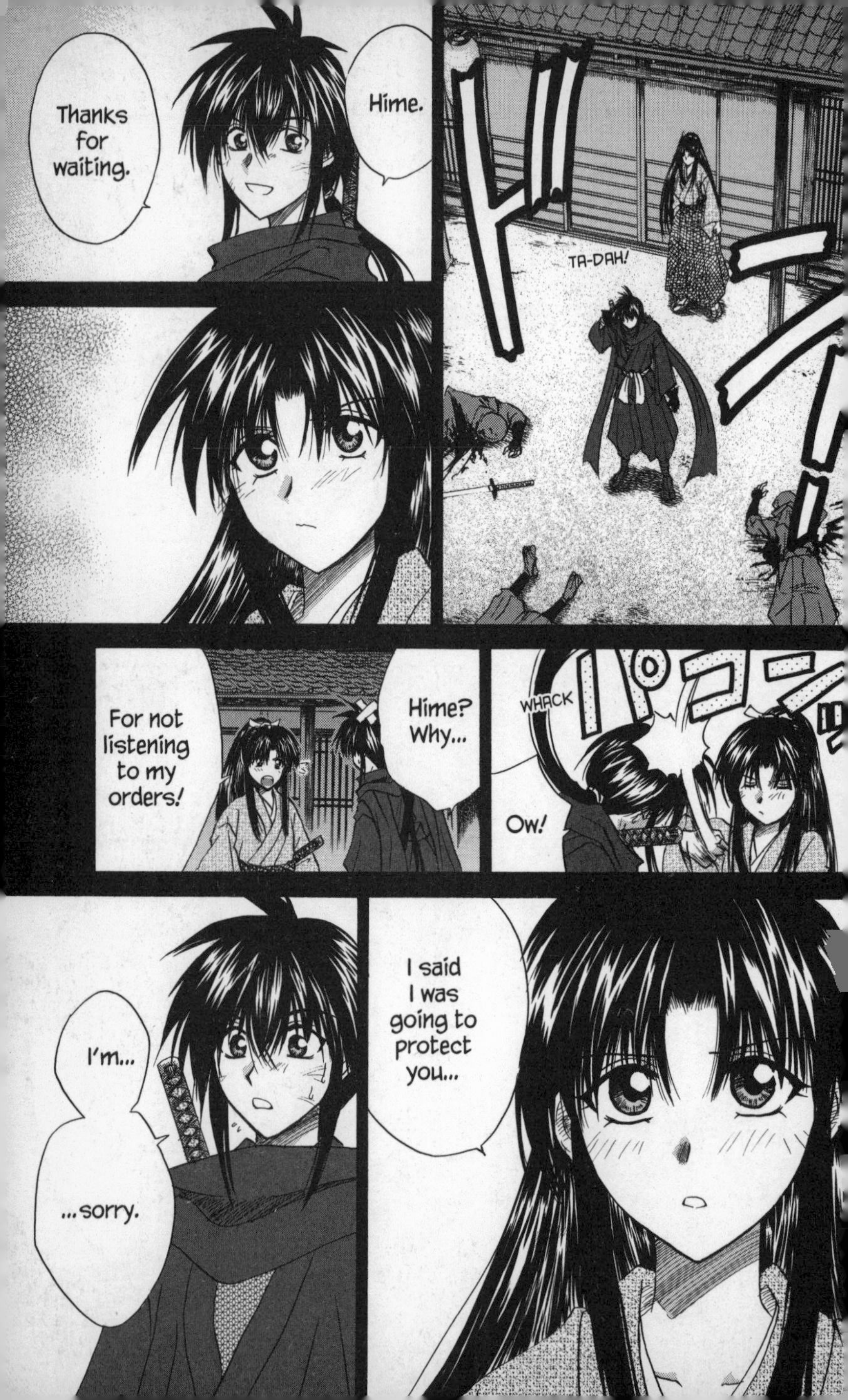
TA-DAH!
Hime.
Thanks for waiting.
WHACK
Ow!
Hime? Why...
For not listening to my orders!
I said I was going to protect you...
I'm...
...sorry.

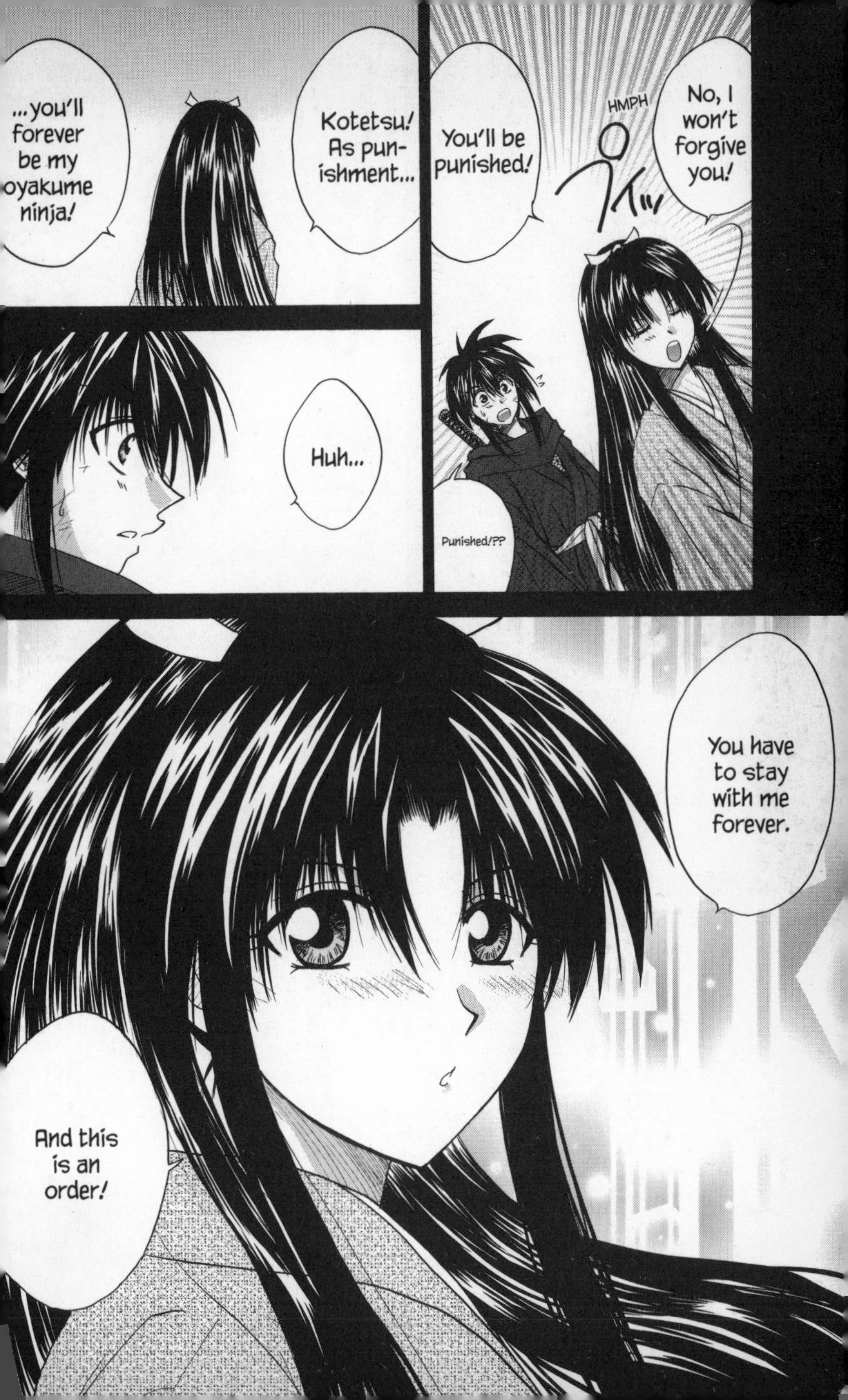
HMPH
No, I won't forgive you!
You'll be punished!
Punished!??
Kotetsu! As pun-ishment...
...you'll forever be my oyakume ninja!
Huh...
You have to stay with me forever.
And this is an order!

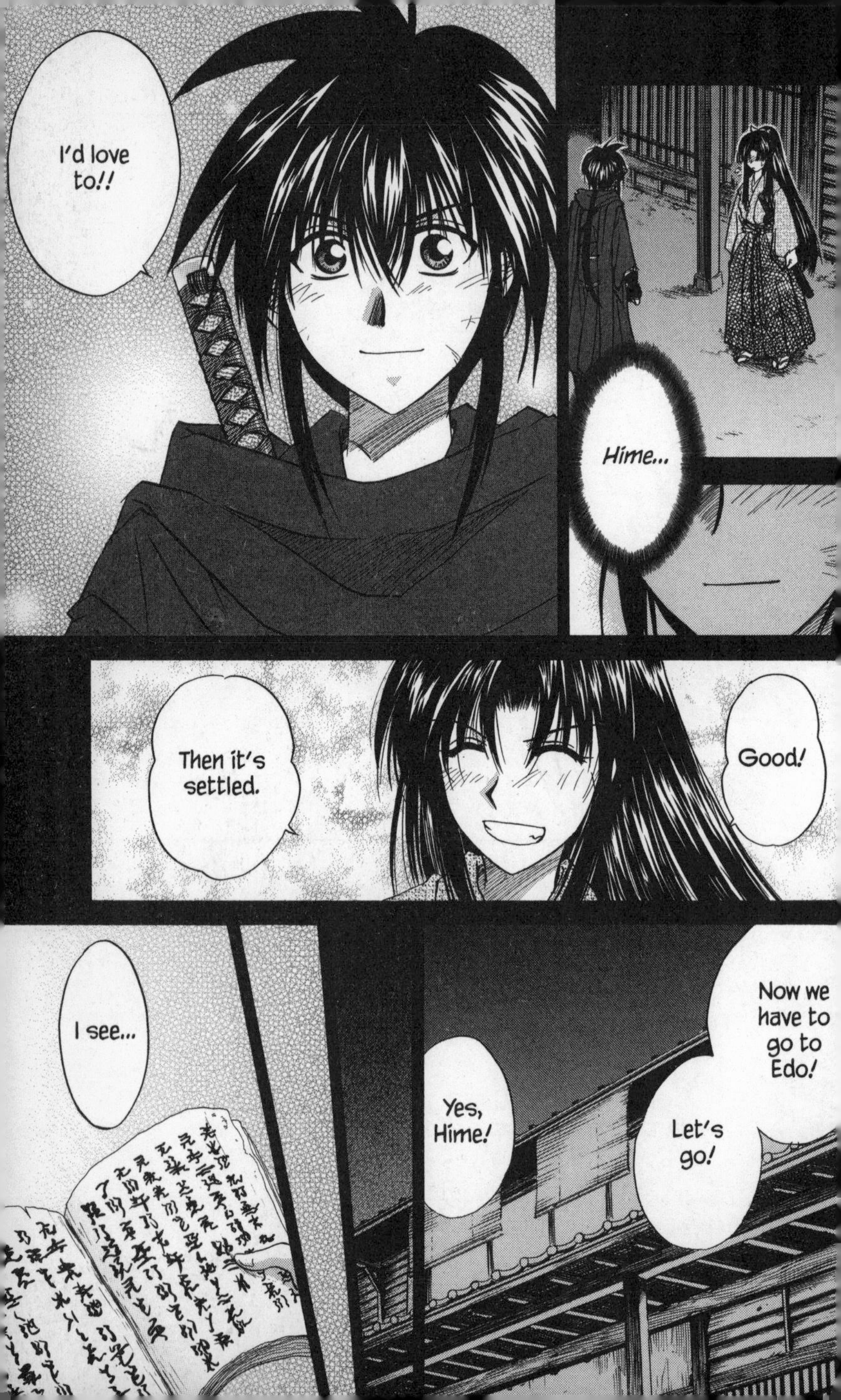
Hime...
I'd love to!!
Good!
Then it's settled.
Now we have to go to Edo!
Let's go!
Yes, Hime!
I see...

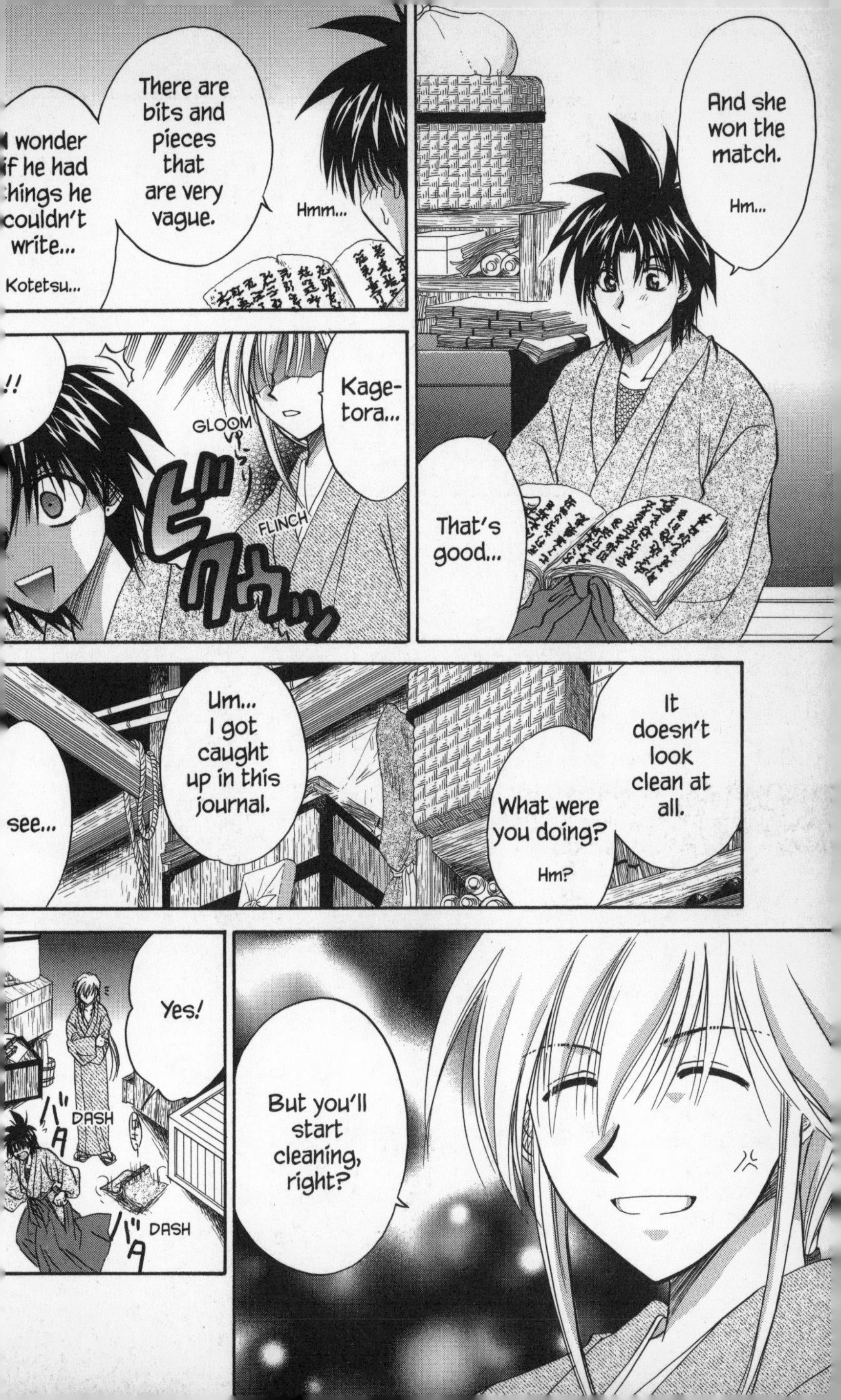
And she won the match.
Hm...
That's good...
There are bits and pieces that are very vague.
Hmm...
wonder if he had hings he couldn't write...
Kotetsu...
Kage-tora...
GLOOM
FLINCH
!!
It doesn't look clean at all.
Hm?
What were you doing?
Um... I got caught up in this journal.
see...
But you'll start cleaning, right?
Yes!
DASH
DASH

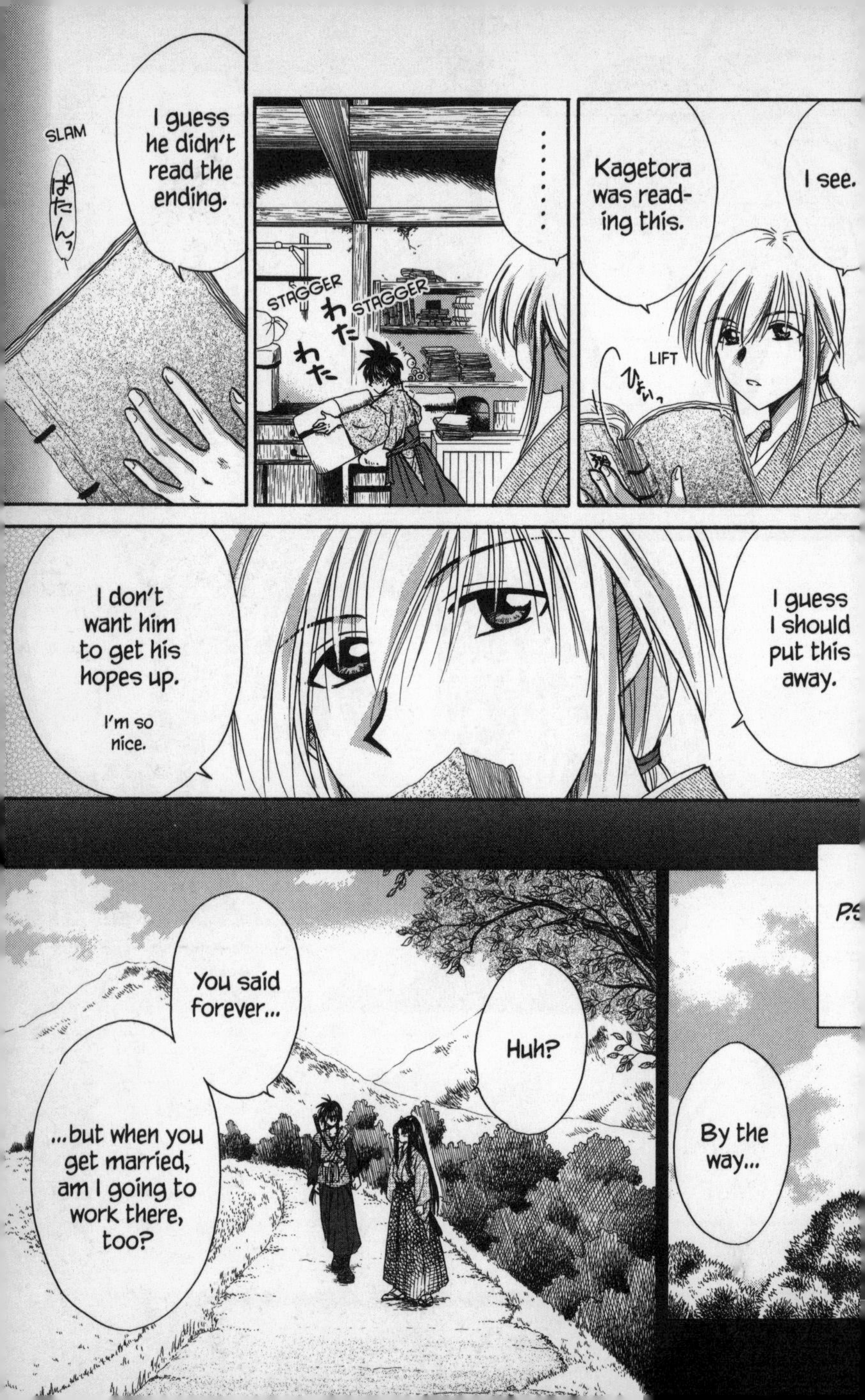
I see.
Kagetora was reading this.
LIFT
......
STAGGER
わた
STAGGER
わた
I guess he didn't read the ending.
SLAM
ぱたんっ
I guess I should put this away.
I don't want him to get his hopes up.
I'm so nice.
P.S
By the way...
You said forever...
Huh?
...but when you get married, am I going to work there, too?

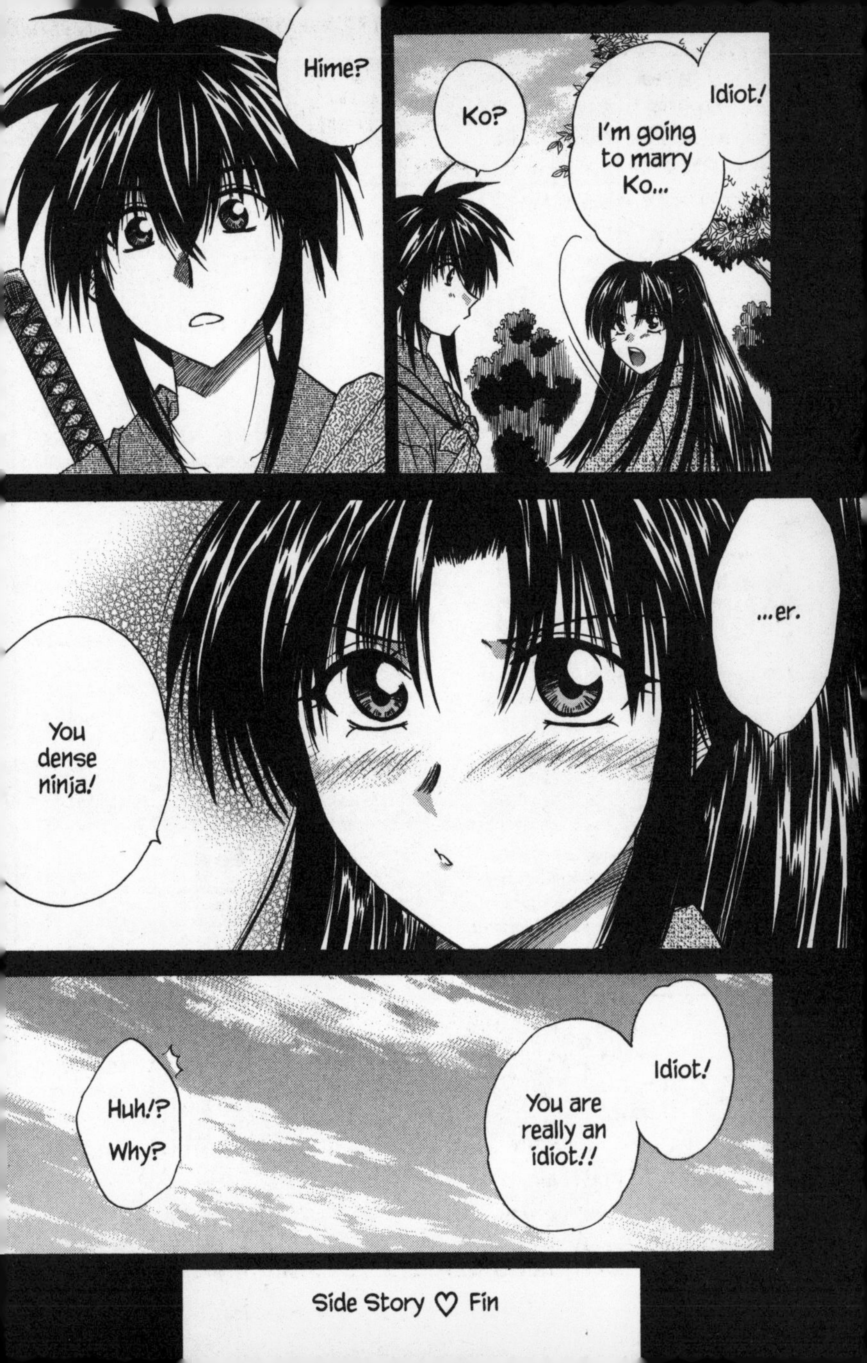
Idiot!
I'm going to marry Ko...
Ko?
Hime?
...er.
You dense ninja!
Idiot!
You are really an idiot!!
Huh!? Why?
Side Story ♡ Fin

Bonus Page

This is Segami. There are a couple of things that happened for this volume. Like the inclusion of a story I did before... Well, as long as you enjoyed it, that's good enough for me. (laugh)

About Ninjas - Part 7
I have a lot of ninja materials now. I have interesting things. I have weapons and books, of course, but I have videotapes, too. What's funny is that it has a cautionary note in there, too. "Please do not try any of the things introduced in this video because it is dangerous." I can't do anything in the video anyway...maybe poking eyes, but that's about it. I guess I can't become a ninja.

About Traveling
I went to Aichi prefecture to eat blowfish. It was really good...On the way there, I stopped by a bird park. I was able to touch a penguin! A penguin! I was so happy!! I always wanted to touch one!! It was a little slippery...The park was fun. You get to feed different birds. But I don't think that's safe. Sometimes it hurts...And I think it's a little dangerous to leave peacocks out, too. But it's fun.

About Cats
The cat I wrote about in volume 3—the little one—died...(cry) He tried his best until the end... The most difficult thing about having pets is when they go. But he gave me many memories. So I would like to be thankful.

About Moving
I moved again. I am now closer to the publishers. I used the same movers as before. I was watching them, amazed by how efficient they are, when I heard a loud noise. They knocked the naginata against the sword sheath. Now there's a small mark on my naginata...(cry)

Thank You
Thank you very much for your letters! I have readers who saw my ad in the *Weekly Shonen Magazine* and started reading. It makes me happy to hear that! I'm also happy when readers tell me they were accepted into college (laugh) and I enjoy reading the letters. I'll continue to work hard writing back ~ ♪

Special Thanks

Assistants:	Tanaka-kun, Oshima-chan
Helper:	Takaeda, Keisui-sama
Editor:	Mr. Morita
Comics Editor:	Houjou-san
And all the readers ♡	

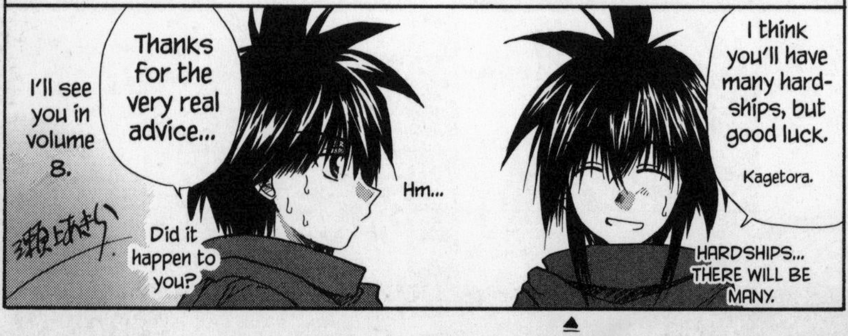

I think you'll have many hardships, but good luck.
Kagetora.
HARDSHIPS... THERE WILL BE MANY.
Hm...
Thanks for the very real advice...
Did it happen to you?
I'll see you in volume 8.

▲ Kotetsu

I took time off from Magazine Special No. 2 and No. 3 for 2005 and was drawing KAGETORA for Weekly Shonen Magazine.

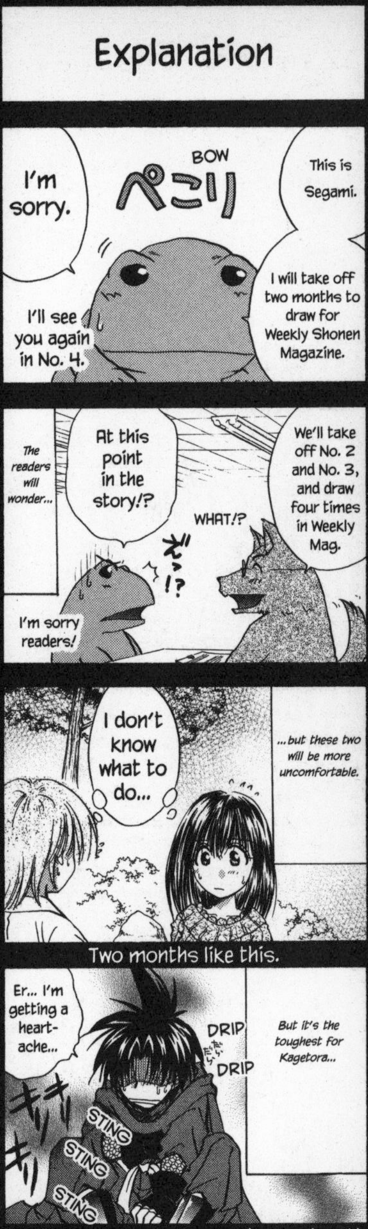
Explanation
This is Segami.
I will take off two months to draw for Weekly Shonen Magazine.
BOW
ぺこり
I'm sorry.
I'll see you again in No. 4.
We'll take off No. 2 and No. 3, and draw four times in Weekly Mag.
WHAT!?
ぞっ !?
At this point in the story!?
The readers will wonder...
I'm sorry readers!
...but these two will be more uncomfortable.
I don't know what to do...
Two months like this.
But it's the toughest for Kagetora...
DRIP
DRIP
Er... I'm getting a heart-ache...
STING
STING
STING

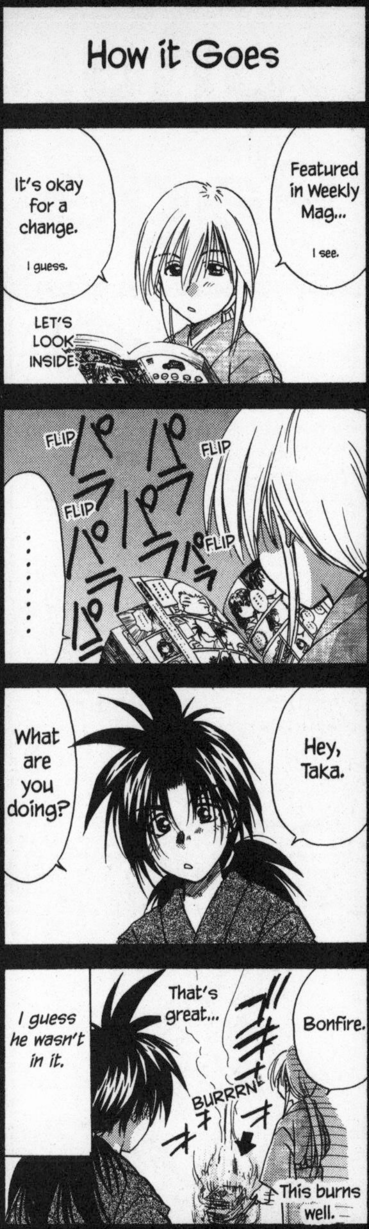
How it Goes
Featured in Weekly Mag...
I see.
It's okay for a change.
I guess.
LET'S LOOK INSIDE.
FLIP
FLIP
FLIP
FLIP
......
Hey, Taka.
What are you doing?
Bonfire.
That's great...
BURRRN
This burns well.
I guess he wasn't in it.

This four-panel comic was drawn when the author took a break from No. 2 and No. 3.

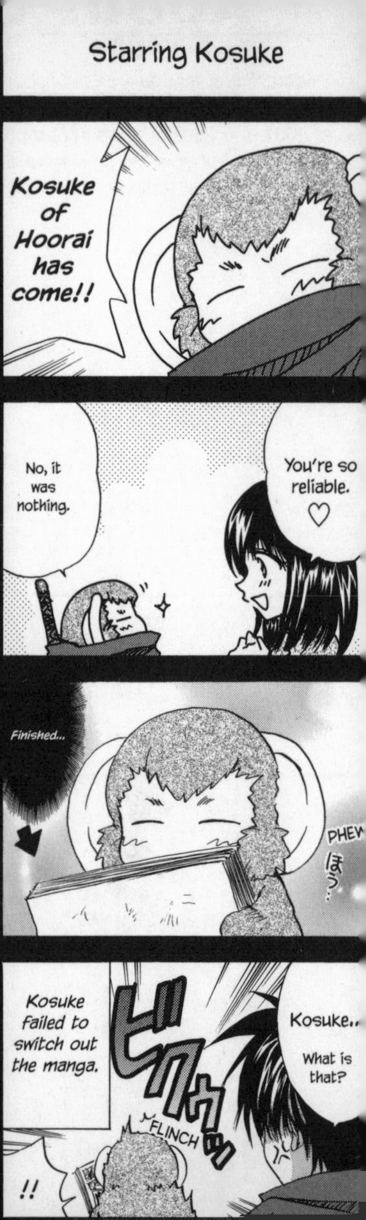
Starring Kosuke
Kosuke of Hoorai has come!!
You're so reliable. ♡
No, it was nothing.
PHEW
ほう…
Finished...
Kosuke.. What is that?
ビクゥッ
FLINCH
Kosuke failed to switch out the manga.
!!

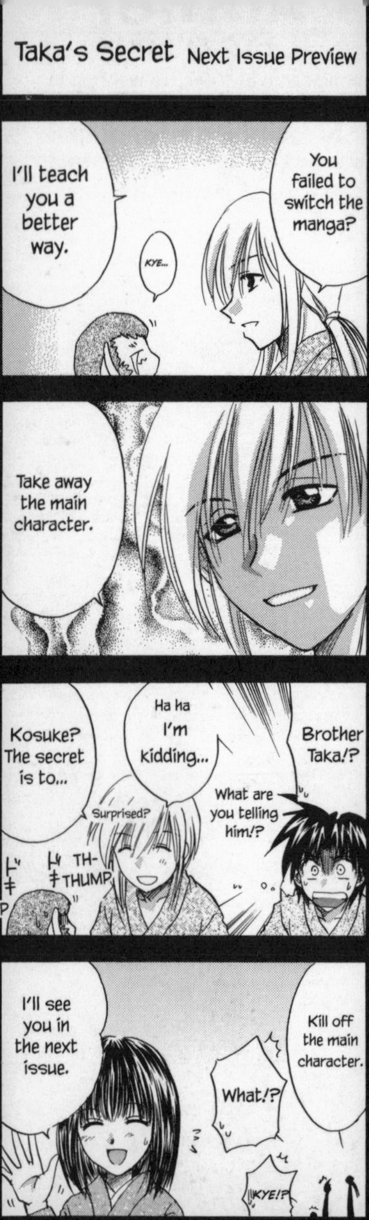
Taka's Secret Next Issue Preview
You failed to switch the manga?
KYE...
I'll teach you a better way.
Take away the main character.
Brother Taka!?
What are you telling him!?
Ha ha I'm kidding...
Surprised?
Kosuke? The secret is to...
ドキ TH-THUMP
ドキ TH-THUMP
Kill off the main character.
What!?
KYE!?
I'll see you in the next issue.

We'll have those episodes in the comics, so please look forward to them!

About the Author

Segami's first manga was published by Shogakukan in 1996. He went on to do a few other small projects, including two short stories entitled "Kagetora" in 2001 and 2002. The character proved to be popular with fans, so Segami began his first ongoing series, *Kagetora*, with Kodansha in 2003. The series continues to run today.

Translation Notes

Japanese is a tricky language for most Westerners, and translation is often more art than science. For your edification and reading pleasure, here are notes on some of the places where we could have gone in a different direction in our translation of the work, or where a Japanese cultural reference is used.

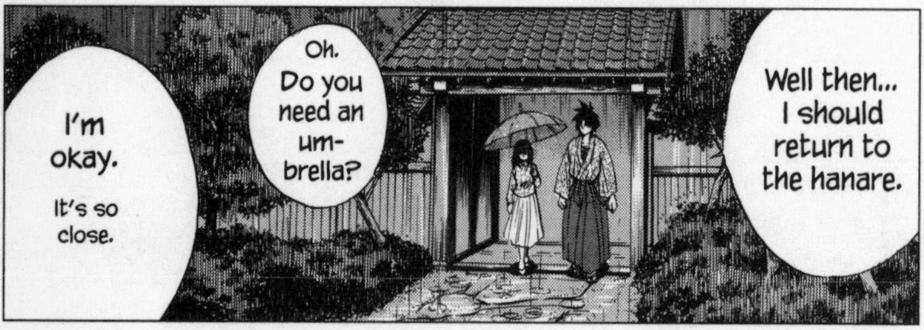
Well then... I should return to the hanare.
Oh. Do you need an um-brella?
I'm okay.
It's so close.

***Hanare*, page 5**
Hanare is a detached building, separate from the main building in classical Japanese homes. Usually farm machines and implements are kept inside the *hanare*.

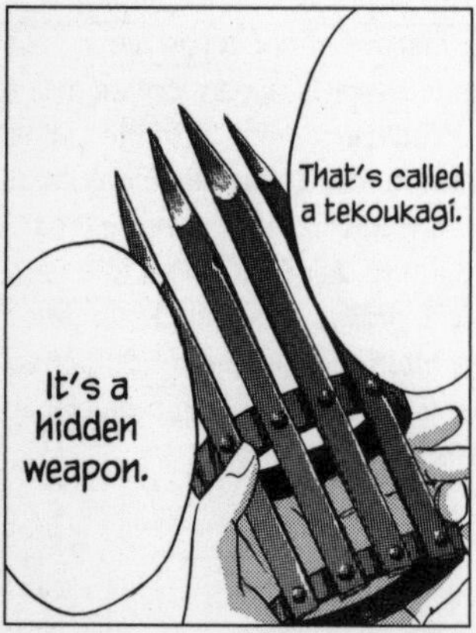
That's called a tekoukagi.
It's a hidden weapon.

***Tekoukagi*, page 14**
Tekoukagi is a weapon ninjas put on their hands. They can use it to climb trees or claw into wood, or they can use it to attack enemies.

Makibishi, page 15

Makibishi is a weapon ninjas leave on the ground when they are being chased. Ninjas usually carry them in bamboo tubes.

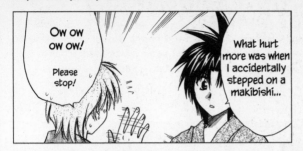

What hurt more was when I accidentally stepped on a makibishi...
Ow ow ow ow!
Please stop!

If there was nothing fishy, you should be fine.
Even if they find out, it doesn't affect your "oyakume."
KYE?

Oyakume, page 28

Oyakume translates as "a duty." Its use in this book is more formal, suggesting a specific and honored duty.

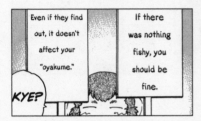

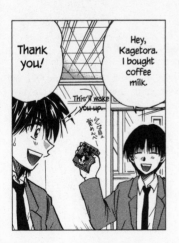

Hey, Kagetora. I bought coffee milk.
This'll wake you up.
Thank you!

Coffee milk, page 30

Coffee milk is similar to chocolate milk. However instead of chocolate syrup, coffee syrup is used. In Japan, coffee milk is often drunk at public baths. In the United States, coffee milk is hard to find outside of the New England region (where it can be found in the dairy case next to chocolate milk). Travelers requesting it in other areas are often mistakenly served coffee with milk. Interestingly, it is the official state drink of Rhode Island.

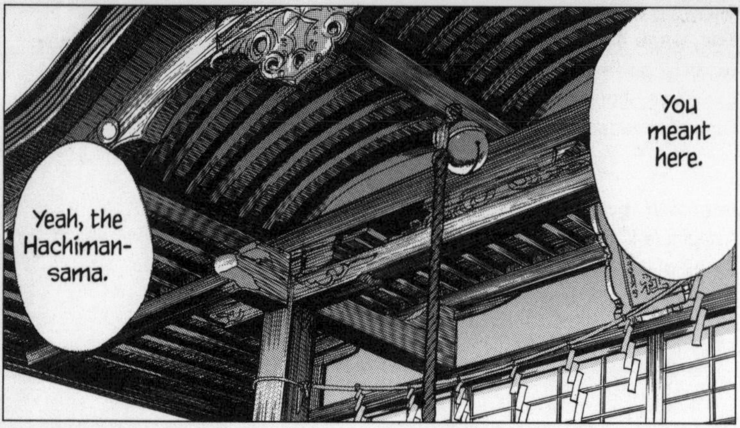
You meant here.
Yeah, the Hachiman-sama.

***Hachiman-sama*, page 118**
Nao and Kagetora are visiting the Tsuruoka Hachimangu, a famous shrine in Kamakura. Nao calls the god *"Hachiman-sama"* for short.

Kotetsu and Yuna, page 158-159
Kotetsu's name has the same kanji for "tora" in Kagetora's name. Yuna's name has the same kanji for "Yu" in Yuki's name.

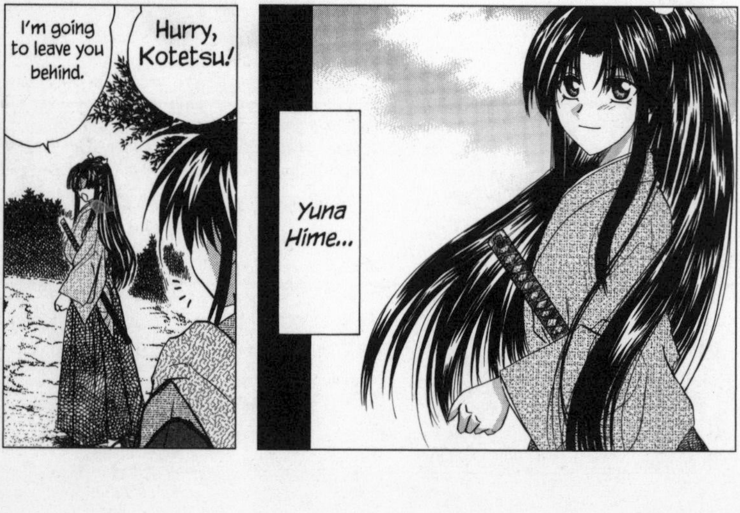
Yuna Hime...
Hurry, Kotetsu!
I'm going to leave you behind.

Edo, page 158

Japan's Edo Period lasted from 1603 to 1867. It was governed by the Tokugawa Shogunate. Edo is also the name of old Tokyo, where Kotetsu and Yuna are headed for the match.

Naginata, page 189

A *naginata* is a long-handled sword. It looks like a spear with a short sword at the tip of it. In modern Japan, it is often used in martial arts for women.

Preview of volume 8

We're pleased to present you a preview from volume 8. Please check our website (www.delreymanga.com) to see when this volume will be available in English. For now you'll have to make do with Japanese!

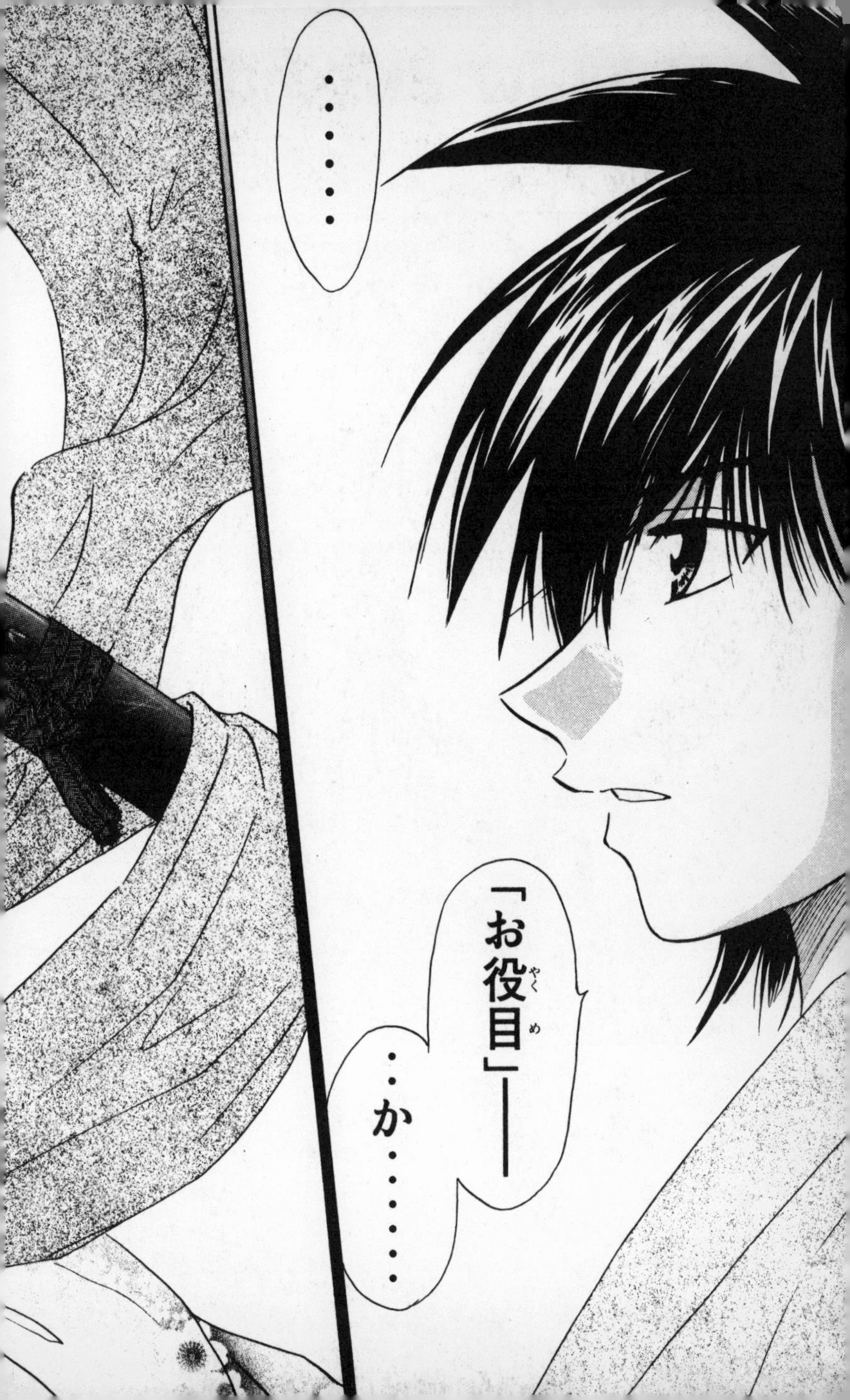
……
「お役目(やくめ)」――
……か……

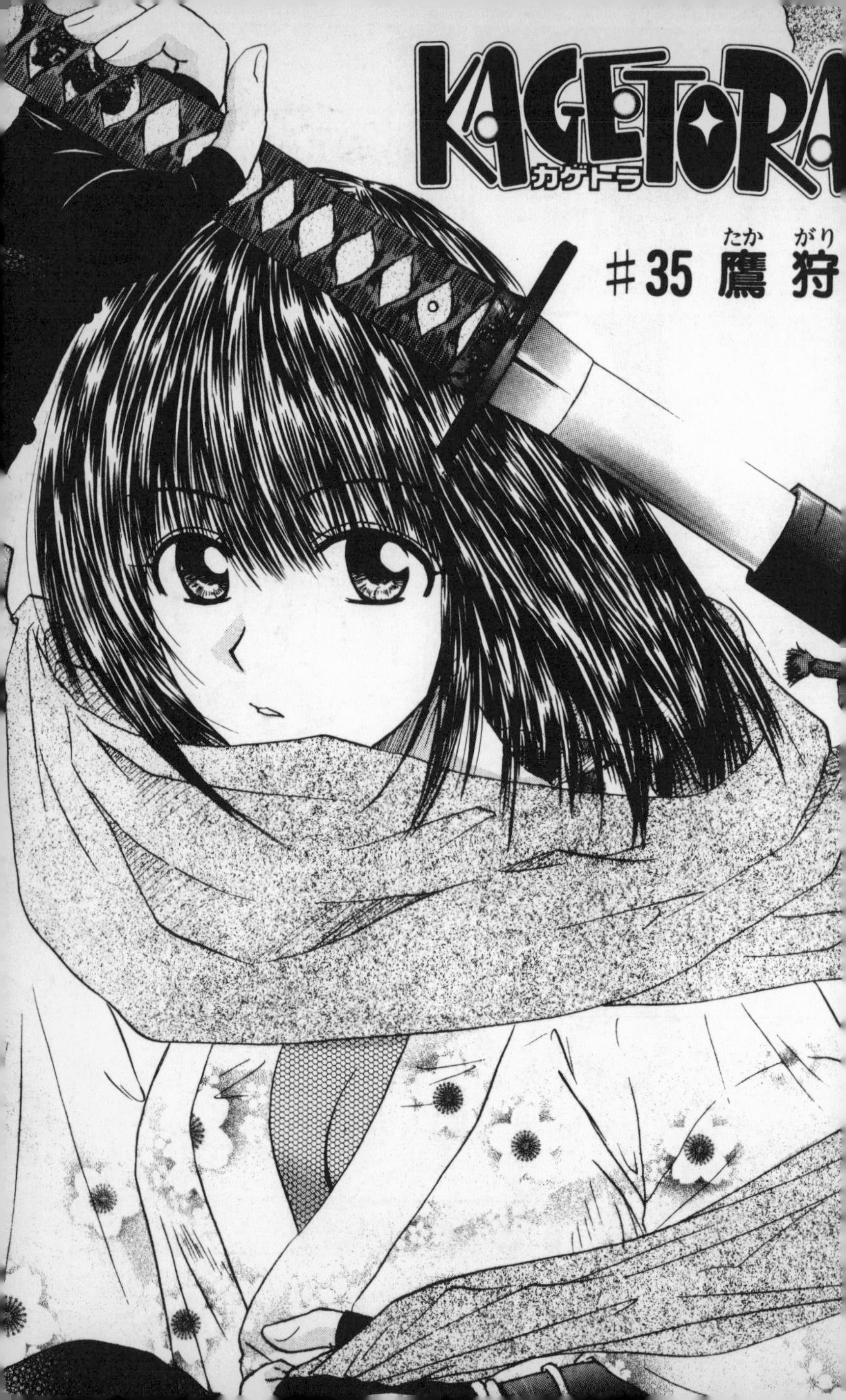
KAGETORA
カゲトラ
＃35 鷹狩

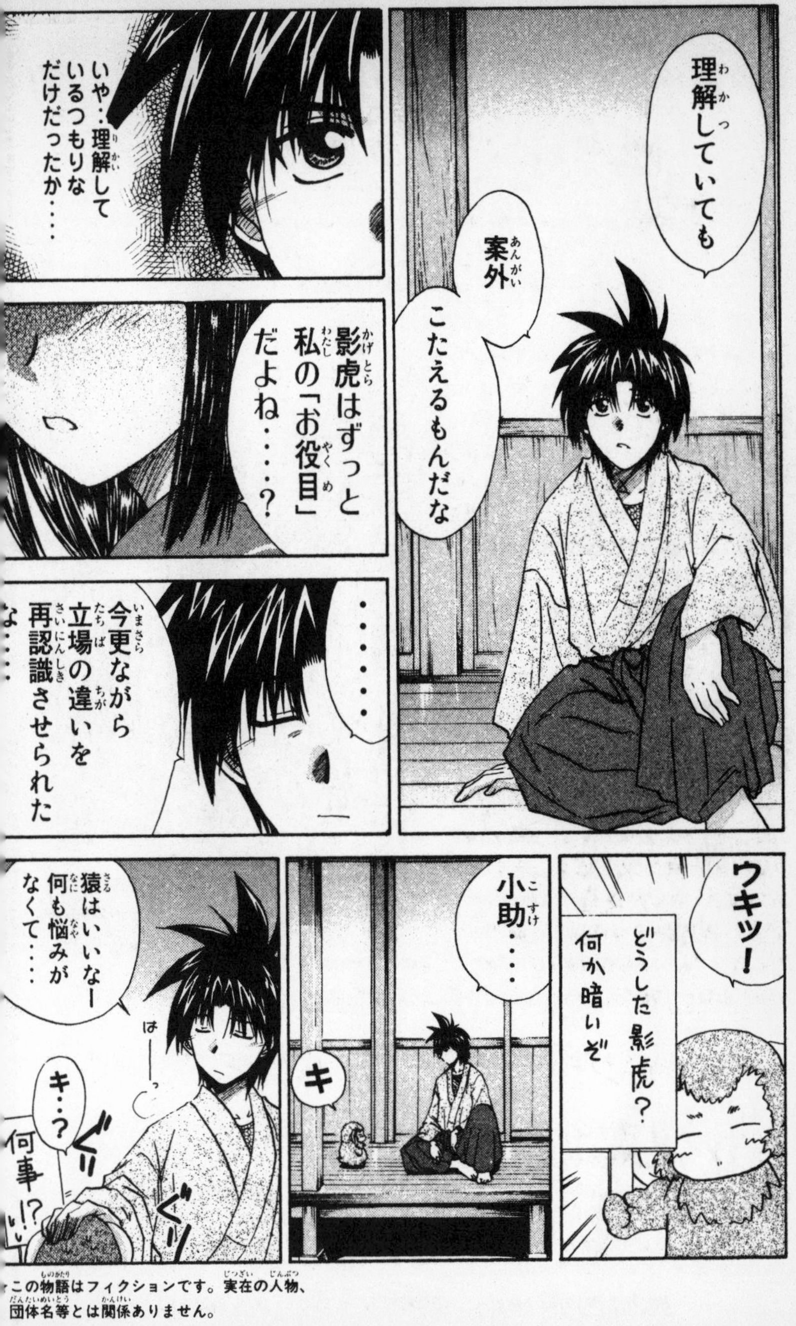

理解していても
案外こたえるもんだな
いや…理解しているつもりなだけだったか…
影虎はずっと私の「お役目」だよね…？
……
今更ながら立場の違いを再認識させられたな…
ウキッ！
どうした影虎？何か暗いぞ
小助…
キ
猿はいいなー何も悩みがなくて…
はーっ
キ…？
グリ
グリ
何事!?

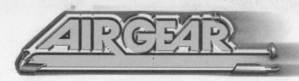

AIRGEAR

BY OH!GREAT

AIRGEAR
1
Oh!great

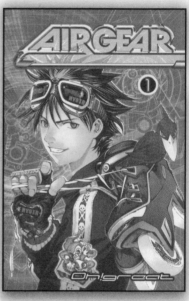

Itsuki Minami needs no introduction—everybody's heard of the "Babyface" of the Eastside. He's the strongest kid at Higashi Junior High School, easy on the eyes but dangerously tough when he needs to be. Plus, Itsuki lives with the mysterious and sexy Noyamano sisters. Life's never dull, but it becomes downright dangerous when Itsuki leads his school to victory over vindictive Westside punks with gangster connections. Now he stands to lose his school, his friends, and everything he cares about. But in his darkest hour, the Noyamano girls give him an amazing gift, one that just might help him save his school: a pair of Air Trecks. These high-tech skates are more than just supercool. They'll enable Itsuki to execute the wildest, most aggressive moves ever seen—and introduce him to a thrilling and terrifying new world.

Ages: 16 +

Special extras in each volume! Read them all!

DEL REY

VISIT WWW.DELREYMANGA.COM TO:

- Read sample pages
- View release date calendars for upcoming volumes
- Sign up for Del Rey's free manga e-newsletter
- Find out the latest about new Del Rey Manga series

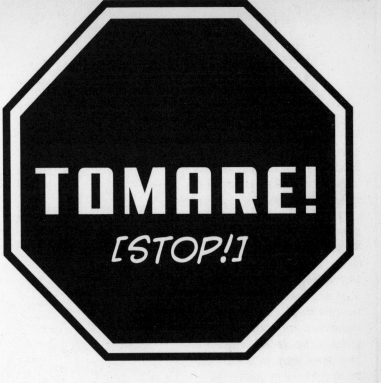

You are going the wrong way!

Manga is a c̶ ̶ ̶ ̶ ̶
type of re̶ ̶

To start at the be̶ ̶

That's right! Authentic manga is read the traditional Japanese way—from right to left. Exactly the *opposite* of how American books are read. It's easy to follow: Just go to the other end of the book, and read each page—and each panel—from right side to left side, starting at the top right. Now you're experiencing manga as it was meant to be.